THE EPIC OF AMERICA

By James Truslow Adams

THE FOUNDING OF NEW ENGLAND

REVOLUTIONARY NEW ENGLAND

NEW ENGLAND IN THE REPUBLIC

JEFFERSONIAN PRINCIPLES

HAMILTONIAN PRINCIPLES

THE ADAMS FAMILY

THE EPIC OF AMERICA

James Truslow Adams

Simon Publications

2001

Originally published byLittle, Brown & Co.; Boston

Library of Congress Control Number: 31025405

ISBN: 1-931541-33-7

Printed by Lightning Source Inc. La Vergne, TN

Published by Simon Publications, P. O. Box 321, Safety Harbor, FL 34695

SAIL — sail thy best, ship of Democracy!
Of value is thy freight — 't is not the Present only,
The Past is also stored in thee!
Thou holdest not the venture of thyself alone — not of the western continent alone;
Earth's résumé entire floats on thy keel, O ship — is steadied by thy spars;
With thee Time voyages in trust, the antecedent nations sink or swim with thee,
With all their ancient struggles, martyrs, heroes, epics, wars, thou bearest the other continents;
Theirs, theirs as much as thine, the destination-port triumphant;
Steer then with good strong hand and wary eye, O helmsman — thou carriest great companions,
Venerable, priestly Asia sails this day with thee,
And royal feudal Europe sails with thee. . . .

How can I pierce the impenetrable blank of the future?
I feel thy ominous greatness, evil as well as good;
I watch thee, advancing, absorbing the present, transcending the past;
I see thy light lighting and thy shadow shadowing, as if the entire globe;
But I do not undertake to define thee — hardly to comprehend thee.

— WALT WHITMAN

PREFACE

THERE is no lack of excellent one-volume narrative histories of the United States, in which the political, military, diplomatic, social, and economic strands have been skillfully interwoven. The author has had no wish to work in that somewhat crowded field in writing the volume now offered. He has desired rather to paint a picture, with broad strokes of the brush, of the variegated past which has made our national story, and at the same time to try to discover for himself and others how the ordinary American, under which category most of us come, has become what he is to-day in outlook, character, and opinion.

His own ancestors, in one line, came from Spain to settle in South America in 1558; in another line, that of his name, from England to settle in Virginia in 1658. He himself was Northern in birth and upbringing. He has spent, in the aggregate, a fair number of years in residence in lands other than his own. His family have played their parts in the settlement and development of the two continents of the New World; and he himself has lived enough in the Old to be able to realize the differences which now divide the citizens of the one from the other. Conscious, on the one hand, of no sectional prejudices, but only of being an American, on the other he has grown increasingly conscious of how different an American now is from the man or woman of any other nation. He has been equally interested in the whole colorful pageant of the great epic which is our history, and in trying to discover how we became what we have become. This book was written from these two standpoints. He has endeavored in particular to trace the beginnings at their several points of entry of such American concepts as "bigger and better," of our attitude toward business, of many characteristics which are generally considered as being "typically American," and, in especial, of that American dream of a better, richer, and happier life for all our citizens of every rank which is the greatest contribution we have as yet made to the thought and welfare of the world. That dream or hope has been present from the start. Ever since we became an independent nation, each generation has seen an uprising of the ordinary Americans to save that dream from the forces which appeared to be overwhelming and dispelling it. Possibly the greatest of these struggles lies just ahead of us at this present time — not a struggle of revolutionists against established order, but of the ordinary man to hold fast to those rights to "life, liberty, and the pursuit of happiness" which were vouchsafed to us in the past in vision and on parchment.

For permission to quote the verses through the text, the author's most hearty thanks are due to Mr. Carl Sandburg and his publishers, Messrs. Harcourt, Brace and Company, for the quotations from *The American Songbag;* to the Grafton Press for those from George G. Korson's *Songs and Ballads of the Anthracite Miner;* to John A. Lomax, Collector and Editor of *Cowboy Songs*, and to Mr. Vachel Lindsay for the lines from his poem, "The Santa Fé Trail" — both volumes published by the Macmillan Company; to the Harvard University Press for quotations from Newman I. White's *American Negro Folk Songs;* to Houghton Mifflin Company for those from the works of Lowell and Whittier, and for the passage from *The Letters of Sir Cecil Spring-Rice*. To Harms, Incorporated, he is indebted for special permission to quote the words of "Ol' Man River." Professor Allan Nevins, of Columbia University, Mr. Edward Weeks, of the Atlantic Monthly Press, and Mr. M. A. DeWolfe Howe have made many valuable suggestions, which are cordially acknowledged.

JAMES TRUSLOW ADAMS

WASHINGTON, D. C.
May 1, 1931

CONTENTS

PROLOGUE

PROLOGUE

I. FROM TIME IMMEMORIAL

No date marks the beginning of our tale. With the exception of the Aztecs and the Mayas, no aboriginal American knew a calendar, and for all those who lived within the bounds of what is now our country, time was dateless. It simply flowed as it had always flowed from time immemorial, marked by the seasons, by birth and life and death. How long the Indians had been here or whence they came, we know no more than they.

The continent on which they dwelt, on which beyond the furthest reach of native myth they had forever worked and played, loved and warred, had remained unknown to all the world except themselves. Its northern limits stretched into the frozen death of arctic ice. Its eastern and western shores were washed by limitless seas. Lying like a vast triangle with its base at the north, its apex rested upon the base of another vast triangle at the south — its sister continent, whose apex in turn pointed to the southern pole.

Its structure was simple as its extent was vast. Within the

limits of our own land, which was in time to stretch across it in its more temperate zone like a colossal band, there is a comparatively narrow coastal plain, flanked on the west by the rampart of the Appalachian range of mountains. Beyond that is the gigantic valley drained by the Mississippi, flanked in its turn by the successive ranges of the Cordilleras. Westward once more is the slope to the Pacific. Of the three thousand miles from shore to shore, more than one third is occupied by the great central valley, the most spacious habitation for human life to be found in the world. In the centuries of which we are writing, one million three hundred thousand square miles of the continent — most of it, indeed, except the central prairies and plains, the western mountains, and the arid regions to the southwest — were covered by primeval forests of great density. A squirrel might have leaped from bough to bough for a thousand miles and never have seen a flicker of sunshine on the ground, so contiguous were the boughs and so dense the leafage.

The varied surface of the land was modeled by a giant hand. In the north a group of great lakes, covering nearly a hundred thousand square miles, held half the fresh water of the entire world. The falls where these waters from the first four tumbled into the last of the lakes were over a mile wide. In the great central valley of the Mississippi, drained by a river system four thousand miles long, one could travel in a straight line for a couple of thousand miles across rolling prairies and plains, from the heat of the great Gulf to the cold of the north. The whole valley slowly rises from east to west like a tilted floor until in the Far West the level ground is five thousand feet above the sea. It is there closed in on the west by range after range of one of the great mountain systems of the earth, rising to heights of over fourteen thousand feet and traversable by man at only a few points. On the western side of the watershed, the Colorado River tears its way to the narrow Gulf of California at the bottom of canyons of which one is twenty miles wide, three hundred miles long, and averages over a mile in depth, forming what has been called by scientists the "grandest natural geological section known." In places on the Pacific slope trees grew to a height of far over two hundred feet, and one still standing, with a girth of ninety-three feet, is estimated to be four thousand years old, perhaps the oldest living creature in the world.

In a country of such vast extent, the scenery and local conditions varied greatly. The Northeast of rolling hills and low mountains, wholly covered with forest and dotted with a thousand gem-like lakes, had nothing in common with the waterless cactus-spotted deserts of the Southwest; nor had the Southeast of low-lying sandy pine barrens, humid swamps, and slow-moving mud-brown rivers with the Northwest of bright cascades, snow-capped mountains, and highlands reaching down to the blue Pacific. There was equally striking contrast between the wide horizons of the ocean-like plains and the endless complexity of the barren and forbidding western mountains. The climate was also of infinite variety, from the tropical and moist heat of the low-lying gulf coasts to the dry air of the high western plateaus or the long cold of the Maine winters and the blizzard-swept plains of the northern central valley.

The distances between these different sections were vast, as were the extents of the several sections themselves. Moreover, owing to the simplicity of the continental structure and the fact that the mountain barriers lay from north to south, the climate of almost all sections was one of extremes. More particularly up and down the Atlantic Coast and the central valley there was nothing to break the force of winds sweeping southward from the Arctic or northward from the equator. Even in most of the parts furthest south there could be killing frosts in winter, while the inhabitants of the furthest north could swelter with the heat of summer. For the most part throughout the continent the climate seems always to have been one which tended to produce a high nervous tension in the living beings subjected to it, even the savages, not only from its sudden changes, but from some quality which we do not know. In every way the land was one of strong contrasts rather than of softly graded tones, a land of dazzling light and sharp shadows, of drought and overwhelming flood, of sunshine and appalling storm.

Deep in its soil, all but unknown to its first inhabitants, were fabulous riches of coal and iron, of silver and gold, of copper and oil, and other things of which for the most part the savages neither felt the need nor knew the use. Far more important to them were the vast herds of buffalo which roamed the plains by millions; the myriads of fur-bearing animals of smaller size; the pigeons which at times fairly darkened the sky in flocks which extended from horizon to horizon; the fish with which the lakes and rivers swarmed. Animal enemies there were in plenty, too, from bear and panther down to the rattlesnake and insects which made some sections practically uninhabitable.

In the extreme lower end of the apex of the continental triangle in what we call Mexico, the varieties of scenery and climate were more closely squeezed together. There the distance was comparatively short between the dense jungle of the tropical seacoast and the cool air of the mountains and central plateau where snow-capped volcanoes reared their crests. Here also, in yet more concentrated form, were vast deposits of precious stones and metals. Such was the gigantic setting, rich in all that man needs for his latest type of civilization, in which one of the noblest dreams of his long and troubled rise was to take form and deeply to affect the thought and life of the inhabitants of all the globe.

In the prehistoric era of which we are now speaking, however, the huge continent north of Mexico was so sparsely inhabited as to have supported only about a half million savages or barbarians of the race we call Indians. The descriptive adjective "red" is a misnomer, for they varied merely from a dark skin to one of light yellow. Although of one generic race, they were divided into a considerable number of stocks, and again into a far greater number of tribes. Originally there had probably been migrations on a large scale, but at the time our story opens, the Indian had developed a settled and not a nomadic habit of life.

It would be both needless and impossible to differentiate carefully between the various tribes. In their numbers, their arts and crafts, their ways of life, they varied to some extent with locality, but their general characteristics will suffice us here. They were in the hunting and fishing stage, although they also raised maize and some other vegetables. The density of population in any one section depended mainly on the food supply, being greater, for example, upon the Atlantic Coast than on the plains. Chatty and sociable in ordinary life among themselves, they held to a convention of extreme gravity on all public and ceremonial occasions. Their nervous systems were unstable and they were of a markedly hysterical make-up, peculiarly susceptible to suggestion. Cruel and revengeful, they could school themselves to stand pain as a matter of social convention, although when unsustained by that they were childishly lacking in self-control.

Their weapons were bows and arrows, tomahawks, and clubs. As we pass southwestward toward the Indians of New Mexico and Arizona we find an increase in skill in such arts as pottery and weaving, although the finest designing was on the northwest coast. The houses were rude, ranging from mere wigwams and tepees to the "long houses" of the Iroquois, until again we reach the Southwest, where we find the stone or adobe communal dwellings of the "pueblo" Indians and the "cliff dwellers," which, unlike almost any other primitive dwellings, sometimes rose six stories and contained great numbers of rooms. Defense was a primary object in such buildings as these, and they were often located far from the fields which were tilled by the community.

The country was sparsely settled, considering its size and the number of inhabitants, but we must recall that it takes a large area to support a people in the hunting stage of culture. Although in many cases the roughly defined hunting grounds for each tribe were vast, they were considered none too large by their possessors, who sometimes traveled great distances within their own territories, having occasionally, as in the case of the Iroquois, to pass through the territory of a hostile tribe. War between tribes, save when treaties had been made for a period, was the normal state of existence, and, almost as much as gathering food, was the chief occupation of the men. For purposes of both the peaceful migrations and the war expeditions, the Indians had clearly marked trails extending practically over the continent, through the forests, over the plains, and along portages connecting their navigable streams and rivers, the routes chosen being scarcely capable of betterment by a modern engineer. The length of time taken to locate them must be reckoned by centuries when we consider the vastness and difficulties of the land and the fact that there were thousands upon thousands of miles of these trails.

For unknown ages this life had been going on in the American forests, along its coasts, on its vast plains, even in its desert stretches. Whether the culture was advancing or retrograding we cannot say, but as we go still further south, to the apex of our triangle in Mexico, we reach a higher stage. Indeed we reach up to time and dates.

In the southeast of Mexico and on the peninsula of Yucatan there had dwelt a mysterious people whom we call the Mayas. They had stone cities, had developed a method of writing, constructed a calendar, and to some extent we can trace their history back to 418 A.D., perhaps even earlier, from their own records. From some cause their civilization fell, but another, that of the Aztecs, further north in the higher lands of Mexico, arose, based seemingly on that of the Mayas. Unlike the sparse hunting population of the larger part of America, here we find a population so numerous as to be almost incredible, it being reported by early writers that twenty thousand human sacrifices were offered in one celebration alone.

These Indians, who had built up so densely populated and highly organized an agricultural State, had probably wandered down from the north about the year 1000, and come into contact with the earlier Mayas. They too had a system of writing and a calendar, and have left manuscripts for us to read. Unlike the northern tribes, they had learned how to smelt metals, and although they had no iron, the splendor of their gold and jeweled ornaments and dress sounds like a tale from the *Arabian Nights*. The palace of the king was of such extent that one wrote of it that, although he walked through parts of it several times until he was tired, he had never seen the whole of it. The nobles wore solid golden cuirasses under their feathered robes, and the rich wore ornaments of precious stones set in the same metal, exquisitely chiseled. In one grave alone four hundred and eighty ounces of gold were buried with their owner, and a hoard found in one storage place was worth $750,000. Instead of the shell money of the northeastern Indians, quills filled with gold dust were used for "small change." Great markets were held which twenty to twenty-five thousand people were said to have attended, and at which, besides all sorts of food, clothes, feathers, plumes, obsidian swords, and other things which could be found for sale, there was a section given up to those who sold gold by weight and all sorts of ornaments in the form of birds and animals made of gold and jewels.

In spite of the splendor of the civilization and its high social and economic organization, it differed only in degree from that of the North, and its religion was ghastly in its cruelty. The especial deity of the Aztec, however, Quetzalcoatl, a bearded god of white skin who had given them all their arts and crafts, was supposed to have been averse to human sacrifice. Long, long ago, so their legend went, he had gone down to the sea-coast, sailed to the east, and been seen no more. But he had promised to return and was still awaited.

II. THE RETURN OF QUETZALCOATL

Centuries had passed and the "white god" had not returned to make good his promise to his people. The Mexican calendar had cycles of years, and the same names were given to those which occupied the same position in the successive cycles. Quetzalcoatl had said that he would reappear in the year *ce acatl*, but an almost countless number of those years had passed without him. He was still worshiped, and professional thieves would carry his protective image when they plundered a house. But he did not come. At length, however, a generation arrived in which strange things began to happen. In 1492, according to a calendar unknown to the Indians, three boats of a size undreamed of, with great wings, were seen by the naked inhabitants of a little island in the Bahamas. They hurriedly ran to the shore, and soon small boats were put off from the big ones and strange men with white skins landed on the beach, where they erected poles with gorgeous banners and seemed to be performing a ceremony.

The strangers stayed for many days, and what appeared to interest them most were the little rings of gold which the natives, otherwise stark naked, wore in their noses. So, by signs, the inquisitive strangers were told that far to the south, overseas from the island, dwelt a people who had vast stores of golden utensils and ornaments. Then the white men soon departed, and after that several of the natives could not be found. But not long after, the savages in Cuba were disturbed by the apparition of these same strangers, who tarried and then disappeared. They were next seen from the island of Hayti, on which the largest ship was wrecked, but the natives saved all the cargo for them out of kindness, and when the other two ships left, forty-four of the strangers remained behind. None of these island cannibals had ever heard of Quetzalcoatl. They were merely mystified by the white men and terrified by the thunder and lightning which they wielded from instruments in their hands; but the demands of the forty-four, dictated by hunger and lust, became intolerable. Then dark deeds happened in the jungle.

One day a great ship reappeared and from black objects on her deck came a deafening roar and flashes of light, but when Columbus landed once more there were none of his Spaniards to greet him. This time he had brought strange animals called horses, pigs, and chickens, strange vegetables to grow, such as wheat and sugar cane, and it was evident he intended to remain. The natives decided to kill the intruders. Bloody war settled down on the island. In three years two thirds of the savages were dead. They could not fight against the lightning of the white men.

From time to time this Columbus appeared at other islands, and in 1497 the natives of the far northeast coast of America were similarly surprised by the appearance of a white man who called himself Cabot and was in the employ of a great chief of a tribe known as English. With more and more frequency along the coasts of North and South America did these strangers begin to appear from nowhere across the sea. They began especially to conquer the islands of the Caribbean and at a few places to establish settlements on the mainland. After the failure of one of these at Darien, a Spaniard named Balboa, in 1513, managed to climb a mountain on the isthmus from whence he could see the Pacific, and this sight seemed to whet the desire of the white men to continue their depredations. Six years later one called Alonso de Pineda sailed all along the coast from Florida to Vera Cruz. Two years after that another, Ponce de León, tried to settle a colony at Tampa Bay. Others made the attempt at the mouth of the Savannah River, and the Spaniards now began to hunt as far up as South Carolina for slaves to take back to their islands. But most of all they wanted gold.

In 1524, Estevan Gomez, who was a Portuguese, searched the coast from somewhere in the north down to about the bay of the Chesapeake, but was discouraged by its bleakness and poverty. With all their exploration for over twenty years, gold had eluded them — that gold which, as Columbus wrote, "is the most precious of all commodities; [it] constitutes treasure, and he who possesses it has all he needs in this world, as also the means of securing souls from purgatory, and restoring them to the enjoyment of Paradise." But if it had not yet been found, it had always seemed at the end of the rainbow, and in 1517 Diego, the son and heir of Columbus, had undertaken to carry exploration further into the mainland. In Yucatan the natives who lived in cities with paved streets and stone temples were surprised one day, when their altar was still dripping with the blood of a sacrifice, to find the white men among them. In a sudden battle the intruders were driven off, and after various adventures further along the coast they disappeared.

In less than two years, however, in 1519, the unwelcome white men appeared again, under the ablest leader they ever had, Hernán Cortes. There were eleven ships this time, carrying five hundred and fifty Spaniards, two or three hundred Indian retainers, and sixteen horses. The first inquiry that the white men made was after eight of their countrymen who they had heard had been shipwrecked and taken prisoners eight years before. Nothing could be learned of them, and the fleet set sail. Damage to one of the vessels required their return, and as they were lying at anchor one of the sought-for prisoners, who had been kindly treated, paddled out in a canoe and was received with joy. During his captivity he had learned the Mayan language and thus gave an invaluable gift to his rescuer.

Further along the coast, in Tabasco, a battle took place, in which the white men's victory was due to the confusion into which the Aztecs were thrown by the appearance of the horses, although the natives far outnumbered the strangers. The Aztecs were so won, however, by the clemency which their conqueror showed them that they presented him with twenty young women, among whom was a pretty young girl with a sad and romantic history. She could speak both Aztec and Mayan, and Cortes, whom she successively served as slave, secretary, and mistress, thus received another invaluable ally. His goal was the conquest of the Aztec kingdom, the existence of which had been gradually growing from rumor to reality for the Spaniards.

That kingdom had recently been widely extended by conquest, and at the time reached from the Atlantic to the Pacific and far up and down Mexico and Central America, with its capital at Mexico City, where dwelt the king, Montezuma. The very extent of the conquests and the vast number of the population, large sections of which were hostile to the claims of the king, made for weakness. Moreover, he had antagonized a great part of his subjects by his pride and ostentation, and by the heavy taxes imposed to satisfy his pomp and luxury.

During the last decade, also, strange portents had been seen and heard in Mexico. From time to time tales had been received from the distant and far-separated points we have noted of the coming of a strange race of white men. In 1510, without earthquake or other tangible cause, the large lake of Tezcuco had suddenly been disturbed, flooded the capital, and destroyed a considerable part of it. The next year one of the temples had taken fire without cause and all efforts to save it had been in vain. Three comets had appeared in the sky, and not long before Cortes landed a strange light had flared in pyramidal shape all over the eastern heavens. The feeling had been growing that at last Quetzalcoatl was to return, and then, in the year *ce acatl*, Cortes landed at Vera Cruz.

He and his followers waited there a week, while all was in confusion in the capital, to which the news had been carried. Meanwhile they were treated with great courtesy and hospitality by the local governor. At the capital the question was hotly debated: Was Cortes Quetzalcoatl, or was he not? Opinions were divided, and Montezuma determined on a halfway course — to send an embassy with rich gifts and to forbid any nearer approach to his city. At length the embassy arrived, and the Spaniards were rendered breathless by what was spread before their eyes. Cortes had sent a Spanish helmet to the king, and this was now returned filled to the brim with gold dust. There were thirty cartloads of cotton cloth, fine as silk, quantities of birds and animals cast in gold and silver, crests of gold and silver thread covered with pearls and gems, circular plates of silver and gold, one of which the "fair god" estimated as worth a sum equivalent to-day to about $225,000.

These gifts were accompanied by a message regretting that Montezuma could not comply with the stranger's invitation for an interview, as the fatigues and dangers of the journey were too great, adding the request that the strangers should now retire to their own home with the tokens of the king's friendship. Cortes returned the obvious word that Montezuma's munificence had only made him the more anxious to meet the king and that he would come to Mexico City. If the Aztecs had known "Quetzalcoatl" better, they would have been able to predict that no other course would be considered.

It is impossible to recount again that most romantic of all historical tales, the conquest of Mexico by the Spaniard, already incomparably told by Prescott. The Aztec slave girl played her part, but with all the fortuitous circumstances in his favor, so remarkable as to be thought miraculous in his day, one cannot withhold admiration from the great Spaniard who with a handful of followers, divided and mutinous, conquered a large country with a vast and highly organized population in less than two years, and who showed himself statesman as well as conqueror. The riches that he found appeared inexhaustible. The El Dorado of the white men had been reached. An empire was founded. If all this had been discovered within a few days' journey of the coast, what infinite treasure might not yet lie within the continent the vastness of which was beginning to be understood, though vaguely enough.

In 1524, the savages dwelling at the mouth of the Hudson River probably saw one of the strange ships arrive with a commander named Verrazzano, an Italian in the employ of a people called French, and ten years later more French under command of Cartier appeared to the natives on the St. Lawrence, and for a couple of years they tried to found a colony there. The savages on Newfoundland now saw year after year innumerable boats filled with uncouth white men who came to take huge quantities of fish, and landed on the shore to dry and cure them.

Meanwhile, having conquered Mexico, the Spaniards sent out many expeditions thence, and in 1533 a cruel leader called Pizarro went far south and conquered the native kingdom in Peru, which proved to be almost as rich in gold and silver and precious stones as Mexico itself. At the same time the natives of Florida were again disturbed by the appearance of white men near Tampa under Pánfilo de Narvaez, and fought them off, forcing them to travel along the coast of the Gulf through forest and swamp. Finally the Spaniards built boats, and fifteen survived to reach the shore of Texas, where they were captured by the natives of that coast. The Indians could not be sure what sort of beings they had secured, and tried the experiment of making one of them, Cabeza de Vaca, a medicine man. Thanks perhaps to the suggestibility of the natives, wonderful cures were made by the white medicine men, for others had become such also, and for five years they had to serve their native owners. At length De Vaca and three others escaped to another tribe, where they also performed seemingly miraculous cures. After about eight months they were allowed to depart westward, but so great had their reputation become that they were accompanied at times by several thousand of the savages. The procession, living on plunder and food which had to be breathed upon by De Vaca to sanctify it, wound its way across Texas to the Rio Grande, and finally, after ten months' journey through the wilderness, De Vaca himself reached the city of Mexico, having touched the coast of the Pacific on his way. He had been gone nine years, and began to tell marvelous tales about having found in Florida the richest country in the world, so laying the foundation of a long-lived myth. The rumor was believed by Hernando de Soto, who had returned to Spain with about $300,000 in gold from Peru.

In May 1539, the long-suffering natives at Tampa, who had now become used to fighting off the white men, saw nine vessels arrive, from which were disembarked over six hundred men and two hundred and twenty horses. Much to the relief of the natives, the whites set off on a march late in the summer and disappeared into the wilderness.

During the next two years the natives on the Savannah River, and others on a long route that lay through Georgia, Alabama, and Mississippi, were surprised by these strange men with white skins who were accompanied by great droves of hogs and huge animals with long tails such as had never been seen before. Everywhere the savages attacked the intruders, whose numbers slowly dwindled. In 1542, the natives had a great victory in northern Mississippi, where the whites had settled into winter quarters. The savages set fire to the camp, killed nine men, and burned fifty horses and several hundred hogs.

The intruders set out on the march again, and on May 8, 1541, they discovered the "great river" somewhere near Memphis. Having crossed in barges which it took a month to make, the next natives to see them were the roaming bands on the prairies, probably in Arkansas. The savages and disease had reduced the number of the intruders by two hundred and fifty, and after a winter of great severity they retreated again to the Mississippi, where De Soto fell ill and died. Sharp-eyed savages lurking on the bank to watch the movements of the strangers may have seen a body wrapped in cloaks weighted with sand dropped into the middle of the river; and rejoiced that the leader of their enemies, who had told them that all white men were immortal, was dead.

The remainder of the intruding band now started southwestward for Mexico, but provisions were scarce and the savages were menacing all along the way. They were successful in turning the strangers back again to the river, where they built seven small ships and, after liberating over five hundred Indian slaves whom they had taken, disappeared from view downstream. Before they did so it had been noticed that the power to control the thunder and lightning from the death-dealing weapons they had held in their hands had left them. Four years and a quarter from the time they had started, exactly one half of their number reached Mexico again.

Meanwhile the Indians of the plains and the Southwest had been busy trying to repel other intruders. Tales had been told of the "Seven Cities of Cibola" of surpassing size and wealth in the land of the pueblos, and presently the natives of southwestern Arizona were disturbed by the invading bands of a great expedition under Coronado, numbering three hundred white men and eight hundred Mexican Indians. These found the Colorado River and the Grand Canyon, but none of the Seven Cities; constantly attacked by the natives, they worked their way as far north as Kansas, where at one time, unwittingly, they were only nine days from De Soto's force. The natives had to deal with this new menace for a little over a year until the expedition returned to Mexico. The next year, however, 1543, the natives all along the coast of California, nearly to Oregon, saw the strangers sailing along in ships under command of Cabrillo, occasionally having to fight them when they landed.

We cannot recount all the places at which the white men now began to be encountered by the natives with increasing frequency and foreboding. The strangers were showing more determination to settle along the Atlantic Coast, and the Indians, with occasional fighting, watched abortive efforts of the Spanish to settle at several spots as far north as North Carolina, until in 1565 they finally did effect a permanent settlement at St. Augustine in Florida, near where the French had also tried twice to settle. In the course of the second French effort it must have afforded the natives some hope to see the white men turn to killing each other when the Spanish who founded St. Augustine slaughtered the French colonists at the mouth of the St. Johns River. Five years later the Spanish had secured a temporary hold on the coast as far north as Chesapeake Bay, and in 1581 built a fort at St. Augustine with the help of negro slaves imported from Spain.

In 1584, the savages on the North Carolina coast were busy watching the English try to establish settlements in their land, and were well content to see them all sail off again two years later. Only a couple of days afterward, however, more ships arrived, and fifteen men remained when these sailed away. This time the Indians fell upon them, killed one, and drove the rest to sea in a small boat. The savages had again cleared their land, for these white men were never more heard of by them or anyone. The next year, 1587, more of the persistent English came, a hundred and fifty of them, of whom twenty-five were women and children, the like of whom had never been seen in North America before. Soon there was a white girl baby born who was called Virginia Dare, and not long afterward the ships set sail and left the colony to fend for itself. What course the savages took with these colonists we do not know, but four years later, when ships again arrived, not a trace was to be found save an empty fort, on the wall of which was scrawled the word "Croatan."

The English had now for the first time appeared to the savages on the west coast also; in 1579 a ship called the *Golden Hind*, commanded by one Francis Drake and loaded with gold and silver plundered from the Spaniards, slowly made her way up the California coast to Oregon, stopping for some time in the bay of San Francisco, where the savages watched a ceremony intended to transfer their entire land from themselves to some stranger named Elizabeth.

During three generations the Indians north of Mexico had had more than enough of this strange new enemy who was likely to descend on them at any moment, but their life had not been greatly altered by the skirmishings that had taken place. In Mexico the case was very different.

The Spaniards had come seeking gold. They had not only found it, but they had also found a highly organized society of barbaric splendor. If the white men robbed the Indians of their independence and wealth, they also felt that they had a gift of priceless value to bestow in return — the gift of the Christian religion, as they understood it, and of eternal salvation. With all their cruelty, it never occurred to the Spaniards but that the Indian was a human soul to be saved, as well as exploited. In the new empire that Cortes built up, the Indian might be socially and economically subordinate, but he had his rights as an integral part of the common society, and Spanish civilization as transplanted to Mexico was a civilization in which the Indian was included and in which he survived, mixing his blood in marriage with the whites. That fact was of prime importance for the savage and the white man both.

Within a century from the time the first Spaniard arrived, the change from the Indian point of view had been immense. He had been taught the Catholic faith, and if it was not very well understood, perhaps, by either race, nevertheless the bloody sacrifice of life of the old religion had become a thing of the past. No longer were vast numbers of victims slain at one ceremony to appease an angry god. A new civilization had arisen with startling rapidity, a civilization in which the Indian was expected to take a part, albeit it was to a great extent an exploited and unhappy one.

By 1574 there were about two hundred Spanish cities and towns in America with a population of a hundred and sixty thousand Spaniards, mostly men. Schools for the Indians were spread broadcast in the Indian villages, and as early as 1522 one attended by over a thousand Indian boys was established in Mexico City, where the pupils were taught handicrafts and the fine arts as well as the usual branches of learning. Thirteen years later the first institution for higher learning in the New World was established especially for natives in the same city, where there was also a college for Indian girls. In 1551 the University of Mexico was founded, one of the chairs being that of the Indian languages, and among the important books published on Mexican printing presses, of which there were seven or eight in this century, were grammars and dictionaries of the Mexican tongue.

The civilization which was opened to the Indians, and in which in many cases they rose to local offices, at least, of importance, was an amazing one to be projected in so short a time. There were over fifty booksellers in Mexico in this first century, in the last quarter of which over thirty thousand books were imported from Spain. Others of great and lasting importance on anthropology, linguistics, and history were written in Mexico itself by its own scholars. A large number of works, mostly religious, were printed in the native languages. In 1573, the foundation was laid for the Cathedral of Mexico, the greatest among the innumerable churches which had been built throughout the country, and which yet remains the largest and grandest church building in North America. In these buildings the Indian often saw examples of European painting in the pictures hung over the altars, and in this century a Mexican school of art led by Alonso Vasques and Rodrigo de Cifuentes had already sprung into life. Another indication of the vigor of the interest in the arts is to be found in the fact that in 1585 over three hundred aspiring authors contested for a prize in literature.

The Spaniards had also done much to increase the resources of the country. They shipped in so many cattle and horses and jennies for breeding mules that within a few generations these were running wild all over the country and were hunted instead of being bred. Cotton and sugar were planted, and by 1590 the sugar mills were exporting two hundred thousand pounds a year from Santo Domingo alone, where the Indians had learned to eat beef instead of human flesh, and to work at agriculture instead of hunting and war. Flowers of all sorts were introduced, and in 1552 Mass was said at one of the churches over the seeds of roses on the altar, which were soon to make all New Spain rich in fragrant blossoms.

But gold and silver were still the compelling lure. Annually the great fleet carried about fifteen million dollars in gold and treasure to Spain. Thousands of unhappy Indians toiled in the mines of Potosi and others almost as rich. But north of the Mexican border life was going on unchanged, as it had from the beginning, except for occasional appearances of white men to be humored or killed. The only change was that cattle and horses, which the Spaniards had brought and which were now roaming Mexico by the hundred thousand, were found, as they strayed, by northern natives, and the wild Sioux and other plains Indians now swept on horseback over the ground on which they and their ancestors had painfully trudged for countless ages.

Meanwhile, unknown to the savages, the English and the Spaniards whom they had so often repulsed from their shores had met in fierce fight in more ships than the Indian had ever dreamed of, on a narrow strait three thousand miles away. By the night of the twentieth of July, 1588, the Spanish Armada was in full flight in the English Channel. The fate of the unwitting North American savage had been sealed.

THE EPIC OF AMERICA

I

THE MEN OF DESTINY

Whence and why had come these white men who had already so profoundly altered life for the North American savage? Three thousand miles across the sea was the continent of Europe, filled with energetic, restless peoples. They had often fought among themselves for political and economic advantages. They were of various religious beliefs. The fifteenth and sixteenth centuries had witnessed a marked increase of energy among them, the tempo of their lives having suffered an inexplicable but very noticeable rise. The forces of trade, religion, and nationalism were the dominant ones, and the conflicts were increasing in intensity.

Just about the time that the increase in energy became notable, one outlet for that energy was blocked by the Turks' obtaining control of all the overland routes to the marvelously profitable trade with the Orient. That, combined with the need in any case for new outlets for the increased energy, inaugurated an era of exploration by sea to find new openings for trade and especially a new way to the closed Orient. For twenty years before Columbus was seen by the savages in the Caribbean, Portuguese sailors had been coasting down the African shore. If all this was unknown to the American Indian, equally were he and the very existence of his continent unknown to the European. When Columbus conceived the idea of reaching the Far East, "the Indies," by sailing west, the prevailing winds carried him by chance, not indeed to that Orient which he always believed he had found, but to the front door of the very section of North America which held the one rich civilization of its inhabitants. With a minimum of balked effort, Spain, in whose employ he had sailed, thus obtained a source of fabulous wealth, and hence of power, which completely upset the balance among European nations.

In no country of Europe, however, was the increase of energy more marked than in the England of Queen Elizabeth. Moreover, England had become passionately Protestant in religion and hated the Catholic Spaniard with a glowing hate. To see him rise to the very pinnacle of power, to watch his galleons bring their millions in gold with every fleet from the new land in the West, to have the Catholics lord it over the world, was more than the bounding new energy of the English could brook. In 1584, Richard Hakluyt was writing to plead that if the English colonized and fortified some points in America and preyed on the Spanish plate fleets, "no doubte but the Spanishe empire falls to the ground and the Spanish king shall be left as bare as Aesops proude crowe . . . with such a mayme to the Pope and to that side" as had never been given before by anyone, for "if you touche him in the Indies, you touch the apple of his eye," and the Spaniard's armies and pride would fall with his wealth.

The English sea dogs — Hawkins, Drake, and the rest — were in full cry after the hated and gold-laden Papists by sea. Enormous plunder was captured, and the Spaniard, touched in "the apple of his eye," turned snarlingly to give the English a fatal blow by overwhelming them in their own Channel. But the English won the day, and a wild storm completed the total destruction of the Spanish fleet. The defeat of the Armada, with the subsequent decline in the power of Spain, meant that that nation's American empire would be practically limited on the north by the Mexican border and would never spread into the wide expanse of the continent claimed beyond. That was too vast, and the frontier line too extended, to be held by a declining nation. The way was open for the boldest plans of the English Of the Spanish empire in America as it was, and the type of civilization so brilliantly planted there, the English knew and cared nothing, nor did their American sons for the next three centuries. Competition, ignorance, dislike, and religious fanaticism all combined to make Spain and her empire in their eyes merely an enemy and a prey. To have conquered New Spain from Old would have been too great a task for even the rising England of Elizabeth, and efforts at colonization were thus all diverted to the North, where it was hoped gold and vast riches might also be found.

Gilbert and Raleigh had tried in vain to found their colonies, but, if success had not come, their courage had not been damped. Of America, which had been his undoing, Raleigh said when near death, "I shall yet see it an English nation," and Gilbert's remark after his own failure was equally indicative of the spirit now abroad: "He is not worthy to live at all that for fear of danger or death, shunneth his countries service and his own honor." More powerful companies were formed to finance the planting of colonies, and the work went doggedly forward.

In 1607, a renewed attempt was made to plant a colony at Jamestown, Virginia — thirty miles up the river to avoid surprise by the Spaniards. This time it was successful, in spite of the horrors of "the starving time," in which one husband was reported to have killed his wife, eaten part of her, and salted down the remainder. By the end of the first dozen years the settlement numbered about a thousand. How precarious it was, nevertheless, is indicated by the fact that although between 1619 and 1622 about three thousand new settlers arrived, by the end of the latter year there were left only about twelve hundred in all, old and new, and of these about four hundred were soon to be massacred by the Indians. Sickness and hardship took a frightful toll, but the struggling colony managed to survive. The English stock had been grafted on the American continent. Self-government had, also, for the governor, Yeardley, who arrived in the spring of 1619, was instructed not only to replace martial law with civil government, and to make grants of land to all free immigrants, but also to summon an assembly in which the elected representatives of the people should make such laws as might "by them be thought good and profitable." A new nation had been founded, though the fever-infested, squalid colony seemed to hold little promise of greatness. Little indeed; for Spain, which would have quickly wiped it out, left it alone because the Spanish Ambassador in London advised paying no attention to it, as it would surely die by itself.

Far to the north, in Maine, another company had tried to establish a colony, which *had* died by itself. But in 1620 the little band of English "Pilgrims," who for their religion's sake had been living self-exiled in Holland for some years, arrived by the *Mayflower*, settled themselves on the inhospitable shore of Plymouth, and with rugged devotion grafted another bud of the English nation on the continent. They were a simple and gentle folk, but their courage was no less and of a finer quality than that of the most swashbuckling of the "sea dogs." A couple of years after the founding of their settlement, William Bradford, leader and historian of the colony, answering a list of objections which had been brought in England against the colony, noted that the settlers were said to be much annoyed with mosquitoes. "They are too delicate and unfitted to begin new plantations," he answered, "that cannot endure the biting of a muskeeto; we would wish such to keepe at home, till at least they are muskeeto proof."

One had indeed to be much more than "muskeeto proof," as Bradford ironically wrote, to be an American pioneer. Sickness, incessant and unremitting labor, hunger, attacks from savage men and savage beasts, were among the "mosquito bites" that these first founders, north and south, had to face and endure. In the first winter at Plymouth, half the little company of a hundred died from sickness and hardship. At times there were but six or seven strong enough to hunt, cook, and care for the entire company, who, nevertheless, "to their great commendations," as Bradford wrote, "spared no pains, night nor day, but with abundance of toyle and hazard of their own health, fetched them wood, made their fires, drest them meat, made their beds, washed their loathsome clothes, cloathed and uncloathed them . . . all this willingly and cherfully, without any grudging in the least, shewing therein their true love unto their friends & brethren."

Here and there more came. Some settled around the shore of Massachusetts Bay. A little fishing settlement was founded at Cape Ann. The Virginians had been granted the right to make their own local laws by the King himself, but these northern settlers had come without charter or written right. The novel situation of being free from all laws whatever faced the Pilgrims even before they landed from the *Mayflower*, and there were some unruly members in the mixed company. There was no one set over them to govern them. Some government was needful. It was clear that they must therefore govern themselves; and, impelled by the simple logic of their situation, they drew up a compact which all signed, agreeing that they would "submit to such government and governors as [they] should by common consent agree to make and choose." Simple as were both the logic and the document, the decision was peculiarly English, and in time to come was to be characteristically American also. Those who signed had no intention of creating a "democracy" or of changing any government in the world. They simply avoided the possible dangers of anarchy or an iron dictator by agreeing to abide by the expressed *common* will. Simple as it was, no group of men other than English at that period would have chosen the same solution; and it was the solution that was to occur over and over again in a thousand situations in the later history of the country.

By 1628 it had been made certain that English colonization

of the Atlantic Coast, although toilsome and hazardous, could be undertaken with success. The Virginia colony was by then twenty-one years old. It had had to stand on its own feet after the royal dissolution of the company which had backed it, and yet the colonists had felt themselves strong enough to insist upon the reëstablishment of the Assembly when the King threatened it, and they had won. The Pilgrims had always stood on their own feet, and in spite of much hardship and little profit had also won through. Owing to these examples, as well as to conditions in England, a great movement of population toward America, a migration such as in its entirety the world has never seen elsewhere, was now about to set in. By 1630 there were almost seven thousand English settlers on the American coast and about four thousand in Bermuda and the West Indies. Soon after 1640 the total was to be increased by about sixty-five thousand, of whom about two thirds were on the islands and one third on the mainland.

For various reasons, economic conditions in England were very bad, both gentlemen and poorer people of many sorts finding themselves hard pressed either to keep up their accustomed scale of living or to make any living at all. The opportunities of the New World were painted in glowing colors, and those who were sinking in the social and economic scales in England began to look toward it as a land of refuge and of hope. Not only, however, were economic conditions bad, but so also, for great numbers, were the political and religious outlooks. Politically, the tyranny of the Stuarts had begun, and, religiously, the promise of greater persecution of the Puritans filled many with dark forebodings, for a considerable part of the nation had become Puritan. On account of all these causes, — poverty, fear of religious persecution, political dangers, and the general hope of bettering themselves, — a veritable exodus of English men and women took place to Ireland, which was then also being colonized, to the Atlantic Coast of America, and to the West India islands. Our customary preoccupation solely with continental "American" history usually makes us overlook the fact that, of the possibly seventy-five thousand persons who left the old home, only about one third came to *our* America. It was a vast emigration of which only this fraction impinged on our own shores.

The American dream was beginning to take form in the hearts of men. The economic motive was unquestionably powerful, often dominant, in the minds of those who took part in the great migration, but mixed with this was also frequently present the hope of a better and a freer life, a life in which a man might think as he would and develop as he willed. The migration was not like so many earlier ones in history, led by warrior lords with followers dependent on them, but was one in which the common man as well as the leader was hoping for greater freedom and happiness for himself and his children. English-like, it was for particular liberties for themselves and not a vague "liberty" in itself that they crossed the sea. The dream was as yet largely inchoate and unexpressed, but it was forming.

In 1628 the Company of Massachusetts Bay, in which many Puritan peers and gentlemen were interested as promoters, received a patent from the Crown, and a charter the following year. After an advance party had settled on Massachusetts Bay under the lead of John Endicott, a larger party, numbering about a thousand, came out in 1630 under the lead of John Winthrop, with all the needed cattle, tools, and supplies for settlement on a large scale. The first winter, as usual in all such ventures, was one of great hardship and suffering, but colonizing was now better understood, and the days of failure were past. Within a decade there were to be about fifteen hundred settlers well-rooted in Maine and New Hampshire, fourteen thousand in Massachusetts, three hundred in Rhode Island, two thousand in Connecticut fifteen hundred in Maryland, and eight thousand in Virginia. The whole coast from Maine to Carolina, east of the Appalachians, was by then firmly in the possession of the English, with the exception of the claims of a small body of Dutch who had founded New York, and of some Swedes who had established themselves in Delaware. Before the beginning of the eighteenth century these had been swallowed up by conquest or the irresistible tide of increasing English population, and the colonies of Pennsylvania, the Jerseys, and the Carolinas had also been strongly settled. Many religious sects were now represented, for not only were there the Puritans in New England and the Church of England men in Virginia and the South, but Maryland had been settled as a refuge for Roman Catholics and Pennsylvania for the Quakers.

Internationally, the competition for empire was far from having been determined. France was powerful and ambitious, and was fired by missionary zeal for spreading Christianity among the natives, in exchange for furs. In 1608, she founded the fortified post of Quebec, and from thence for decades missionaries, fur traders, and intrepid explorers pushed their way into the wilderness to the west and southwest. With the successive discovery of the Great Lakes and the exploration of the entire length of the Mississippi by La Salle in 1682, she laid claim to the two great waterways of the continent and the whole of the great central valley. By the end of the first century she had a fort at Niagara and had settled Sault Sainte Marie (fourteen years before Philadelphia), Detroit, Kaskaskia, Vincennes, Duluth, and other places in the Mid-West.

There were missions of the indefatigable Jesuits at many points, and the intoning of the Mass was heard by savage auditors here and there along the whole network of waterways and Indian trails, where the French followed the routes laid down centuries before by the natives. French and Indians fraternized and understood one another. "When the Frenchmen arrived at these falls," said a Chippewa chief in 1826, lamenting the change to American conditions, "they came and kissed us. They called us children and we found them fathers. We lived like brethren in the same lodge, and we had always wherewithal to clothe us. They never mocked at our ceremonies, and they never molested the places of our dead. Seven generations of men have passed away, and we have not forgotten it. Just, very just, were they towards us." One exception there was — the fierce Iroquois of western New York and Ohio, who always preferred the English, and who from their hostility to the French deflected the stream of French exploration and trading to the north of their territory.

Meanwhile the Spaniards were not idle. In 1608 they founded Santa Fé in New Mexico, which is thus twelve years older than Plymouth, and by the year of Winthrop's landing they had twenty-five missions in their new State serving ninety pueblos, with, as they claimed, a thousand Indian Christians in each. The story of our New Mexico for a couple of generations was that of highly colored and picturesque conflicts between the civil (usually very uncivil) governors and the friars — the former, as slave raiders, being as bent on capturing the bodies of the savages as the latter were upon saving their souls.

To offset threatened entry by the French, missions were also established in Texas, where San Antonio was founded in 1718. The need for establishing settlements in California had also been felt, as English freebooters preyed on Spanish ships off the coast, and in 1697 the whole project of Californian settlement was placed in the sole hands of the Spanish Jesuits, who established several missions in the South.

The contrast between the three nations now laying claim to large stretches of the continent was a fascinating one. The imagination of the French had soared to dizzy heights when they saw their empire embracing the vast valleys of the St. Lawrence and the Mississippi, whose waters had been explored by gay-hearted traders or black-robed priests. Agriculture and the plodding ways of backwoods settlers made little appeal to these men who thought in terms of the Kingdom of Heaven and an earthly empire of nearly as great an extent. New France, with a population numbered only in thousands, always remained to some extent dependent on importations of food, whereas the Spaniards in the South supported a population of over five millions on domestic agriculture. The French settlers remained for the most part humbly poor and absurdly few in numbers, considering the empire to which they laid claim, and could scarcely be said to have established more than an outpost of civilization in a wilderness. The Spaniards were numerous, some of them incredibly wealthy, and the civilization they established was to be that of more than the entire southern continent. The French, by love of adventure and the character of their basic industry, the fur trade, were lured ever deeper into the forests, while the Spaniards were busy consolidating a densely populated mining and farming country, with great cattle ranges and ranches. Neither had any race prejudice against the native population, but whereas the French had chiefly amours with the Indian women, and, owing to small numbers, left but little genuine impress upon the native culture, the Spaniards built up a new nation of mixed bloods and transformed a very large part of the great native population from barbarism to civilization. The French dreamed an imperial dream; the Spaniards built an empire.

When we turn from the French Jesuit and gay *voyageur* and explorer, paddling their almost solitary way through thousands of miles of forest streams where white men never had been seen before, or from the Spaniard of great agricultural estates or mines and ranches, to the plodding English in their settlements huddled along the Atlantic Coast, we seem to leave romance for drab reality. It is true that the English also had, to a considerable extent, been lured by dreams of wealth and power, for the myth of the Seven Cities or other great sources of gold and jewels somewhere in the centre of the continent was long to persist. But after a few fruitless explorations the Anglo-Saxon adventurers turned to fish and tobacco and steady hard work to wring their living from sea or soil. In the North they built compact little villages, in the South they scattered more widely on solitary plantations, but all were within reach of seacoast or short stream. At the farthest to the westward, they were but three hundred miles, and usually less, from the great barrier of the Appalachians which hemmed in their land in that direction, and through which only one river, the Hudson-Mohawk, found its way and gave easy passage. Empire builders though they were, they seemed to think and move in inches, tilling their farms or plantations in serried ranks as they advanced. No mines of Potosi, disappointingly but fortunately, turned their minds from the steady work of daily toil, nor did it occur to them to go on wild expeditions merely to trace the course of rivers a thousand miles from where their shops needed tending or their fields tilling.

Nor, again, although a goodly number of them, especially in New England, had come into the wilderness in order to worship God in the only way in which they believed He should be worshiped, were they fired with any missionary zeal. There was some talk now and then of the glory of converting the heathen, but for the most part little or nothing was ever done toward that end. The Reverend John Eliot, in Massachusetts, did attempt it, and translated the Bible into the Algonquian tongue, but he was almost the only person who ventured to think of the Indian as a soul to be saved rather than a child of the devil to be fought when need be — "devilish men who serve nobody but the devil," as Dominie Michaelius called them.

Race consciousness and a sense of superiority were strong in the settlers, and in their minds it was the hand of God that slew Indians for them. Speaking of the disease which had decimated the savages around Plymouth before the Pilgrims landed, a Puritan characteristically noted that "by this means Christ made room for his people to plant." Unlike the French and Spaniards, the English were strengthened in their race consciousness by contact with both Indians and the later negro slaves, and although there was some illicit miscegenation, there was never any social countenance given to racial admixture. In marked contrast to the Latin colonies, English wives and children shared the perilous adventure of their husbands and fathers.

Many a war, however, was fought with the savages, two of the most notable being the Pequot and King Philip's wars in New England. Everywhere, except in Pennsylvania, where for a while the Quakers maintained friendly relations and fair dealings with the natives, the settlers were in constant danger from attack, and at any moment the dreaded war whoop might resound, and fire and ravage follow. The original inhabitants, who had first seen the white men arrive in small scattered bands, now began to find themselves overwhelmed and driven back step by step from their accustomed hunting and camping grounds, their springs and fishing places, their streams and old wigwam sites. As they began drearily to surmise, the pressure from the unknown lands across the sea was to become incessant and relentless.

Although there was a goodly sprinkling of mere adventurers and ne'er-do-weels, the larger part of the English came with the purpose of establishing homes where they could better their condition either from the point of view of religious conditions or, more frequently, merely in the social and economic scale. Even in the New England migration, which was more motivated by religion than any of the other continental ones, such a leader as Winthrop, one of the richest to come, listed among his reasons for the move the facts that his estate had so greatly diminished as to preclude his living longer in his accustomed style at home; that he had lost his office; and that the prospects in England were such as to indicate that he would not in the future have there the scope he wished for the exercise of his talents and ambition. Throughout all the colonies there was a strong Puritan tinge, however, to thought, morals, and the codes of local laws. Puritanism in its widest sense, as a movement of moral reform and purification, was in the air, and received widespread acceptance among the classes who came to America and became the leaders there. Many of the "blue laws" of New England had their counterparts in Anglican Virginia and other colonies.

If the dreams of the early imperialists had been to create an empire, to singe the beard of the king of Spain and to make a shrewd thrust at the Pope, the hope that now dwelt in the breasts of the individual emigrants of all classes was to escape from conditions overseas and to prosper in a new land. They came from prisons, from hovels, from little farm cottages, from town shops, from country manor houses and rectories, but never from palaces. The aristocracy remained in England, and, with scarcely an exception, the thousands who came were from the middle and lower classes, fleeing from persecution or hard social and economic conditions. These men and women of the first few generations were not frontiersmen, and had no qualities in common with those who later were so important and formative an element in American life. These earliest Americans were laborers, tradesmen, artisans, and such, with a slight sprinkling of moderately well-to-do and educated gentlemen. They were lured in large part by the prospect of owning land, but the land that lured them was that nearest at hand and not in the distant wilderness. They came to make homes.

All at first was wilderness, however, and had to be subdued. In that process the man with money found himself brought far nearer the level of the laborer than he had ever dreamed of being in England. At the beginning of most settlements it was "root, hog, or die" for all. It was an omen of deep influence in American life that, when the Winthrop party arrived, food was so scarce that a hundred and eighty indented servants had to be given their liberty, at a cost of nearly £400, because their masters could not feed them. Even when Germantown was established, Pastorius wrote of the Germans arriving in the settlement that all "have to fall to work and swing the axe most vigorously, for wherever you turn the cry is, *Itur in antiquam sylvam*, nothing but endless forests."

This insistence on work is heard all through the period, from every colony. Among the first laws in Virginia it was enacted that if any man be found an idler, even though a freeman, he should be assigned to someone by a magistrate and made to work for wages "till he shewe apparant signes of amendment." A describer of Maryland in 1666 says that "the Son works as well as the Servant, so that before they eat their bread they are commonly taught how to earn it." Even little children under twelve worked in the fields, just as those of our latest immigrants the "Polacks" and others do. The settlers had come from a land with a strongly stratified social scale. They were not engaged in building a Utopia. Their hope was for a civilization which should be, as soon as might be, like that they had known, but in which they would each be freer, richer, and more independent. As the settlements were founded, class distinctions remained, but the unending need for work unconsciously altered the attitude toward labor for gain.

Moreover, as the decades passed, the scarcity of men who would work for wages tended to raise the relative position of the worker. With free land easily obtainable there was little or no reason why a hard-working ambitious man should have to work for another instead of for himself. He could apply for his own bit of land, either freehold in the North or subject to a small and often uncollected quitrent in the South, clear it of trees, build a house with the help of neighbors, and become lord of his own life. There was plenty of land near coast and stream everywhere. On the other hand, there was a tremendous demand for hired labor, on farms, in shops, in the fisheries, and in every sort of occupation in which incipient capitalists were anxious to increase the scale of their operations beyond that possible merely by their own personal exertions. Winthrop's note in 1633 that "the scarcity of workmen had caused them to raise their wages to an excessive rate" was merely a premonitory symptom of what was to become a fundamental tendency of vast importance in American life. Although there was occasional grumbling from discontented settlers of the laboring class, we have not a few letters of this period which indicate how great were the possibilities for them in the new country as contrasted with England. "Wages here are three times as high as there," wrote one. Another wrote that for working people it was much better living here than at home, adding, "I live a simple life and hath builded a shop, and doth follow the weaving of linen cloth, but I have bought 450 acres of land in the woods."

It was this "land in the woods" as a possibility for almost every inhabitant of America that was to prove one of the most powerful of the forces which worked toward a democracy of feeling and outlook, toward the shaping of our American dream. The English mind is essentially a practical and pragmatic one. On the one hand, English rulers never laid down vast and logical (and unworkable) schemes for colonial administration as did the French and Spanish. On the other, also, the citizenry never attempted to make all things new at a stroke of the pen, as the French did in their Revolution. None of the leading men of the English colonists who came over to settle expected or wished for any democratizing of either social or political life. Most of them, like the Reverend John Cotton and John Winthrop, feared and detested democracy. The latter, indeed, cursed it as the "meanest and worst of all forms of government."

But the fact was that in these small new communities, weeks or months from England, local government could function and anarchy be averted only by the consent of the governed, as the signers of the "Mayflower Covenant" had perceived, not as a theory but as a practical exigency. In these small coast villages or groups of plantations, the gentleman and moneyed man might still have various social privileges, but where there were few luxuries to be bought with money, where service was hard to hire, where almost everyone owned his own house and bit of land, where there was as yet little distinction between the houses of rich and poor, where work was a heavy leveler, where almost all had a stake in the community, it was impossible that the ordinary man should not assert himself and become a power.

To a great extent "government" was of a parochial sort, and the questions that had to be decided were such as came home directly to every householder and which he felt as competent to discuss as the "gentlemen." Government was largely concerned with such matters as allotting lands to settlers, laying out highways and working on them, raising money for the support of the town or parish church, arranging for sentry duty, or organizing a small force against the Indians. The French and Spanish settlers were not self-assertive. They accepted the vagaries of aristocratic or imperial overseas government as they did those of hurricane or drought, but the English in their own homeland had developed a different sort of reaction toward life. When an Englishman had taken all the risks of a crossing to the colonies and had gone through the trials and labors of the first years of clearing his land and establishing his little home, it was not in his nature to sit by and allow his daily life to be governed by a few neighbors who, in the wilderness, had lost a good deal of the authority and advantages of mere money or social position which had set them apart in England, and who had come a long way toward his own status of a simple human being struggling to clear a forest. When therefore we find in colony after colony a steady increase in the demand of the ordinary man to be heard in the affairs of his local government, and a widening of the franchise to permit him to do so, we are simply watching the inevitable reaction of English character to circumstance, not the development of any consciously held theory of politics.

The increasing demand for freedom and self-government can be seen clearly at work in Massachusetts in the very first decade of the Puritan settlement. The Puritan leaders had led their hosts of several thousand into the wilderness with the intention of being free to worship as *they* chose and to escape from political and economic conditions in England. The leaders had brought with them to Massachusetts the original charter, intended to be that merely of a trading company, and by a skillful interpretation of its clauses they had made it into a sort of constitution for a self-governing State. This act in itself was for more than a half century to afford them a remarkable training in self-government, but they had no intention of allowing democracy in their government or liberty in worship. The American dream owes more to the wilderness than to them.

Almost at once the influence of conditions in the new and empty land began to make itself felt. The demands and protests of the men of Watertown in 1634 showed clearly that the plain man with his farm cleared by his own labor was going to insist upon a voice in making rules to govern himself. A year later, when Roger Williams was banished and fled to Rhode Island, it was to establish there in time a colony committed to the belief in complete freedom from all dictation in matters of religion. In 1638, when Connecticut had been settled for a couple of years by newcomers from England and discontented inhabitants of Massachusetts, the Reverend Thomas Hooker preached his famous sermon in which the fundamentals of government in the new settlement were proclaimed to be that "the foundation of authority is laid, firstly, in the free consent of the people . . . those who have the power to appoint officers and magistrates, it is in their power, also, to set bounds and limitations of the power and place unto which they call them." By the end of the century we find John Wise, a minister but the son of an indented servant, writing in Massachusetts, although ahead of his time, that government is based on "human free-compacts" and not on divine authority, that its only end is "the good of every man in all his rights, his life, liberty, estate, honor," and that "all power is originally in the people."

The common man had taken a vast step forward. In the forests of America he had become perhaps a freer individual than he had been at any time in the thousand years since his Anglo-Saxon ancestors had dwelt in the forests of Germany. The English government, because it was itself the freest at that time in the world, had helped along the American tendency by giving the colonies local governments in which the lower houses or assemblies were elected by the people. No such gift was given to the inhabitants of New France under the feudal régime in force there, nor to those of New Spain.

But if the common man was rising more rapidly toward freedom and self-government in the English than in the French and Spanish colonies, it is instructive to contrast the three at this period in another respect. All were engaged in attempting to transplant their European culture to their portions of the New World. The French laid their main stress on the religious element, and the effort to convert the savage. In this, in spite of the almost superhuman courage and devotion of the Jesuit priests, they failed, in part because the work of a few was dispersed over thousands of leagues. Moreover, in the small French settlements on the St. Lawrence, the poverty and the paucity of numbers prevented the building up of any genuinely cultured communities. In New Spain, on the other hand, as we have seen, a rather brilliant æsthetic and intellectual civilization, although barbaric, had been found, highly organized and very wealthy. The Spaniards, who amalgamated this with their own, became a sort of ruling caste, the Indians performing most of the labor. There thus sprang into existence almost at once a class which possessed wealth, leisure, and power, and it was through them that the arts were introduced. It was they who were responsible for the amazing transplantation of a full-fledged cultural life.

When we turn to the English colonies, we find an entirely new set of conditions, which caused the English to take a place between the cultural failure of the French and the success of the Spaniards. To develop the higher life of a civilization requires both wealth and leisure — that is, accumulated resources which will permit men to have some time free from the grinding toil of merely feeding and sheltering themselves. The savage, with his low standard of living, often has more "wealth and leisure" than the white man. Because his list of wants are few, he may have ample time to interest himself in his primitive arts.

What the English were trying to do was to establish in the wilderness as quickly as possible, and even in individual cases to better, a standard of life to which they had been accustomed in England, with its centuries of accumulated resources. Owing, as we have said, to poverty of resources and the smallness of the population, such an attempt would have been bound to fail in New France. It succeeded in New Spain because of the conditions we have noted. It proved too much for the English in this first century. They had been met by no such wealthy and organized native civilization as had the Spaniards, and in any case their racial pride would have prevented their building their own civilization upon it as an amalgam. They had, as we have noted, no interest in the Indian as a human being. They regarded him, indeed, as somewhat higher in the scale than the wolves, but nevertheless as something to be cleared from their path, by war or treaty, as rapidly as might be. If they cared nothing for saving his soul, neither for the most part did they about enslaving his body for labor, although they tried it. For labor they depended solely on themselves and such servants, indentured for a few years to pay their passage, as they could get. The few negro slaves were of no importance in this period.

In many cases splendid effort was made to transmit the English standards of life and thought, but as the struggle with the savages and the wilderness continued, it became evident that these standards could not be maintained when energy was continually being diverted and consumed by the incessant toil of wilderness breaking. Something had to be cast overboard, and it proved as always to be the less immediately "useful" parts of man's life, the æsthetic and intellectual. More particularly in New England we may see the two tendencies at work — that of the increased demand of the common man to share in the good things of life, and that of the down drag of the wilderness.

The ideal of the possibility of at least an elementary education for everyone came into being, and at the same time the education of the higher class slowly declined. We make much in our history of the founding of Harvard in 1636, but this remained the only institution above an ordinary school in the colonies for nearly sixty years, and was pitiably unimportant in the training it afforded and the scholarship it produced as compared with the universities in New Spain. In fact nearly two hundred years were to pass before any English institution in America reached the point which the Spanish had attained even before the English had settled at all. As we shall see, other races, white and black, were to come to take off the shoulders of the English some of the weight of mere physical toil, but during this first period, when they essayed the task of doing everything for themselves, they gradually sank, until the decade of about 1700 to 1710 marked the lowest period of English culture reached in America before or since.

To some extent the period, like that of every recurring frontier, was to leave a lasting scar. It was not merely that the folk arts, such as wood carving, painting of furniture, artistic weaving, were more or less abandoned in the hard struggle to have anything at all, even if it were not beautiful. This was, indeed, also a permanent spiritual loss in itself, but the scar that lasted was the feeling developed among the ordinary people that such spiritual satisfactions as the arts can give are mere trimmings of life. It could be truly said in 1719 by an early authentic American voice that "the Plow-man that raiseth Grain is more serviceable to Mankind than the Painter who draws only to please the Eye," but under other conditions of life, when a surplus has been accumulated, the statement has its falsity as well as its truth. A long struggle with the frontier was to make it seem true to most of us *semper et ubique*.

Scattered throughout all the colonies were men of education and cultivated tastes, but, on the whole, life became extremely small and petty in all the length of these coast settlements. Practically all the settlers at first had belonged to the middle or laboring class, with the somewhat narrow point of view that belongs in general to them. This narrowness was greatly emphasized by the lack of interests and by the gossipy, prying habits of village life everywhere. This latter quality was in turn emphasized by that tendency of the Puritan mind which makes each one his brother's keeper to an unholy extent. The thoughts of the settlers tended to become ingrowing. Because recreation was scarce, even when not frowned upon or prohibited in many of its older forms, the settlers occupied themselves too much with their neighbors' morals and habits. The common man, who was now finding himself in the rôle of lawmaker, enjoyed his new importance to the full. Moreover, the self-made man is proverbially self-satisfied, and in a sense all Americans in this period were self-made. They had performed a great task, had shown courage and endurance, but they were aware of it. In the more strictly Puritan colonies, Puritanism, with its assertion that its members are a chosen race, added fuel to this burning belief in their own superiority, and left us an unhappy inheritance from its believers. "God hath sifted a whole nation, that he might send choice grain into this wilderness," wrote Stoughton. "We are as a city set upon a hill," wrote Bulkeley, "in the open view of all the earth, the eyes of the world are upon us, because we profess ourselves to be a people in Covenant with God." In the middle and southern colonies, fortunately for leavening America, people took themselves less seriously.

This first American frontier along the fringe of coast was never really a frontier in the later American sense, but in the formative stage of the old colonial life it did acquire some of the impresses of all frontiers. Man rationalizes and idealizes the sort of life that is imposed upon him. In the absence of any rich stores of gold or precious stones, and of an adequate labor supply, the only way open to the English was plain hard work. The machinery of life — farms, houses, capital of all sorts; in a word, money and comfort — had to be created as the most pressing task of all. Hard work became transmuted into a moral virtue and leisure into evil. Mere ease and wealth, because so hardly won and won by the exercise of the moral virtue of work, took on exaggerated importance and became God's blessing. That first frontier began to set its stamp on America. Again and again and again, on successive and more genuine frontiers, some of these stamps were to be forced down harder and harder.

Meanwhile, the Atlantic seaboard had become definitely English. By 1700 there were about two hundred and sixty thousand Englishmen in the colonies, or about a hundred thousand more than there were Spaniards in New Spain, whereas there were only about thirteen thousand French on the whole continent. The English, moreover, were compactly settled, scarcely anywhere more than a hundred miles from the shore, with the Appalachians hemming them in everywhere on the west. Ninety per cent of them lived and worked on farms or plantations. The rest were fishermen, sailors, clergymen, merchants, lumbermen, or what not. Under pressure of circumstance most of them had also become Jacks-of-all-trades who could turn their hands to making or doing almost anything. There probably was not a gentleman of leisure on the continent, north of Mexico, unless he were a jailbird or a redskin.

In a few places towns had grown populous. Charleston, the only one of importance in the South, may have had fifteen hundred people. Philadelphia, which had been laid out only in 1683, had grown with amazing rapidity and numbered, like New York, about four thousand, whereas Boston, the metropolis of the colonies, had possibly seven thousand. But everywhere, although pushed back from the coast, the Indian formed a long encircling line behind the settlements, hostile or friendly by turns, making war or treaties. In village or lonely cabin on the outer fringe of settlement the war whoop sounded and men slept with their guns beside them. Slowly, doggedly, these English felled the forest and the foe. Strong in their racial pride, detesting the Indian and other "vermin" that barred their way, consciously elect of God, bent on winning lands and homes — these were the men of destiny.

II

A CIVILIZATION ESTABLISHED

History has concerned itself greatly with forms of government and the records of politicians and parties. These have their place and importance, but more deeply essential is the character of a people. The same republican, parliamentary system conferred upon Englishmen, Frenchmen, or East Indians would become completely different within a few generations. Under all the machinery of life devised or evolved, the varieties of humanity twist and turn and end by impressing their own idiosyncrasies on the machine, although in the process they may themselves be materially influenced. This was the case in the colonies.

The English mind had long been accustomed to the triple combination of King, Lords, and Commons; and in general this type was reproduced in America, with local variations. In the experimental stage, when the colonies were first being planted, various sorts of government were imposed or developed, but, especially after the return of the Stuarts from exile in 1660, there was a strong tendency toward increasing the imperial control and making the governments more uniform, a tendency which was notable in the forfeiture of the old Massachusetts charter in 1684. In general, though Rhode Island and Connecticut remained almost independent, there was in each colony a Royal Governor, appointed by the Crown, who represented the King; a Council, or Upper House of the Legislature, which tended to be undemocratic owing to the methods of selecting its members, and for other reasons; and an Assembly, or Lower House, which was popularly elected, as popular election was then understood, and which was the chief fighting ground of the ordinary people. The Assemblies were splendid arenas for the play of popular politics and feeling, and the parliamentary battles of old England, such as that for the control of the purse, were fought over again in almost every colonial government.

If these governments, however, in their triple form much resembled the King, Lords, and Commons of England, there were new factors involved which greatly affected the comparison. For one thing, the Royal Governor, too often a needy and broken politician from home (though there were notable exceptions), was invested with none of the sanctity and reverence which hedged the monarch himself. The Englishman at home felt quite differently toward a King Charles or William or George from the way a colonial felt toward his Governor, Cornbury, Burnet, or Andros. These latter were mere men, and were fair game in a rough-and-tumble political fight. Moreover, although local laws were enacted by the local governments, Parliament, across the seas, also enacted laws, and in that body the colonists were in no way directly represented. And there were three thousand miles of perilous seas between the old mercantile homeland and the new lands producing chiefly raw materials — furs, lumber, fish, tobacco.

Several important results flowed from these conditions. In the first place, the ordinary man represented in the Assemblies, who, as we have seen, had risen considerably in his sense of independence and self-esteem in America as contrasted with England, felt a good deal freer to fight a parliamentary battle against a governor than his fellow commoner in England did to fight one against the King. Moreover, it was a good bit safer to play a skillful hand against even His Majesty himself when he and his power were on the other side of the Atlantic. All passions grow by what they feed upon, and at that time the colonists were the freest people anywhere in the world in playing their political games in their Assemblies. There was no lack whatever of loyalty to monarch and mother country, but in a sense both King and Parliament were absentees, and the colonists were quite naturally convinced that neither knew what was good for them as well as they knew it themselves. The governors, as representing this absentee government, came to represent in the minds of the people an almost foreign power, which might, and frequently did, thwart their own will; and so there arose that profound and often unwise conviction in America that executive power must always be dreaded, whereas full confidence can be reposed in the legislative.

In this same situation was evolved the germ of another and even more serious trait in American character. A sense of law and respect for it is one of the deep-rooted traits of Englishmen. It was amply displayed in the Mayflower Covenant and other acts of the first comers. If a good many (though not many in comparison with the total) of the immigrants in the first century were taken from English jails, it does not mean that they were criminals. They had been jailed mostly for debt, vagrancy, or trifling thefts, at that time cruelly punished. Under better economic conditions, crimes against person or property became extremely rare in the colonies — so rare that, in spite of the lonely roads through the woods connecting almost all the settlements, I have found only one case of highway robbery in the entire colonial period.

Had the colonies not formed part of an empire, but been wholly free to enact their own laws for themselves, it is likely they would have continued to respect them, though excess of puritanical zeal by the new lawmakers might here and there militate against it. Such an unenforceable law, for example, as that in Connecticut which called for the putting to death of any boy above sixteen who would not obey his mother was, like so many of our later ones, not calculated to maintain the majesty of law itself. But the colonies were parts of an empire, and as laws, some wise and some unwise, were passed overseas, protecting the forests, reserving trees suitable for masts for the royal navy, regulating trade, manufactures, and otherwise interfering with what the colonists considered their legitimate interests and profits, they disobeyed them when they chose. The right of Parliament to make laws was not at this time denied, but, what was more serious, the colonists got in the habit of deciding for themselves as individuals which laws they would obey and which they would ignore or even forcibly resist.

If a case were brought by a royal official to the courts, juries would find for their neighbor and not for the King. Lawbreaking of some sorts was not serious. The court records are full of cases of fines for cursing, slander, fornication, and so on which took their appointed course. The serious matter was the drift of mind of the rich and leading men of the community as well as the common people toward the belief that if a law interfered with their business and profits it need not be obeyed, and that they were morally justified in nullifying it if they did not personally like it. In some cases, as in that of the Molasses Act of 1733, such a law would have meant general ruin for certain colonies, and as repeal was shown to be impossible, this seemed to sanction the general theory of selection and nullification which came to be stretched to cover any law which might mean trouble or decreased profit, or even which merely gave the nullifier an advantage over the man who obeyed it. This is perhaps the most damaging legacy left to us from this period, emphasized by the frontier life of later epochs to come.

On the whole, however, the system of colonial government as exercised by England did not work badly until after the end of the Seven Years' War in 1763. Certainly it gave the Americans an incomparable schooling in political life. Under it, they prospered exceedingly, and by the date named had built up a strong and vigorous civilization. Adventurous life on the outskirts of the world unquestionably breeds a hardy and courageous type of men, but for civilization as we know it both wealth and a settled way of living are essential, and these the colonies enjoyed during the period from 1700 until 1763. It is true that on the edge of settlement, as they pushed ever farther and farther back from the sea, the savage was a constant menace. The terrible massacre of the inhabitants of Deerfield was but one incident in the constant clashes of white and red along the whole border from Maine to Georgia. Off the coasts lurked pirates with their headquarters in Carolina bays or Caribbean Islands. Sometimes in league with the English authorities and the less scrupulous American business men, they even swaggered the streets of little New York, and not a few money chests of New Yorkers in high standing were filled with "Arabian gold." Teach, Blackbeard, the notorious Captain Kidd, and others gave color to the scene, and helped to build up our legendary past in which explorers, pirates, savages, western-trekking pioneers, covered wagons, gold seekers, bad men, and cowboys pass in endless file across the screen.

Violence, however, was incidental, and a culture along English lines, but indigenous to America, quickly arose, and with it came not only a much greater richness of life but a fast-increasing differentiation between the various groups of colonies. During most of the seventeenth century, although New England was more given to overseas trade, and more insistent upon the utility of a cash balance and of being the elect of God, than were the Southern colonies, nevertheless the population of all was over 90 per cent agricultural and there was little difference in that field. The unit of plantation size in Virginia was about the same as in Massachusetts, and even at the end of the century, when negro slavery had begun, over 60 per cent of the Southern plantations were as yet small enough to be tilled by the owner himself, when he possessed neither black slave nor white indented servant. The chief agricultural difference, and it was an important one in its eventual effect, was that from Maryland southward it had become apparent that profit lay only in raising one staple crop, whereas in the North, owing to different soil and climate, the crops were diversified. From 1700 or thereabouts, however, three sections emerge, the social and economic characteristics of which become markedly different as the century advances.

One of the fundamental needs in America, if a civilization was to arise, was the accumulation of capital — that is, of resources greater than those consumed in daily living. The Spaniards, as we have seen, had found a vast store of capital ready to their hands in New Spain, due to the accumulations of the earlier civilization, and also an unlimited supply of labor for the accumulation of more. The English found none of either. By the hardest sort of toil the first settlers provided themselves with cleared fields for food and small houses for shelter, but beyond that the building up of capital was bound to be slow if every individual merely tilled his own fields, the results of such toil barely providing for more than the subsistence of his household. Such a state of society might breed certain virtues of its own, and would certainly be equalitarian and uniform, but it would not develop a variegated and spiritually rich civilization. In the absence of machinery, the only way in which an energetic, ambitious, able man could extend his wealth-producing power was by the use of hired or other labor, a part of whose produce would go to the laborers and the surplus to himself. By gift or graft he might win from governors or legislatures vast grants of land. But so long as he could use only such part as he could till or clear by himself, it was of no use to him, save as he might look forward to a labor supply or to new settlers to whom he might sell, at low prices.

For the reason already given, free labor in all the colonies was extremely scarce. A man of any value who was free to do as he chose would naturally not be a wage earner when, with no more labor than if he worked for someone else, he could get a house and farm of his own, and by so doing put himself socially and economically on a par with the overwhelming proportion of his fellow citizens. For the first few generations, all the colonies experimented with the use of indented servants, whose time and service were bought for a term of years by paying their passage over. After a while the traffic became a business, and the colonists would buy the servant from the sea captain who had secured him or her in England and who sold their time on arriving in America. In all the colonies, New England as well as south, Indian slavery was also tried on a small scale, but proved unprofitable, the Indian, unlike his Mexican fellow, not being used to a settled life and proving intractable in confinement.

Next, all the colonies tried to solve their labor problem by negro slaves, and this proved effective in the South of the single staple crop. A white indented servant was more intelligent, but he cost from two to four pounds a year for his period of service, at the end of which, lured by the free grant of fifty acres from the government, he could, and usually did, leave his master. On the other hand, a negro slave could be bought for eighteen to thirty pounds. If he lived for a similar number of years, the cost would be only one pound annually during his service, and in addition the master owned all his children, which added a considerable unearned increment to his capital. The negroes, particularly the women, of the more docile tribes imported made excellent house servants, though the men were not so useful unless their work was simple and more or less uniform in nature. This was just the case, however, in the cultivation of tobacco, in which the process, easily learned, continued forever without variation. In 1698, there were more white indented servants in Virginia than there were blacks, and the number imported was greater. Then the tide began to turn. With the granting by Spain to England of a monopoly of the Spanish slave trade in 1713, a flood of slaves began to be shipped to the colonies, the New Englanders, for reasons we shall note later, eagerly seizing upon the profit to be made in the traffic.

The type of life which now evolved in the South was in many ways the most delightful America has known, and that section has become in retrospect our land of romance. It was the period of the building of the "great houses," though they were not in reality so very "great," charming as they were. The

Byrd family, which had built their first house in 1690, built the present beautiful "Westover" thirty years later, and when we think of the "old South" it is of the lives led in such places as these; we forget the other side of the picture.

Great landed estates, whether in England, the West Indies, our old South or elsewhere, develop certain qualities in their owners. The man who has a thousand tenants on his estate or a thousand slaves on his plantation develops a sense of responsibility and of easy mastery and leadership. It is a patriarchal life, quite different from that of an employer of labor on even a far larger scale when that labor consists only of a shifting body of daily wage earners. On an estate one has to look after "one's people" from birth to death, from generation to generation, in work and in sickness. In the South there was always also the need for sudden command in case of a slave insurrection.

There is something, moreover, that fosters the aristocratic virtues and outlook in the mere fact of living in a large house, affording space and privacy, in the midst of one's own vast domain. A social life is bound to emerge of a type quite different from that in a bustling town where all one's friends live within five minutes of one another. The peace of the great estates, the distances between them which made a "call" usually a stay overnight if not of several days, tended toward a leisurely and unhurried form of society, and the need for social intercourse was all the greater for the semi-isolation in which all lived. Life took on a comeliness, a grace, and a charm that it can never have in a confused, hurried existence. Moreover, although it is the way of great planters everywhere to run into debt and believe themselves far richer than they are, the mere largeness of their operations, the shipping once a year of a great staple crop the value of which runs into high figures, lends a feeling of amplitude and scale to their lives. Hospitality becomes as unstinted as it is cordial. When the owners of such estates are men of cultivated tastes, the character of their minds is apt to be philosophical, and their culture broad. It is noteworthy, in connection with the qualities sketched above, that when the need arose for a man who could lead and inspire an army he had to be sought in the great slave owner of Mount Vernon, and that the philosopher of the Revolution was the great slave owner of Monticello.

Although there had been a strong Puritan tinge to the thought of the colonists everywhere, there had not been in the South that harsh and determined Puritanism which grew steadily more narrow and bitter in New England. The "New England conscience" was not found among the first settlers in the South. It would probably not have survived the climate even if it had been there.

The Southerners, moreover, maintained a closer connection with old England than any of the other colonists. Living on their estates, fox hunting, dancing, visiting, playing cricket, they were closely allied in sympathy and tastes to the Tory gentry of the English county families. They were also in constant relation with the great mercantile firms of London, not merely as buyers and sellers, but as permanent clients whose cash balances, or, much more often, whose debits, remained on the books of their correspondents for a generation or more. Owing to their scattered plantations, any school for a group of families of the upper class would have been difficult, so the children were taught in their own homes by tutors who were usually imported from England. When older, the boys not seldom went to Oxford or Cambridge to finish their education, and to the Temple to study law and be admitted to the bar. The sons of these American planters were no rare visitants in London society, and brought home with them, when they returned, English social training and English tastes.

Once back in South Carolina, Virginia, or Maryland, the young man found himself a member of a distinct governing class, which had originally derived its power from being a small clique, controlling the Council and in close relations with the governor, but which gradually transferred its activities to the House of Burgesses as class distinction took the broader basis of slave owners or non-owners. He would find also a dignified house of Georgian type, modified in its architecture by the local conditions of climate, with long avenues of trees leading up to it and flower gardens in the English style about it. Within were numerous slaves to wait on him, a few books, or in some cases well-stocked libraries, to browse in, beautiful furniture from England, silver plate and family portraits, and in the stables horses to his fancy. The places had not yet been mellowed by time, and the country was still new and a trifle raw, but life was full, rich, and urbane for the young squire as compared with what his father and grandfather had known.

As we pass northward to the middle colonies, — Pennsylvania, the Jerseys, and New York, — we find quite a different type of culture. The tobacco fields disappear, and the slaves are less in evidence except as house servants, for the simple reason that they have not proved so profitable in the economic life of these colonies. There have been some large land grants, colossal indeed in New York, as we shall see; but without a plentiful labor supply and without large immigration these have not yet proved so profitable. We find instead the comfortable farms of Germans and Welsh as well as English, and the beginnings of manufacturing, notably iron furnaces, which were already beginning to be sources of wealth.

Philadelphia and New York, as ports, were also rapidly outdistancing Boston, and much of young American commerce was beginning to pass through them. New York, already cosmopolitan with eighteen languages to be heard in it, would have grown much more rapidly had the Van Cortlandts, the Van Rensselaers, and others, who had secured enormous tracts of lands up the Hudson Valley, been willing to encourage settlement, in which case the back country of the Hudson and the Mohawk would have become populous and rich. Their policies, however, were selfish and shortsighted, and New York alone of the colonies still depended to a great extent upon its fur trade. Had this been properly conducted, a vast sphere of influence among the Indians might have been developed to the west; but, in direct contact with the savage, the French were better traders than the New Yorkers, who to a great extent found it more profitable to sell their trading goods to the French at Montreal than to exchange them directly with the Indians for furs.

The English governor, Burnet, saw the danger of giving the French the advantage of making the Indians dependent upon them, but the merchants, preferring their immediate profits to any farsighted policy of statesmanship, disobeyed the laws prohibiting the French trade, and finally secured the recall of the governor. The impression one gets of New York in this period is of a hustling, moneygrubbing, rather corrupt community, the leaders of which were anxious to get rich quickly by any means, however unsocial, even to allying themselves with pirates and strengthening the Indian foes. From these conditions a rough-and-ready, overbearing, bribing, and unscrupulous type of business man was beginning to emerge. Although the town had its theatre and even art exhibitions, one does not find in it either the culture of the best families in the South or the intense if narrow preoccupation with intellectual matters that one finds in the Boston circles.

In New England, the poor soil, the harsh climate, and the necessity for diversified crops had utterly precluded the success of slave labor out of doors, for which, otherwise, the New Englanders would have been grateful enough. They had not the slightest objection to slavery as an institution in this period, and used slaves when they could afford them and where they found them profitable, as in housework. When it became apparent that farming in New England was always to remain a small and unprofitable business, owing to the soil, the inability to get white labor, and the impossibility of using black, those ambitious to grow rich turned largely to overseas trade, one of the profitable branches of which was importing slaves from Africa for use in the West Indies and the South. The chief currency with which they secured the slaves was rum, and this was distilled from molasses, bought mostly in the West Indies. In exchange for this, they exported to the islands great quantities of lumber, staves, horses, and produce of various kinds. To pay for their large importations of manufactured goods from England, and of wines from the wine islands, they exported their dried fish and every conceivable commodity they could raise or procure which would have a market anywhere.

The balance of trade was always in imminent danger of going against them, and, without any staple crop such as enabled their richer Southern cousins to live at ease, even when in debt, they had to sharpen their wits to drive every possible sort of bargain. Although the total volume of their trade was large, it was in small lots in small ships, and partook of the nature of huckstering. Almost every village which could be reached by a small boat, even those far up the Connecticut River, took part in it, but Newport and particularly Boston were the centres, the latter always remaining the metropolis of the entire group of New England colonies.

The type of mind and character developed by all the New England conditions was in marked contrast to that of the South. By force of circumstances, "work," as we have seen, had early become, as it was to remain, one of the cardinal American virtues. If life was to become something more than a mere scrabble for existence, capital was necessary in New England as well as anywhere else. That section possessed no rich natural resources (except fish in the sea), no iron ore for manufacturing, no labor, free or slave, to be exploited. There was only one way out. One penny would somehow have to be made to do the work of three, and every possible profit must be squeezed out of a bargain with fellow citizen or foreigner. As always, the necessity was rationalized to make it attractive; and thrift and shrewdness were added to the list of essential virtues. It became sinful to spend freely, just as it was sinful not to be forever at work, except on the Sabbath; and when the catch of fish or slaves was good, God had smiled on one of his saints. It was all very natural and very human.

The New Englanders were, indeed, very human. Many writers have tried to prove this platitudinous thesis by showing that they liked gay clothes, that they did occasionally read frivolous poetry, that their youths were as amorous as those elsewhere, or in such other like ways. A much simpler method of observing the obvious truth is to note the manner in which they received the impress of their times and surroundings. When the great immigration took place, Puritanism was one of the absorbing movements in the life of the English nation. For the most part the New England immigrants came from the extreme Left Wing, and were Puritans of the Puritans, so far as their leaders were concerned. A large part of the general mass was not, but from the first the colony, with a good bit of rebelling now and then, was forced to take the impress of the clerical and lay Left Wing leaders. About the same time that Massachusetts was settled, a similar migration under the same auspices had gone to the Caribbean, but there the climate proved stronger than Calvin. In New England the soil and climate ruggedly backed up the theology of the dominant group.

As time went on, the gristle of conscience, work, thrift, shrewdness, and duty became bone. There were no influences making for suppleness. It was good bone, all too lacking to-day, but the flesh was missing about it. There was no softening effect of climate. Indeed, some of the New Englander's preoccupation with hell fire may be accounted for by the severity of his winters and the depth of his snowdrifts. There were no broadening contacts with the outside world. For nearly a century from 1640 there was to be no further immigration of any amount. When on one occasion a few misguided Scotch-Irish did venture to intrude, they were promptly made to feel that they were not wanted.

In any society the influence of the life and outlook of those at the top is almost immeasurable. Throughout its first century and more, the leaders in New England steadily declined in humane culture. In the first migration, narrow as we may think many of them, there had been an ample number of men of affairs who had been in contact with many sides of the rich life of England in the seventeenth century. In 1643, for example, of the eighty ministers in New England over half were graduates of Oxford or Cambridge. Fifty years later, of the one hundred and twenty-three in Massachusetts and Connecticut, one hundred and seven were graduates of Harvard. The freshening airs had ceased to blow, and there was none of that frequent contact with the culture of the Old World that there was in the South. Lack of intercourse with others tended to emphasize the New Englander's deep-rooted belief in his own superiority as the chosen vessel of God for the regeneration of the world, the "city set on a hill," with a consequent increase in his aloofness and provinciality. The intellectual life that remained came to be pedantic and narrow rather than humane and broad, with both conscience and thrift operating against much that is valuable in social life and the arts.

There were thus forces at work tending strongly to differentiate the character of the various sections. There were also others which were common to all, and which resulted during this period in the formation of the first genuine American frontier, which came to stretch, like a selvage edge, at the back of all the varicolored colonies.

If capital is essential to civilization, it is also obvious that, whatever the future of a machine age may be, there cannot be, without machines or some very different form of social organization than mankind has ever yet been willing to venture upon, any concentration and large accumulation of capital without labor. In all history so far, civilization has rested upon accumulated capital, and capital upon exploited labor; and as labor made the American frontier, and the frontier has largely made America what it is, we are bound to trace the first beginnings.

There had, of course, been some differences in wealth in the colonies from the very beginning, but these had been unimportant so long as there was always free land only a few miles beyond the line of settlement and little or no labor to be hired. At the very opening of the period of this chapter we come upon a somewhat different situation. In a little less than a quarter of a century before the Peace of Utrecht in 1713, the population of the colonies had increased from about 213,000 to 357,000. The period had been one of constant danger from the French and Indians, and there was no incentive to move beyond the line of strong settlements. In fact, that line had actually retreated. The result was that the density of population had nearly doubled. This would in itself have created new problems had not the year in which the war ended seen the emergence of new forces that were to affect us profoundly. Although the rise of the capitalists, and the discontent of the poor, were common to all the colonies, we must consider the different sections in their local aspects. In the preceding period capital had been accumulated in various ways, such as planting, fishing, fur trading, operating a mill, merchandising, but all on a small scale. Farsighted men everywhere had secured for themselves large land grants, but had been unable to develop them profitably. Now all was to change.

In Virginia, for example, to begin again with the South, William Fitzhugh in 1684 had twenty-four thousand acres of land with only three hundred under cultivation. He had a mill, two stores, and raised cattle and hogs. He was one of the very rich men of his day, but his land could not produce income without labor, and he had only twenty-nine slaves for all his enterprises. Control of labor was control of power, like water, steam, or electricity, and as usual it would enure to the benefit of those who could first preëmpt a share in it. Up to the beginning of the eighteenth century there had been poor white men farming in the South, but no "poor whites." The relation of a vast plantation, with its equipment of several hundred slaves, to a single-handed farm, however, was soon to be similar to that of a modern textile mill to the cottage of the hand weaver. Such a vast plantation called for two things — land and slaves.

The large landholdings were for the most part got in devious ways, through official position, influence with the aristocratic Council, or "friendship," so to say, with the Royal Governor. But all of this required a social position, connections, and a finesse wholly beyond the sphere of the ordinary settler. Once the land was got, moreover, the purchase of slaves on a considerable scale called for capital which only those who had secured it by marriage or in the various ways noted above would possess. The quality of the tobacco raised by the white farmer on his few acres was far better than that raised on the big plantations by slave labor, but the small farmer became helpless when it came to disposing of his crop in the face of such competition. As in all large-scale businesses, economies could be effected, connections made, and terms arranged which are beyond the reach of the small individual. Moreover, as the land became absorbed by the fortunate and the new source of black slave power was applied to it, the price went up, and it became more difficult for the poorer man to secure good and convenient acreage for himself or his children.

Meanwhile the rich grew richer, intermarried, controlled the Council, formed a clique with the governor, and for them all went merry as a marriage bell. A hitherto unknown gulf began to separate these "first families" from the farmers tilling their own soil behind their mules. The great plantations became self-sustaining units, making their own harness, clothes for slaves, raising up their carpenters, wheelwrights, and every sort of handicraftsman. Not alone was the competition killing, but racial pride came into the problem, and the poor white farmer or artisan was put down to a hopeless position as compared with the rich — on a level with the negroes, unless he owned some. In increasing numbers these new poor whites gave up the fight, left the old farm, and trekked up to the high lands of the western part of the colony to begin again on a frontier.

In Maryland the same tendency was at work, with variations. Slaves were brought in, but men like Carroll and Dulany, who had acquired enormous tracts of land, preferred in part to settle them with tenant farmers, and so carry them until the increase in population should give them enhanced value. The possibility of owning land in fee simple had always been, and long remained, one of the chief inducements to undertaking the great risk and hardship of immigration to the New World. Even a nominal quitrent was greatly disliked, which may account in part for the first heavy migration to New England. It was still more difficult to find men who were willing to become tenant farmers, as in the Old World, and it was only a special set of circumstances, all militating against the poor, which enabled the large Maryland proprietors to build up their estates around 1730 to 1745 with tenants of a foreign race.

For long there had been distress of the most appalling sort in both Germany and Ireland. In the first, the results of the Thirty Years' War, which ended in 1648, had been ghastly beyond comparison with even the recent Great War. One county alone had lost 85 per cent of its horses, over 80 per cent of its cattle, and 65 per cent of its houses, while 75 per cent of its population had been killed. In the latter part of the century, sections of the country were harried by the French, and the unfortunate peasants, trying to build up some sort of life again, sowed their crops only to have them destroyed by the enemy. To all this was added political and religious persecution. Between 1683 and 1727, probably about twenty thousand of these unfortunate Germans emigrated to Pennsylvania. Those first coming found ample lands on which to settle near Philadelphia, but as these were taken up or the price advanced, the later comers were forced further into the wilderness, and, by way of its northern end, began to settle in the valley of the Shenandoah.

Ireland had been nearly as badly off. Ulster had been settled largely by Scots, but the Revolution of 1689 in England left them crushed. Ten years later they were hard hit by the law against woolen manufacturing. In the second decade of the eighteenth century, in the midst of almost hopeless economic depression, great numbers of long-time leases fell in and the landlords insisted upon renewing them at double and even treble the old rents. There were wholesale ejections, and drought, sheep rot, and epidemics of smallpox added to the unspeakable misery of the Protestant population, whose standard of living had been higher than that of the Catholic Irish. By 1729 perhaps seven or eight thousand had emigrated to America, mostly to Pennsylvania, but in that year six thousand landed at Philadelphia, and two years later Logan wrote that it looked as though Ireland were about to dump her entire population on the colony. Partly on account of their extreme poverty, these immigrants at once sought lands at little cost or none on the extremest frontier yet settled, in the Susquehanna and Cumberland valleys, up the Juniata, and down into the Shenandoah.

It was out of the misery of Germany that the Maryland landlords determined to build up their tenantry. Agents were sent abroad and went through the Palatinate and other sections where the suffering and discontent were greatest, preaching the wonderful opportunities in the New World. The operations were on a large scale and costly. They proved, however, extremely profitable. Dulany's great tracts in Frederick County had been unbroken wilderness in 1730, but in fifteen years he had laid out the town of Frederick and the county had become the second most populous in the colony. These leases enabled the landlords to carry their land and reap a colossal harvest as the country filled up, and land tripled in price between 1730 and 1760. In 1774, when John Adams met Carroll's son at the Continental Congress, he noted that he was "of the first fortunes in America. His income is ten thousand pounds sterling a year, will be fourteen in two or three years, they say; besides his father has a vast estate which will be his."

In New York at the beginning of the eighteenth century, leading business men and politicians, such as the Schuylers, Beekmans, and Livingstons, had secured enormous land grants by connivance with disreputable governors, notably Fletcher and Cornbury, and it was said that by the time Fletcher left, three quarters of the entire available land in the colony had been granted to thirty persons, one grant, under Cornbury, being for two million acres. Schuyler and his associates obtained another in the Mohawk Valley fifty miles long. In various ways Robert Livingston secured an estate sixteen miles wide and twenty-four long. The New Yorkers, however, were too grasping in their terms and the treatment they meted out to settlers, and after some attempts the Germans gave the colony a wide berth, while it was obviously no place for the Scotch-Irish. Some settlements were made out on the frontier, but these were perpetually harried by the demands of the landlords.

In New England, although the grants obtained from complacent legislatures were smaller in extent, so also was the amount of tillable soil, and as the century advanced and population increased, the people found themselves hard put to it to find speculative townships on the frontier where they could make their homes, and when they did so they suffered from the exactions of the proprietors under the New England system. Even so worthy a citizen as Ezra Stiles saw to it, when he helped to promote such a speculation, that the proprietors should hold all the shares that carried control of taxation, although such proprietors often never even saw the place itself.

The new frontier, which for all these reasons was being formed all along the colonies, beyond the back line of the old settlements, was quite different in spirit from that of the first seaboard plantings. In the beginning, opportunity had been more or less open to all, and there was a feeling that all were united in an arduous and dangerous enterprise. By the middle of the eighteenth century, opportunity appeared to a great extent to have been monopolized by the rich and influential, and many of the poorer people felt that even here in the New World they were being shut out not only from a chance to rise, but from opportunity to maintain their living on a small scale. The advancing wealth of society as a whole had affected the poorer people chiefly adversely, when it had done so at all. Their farms were no larger, their houses and furniture no better. Their labor had not been lightened. No inventions or machinery had come into being which altered the routine of their lives. On the other hand, there was evident to any observer an immense increase in the wealth, luxury, and leisure of the fortunate rich. Yet what all classes desired was comfort, stability, and safety in a home life, whether in a village or on their farms.

There was as yet no genuine frontier spirit, not even among those who were forced out by economic maladjustment or misfortune into the renewed danger and hardship of the wilderness and the Indian country. If, when they tramped westward with their families and few belongings, they held courage and hope in their hearts, they also lodged bitterness there against the colonial rich whom they deemed responsible for their plight. Moreover, on the first fringe of settlement, which had never really been an American "frontier," rich and poor, learned and ignorant, had worked and lived in the same community. This newer frontier sheltered only the poor and the comparatively ignorant. The original settlers had been looked down upon by nobody, but now the inhabitants of the older settlements did look down upon the frontiersmen, who came to be termed "buckskins" and who were made to feel their inferiority in sophistication.

One other important factor in the new situation must be noted. If the rapid and, it must be added, essential and fortunate creation of capital was bringing about a distinction between rich and poor in the old settlements, if a frontier was coming into existence with grievances against the seaboard and its culture, there was also an element of no little significance in the character and circumstances of the new immigration. By the middle of the eighteenth century there may have been 80,000 Swiss and Germans and 50,000 Scotch-Irish in the colonies, these groups forming over 10 per cent of the total population. In this large leaven, the Teutonic portion had no attachment whatever to England, and, indeed, not the slightest interest in her. If they had taken any interest in Anglo-colonial relations, it could only have been to regard England, not as the mother country to which they were bound by ties of sentiment and descent, but as a foreign and unknown power. On the other hand, the Scotch-Irish had left their old homes with a deep, bitter, and abiding hatred of England and her ways. From her had come all their woes and the need of abandoning their homes.

Moreover, these people had become thoroughly embittered against the political and economic power of those above them in their old lands, and their experiences on their way to America and when they landed did nothing to assuage this. We have heard much of the horrors of the "Middle Passage" for the negro slaves captured in Africa and herded into ships for transportation across the sea. But the Scotch and Germans fared little if any better. On the voyage the food was often so rotten and maggoty as to be uneatable. Delay from calms brought the immediate spectre of death by starvation or thirst. In many instances they fought for the dead bodies of rats, and in at least one case, officially reported, they had eaten six human bodies and were cutting up a seventh when sighted by another ship and supplied with a little food. There were almost no sanitary arrangements and the filth and vermin were unbelievable. On one immigrant ship three hundred and fifty passengers died out of four hundred, and these figures can be almost duplicated in many other instances. The mortality was always frightful. Costs were piled up on the immigrants unexpectedly and to such great extent that on landing, when the living would be held accountable for the passage money of the dead, they would often have to sell themselves into bondage, and families would be torn apart and sold to different temporary owners as if they had been negro slaves.

It is not surprising that when these famished creatures finally got away safe from the clutches of every kind of sharper and made off for the wilderness, — if they were so lucky as to be able to do so, — they would have little regard for land titles, and would soon begin to develop a "frontier" spirit, and claim that "it was against the law of God and nature that so much land should be idle while so many Christians wanted it to labor on and to raise bread." If capital is essential for civilization, it is well not to forget the price that humble humanity pays for it.

Meanwhile a civilization had developed, and Franklin could say in 1756 that the "English settlements, as they are at present circumscribed, are absolutely at a stand; they are settled up to the mountains." To the south of the colonies, in Florida and along the Gulf, was Spanish territory. Everywhere else, west of the Appalachians and north of New England, was the power or the shadow of the claim of France. A few bold spirits like Captain William Bean and Daniel Boone had penetrated into Kentucky, but only the seaboard was English, and that had now become fairly populated, wealthy, safe, and cultured.

Boston could not have been distinguished, had one been set down in it without knowing where he was, from a provincial town in England. The fields, the elms, the whole landscape about it, as in the Connecticut Valley, were taking on the aspect of the peaceful English countryside. In the South, a young Englishman would have been completely at home in the country family life, except for the presence of the black slaves. American newspapers, such as the Maryland and Virginia *Gazettes*, were quite as good as those of the same period in England. After the middle of the century there were frequent orchestral concerts in New York and the Southern towns — Charleston, South Carolina, being a centre for music as for the other arts. From 1750 to 1770, Mr. and Mrs. Hallam, noted London actors, and their troupe, gave repertoires all through the colonies as far north as New York, consisting of the best plays then in the language — by Shakespeare, Addison, Congreve, Steele, Farquhar, and others. In painting, Copley was beginning his career, and in Benjamin West the New World was to give a president to the Royal Academy in England. In 1757 there was an exhibition of paintings in New York, all of which were by American painters. There were also the beginnings of sculpture. Many men were busying themselves with scientific discovery, Franklin with his experiments in electricity being merely the most notable. The colleges of Harvard, William and Mary, Yale, Princeton, Dartmouth, Rutgers, and Brown had all come into being. The movement for public libraries, in which America has always led the world, had also got started, and I have found twenty-three all the way from Maine to Georgia by 1763.

If a distinction had developed between rich and poor, nevertheless even the poor were better off, freer and more independent than they had been in Europe. Above all, they had glimpsed the American dream. English, Irish, Scotch, Germans, all who had come to our shores, had come to find security and self-expression. They had come with a new dynamic hope of rising and growing, of hewing out for themselves a life in which they would not only succeed as men but be recognized as men, a life not only of economic prosperity but of social and self-esteem. The dream derived little assistance from the leaders in America. It was arising from the depths of the common mass of men, and beginning to spread like a contagion among the depressed in the Old World. It was already beginning to meet with opposition from the "upper classes" in the New, but it was steadily and irresistibly taking possession of the hearts and minds of the ordinary American. It was his Star in the West which led him on over the stormy seas and into the endless forests in search of a home where toil would reap a sure reward, and no dead hands of custom or exaction would push him back into "his place."

If American culture was as yet a little thin, it was genuine, though European. In many ways, perhaps, Franklin typified it best. Making Philadelphia his home, though born in Boston, he occupied in more ways than geographically a middle position in colonial life. Shrewd, practical, always alive to the main chance, anxious to make money and rise in the world, yet keenly alive to a life above moneygrubbing, he had, on the one hand, none of the genuine depth or the religious fervor of the New England intellectual (nor his conscience), and, on the other hand, none of the humane quality or natural gentility of the Southern gentleman. Always something of an actor, with genuine ability, a self-made man in every way, he was ever ready to make the best of every situation and, *if* there were two, of both worlds. Complete intellectual disinterestedness was as foreign to his nature as religious exaltation. He could draft a plan of union for the colonies, or invent a stove or a lightning rod, yet there was also that in him which brought the French to pay homage to him as a philosopher. If we were as yet able to say what an American is, we might name him as the first.

In any case, the time seemed to have come in America, as he said, to think of other things beside exploiting and settling the wilderness. There appeared no reason why the colonial civilization and culture should not progress indefinitely on the lines already so well begun. Had the waves of the Pacific instead of the fleeting power of France been all that lay on the western side of the Appalachians, this might have been the case. But there had been a rise in the potential of power and ambition in the American English, rich and poor; instead of a waste of waters behind the mountain barrier there were nearly three thousand miles of virgin continent; and forced by defeat, in 1763, France by a stroke of the pen renounced all claim to the New World. In the next half century, the mass of the American West was to deflect the apparently established course of American culture and eventually to drag the entire world into the maelstrom of strange ideals.

There was no "standardization" at this time, and it was a varied scene that was composed of our different sections. In New England, merchants sat in their countinghouses, figuring the gains from rum and slaves and English goods; small farmers tilled their few and stony acres; and on Sundays both united in singing in their meetinghouses verses equally stony from the old *Bay Psalm Book:* —

> "The earth Jehovahs is,
> And the fullness of it:
> The habitable world, & they
> That thereupon doe sit. . . ."

In the South the Virginian gentleman lived his English country life, raised his tobacco, hunted his foxes, or hung over the spinet while his sweetheart sang an old Cavalier song of the Pretender: —

> "Oh! send Laurie Gordon hame,
> And the lad I daurna name;
> Though his back be at the Wa',
> Here 's to him that 's far awa'."

Outside in the dusk from the slave quarters came the throaty voices of negroes singing in the dialect of their new tongue, with overtones of the swish of an overseer's lash or the beating of remembered far-off tom-toms in the jungle. It might be a gay jingle or one of the plaintive melodies that the slaves had made their own: —

> "De night is dark, de day is long,
> And we are far from home.
> Weep, my brudders, weep!"

Along the Mississippi and the rivers of the North, the French voyageur plied his paddle, gathering furs for the storehouse in Montreal, humming while he dreamed of the old Norman farm: —

> "Fringue, fringue sur la rivière,
> Fringue, fringue sur l'aviron."

Far to the southwest and over the Rockies in California, the bells of Spanish missions among the roses called the faithful to Mass, or young men sang under windows from which black eyes peered out: —

> "Lo que digo de hoy en día,
> Lo que digo le sostengo,
> Yo no vengo a ver si puedo,
> Yo no vengo a ver si puedo,
> Yo no vengo a ver si puedo,
> Sino porque puedo, vengo!"

Varied, colorful life in far-scattered regions. But the America of the future was to stem from none of these. A bit of all of them was to be mingled in the melody of the twentieth century, but sternly dominant over all we hear the *stroke, stroke, stroke* of the axe on trees, the crash of the falling giant — advancing woodsmen making their clearings; Democracy; "business."

III

AMERICA SECEDES FROM THE EMPIRE

DURING the colonial period, as well as for long after, the wars between European nations always involved their nationals in America in the strife. What we call the French and Indian War, which ended in 1763, was merely the American phase of the Seven Years' War abroad. When peace was made by the Treaty of Paris, France ceded to England all of her American territory east of the Mississippi River, except the town of New Orleans, which, with whatever rights she possessed west of the Mississippi, she transferred to Spain on the same day. Thus, with the exception of Spain's claims along the Gulf coast and in the far West, England came into possession of the entire North American continent up to the Arctic and east of the great river. The Spaniards were not idle, however, and were soon pushing settlement up the Pacific Coast, founding the city of San Francisco almost at the very moment when English and Colonials were slaughtering each other on the slopes of Bunker Hill.

Nations seldom if ever pass through great conflicts without some change in outlook, and the Seven Years' War, following immediately on the War of the Austrian Succession, had been one involving almost every great State in Europe — England, France, Spain, Austria, Russia, Sweden, and the various ones now included in Germany. It was almost a "world war," involving all European and American civilizations. It left Europe with altered ideas, new fears, and in unstable balance, much as did the last great war.

One of the changes in ideas, though not clearly perceived by all, was an alteration in the theory of empire. Hitherto all nations had looked upon their colonial possessions as sources of raw materials, — gold, furs, sugar, tobacco, or what not, — and as consumers of the manufactured goods made in the old countries. The theory was almost exactly that of a great modern trust that tries to combine all branches of business from raw materials to final sale in its own organization. For some time, however, European nations had been drifting into the rôles of world powers. Vaguely but actually, a new feeling of imperialism was coming into being. It was long debated in both the English cabinet and the public press whether England should demand of France her rich West Indian islands or Canada as one of the spoils of victory. The sugar islands fitted into the old mercantile theory of what the empire should be. Possession of Canada belonged to the new imperialism. The die was cast for the latter. A profound change, little recognized, had come into Anglo-American relations.

Under the old system, the whole fabric of colonial administration had been organized for the purpose of seeing that the colonies remained in their appointed rôles in the imperial structure, as producers of raw materials and consumers of manufactured goods. Most of the laws passed in England had had this for their purpose. Although objected to now and then in specific cases, they were accepted by the colonists, who had no aversion to the system itself, but only to certain manifestations of it when they were galled too severely on a sore spot. England had had no occasion to spend much money on her colonies, or, except in the normal course of colonial trade, to draw any from them. In the beginning they had been largely business ventures. The English colonies had mostly planted themselves. They had fought their own local fights with the Indians on their frontiers. They had settled little by little land which their numbers could hold against local foe — savage, French, or Spaniard.

Now, however, all was altered. International relations had gone a long way toward modern conditions since the time when English buccaneers could undertake almost single-handed to "singe the beard" of the King of Spain, while the English monarch looked on complacently ready to share plunder if all went well, or to jail or behead the offender if the case got too hot. The modern State and modern international relations were fast emerging. England had gained by war a territory encircling the original colonies and of more than double their extent east of the mountains. This enormous expanse of Canada and the Mississippi Valley, with perhaps two hundred thousand Indians on it hostile to the new régime, needed governing. There were also eighty-five thousand conquered French, of whom twenty-two thousand probably were capable of bearing arms. France herself, defeated but not broken, was known to be hungering for revenge when the chance might come. The colonies had always shown themselves jealous of each other and unable to unite in any war against a common foe or in any general Indian policy. In the war just ended, England had had to send nearly twenty thousand troops to America to help the colonies against the French. Quite apart from the desire to govern the empire from the centre, no sane government could have turned over the problems of defense and Indian policy in the new domain to the thirteen separate colonies to handle with their own resources. The colonists had never managed the Indians well and usually managed to incur their hatred, with the exception of the Iroquois. If, according to the old theory of empire, the fur trade must be made to yield its raw material, so, according to the new, must this acquisition of a half continent be held and policed. The French, though now subjects, could not be counted as loyal, and almost the entire population of savages were under their influence.

It was calculated that ten thousand troops would be none too many to police the new realm. It was obvious that the colonies would not raise any such number or pay them if they did. The new imperialism was going to cost a lot of money. It was also evident that the replacement of French by English rule in the newly acquired territory would be of great eventual benefit to the colonies already bordering on it. It was again evident that the English debt was colossal as the result of the long struggle, and that if empire were going to prove costly beyond the ability of England to carry alone, the colonies, who shared the benefits, should share to some extent the cost. The members of the successive British governments of the next few years were none too clever, but these ideas gradually began to take root in their minds, mixed with the old feelings that the colonies existed chiefly for the benefit of the mother country and owed obedience to her.

At the time the treaty was signed in Paris in 1763, French diplomats predicted, as occasional foreign observers like the Swede Kalm had before, that, the French menace having been removed from the colonial frontier, the colonists would have no more need to rely upon England and would quarrel with her whenever it suited their convenience. Although this view has been adopted by many American historians, I do not think that this point had much influence upon Anglo-American relations. In point of fact, easily accepted as the theory has been, I do not find any expression in American public opinion of the day to warrant the belief that the expulsion of France had anything to do with the subsequent war with England.

America had, for other reasons, been becoming more self-conscious and sure of herself. As early as 1701, Governor Nicholson in Virginia had noted that the country was then mostly populated by colonial born, and that the people were beginning to "have a sort of aversion to others, calling them strangers." During the next decade, the united efforts of English and colonials to conquer Canada, in which the English showed up very badly, gave the colonials a very good opinion of themselves in contrast; as did also the mismanaged Cartagena expedition of 1741, in which over thirty-five hundred colonial troops took part, and the capture of Louisburg by the New Englanders in 1745. The Seven Years' War had begun without formal declaration, and in the beginning over four of the five thousand troops engaged in America were colonials, although later the overwhelming number were British, Wolfe having only seven hundred colonials among his eighty-five hundred regulars at Quebec, and Amherst only one hundred among his eleven thousand. The disastrous Braddock campaign, however, had left an indelible impression.

The question of relative Anglo-American strengths or of the presence or absence of the French had little to do, nevertheless, with the conflict now looming, except in so far as the Americans had grown more conscious of being a people who had rights and who were used to governing themselves. Indeed, it has been said that England's chief blunder was in not recognizing a nation when she saw one. It must be said, however, that the Americans themselves did not, in fact, see "a nation." They were merely Virginians, or Pennsylvanians, or New Englanders, who came to feel certain grievances which they undertook to resist. There was no nation on the horizon, then — merely two million sturdy, prosperous people scattered under thirteen different governments, in each of which, in innumerable local conflicts with their governors, the colonials had usually been allowed to gain their own way in the end, a way which they had become incurably sure of having.

Except for sections on the frontier which suffered from Indian raids, the colonies had not been the seat of any of the military operations of the Seven Years' War, which ended, as far as America was concerned, in 1760. As always happens in a war, a good many new fortunes had been built up. Privateering frequently proved exceedingly profitable, and the great prizes brought in encouraged speculation. Army contracts — such, for example, as one for two million pounds of beef and two million pounds of bread, among other supplies — lined the pockets of the contractors, who always emerge rich from such troubled periods. Business of all sorts had come to be conducted on a much larger scale, and we can clearly trace the growing connection between business leaders and subservient or participating legislatures, even one so close to the people as that of Connecticut. Lawyers were rising into prominence as business affairs became larger and more complex, and they also began to appear in legislatures.

For a while the farming and laboring classes had shared in the war-time prosperity; the farmer had got war-time prices and the laborer's wages had risen rapidly as the scarcity of labor had increased and floods of paper money had worked their usual inflation. But when the bubble broke, all of these classes suffered severely. Taxes had risen rapidly with the debts contracted by the several colonies. The currency became heavily depreciated. General business fell off sharply. The price of farm produce crashed. Many of the laborers and farmers had to abandon their homes. There was a severe decline in the price of farm land in the older settlements, many foreclosures of mortgages, lawsuits for debts which wiped out all equities. Once more the frontier seemed to offer the only hope to many of the poor who could not weather the storm.

But in 1763 came a stunning blow. England by proclamation forbade any colonials to cross the watershed of the mountains to settle. This was the British government's solution of the Indian problem, one of the first which required to be settled with respect to the new Canadian and western territory. The Ministers feared — not without good cause, as Pontiac's conspiracy was to show — that, with the savages already hostile to the English régime and perhaps stirred up by the French, there would be constant trouble on the frontier if the settlers pressed into the Indian hunting grounds. The valuable fur trade had to be preserved, and England had no wish to garrison a frontier of perhaps twelve hundred miles. As a temporary expedient, the government lit upon the idea of holding back immigration to the western country, and, in order to keep the Indians quiet, to erect for the present a large Indian territory. Unfortunately, with the procrastination in government affairs characteristic of the times, what was intended to be only a temporary expedient was never seriously considered again. The Americans felt that they had given considerable help in conquering America from the French, and were furious at being told that they must not enter the promised land. The population was doubling every twenty to twenty-five years. The post-war suffering was keenly felt. Canute might as well have commanded the waves not to advance as for the British government to forbid the Americans, in their distress, to seek new fortune across the mountains — except that the waves would not have resented it, whereas the colonists did.

We have already seen that there was plenty of resentment on the frontier in any case — resentment against New England land speculators, against the all-engrossing land-grabbers in New York, against the new slavocracy in the South; resentment on the part of the new immigrants against those who had cheated and ill-used them; resentment against the landlords of England by the Scotch-Irish. Typical of the feeling of the latter was the inscription that was carved on the tombstone of one of them in the Shenandoah Valley. "Here lies," so it read, "the remains of John Lewis, who slew the Irish Lord, settled Augusta County, located the town of Staunton, and furnished five sons to fight the battles of the American Revolution." There is ample evidence that the frontier was full of combustible material — lawless, resentful, radical, and independent. Moreover, in the older settlements the poorer people were full of trouble and grievances at this time and quite ready to father them upon anyone. Even the rich were beginning to feel hard times. If more grievances came, it would not be very difficult to stir sedition into a flame. There was a flare-up in 1761 when the Courts in Boston were asked by the revenue officers to issue new "writs of assistance," all the old ones having expired with the death of George II. These were of the nature of general search warrants, not naming the particular place to be searched or the object to be searched for, and had been used for some years, at the suggestion of Pitt, chiefly to try to prevent the illicit trade between Boston merchants and the French enemy, which had been prolonging the war. James Otis, who argued against them in a fiery speech, although he lost his case, took the proper ground that they were destructive of liberty, and John Adams once said that the American Revolution began then and there.

The first move made by the English government to reorganize the administration of the empire was along the lines of old legislation accepted by the colonists in principle though not complied with in practice. In 1764, in an effort to secure some customs revenue, which heretofore had sufficed only to pay a quarter of the cost of collection, the Sugar Act was passed by Parliament, followed by two others in the next two years.

These three Acts might have seriously demoralized commerce, but as their incidence happened to be almost wholly on the trade carried on by New England, the issue was not felt by all the colonies. The Stamp Act in 1765, however, as being internal taxation, affected every colony alike, though not to equal extent financially, as did also the Townshend Acts of 1767, which included duties on imports of manufactured articles from Great Britain. Moreover, both these last were especially designed to transfer a revenue from the colonies in sterling or bills of exchange, when it was difficult enough to find sufficient of either to make good the annual adverse balance of trade. They also marked a new sort of legislation, different from the mere trade regulation of old.

The excitement during these years was intense. The economic structure of the colonies, already seriously affected, was threatened with ruin. Business grew rapidly worse, and the passage of the Stamp Act had given a focus for every possible form of discontent. The reaction expressed in varying tones from Patrick Henry's well-known speech up to the dignified papers drawn up by representatives of the various colonies in the Stamp Act Congress, as well as the mobbing and burning of houses in various towns, made the British government realize it had gone too far as a matter of expediency. Both the Sugar Act and the Stamp Act were soon repealed, and in 1770, after a non-importation agreement, enforced in the colonies, had reduced imports from Great Britain by nearly half, the Townshend Acts also were largely modified, leaving only a trifling tax on tea as a symbol of the power of Parliament. The much disliked Act quartering British soldiers on the colonists where garrisons were maintained was also allowed to lapse without being reënacted. The British government pledged itself to attempt to raise no further revenue in America; the non-importation agreements were rescinded; and American imports from England rose from £1,634,000 in 1769 to £4,200,000 in 1771. Here and there in various colonies there were local grievances against England, but prosperity had returned to America, and the wealthy, as well as many of the classes dependent on them, were inclined to forget the quarrel with the mother country.

Meanwhile, however, much that was ominous for the future had happened. The merchant and other wealthy and conservative classes had been chiefly anxious to avoid trouble and merely to get the obnoxious acts rescinded. The English mind which America inherited has nearly always preferred adjustment and working compromises to declarations of abstract principles. The wealthy men had been willing to fight their cause on the grounds that the new laws were inexpedient and that they would damage the business interests of England as well as their own, a line of argument in which they received the cordial support of the mercantile interests in London who did business with them, and who agreed with their point of view. In fact, the repeal of the various acts was due more to the English mercantile influence brought to bear on Parliament than to either the mobbing or the constitutional arguments in America. What the English merchants and the richer men in the colonies wanted above all was good business and as little political friction as possible.

On the other hand, as we have seen, there was a vast mass of smouldering discontent among the poorer people everywhere in America. The line of economic class cleavage was beginning to be more clearly defined, and the lower in the scale were beginning to look to men from among their own ranks to lead them politically. When, for example, Patrick Henry tried to secure the passage of his Stamp Act resolutions in the Virginia House of Burgesses, he was unanimously backed by the poor electors, whereas he had to overcome the almost solid resistance of the rich. However, the greatest master in manipulating the masses whom America has ever seen, except possibly Bryan, arose in Boston. Opinions will always differ regarding Samuel Adams, but there can be no difference of opinion as to his consummate ability as a plotter of revolution. In all else he was a failure throughout his life. Before the years in which his manipulation of the inflammable material among the public was to give him a lasting place in American history, he had failed in law and business and public office. In after years, when constructive work had to be done in Congress in constitution making or as governor of his new State, he played a wholly insignificant part. He could tear down, but not build up. He was a fanatic, as most men are who change history, and with a fanatical hatred of England he strove to break all ties with her. Had he lived a century earlier he would have been one of the stern Puritan leaders of the type of Endicott, unyielding, persecuting, convinced to the very marrow of his bones of the infallibility of his own beliefs. But although he was a Puritan of the Puritans, the times had changed. They had become political, and in Adams's mind England and her rule had become the principle of evil in the lives of the people of God, to be fought day and night and with every weapon in his arsenal. Even when others had no wish to secede from the empire, but merely to be left in peace or to have certain inimical laws repealed, Adams early conceived the belief that the one end to work for was immediate and complete independence.

As he surveyed the field of public opinion in which he would have to operate, he saw clearly the two classes of rich and poor and realized that their interests were different. The rich were conservative, the poor radical; the rich were desirous of as little change as possible, the poor clamored for any change that would better their condition; the rich would be influenced mainly by arguments of compromise and expediency, the poor by appeals to their rights for a greater share in the political and economic life of their communities. If these two classes could be brought to work together, public opinion would be a unit, but if they could not, then the greater reliance must be placed on the poorer classes, who constituted the overwhelming mass of the population and who could more readily be stirred to anger and radical action. From about 1761 until independence was declared by the colonies in 1776, Adams worked ceaselessly for the cause to which he had devoted his life, manipulating newspapers and town meetings, organizing committees of correspondence throughout the colonies, even bringing about happenings which would inflame public opinion. At one period it looked as though his efforts would be in vain, but in the end the stupidity of the British government won the day for him.

It is a great mistake to think of public opinion as united in the colonies and as gradually rising against British tyranny. Public opinion is never wholly united, and seldom rises to a pitch of passion without being influenced — in other words, without the use of propaganda. The Great War taught that to those who did not know it already.

The years preceding the final secession of the colonies may be divided into three periods. During the first, from the passage of the Sugar Act to the practical repeal of all obnoxious legislation in 1770, the different groups were by force of circumstances united in opposition to the policy of England. The merchants needed no propaganda to realize that their business was being seriously interfered with, though they cared little about the popular catchwords that were being used by the new leaders of the people to inflame them. The Stamp Act, however, with its threat of internal taxation, did, during its one brief year of life, bring the whole problem for a while from the realm of mere business to that of constitutional questioning. But by 1770 the merchants' grievances were settled, and from then until 1773 all desire for agitation and "rocking the boat" disappeared among the richer classes. Up to that point, the popular anger had served their own cause. For the next three years their cause was peace, and popular agitation and attacks on England became a menace and not a help to them.

From the first, Adams and those working with him had realized the necessity of democratic slogans in the creation of a state of mind. While the merchants were busy pointing out to their London correspondents that the new laws would hurt the business of all alike, Adams at once struck boldly out to inflame the passions of the crowd by threatening that it was to be reduced to the "miserable state of tributary slaves," contrasting its freedom and moral virtue with the tyranny and moral degradation of England. He proclaimed that the mother country was bent on bringing her colonies to a condition of "slavery, poverty and misery," and on causing their utter ruin, and dinned into the ears of the people the words "slavery and tyranny" until they assumed a reality from mere reiteration. His political philosophy was eagerly lapped up by a populace smarting under hard times and resentful of colonial even more than imperial conditions of the moment. The establishment of government by free consent of all had become imbedded in the mind of the average man, as an essential part of the American dream. Adams himself had seen the vision, but had glimpsed it with the narrowness and bitterness with which the more bigoted Puritans had seen the vision of an unloving and revengeful Hebrew Jehovah. Like them he felt that he alone, and those who believed as he did, were in possession of the truth, and that those who differed from him were enemies of truth and God. Because, however, the American dream had so deeply affected the hopes and aspirations of the common men, the more radical among them, in town and on frontier, echoed with wild enthusiasm such pronouncements of Adams as that "the natural liberty of man is to be free from any superior power on earth, and not to be under the will or legislative authority of man, but only to have the law of nature for his rule."

Such talk as this could only make England fearful of how far the people might try to put such precepts into practice. The upper classes in the colonies also began to be uneasy. Up to 1770, when their own grievances were redressed, they might allow such ideas to be disseminated, considering themselves in control of the situation, but after that it became clear that they were losing control. Whereas such men as John Hancock and John Adams wanted quiet, and retired from public affairs to the management of their own, Sam Adams and the lesser radicals worked harder than ever to keep public opinion inflamed.

With the upper classes become lukewarm or hostile to his continued propaganda, with the obnoxious legislation repealed or modified, he had to trust to generalizations and emotional appeals. A good example of his use of the latter was the affair called the "Boston Massacre." As part of the general imperial policy following the war, the British government had stationed some regiments in Boston. They were under good officers and good discipline, and there was no more reason why they should have made trouble there than in any provincial garrison town of England. Adams, however, was continually stirring up the public mind against them; John Adams reported finding him one Sunday night "preparing for the next day's newspaper — a curious employment, cooking up paragraphs, articles, occurrences, etc., working the political engine." Finally, one March evening, as a result of more than usual provocation given by taunting boys to soldiers on duty, an unfortunate clash occurred. There was confusion, a rioter's shout to "fire" was mistaken for an officer's command, and several citizens were killed. The officer surrendered to the civil authorities, was tried, defended by John Adams and Josiah Quincy, Jr., and acquitted. But Samuel Adams at once saw the value of the incident. Every emotion of the mob was played upon. The affair was termed a "massacre," and in the annual speeches given for a number of years to commemorate its anniversary the boys and men who had taken part in the mobbing were described as martyrs to liberty and the soldiers as "bloody butchers." Although there is no recorded instance of a soldier having offered the slightest affront to any Boston girl, orators ranted about "our beauteous virgins exposed to all the insolence of unbridled passion — our virtuous wives, endeared to us by every tender tie, falling a sacrifice to worse than brutal violence, and perhaps, like the famed Lucretia, distracted with anguish and despair, ending their wretched lives by their own fair hands." At the request of the citizens the troops were removed from the city, but such talk, which served its intended purpose, was kept up for years after. The incident was unimportant in itself, and its chief interest is in how the radicals, after having provoked it, made use of it.

America was, indeed, more or less in ferment, quite aside from the question of Anglo-American relations. Pennsylvania was almost on the verge of civil war, feeling having become extremely embittered between the older and newer sections of the colony. The rich seaboard counties had not only been unwilling to help protect the frontier in the late war, but were controlling all the political machinery for their own benefit, the sixteen thousand voters in the three eastern counties having twice as many members of the Assembly as the fifteen thousand in the five western counties. To some extent the mechanics in Philadelphia were making common cause with the frontiersmen against the moneyed class. In Virginia, there was similar feeling between classes and sections, the tidewater counties controlling the much more populous frontier ones. In North Carolina, civil war did actually break out after several years of agitation, and the frontiersmen set up their own organization of "Regulators" to prevent, among other things, the collection of taxes by the men of the eastern counties who controlled the legislature and graft of the colony, and who succeeded in putting down the insurrection only after three years' effort ending in a bloody campaign in 1772.

The Seven Years' War had left society disorganized and unstable. The rich, from 1764 to 1770, had their grievances against England, grievances that were real and deep, but they were also beginning to watch with alarm the rise of radical sentiment among their own people. Everywhere thoughtful, farseeing men were thinking — thinking of the constitutional relations with the mother country which had permitted so serious a crisis to arise as that from which they believed they had just happily emerged; thinking also of the problems of government in the colonies and of what might be in store for conservatism and wealth if the people, by continuing to press their demands for greater share in ruling themselves, should oust their old leaders who had been used to being in control. The more they pondered the Anglo-American constitutional relation, however, the more it became apparent that if the question should ever have to be forced to an issue, the only ground to take would be the broad one of the rights of man as man. Sam Adams was right in that. They had tried to argue from charter rights, and soon found that ground too narrow. Their rights as Englishmen afforded a wider scope, but argument thence tended toward a bog of legalistic confusion. If Parliament should try inimical legislation again, and if a situation should arise calling for a denial of its power to legislate, the broadest rights of man would be none too broad to provide standing room for argument. But this would play right into the hands of the discontented populace, who were already getting too obstreperous, demanding new rights, asking more representation, refusing to pay taxes, getting a bit too much into the habit of backing up their demands by mobbing, even plunging a colony like North Carolina into civil war. It was all bad for business, thought the rich, and holding back the development of the country. However, the quarrel with England was made up for the present. English merchants had seen the light. Perhaps, with better times in America, these agitations on the frontiers and by the lower classes in the big towns would die down, if only men like Sam Adams would know when to stop and would quit throwing oil on the flames. The rich determined to sit on the lid, and carry out a policy of business and politics as usual. Sam Adams and his group also continued their agitation as usual.

For three years, from 1770, in spite of constant discussion in pamphlets and newspapers and declaimings by radicals, things seemed to be getting better. The frontiersmen and town radicals were doing a lot of talking, but getting nowhere. The Regulators' insurrection had been put down. Then suddenly the British government made a colossal blunder which could never be retrieved. Sam Adams saw to that.

The East India Company had accumulated a huge and partly unsalable store of tea, and was on the brink of bankruptcy. In order to prevent the catastrophe, which would have been a financial one of the first magnitude, the British government, with perfectly good intentions from an English point of view, but with an ignorance and a carelessness which are beyond condonation, gave the India Company what was practically a monopoly of selling tea in America. By the elimination of the American merchants as middlemen, the price of tea to the American consumer was expected to be cut in half; but considering the delicacy of Anglo-American relations, and the fact that the American merchant and business class was the chief reliance of England in America, to have struck a blow at it in favor of an English business concern revealed in a flash both the stupidity of the men in power with whom Americans had to deal and the unthinking selfishness of English policy with regard to the colonies. The fat was in the fire now with a vengeance. For three years the conservatives had been trying to maintain good relations with England and at the same time to combat what they considered the dangerous rising tide of radicalism in their own colonies. Now they were forced once more into opposition to England and so into unwilling alignment with the radicals.

The rest of the story is well-known by every schoolboy — how the tea was shipped over and refused admittance at every port; how Adams's followers in Boston raided the tea ship and threw fifty thousand dollars' worth of tea into the waters of the harbor; how Parliament, when it heard of the deed, passed acts closing the port to commerce except in food, until the tea should be paid for, voiding the Massachusetts charter, and placing the colony under the immediate control of the Crown, ordering that British officers or soldiers should be tried only in England (or in a colony other than Massachusetts) for anything done in the line of duty, and providing that troops should be quartered again in the colonies. "The die is cast," wrote George III to Lord North; "the colonies must either triumph or submit."

It is possible that a peaceful solution might have been found when the dull wits of the British Cabinet had become aware of the extent of feeling aroused in America, and of the fact that they had forced the whole population into a united front. But this would have been possible only had the tea not been destroyed, an act that many loyal Americans condemned. Adams had seized his chance. Fifty thousand dollars' worth of British private property destroyed and indemnity refused; Parliament would have to retaliate. If the retaliation should be heavy enough, the door might be closed to peaceful settlement. The retaliation came, swift and crushing, and the colonies were aflame with sympathy for Massachusetts. In the next three years the progress of events was inevitable in its sequence, given all the factors involved. The petitions and their rejections, the calling of Congress, the bloodshed at Lexington and Concord, the final Declaration of Independence in 1776, and the military events of the struggle are too familiar to need retelling.

What concern us more particularly are the abiding influences upon American character and thought.

We have already seen how the wilderness and the colonists' need of erecting governments for themselves had given a considerable spur to the spread of democracy and the belief in government only by the consent of the governed. The colonies, however, had been far from democratic, and with the accumulation of wealth had been growing less so. Belief was still general among the upper classes that political power should rest in the hands of the well-born or the rich, who had knowledge, experience, and a property stake in the community. Many of the poorer classes, especially as we look further to the south from New England and out on any part of the frontiers, were shiftless, illiterate, rather lawless. To increase the political power of such people seemed to the conservatives like inviting anarchy and the spoliation of property. On the other hand, during the gradual shift in the grounds for arguing the constitutional relations toward Parliament, it had been found necessary to base the argument at last squarely on the rights of man. "When, in the course of human events," in the words of the great Virginian, it became necessary to inform the world why they were taking up arms against England, the signers of the Declaration had to announce the theory of these rights to all mankind — mankind including their own "lower classes" at home in America. "We hold these truths to be self-evident," wrote Jefferson in words which rang through the continent, "that all men are created equal; that they are endowed by their Creator with certain inalienable rights; that among these are life, liberty, and the pursuit of happiness. That, to secure these rights, governments are instituted among men, deriving their just powers from the consent of the governed; that, whenever any form of government becomes destructive of these ends, it is the right of the people to alter or to abolish it."

Nothing here about the rich or the well-born; and, as Sam Adams said, the people recognized "the resolution as though it were a decree promulgated from heaven." The upper classes were thinking of their independence as against the exercise of legislative power by Parliament. The lower classes were thinking not only of that, but of their relations to their colonial legislatures and governing class. "No taxation without representation." If that were true as between England and America, why not also as between poor Western frontier counties and rich Eastern seaboard ones, as between the town mechanic and the town merchant, as between the laborer and the planter?

If, as the King had said, the die was cast in imperial relations, so had it also been in American political philosophy. For a dozen years, men like Adams had been dinning this idea of the rights of man as man into the ears of the people. The conservatives had first been of the party, then fallen off, then again had to join it, and now at last the voice of united America in Congress had announced to the world the political equality of all men as the creed of the continent. The dam had been dynamited. After the announcement that all men are created equal, that all men have rights, that all men may revolt against conditions, there could be no turning back. The quarter of a century from the beginning of active agitation against England until the adoption of the Federal Constitution afforded an incomparable schooling in political discussion and training for an entire people, and for the burning into their minds and hearts of the democratic dogma.

There was another aspect of the Revolution which used to receive but scant attention. If, on the one hand, the radical thought of the nation received the intensification noted above, on the other, the conservative body of thought in many sections was greatly weakened. It might be all very well for men like Sam Adams and Patrick Henry to declaim against tyranny, but I have not been able to find anywhere in their writings, or even in those of sounder thinkers such as John Adams, a serious effort to appraise the difficulties of a struggle against the power of England. To conservative men, these might rightly have seemed to be insuperable at that time. Colonial population and resources were advancing with rapid strides, and the time might come when America could defy England. But in point of fact, in spite of the revolutionists, that time had not come as yet. America had no manufactures; she depended almost wholly on overseas markets and commerce. Her people were not united. She had no trained troops. In plain truth we see now that the Revolution was only saved from being an abortive rebellion by two factors neither of which could be counted upon in 1776 — one the character of Washington, and the other the marshaling against England of European powers.

The people at large might shout for the rights of man and tear down statues of George III, but fighting through seven years was a different matter. We had a population of about two millions, with supposedly three hundred thousand in the militia, though that meant little. Out of this population

Washington was never able to raise an army of twenty-five thousand men at any one time and never had more than eighteen thousand in any one battle. By the end of the war his whole army was six thousand, and even his indomitable will and courage admitted that "we are at the end of our tether" unless France should quickly send additional funds. After the capture of Burgoyne's army in 1777, France, for purely selfish reasons, to strike a blow at England when it was reasonably safe to do so (a policy which long hung in diplomatic balance and which could not be counted upon in 1776), had become our ally. When the war was finally won, it was not by the "embattled farmers" of Sam Adams's colony, but by the fleets of that ally against the British far from our shores. Yorktown was the mere acknowledgment of a *fait accompli* elsewhere.

In 1776 the agitator, the mechanic, the small farmer, the man on his clearing in the woods, with limited knowledge, experience, and outlook, might well give these matters no consideration, but the conservative merchant and professional man saw them more clearly. England was, indeed, governing very badly, showing both stupidity and selfishness; but affairs had been adjusted before, and was there not a better chance of getting them adjusted again (so the conservative might ponder) than this wild scheme of revolution and civil war, with uncertain chance of success at the end? America — and this was her chief weakness — was far from united when it came to this point, even John Adams admitting that only a third of the people desired war. In Boston the upper class, almost without exception, were strongly opposed to it, and more than half the upper class throughout the whole colony. It was the same in New York, where the bulk of the property owners were Loyalists. In Pennsylvania a majority of all the people were not only against war and independence in the beginning, but remained so throughout the struggle. In the South the wealthy planters were more generally in favor of the rebellion, but even there it was clearly seen as a local revolution as well as civil war against England. Landon Carter was typical of many when he wished to oppose British oppression, but feared almost equally "internal oppressions and commotions."

As the times became more unsettled, as free speech was abolished, as mobbings and burnings, destruction and confiscation of property became common, the conservatives looked with horror on what might be in store for the colonies even if they won and were given over to the rule of the people without the strong arm of England to maintain order. British tyranny plus British law and order began to seem preferable to turning fortunes and families over to mobs which stole and tarred and feathered. Secession from the empire might be a cure for the quarrel with England, but where would local colonial *revolution* end? We must not forget that there was threat of revolution as well as secession, and it is not strange if the former appeared the more dangerous in the eyes of a large part of the conservatives, who always look with fear on the breakdown of law and order. Considering the extreme die-hard conservatism of the resolutions of the "Daughters of the Revolution" to-day, it seems impossible to avoid the conclusion that very few of them would have been Mothers of the Revolution in 1776, when revolution meant riding the whirlwind of social disorder.

There was, also, even yet much genuine affection for England, still called "home"; and at least a third of the people, to cite John Adams again, were opposed to separating from her. Only in the years preceding the Civil War was there ever to be once more such searchings of hearts as to where one's loyalty was due. However, the die was cast; singly, or in large groups, Tories, or Loyalists, left the country, exiled or voluntarily seeking refuge. The bulk of the poorer ones remained, suffering socially and economically; but from eighty to a hundred thousand left their native colonies. Representing, as a large part of these did, the wealth, culture, and conservative thought of their local communities, the loss was immense. A few eventually returned, but broken in estate and influence, for during the war fifteen million dollars' worth of Tory property, at the very lowest estimate, was confiscated.

The new Ship of State, with sails spread wide to democratic

winds, thus threw overboard a considerable part of its ballast of conservatism and culture, for the people who left had to a great extent been the most distinguished and looked-up-to in their small communities. The only exodus which can be compared to this in modern historical times is that of the Huguenots from France. How much was lost may be inferred indirectly from the fact that the South, where the better class remained to a much greater extent than in New England and the Middle Colonies, was to furnish, during the two generations following the war, a far greater proportion of national leaders than the North. The "Virginia Dynasty" of presidents and statesmen may not be unconnected with the exodus from Massachusetts and elsewhere of several thousands of families who had been prominent in the public affairs of their colonies, many from their founding.

At last the war was over and won, and peace was made in 1783. The secession of the colonies from the empire, and the existence of the United States of America were recognized by England, as they already had been by France and Holland. In the course of a long national existence or a long history as a people, many wars may be fought and injustices suffered without leaving lasting bitterness. But we had no long history as a people or existence as a nation. America had been a house divided against itself in the war, and the thirteen colonies remained jealous and mistrustful of each other and of any national government after it. A national sentiment had to be developed, and a glorious past improvised to begin our history with. The nation had been born in war, and that war would forever after have to be the starting point of our national story. It had been fought against England, with France as our ally. From these simple factors were born our traditional hostility toward England and our sentimental friendship for France. Years later, when a strong and united nation, we could fight Mexico and be friends. We could conquer Spain and be better friends than ever within a decade. But for nearly two generations after we won from England, we were not strong or united, and we had no past. History and literature are among the strongest influences to bind the citizens of a nation together. Our history to that point, like an ordered drama, led up to the bitter struggle to gain our independence from a harsh motherland. Our literature, or all of it that stirred emotion and appealed to the heart, was our literature of oratory, of which the one theme was the tyranny of England, written in the heat of passion. In the process of creating a national sentiment, these orations were to be heard in every schoolhouse in the land, generation after generation. Each child at his most impressionable age was to be nourished on abhorrence of the British tyrant, and in his own small shrill voice hurl in sonorous periods his defiance to England across the sea. This was another legacy of those years.

Independence, however, had been won, and that fact was to be marvelously potent in altering the mind and character of the people. In every colony they had long been accustomed to assert, as far as possible, their own will whenever it might conflict with the instructions of the royal governors or the legislation of Parliament. But now nothing, so it seemed, stood in the way of the complete assertion of that will in any direction they chose. Much the same change took place in the outlook of the colonists as takes place in a boy when he has left home and for the first time really stands on his own feet and looks about at the world which is his to wander in and conquer. For good or ill there come a release of energies and a rapid development of latent powers. Had England governed with superhuman wisdom and complete unselfishness, the mental outlook and temper of the American people as citizens of the province of a European empire would yet have been different when they became citizens of an independent nation in a New World. Far more important than the mere redress of grievances was the breaking down of all spiritual barriers to the complete development of whatever might prove to be fertile, true, and lasting in the American dream. The forces and influences which were shaping it were suddenly increased in intensity by having the hampering connection with the Old World severed. As we shall see, the connection with that world had been not merely political, and it was to take another generation to clear the way completely, but the first great step had been accomplished when secession became a fact. This was the greatest legacy of the period.

Another was the character of Washington. In the travail of war and revolution, America had brought forth a man to be ranked with the greatest and noblest of any age in all the world. There have been greater generals in the field and statesmen in the cabinet in our own and other nations. There has been no greater character. When we think of Washington, it is not as a military leader, nor as executive or diplomat. We think of the man who by sheer force of character held a divided and disorganized country together until victory was achieved, and who, after peace was won, still held his disunited countrymen by their love and respect and admiration for himself until a nation was welded into enduring strength and unity.

There were great patriots in America whose names are inscribed in the story of that time. There were many humble folk whose names have faded from our histories or were never known outside their narrow village circle, who struggled and suffered from the noblest motives. But war brings out the worst as well as the best in men. It is a mistake to think of the America of 1776–1783 as a nation of patriots pressing their services to gain their freedom. It was hard to get men into the army, and to keep them there. Often Washington had neither money nor food nor clothing to offer them. But he always had an army, pitifully small as it was at times, which held the flag flying in the field through love of him and confidence in the character which they sensed in his dignified presence. Without him the cause would have been irretrievably lost, and the thunder of the orators would have rumbled long since into forgetful silence. When the days were blackest, men clung to his unfaltering courage as to the last firm ground in a rising flood. When, later, the forces of disunion in the new country seemed to threaten disruption, men again rallied to him as the sole bond of union. Legacy to America from these troubled years, he is, apart from independence itself, the noblest heritage of all.

IV

THE NATION FINDS ITSELF

INDEPENDENCE had been acknowledged by the world, but the young nation was weak. Indeed, there scarcely was a nation, for the Confederation which bound together the old colonies, now become sovereign States, had neither the reality nor the semblance of power. Practically there was no central government, merely the empty shell of a loose union. Apart from the lack of political cohesion, the whole social and economic life of the people at large had been severely shaken. War, as we have said, profoundly alters life, and the colonies had had scarcely a dozen years to readjust themselves after the end of the Seven Years' War when this new one had broken on them, while the intervening period had been one of constant agitation and much disorder. The slaves in the South had been but little affected. Submerged at the bottom of society, the storm waves had passed over them without being felt. Dependent upon their masters and not upon their own exertions, they worked, ate, and slept their existence away as usual. Apart from them, however, there was no one, rich or poor, whose existence had not been deeply influenced, although the actual loss of life must have been small in proportion to the population, and the destruction of property on land by the enemy was not great. The suffering came from other causes.

In the first place, the proportion of the men who were engaged at one time or another to the total was much larger than the figures of those in the army at any given date would indicate. Enlistments were short, and many were in service only for a few months. Almost all the men in the ranks were of the small farmer class, without means of subsistence for their families other than what was produced by their own toil in the fields. The army pay which they received, when they received any at all, in the depreciated paper was of slight help to their wives and children, who often suffered cruelly from the absence of the head of the household and lack of money. There was no farm machinery. Farm work meant the hardest sort of long physical toil, and when the farmer was in the army his wife and children worked the fields and chopped the wood for winter fires. The loss of the farmer was a dire calamity for his family, and America was as yet 90 per cent agricultural. This was the chief cause of the many desertions and the refusal of men to reënlist when their short terms had expired. During their service, they themselves were called upon to suffer the greatest hardships. There was no sanitary science to protect them against disease; the medicine chests were all too often empty; food was scarce, and at times, as in the dreadful winter at Valley Forge, soldiers had to go unshod and half in rags in killing cold, their torn feet leaving bloodstains as they walked shoeless on the icy ground. It was not the risk of death in a rare encounter with the enemy that called for courage in those seven years, but anxiety over the family at home, and the steady hardship of camp life in which almost everything was lacking that might have made for comfort and efficiency.

There was the usual disorganization of the economic life that is the concomitant of any war on a large scale, emphasized by the complete demoralization of the monetary system. Like the paper mark of Germany a decade ago, the paper money of the United States declined to zero, and the phrase "not worth a Continental" was so impressed upon the people that, unlike the money to which it referred, it gained a lasting circulation. By 1780, gold stood at a premium of 4000 per cent. All the evils of inflation and depreciation were present. Prices, both of commodities and of labor, soared, owing to actual scarcity and to paper money. Profiteering was rife, and reputable merchants of high social standing took from 100 to 300 per cent profit. Incomes based on permanent investments in mortgages and other fixed forms of interest declined to nothing. Captures of ships at sea *by* the British ruined some merchants, while captures *of* the British raised others to wealth. Unscrupulous contractors rose from poverty to opulence. Everywhere new men appeared to replace those whose fortunes had been lost. In the year of peace, James Bowdoin of Boston wrote to ex-Governor Pownall, "When you come you will see scarcely other than new faces. The change which in that respect has happened within the few years since the revolution is as remarkable as the revolution itself."

If the personnel of the richer class had been turned topsy-turvy, the suffering of the poorer was extreme. The State debts had grown to staggering proportions and taxation had been so devised as to bear most heavily on the poor, the poll tax in Massachusetts, for example, accounting for one third of the total sum raised! By 1786 the debt of that State, with her share of the Continental debt, had risen to over £3,200,000, a sum even the interest on which was not being raised. Farm lands were taxed at so much the acre, regardless of their value, and the poorer farmers were being sold out for taxes they could not possibly pay. To a considerable extent the same conditions were found elsewhere with variations. Moreover, the rapidly accumulated wealth of the new rich, and the seemingly high prices paid for labor, with the general recklessness always engendered by war, had brought about wild extravagance on the part of many. As usual, when the war was over, there were a couple of years of hectic but spotty prosperity, and then the crash came, to be followed by a period of wild speculation which ended with our first great panic. Discontent was rife, and an exodus began from the older colonies to the new western frontier. Ruined New England farmers and mechanics poured in an ever-swelling stream into western New York and Pennsylvania and on into Ohio. Southerners streamed over the mountains to Kentucky and Tennessee. The wilderness was a safety valve, but even with that, open rebellion finally broke out in Massachusetts under an officer in the Revolution, Captain Daniel Shays, and paralyzed the courts of the State for some months until finally quelled.

That, in spite of all the mobbing and violence and confiscation of Tory property, the American Revolution did not pursue to the bitter end the course of most revolutions, such as the French or Russian, was due to one simple cause. As we have seen, the revolutionary movement, as contrasted with the secessionist one, came almost wholly from the poorer classes. The normal course is that the moderates who are in control at first have to abdicate in favor of extremists before the end. In all such cases, however, there have been either large proletarian populations dependent on wages and without accumulated capital, or peasants tilling, under intolerable burdens, soil which they do not own.

In America this was not so. In the slave States the slaves had had nothing whatever to do with the revolution, and, as we have said, remained mostly untouched by it. The towns were small and held no proletarian class, even the laborer for daily wages usually owning his own small home. There was no peasant class in the European sense in the entire country, and almost every farmer, however poor and oppressed with debt, owned his own farm. Tory property, running from such vast estates as those of Governor Hutchinson of Massachusetts or the Livingstons of New York down to stray bits of land coveted by a patriot farmer, could be expropriated, but there could be no expropriation of patriot landed property unless the townsman or farmer ran the risk of losing his own. There were few relics of feudalism and no hard and fast class distinction, such as that between a titled nobility and commoners. One man might own fifty acres and another fifty thousand, but there was no sharp line anywhere between them, and (what has been a holding anchor in American life even when radicalism has been in the saddle) the man with fifty hoped that some day by a lucky stroke he might own a thousand. With every man a property owner and hoping to be a greater, there might be a revolutionary demand for political power, but there was little immediate danger of any overturn of property rights. With this condition and the safety valve of the empty West, the young American nation could ride out the storm with impunity.

There had, however, been a thoroughgoing revolution, though the general economic and social structure suffered a minimum of alteration. The civil war of 1775 to 1783 did not end merely with the secession of three million and more citizens from the British Empire, to set up an independent State of the then accepted model for themselves. Had that been the case they would have invited some scion of a royal house to rule over them, some William of Wied to fill a void in their Constitution. The exigencies of government in a wilderness had seen to that. The long line of simple covenants drawn up by simple men to meet practical situations, from the Mayflower Compact, the Fundamental Orders of Connecticut, through innumerable "church covenants" and frontier agreements, clarified by the years of dispute with England, had ended in the preamble to the Declaration of Independence. All men are created equal; all men have the same political rights; government derives its powers solely from the consent of the governed.

America hoped to become a great nation. Every great nation then in the world was monarchical and aristocratical. America began as a republic and had made a long step toward a democracy. That was something radically new, though the political philosophy was not. American thinkers had nourished their minds on the great Englishmen, Sidney, Locke, Hobbes, and others. There was nothing novel in their theory. What was wholly novel was the putting of the theory into practice, and *that* they owed to the American wilderness. They did not need to chop off the head of their king. In the process of a steady chopping down of the interminable forest the need of a king had gone.

At the end of the war, Washington was only the most illustrious of all those who had been engaged who now returned to resume their peace-time life on plantation, farm, or in countinghouse. One great doubt assailed them all — would the experiment succeed? In the years immediately following, this began to look doubtful. England was treating us with contempt and not carrying out the terms of the treaty of peace. Neither were we, and the Confederacy was too weak to force either England or our own people to do so. After its post-war burst of enthusiasm, business had a collapse. The common people were restive, and the rebellion in Massachusetts, which assumed the proportions of a civil war, gave even Washington a severe shock. As he said, "Government is not influence," and all that the Confederation had was influence, and precious little of that. If within five years of gaining her independence America were to drift into anarchy, as she seemed to be doing, it would simply prove that as yet the world needed monarchy to secure order. The men in country taverns on a Saturday night might declaim about liberty till they were hoarse or asleep, but if the States were to leave their debts unpaid, become a mere pack of small republics quarreling among themselves until gobbled up singly by some European power, there would be little liberty worth declaiming about. Yet the jealousies and the dislike of any strong central governing body seemed insuperable. As Washington sat on the verandah at Mount Vernon, sipping his toddy and looking up the beautiful reach of the Potomac, he had ample time to reflect on whether after all he had for nothing risked a noose for his neck and the confiscation of the estate that he loved above all else next to his country. Many others also throughout the new States were pondering the same problem. The situation was becoming intolerable.

At last courage was found to grasp the nettle firmly, and in February 1787 the almost moribund Congress sent an invitation to the several States to elect delegates to a convention to meet at Philadelphia in May for the sole purpose of revising the Articles of Confederation. The group of fifty-five men who met at the appointed time to consider the momentous problem of devising a Constitution for the nation was the most distinguished which has ever been gathered on this continent. The character, ability, and broad mental attainments which they possessed provide an amazing commentary upon the quality of American civilization in the eighteenth century. We must recall that the entire free white population of the States at that time was scarcely double that of the mere city of Los Angeles to-day. Yet out of a colonial population equivalent to twice that of Los Angeles came a George Washington, Benjamin Franklin, Roger Sherman, Robert Morris, James Madison, Alexander Hamilton, C. C. Pinckney, John Dickinson, William Paterson, Rufus King, James Wilson, and others. In 1931, with forty times the population and many thousand times the wealth of 1787, could we have forty groups of similar capacity sitting simultaneously now?

Constitution making had been a favorite sport in all the colonies for the preceding fifteen years. Hardly anyone felt inadequate to the task. One New England farmer had produced a democratically simple one. We do not need, he wrote, "any Goviner but the Guviner of the univarse and under him a States Gineral to Consult with the wrest of the united states for the good of the whole." Grotesque as this seems, it contained some of the chief kernels of public opinion — the fear of a strong executive and central government, and the belief that any government must be for "the good of the whole." Although complete political democracy was not to be achieved, even in form, for several generations yet, the framers of the Constitution found themselves of necessity influenced by the steps already taken toward it, whatever their individual opinions might be. They realized, although American historians were for a long time to overlook it, that a revolution was in progress as well as a secession accomplished. As a contemporary South Carolinian wrote, "There is nothing more common than to confound the terms of the American Revolution with those of the late American war. The American war is over, but this is far from being the case with the American Revolution. On the contrary, nothing but the first act of the great drama is closed."

This first act had been marked for democracy by many forward steps no less genuine because not sealed by the blood of an uprising. Between 1776 and 1784 the situation had forced most of the colonies to adopt constitutions for themselves to replace the old imperial governments. All but one of these, that of New Hampshire, had been drafted and adopted during the war, when radical sent ment was rampant. It had been the radicals who had cast the die for war in the first place, and, with the rise in war psychology, even good patriots came to be looked at askance if they appeared too conservative to "go the whole hog" with their more radical neighbors. It was extremely easy for a patriot jury to brand a man as a Tory, after which confiscation of his desirable estate might follow as quickly as thunder on flash of lightning. We have recently had enough experience of the queer forms that excessive zeal may take in war times to understand the dangerous situation of conservative thought among our patriot ancestors of 1776 to 1783.

We cannot deal with all the fourteen colonial constitutions (counting Vermont, which had set up for itself) separately, but we may note what happened in the two colonies where the internal grievances had been most acute against the rich Easterners before war with England had been decided upon, for these bring out clearly the continuity of grievance which we tried to point out earlier. In Pennsylvania the disgruntled frontiersmen and Philadelphia mechanics dealt a resounding thwack on the heads of the old moneyed class. All qualifications for office holding or voting were swept away except payment of a State tax. This gave the suffrage to practically all the mechanics and other workmen in the city. Representation was apportioned on the basis of the number of taxables in each county, and this at once transferred the political control from the old governing group along the Delaware River to the Scotch and Germans in the western counties. In North Carolina a bitter fight took place between the radical and conservative elements for the drafting of the constitution, in which the radicals scored a complete victory. Practically every adult freeman was given the franchise, and the governor was so stripped of power that it was said he had none left except to "sign a receipt for his salary." The legislature was made all-powerful, and the small farmers were given control of it.

These two States adopted the most radical of the new constitutions, but throughout practically all of them we find advances in democratic doctrine. The famous Virginia Bill of Rights, which was used as the basis for most of the others, began much as did the Declaration, with the words "all men are by nature equally free and independent." In many of the new constitutions, Church became separated from State, and the slave trade was prohibited by all except Georgia. In the Northern States, where fifty thousand slaves were owned, chiefly as house servants, emancipation had become complete by about the end of the century even when not immediately provided for, as in many cases, by the new constitutions. In Virginia and Maryland such men as Jefferson, Madison, Mason, Pinckney, and Martin struggled for emancipation, but without success, and throughout the South at this time most men looked upon slavery as an evil, although a temporary one.

In all the States the revolution brought about a distinct increase in the electorate, although the qualifications for voting differed. The poorer elements both in the town and in the frontier sections increased their influence. The basis of American political democracy has been economic democracy, and at this time, as for long after, economic democracy meant the opportunity to own land. In this respect, the revolution witnessed a notable advance in two directions, the one relieving ownership of certain burdens, and the other increasing the land which could be acquired by the poorer people. All the royal prohibitions with regard to cutting timber were abolished, as were all quitrents everywhere, and whatever relics of feudalism had remained here and there. Entail and primogeniture, without which the perpetuation of great landed estates is impossible, were likewise abolished. In most States it was also provided that the lands of an intestate should be divided equally among his sons, if not all his children. Everywhere the Crown lands and great forfeited estates had come into possession of the State governments, and attempts were usually made to sell these as small holdings. Even in that stronghold of a moneyed aristocracy, New York, a new law discouraged the sale of these lands in parcels of over five hundred acres, and James De Lancey's were settled by 275 persons. In Pennsylvania the Penn family estimated their confiscated estates as worth one million pounds sterling. Yet more important in providing land for settlement and the building up of the economic democracy of the next fifty years was the cancellation of the restriction against westward emigration which had been embodied in the Royal Proclamation of 1763. After much negotiation, the claims of certain States, based upon the vague geographical terms in their old charters, were surrendered to the Confederation, which came into possession of almost all the land west of the mountains and up to the Mississippi. The one great act of statesmanship of the now expiring Congress of the old government had been the Northwest Ordinance, passed in 1787, for the purpose of providing for the governing of this vast tract, which formed a possible colonial empire as large as the Union itself.

Heretofore, in European thought, colonies had always occupied a position inferior to the mother country, and were supposed to be ruled and exploited for her own benefit. The Americans, however, had had their fill of that doctrine. They had smarted under it when they had been English colonials on the east side of the mountains, and those who hoped to settle on the west side of them had no stomach to resume that status again, with the seaboard States instead of England as their rulers. There was, however, no precedent whatever for the solution of the problem. There was, on the other hand, the very serious problem of the size and future population of this

American empire. There was room in it to carve out more States than the original thirteen. "There has already been trouble enough, Heaven knows," thought the conservative Easterners, "with all these radicals who go out on the frontiers and who are already upsetting everything in the old States. If we fill up this western country, as big as our own, with them and give them a voice in our affairs, anything may happen."

The final solution was evidence at once of the remarkable political wisdom of the day and of the strong influence that the democratic elements possessed. The Ordinance, together with that of 1785, provided that the Territory should be divided into townships six miles square, made up of sections of 640 acres each. These sections were to be sold at not less than a dollar an acre. Temporarily the entire territory was to be governed as a unit by Congress, but when it had five thousand inhabitants they could elect a legislature, and, when population increased, three to five States might be created, of not less than sixty thousand inhabitants each, which would be admitted to the Union on an absolute equality with the original Eastern ones "in all respects whatever." One section in every township was reserved for public education, and slavery was forever prohibited. Simple as the solution may seem, it is one of the greatest and most original of the contributions of America to the modern world of political thought, and it provided the only possible way in which the United States of to-day could have come into being. The original Union could never have held the continent under imperial control, but the way was now open for indefinite increase in population and territory with equally indefinite increase in national solidarity and strength. If the Ordinance was a great achievement of statesmanship, so was it a great achievement for the American democracy. The frontier was the seat of democracy, and now, with the opening of a new frontier of staggering size to settlement and eventual citizenship, it could be conceived that some day the conservative East might have to bow to a young, powerful, and aggressive West. The young Revolutionary poet, Philip Freneau, wrote of it in 1785 that

Forsaking kings and regal state,
(A debt that reason deems amiss)
The traveller owns, convinc'd though late,
No realm so free, so blest as this —
The *east* is half to slaves consign'd,
And half to slavery more refined.

It was in this atmosphere of radical success — or perhaps we should say of evidence of radical thought and increasing power — that the members of the Constitutional Convention in Philadelphia began their labors. However opposed some of them, like Hamilton, might be to trusting the people with power, the whole trend of events for the past fifteen years or more showed clearly that the common people would demand to a very considerable extent an embodying in the Constitution of the political philosophy which had been their gospel in fighting for independence, and that they would not be denied. Madison at first started from the premise that government was to be devised by the leading minds of the Union more or less as a problem *in vacuo* without paying the slightest attention to the wishes of the "unreflecting multitude." Hamilton openly admitted that he had no use for a republic, but that in the atmosphere of America nothing else could be hoped for, whereupon he worked for a form of government of extreme centralization and power. Broader and more practically minded members perceived, however, that the Constitution was bound to be framed according to the dogmas of the Declaration, and the problem settled down to how to reconcile the rights of man with the safety of property. The franchise provided a severe test. Many, perhaps wisely, feared that to bestow it upon the classes without property would be to invite venality and spoliation. On the other hand, it was pointed out to them that many States had already provided for voting by citizens who did not own property and that any new constitution would be rejected by them if it took away rights they had already secured.

A precisely similar problem was that of apportionment of representation. Here the old conflict between tidewater and frontier came out clearly. Gouverneur Morris voiced the strong feeling of many of the delegates when he demanded that property as well as population should be taken into consideration, as otherwise, if "the Western people get the power into their own hands, they will ruin the Atlantic interests. The back members are always adverse to the best measures." Elbridge Gerry, who feared the foreign elements, urged that the seaboard should not be placed "at the mercy of the emigrants." This party, however, was confronted by the fact that the new States to be made in the West had already been pledged absolute equality with the old, and the more liberal opinion won. Both these contests show the immense importance of what the radicals had already gained. On every hand the delegates were confronted not by theoretical problems but by accomplished facts. There were gloomy prognostications of what the future might bring when possibly agriculture had yielded place to manufactures, and the cities might be filled with a floating and propertyless population of mechanics. Nevertheless, the people had already gained power, and, as Colonel Mason pointed out, "those who have power in their hands will not give it up while they can retain it." Hamilton found that while "he had been praised by everybody, he had been supported by none." In the Constitution no qualification was mentioned for the suffrage, and representation was based solely on population, with the exception that in the Senate it should be limited to two Senators from each State regardless of numbers, a compromise essential to win the adherence of the smaller of the older commonwealths, and one destined to perpetuate and emphasize the question of States' rights. In some respects the new government was a federal republic made up of sovereign States, but in others it rested directly upon the people themselves. Just as the State governments derived their powers directly from the electorate, so also did the new Federal one derive its directly from the individual voter and not indirectly through the State governments. In this respect it was an entirely new departure in the theory of government.

After more than three months' deliberation the document was complete, the first written Constitution offered to any nation, following in this the precedents set by the several States. It gave no special privileges to any one class or interest, nor did it lodge power in any of them. Unrestricted suffrage, representation based on numbers, and the parity promised to the new States to arise on the frontier, assured as far as any constitution could the growth of economic and political equality. In the course of a century and a half, the Constitution has been greatly developed by interpretation through judicial decisions, but as it stood in 1787 it was considered extremely democratic.

There was, however, much in it that ran counter to the wishes of many. The prohibition against the issue of paper money and of laws impairing the obligations of contracts could be counted on to be opposed strenuously by the whole debtor class. Moreover, national sentiment was still weak as contrasted with State loyalty, and many powers had been taken from the States and given to the central government. The forbidding of the States to levy any import or export duties was to make the United States within itself the greatest free-trade area in the world eventually, and greatly to increase the possibilities of national prosperity, the scale of American business, and to intensify national solidarity, but it seemed a menacing encroachment in 1787.

The decision was reached, in accordance with the theory of the Declaration of Independence, to submit the instrument directly to the people for ratification, and in every State conventions were elected to consider it. Never before or since, perhaps, has an entire people been so well prepared to discuss so momentous an issue. The years of controversy with England preceding the war, and the erection of all the State governments during it, had for twenty-five years kept the public mind centred on constitutional problems. Extremely adroit management, not to say in some cases even political chicanery, was needed before ratification was secured from the first nine States, which had been the number required to put the Constitution into force, but on the other hand the public discussion was maintained on a very high level. The innumerable pamphlets and newspaper articles, of which those gathered in *The Federalist* were merely the most notable, called for a concentration of thought that could hardly be counted upon to-day in a decision by the people at large. At last nine States ratified; the new Constitution was declared in force; and subsequently the other States adhered to it. The old Congress notified the people that their new government would enter upon its duties on March 4, 1789, and then ended its own existence.

We Americans may well take a legitimate pride in the extraordinary accomplishment of those dozen years, for no other nation has ever given in a similar period such an impetus to political thought through practical statesmanship. Many of the ideas were not new, but they had hitherto been for the most part held by closet philosophers. America had proclaimed them as a gospel for all mankind and as a working political programme for a nation. In the Declaration of Independence, made good by war, the gospel of equality, of natural rights, and of government by consent of the governed, had attained an influence and an authenticity that no mere philosopher could secure for it. In the Northwest Ordinance we had shown how colonial status could be transformed into national citizenship for an expanding empire. In the Constitution we had shown how a Federal government could respect the sovereignty of its States and yet derive its sanction and power directly from the body of the people. In the device of a Constitutional Convention we had pointed out a peaceful way for any nation to alter its fundamental law and institutions. We had also showed that a revolution could be held within bounds if the people at large enjoyed a reasonable degree of economic opportunity.

The new government, however, was weak and untried. The Constitution had been ratified in many States by the narrowest of margins, and even if a majority of the people approved of it, the opposing minority was nearly as large. Fortunately the party system in politics had not yet come into being, the only "parties" having been those who were in favor of or opposed to ratification, called Federalists and Anti-Federalists. The young government was thus saved a party contest and a partisan president. It was fortunate that there was one man in the country to whom all eyes instinctively turned. Washington was not elected President by the glamour of a successful career as general, as has happened since, disastrously. Just as in the war it had not been his military genius but his character that won for him the adoration of his men and of the nation, so now it was his character to which they clung again in the crisis of steering the new Ship of State through the shoals and out on the high seas.

There was as yet no government organization or policy. There were no officeholders, no clearly outlined duties, no departments, no precedents, no money on hand. There were the mere piece of paper called the Constitution of the United States of America, a divided people, huge debts, a worthless currency, and George Washington to give stability to it all, if possible.

For his two chief advisers he chose Thomas Jefferson, as Secretary of State, and Alexander Hamilton, as Secretary of the Treasury.

The two men were utterly different from each other in almost every respect, yet oddly enough no other pair opposed to one another have ever in our history influenced so permanently, both of them, our thought and practice as a nation. Hamilton, a West Indian boy, probably of illegitimate descent, had landed in New York with his fortune to make. A lawyer, with an extraordinarily brilliant mind and attractive personality, he won his way, married into a wealthy family, and became a leading figure in the State. Jefferson had been born on the Virginia frontier. Hamilton, living his life among the moneyed class in New York, with its intensely corrupt politics, had no belief whatever in the capacity of the common man to govern himself or others. Jefferson, influenced by the French philosophers to some extent, and living among the yeomanry of one of the best frontier sections of the country, had complete faith in the ordinary citizen, so long, at least, as the nation might remain agricultural. Hamilton was a realist in politics, Jefferson an idealist, although he proved a better party leader and organizer than his opponent. Hamilton believed in a strongly centralized government, deriving its main support from the moneyed class. Jefferson believed in government performing the minimum of functions, in decentralization, and in reliance upon the farmers. Hamilton was the acknowledged leader of the Federalist Party. Jefferson, who had been in France for some years as our representative in Paris, returned to assume office without party. At first the two men succeeded in working together in the cabinet in moderate harmony, but their philosophies were too antagonistic, and it was not long before the inevitable dislike and mutual lack of confidence began to show itself. Hamilton stood for strength, wealth, and power; Jefferson for the American dream.

To some extent the quarrel became sectional. There had long been a certain amount of friction between the growing mercantilism of the North and the planter class in the South. Hamilton's first task was to establish the credit of the new nation, and for this purpose he deemed it essential to pay off the federal foreign and greatly depreciated domestic debts at par, and also to assume the State debts. He likewise wished to build up as rapidly as possible a moneyed class from banking, shipping, manufacturing, and other industries as a support to the government. He advocated a national bank and a protective tariff, and saw no reason why the South as well as the North should not develop an industrial and financial life. In fact, however, it had not done so, and although the future of both agriculture and slavery was doubtful, an event happened the very year after Hamilton offered his Report on Manufactures to Congress which determined the course of the South for a century.

Agriculture in that section had been rather going from bad to worse. The planters had long been in debt, slave labor was wasteful, though the only labor available, and the future was distinctly uncertain. The old crops of rice, indigo, and tobacco were no longer as profitable as they had been, and it did not seem possible to raise cotton, as it took a slave a month to get the seeds out of one bale. A few experiments had been made, but so impractical was American cotton culture considered that in 1784 the Custom House in England seized eight bales on the ground that they "could not have been produced in America." The demand had become enormous, and the world production in 1791 was 490,000,000 pounds, of which only 138,000 were produced in the United States. The next year Eli Whitney, a young Massachusetts lad on a visit to Georgia, invented the cotton gin, which would clean a thousand pounds in the time it took a slave to clean only five. In 1793 the South raised 487,000 pounds, 1,600,000 the next year, 6,276,000 the next, and 35,000,000 in 1800. Cotton had become king, and the slave doomed to his slavery. The type of Southern culture was thus fixed until almost our own day.

Simultaneously with the sudden rise of the Cotton Kingdom in the South, Samuel Slater, a cotton-mill operative from England, was in Rhode Island trying to remember how the textile machinery which he had tended in the old country had been built, for England prohibited the export of any of the machines lest the industry might be set up elsewhere. Slater was successful, machines were built here, and the foundations laid for the growth of the New England textile mills. Great as the differences between the sections had already been, they were to be increasingly emphasized during the next half century.

If America was to be happiest as a great industrial nation, Hamilton's policies were wise and essential. The forces which have made the industrial United States of to-day stem directly from the Hamiltonian principles. On the other hand, in creating special privileges for certain classes, as in the tariff, in building up a moneyed class whose interests would be distinct from, if not inimical to, those of the agricultural and laboring ones, Hamilton's economic and political doctrines assuredly did not derive from the Declaration of Independence. Jefferson, who had penned that document; the farmers, who wanted to buy manufactured goods as cheap as possible; the debtors of all classes; the men of the frontier, who wanted as little interference from government as might be — all who believed in the American dream were antagonized by this wizard in the Treasury who, it seemed to them, was threatening to raise up an engine of despotism and to sink them in the scale as contrasted with his privileged moneyed men and speculators in securities.

Meanwhile, a new section, to be of vast importance within a few years, was arising over the mountains — a new frontier to be followed successively by others for a century. In all of these the ideas of Jefferson and the Declaration were to find their strongest refuge and supporters. It was, in truth, the size of the country that was to save it for democracy. For better or worse, the United States of to-day was cradled in the Mississippi Valley. As I have pointed out before, had the Pacific Ocean washed the western slopes of the Alleghanies, the type of civilization would probably have continued along the lines of eighteenth-century European culture which had so successfully sprung up in the colonies by the period of the war. How fine the fruit of that culture was to prove we have seen in this present chapter, but it was not to be the American type. What was new in the American of that period was chiefly owing to the wilderness, but had the wilderness ended at the mountains, the frontier would have ceased to be an influence, for the land was fast filling up. If the frontier had been closed in 1790 instead of 1890, an entire century of an irresistibly powerful moulding force would have been lost. By 1800, the North Atlantic seaboard was getting started on its way toward an industrial future. The South had been definitively started on its career as a great agricultural area based on the economics of slavery. Neither of these would have produced what we think of as the typical American mind and character of to-day. If we, as Americans, boast too much of our size, it is nevertheless true that that size has shaped us to what we are.

As we have seen, the population had already begun to spill over the mountains before the Revolution, but after independence was won, the trickling streams became a flood. In 1788 nearly a thousand boats, containing over 18,000 men, women, and children, carried settlers down the Ohio. Emigrants were largely from New England, and indeed the section known as the "Western Reserve" became a sort of second New England, with its town meetings and general type of New England life.

Other settlers, however, were also pouring through passes over the mountains from the South, and by 1790 there were at least 170,000 inhabitants in the Western country. Kentucky was admitted as a State in 1791 and Tennessee five years later, both with manhood suffrage for all males over twenty-one, though Kentucky later qualified this by "white."

If ever men were free, these were. The seaboard colonists had not only had their charters, royal governors, and other symbols of imperial rule, but had also had a certain sentimental tie with the mother country. These new colonists who were now so rapidly building towns across the mountains were at perfect liberty to devise their own governments, and that of the United States was too young and too weak to afford much basis as yet for either loyalty or fear. In fact, when many of the immigrants had gone West and built their stockaded village or made their solitary clearing, there was no United States government worthy of the name. Here in the West was a colossal land of surpassing richness which they intended to make their own by their blood and sweat, and in which they planned to do as they chose. Perhaps they would join the United States back East, and perhaps they would not. They had their own problems, and they would see how things turned out. If the United States could help them to what they wanted, well and good. Meanwhile, the world was wide and there was an empire to be won. By 1800 the Ohio country was raising crops for export to the value of $700,000, and building ships for the European trade, by way of the Mississippi and her tributary rivers. In 1803 the *Duane* of Pittsburgh surprised the authorities of Liverpool by arriving there from a place never heard of, and a couple of years later the *Louisiana of Marietta* was trading between Italy and England from the small Ohio town as her home port!

But there were difficulties, South and North. The fast-increasing produce of the West could not profitably be transported eastward across the mountains to the seaboard United States. Its natural outlet and market was down the Mississippi to the Gulf settlements of the Spaniard or overseas to

Europe. But the Gulf coast and the whole of America west of the great river belonged to Spain. Not only that, but she owned both sides of the river at New Orleans, and any traffic which passed between her banks was allowed to do so by courtesy and not by right. The Americans, with new vast ideas of continental expansion, were also beginning to look not merely for an outlet for their commerce but to the great plains of the Southwest, and even the rich civilization and mines of Mexico. Spain had a full realization of this, and felt that the only way to prevent the expansion, with its threat to her American empire, was to push up against the descending flood and try to crowd it back. She refused to surrender Natchez, which belonged to us by the treaty with England, claiming that England's title had been defective, and New Orleans and Natchez became double corks in the bottle neck which was the only outlet for our West. Not satisfied with that, Spain built more posts on American soil, and entered into intrigues with prominent Western Americans. General James Wilkinson, for example, was simultaneously in the pay of the United States army and of the Spanish secret service. The Westerners felt that the new government in the East was not giving them sufficient help and that they would have to look after themselves. They had little respect for Spanish power, and thought that, with some judicious fishing in troubled waters, the time might come when they could conquer a southwestern empire for themselves, made up of the Mississippi Valley, Texas, and Mexico. With the most magnificent and richest part of the whole continent in their possession, they might need to bother no more with the "United States" across the almost impassable mountains. There were also plenty of men in the East who would have had no regrets if the problem of possible invasion of Western radicalism might thus be got rid of.

As the Westerners looked south to the Gulf or west across the river to the farther West, they were thus confronted with a hostile and intriguing Spain. As they looked north to the great region of forests and fur trade, they were confronted with a no less hostile and intriguing England. Both nations worked on the Indians to attack the Americans on their own soil. Moreover England, like Spain, not only refused to surrender her army posts within our territory, but also built new ones. The United States, as we have said, had not carried out all the terms of the Treaty of Peace, notably the one which had pledged the national faith to offer every facility in the American courts for the collection of bona-fide pre-war debts owing to English merchants by Americans. Taking advantage of this dereliction of duty on our side, the English government continued to hold the Northwestern country, collecting furs, influencing the Indian tribes against us, and holding back American settlement. The territory clearly belonged to us, yet was held by the British army. This was all that the Western settlers could see, as they knew little and cared less about unpaid debts to English creditors by seaboard debtors. The frontier spirit in any case would have been on the side of any debtor, especially when the debts were owed to our late enemies. The Westerners hated the Spaniard for his strangle hold on their Mississippi outlet, but they hoped to deal with, and even despoil, him later. It seemed more hopeless to dislodge the English, and their hatred of the latter became intense.

Over the mountains to the east, the new government was not oblivious of what was going on in the West, nor even as to what was in the minds and dreams of the Westerners; but the government was weak, and Washington felt that everything possible had to be done to gain time for domestic loyalty to develop, and to keep out of foreign war. There was a party in England which would have adopted a conciliatory policy toward our new country, but the opposition had won, and our ships had been debarred from the lucrative West India commerce, which had formerly been one of the chief bases of our shipping trade. Moreover, war had broken out in Europe after the French Revolution, and as neutrals we were suffering depredations upon our commerce, none of the belligerents having, because of our weakness, any respect for our rights, which were in any case rather vaguely defined. Washington played the game of diplomacy patiently, but out in the West "Mad

Anthony" Wayne had taught the Miamis and Shawnees and other Western tribes in the battle of Fallen Timbers that perhaps it might not be well for them to rely too much upon their friends the British.

Meanwhile John Jay had been negotiating with England, and in November 1794 signed a treaty by which the English agreed at last to hand over the Western posts and evacuate the country, but at the expense of commercial conditions that enraged the Atlantic seaboard. No other treaty ever made by us has been so unpopular, and it was an act of great courage on Washington's part to sign it. The West, however, had been ransomed, and a breathing space gained from the threat of European war. "If this country is preserved in tranquillity twenty years longer, it may bid defiance in a just cause to any power whatever," wrote the President, "such in that time will be its population, wealth, and resources." Political parties were now being formed, with intense rancor against each other, and during the next two years Washington was bitterly attacked by a portion of the press. Wisely refusing to run for a third time, and thus establishing a precedent, he made his Farewell Address to his countrymen on September 17, 1796. He warned them against cherishing "inveterate antipathies" or "passionate attachments" for any other nations, and urged that we might keep ourselves, in the then condition of the world, from all entangling alliances with Europe, which had a set of interests unshared by us.

When Jay's Treaty was signed, peace had come temporarily to the nations of Europe; and as England had withdrawn from the North, and the times were not propitious for further intrigue, Spain, who had decided that perhaps a definite boundary was preferable to expeditions of Americans into her territory, agreed on the 31st parallel as the southern line of the United States east of the Mississippi, and granted the much-longed-for right of navigation of that river and shipping of goods through New Orleans. By 1798 she had evacuated her posts on American soil, and the Westerners at last came into possession of their territory. Now that the intrigues of both

English and Spanish no longer set the Southern and Northern tribes on the war path, the savages could be more easily dealt with, and the increase in American population became rapid all the way from Georgia to the Great Lakes. The heart of the new Americanism began to find its home in the heart of the continent, in the new empire of the Mississippi Valley. America would not have become what it did in mind and spirit had we clung to the shores of the Atlantic. For better and worse both, the new America was the child of "Ol' Man River," nurtured in the vast domain which had been his through all the ages. It was on frontier after frontier of his vast domain that the American dream could be prolonged until it became part of the very structure of the American mind.

V

AMERICA SECEDES FROM THE OLD WORLD

About 1800 there were three racial frontiers in the West, although we have been apt to think only of the one steadily advancing from the fringe of the United States. Within the limits of our own territory as marked out in the Treaty of Peace, there was still a scattered line of settlements which were French in culture and long remained so. Detroit, which is now the fourth largest city in our country, remained French in character until well into the nineteenth century, and even after the Civil War its French ancestry was clearly noticeable. From there down the Mississippi Valley, through Vincennes, St. Louis, and smaller posts to New Orleans, the French influence and character were strongly marked, all of this string of settlements lying as yet beyond the advancing phalanxes of the Americans, with a broad swathe of undeveloped wilderness between.

At New Orleans, the French met and mingled with the other Latin stream of the Spanish, who extended from Florida to the Pacific. The main body of the Spanish Empire was, of course, in Mexico and South America, but this had a vast and impractically extended frontier line from the army posts in the Floridas, through New Orleans, San Antonio, and other settlements in Texas, Santa Fé in New Mexico, and straggling settlements up the coast of California. Santa Barbara, Santa Cruz, Monterey, San José, San Francisco, had all been founded in the eighteenth century, as well as Los Angeles, now the fifth largest city in the United States. There were many military posts, called presidios, and Jesuit missions along the coast, at which twenty thousand nominally Christianized Indians had been gathered, but the Spanish population within the limits of the present United States was small — not over twelve hundred in California, and probably less than that number in the other northern provinces. The expansive powers of Spain had long since failed, and in any case it would have been impossible to settle thickly a frontier line of such endless length edging an entire continent. Texas, New Mexico, California, were each at the end of a long overland trail from Mexico City, and were mere outposts of empire against Indians, English, French, and Russians, the last threatening southward expansion from Alaska. The culture of the Spaniards, however, — notably in architecture and historical romance, — has been far out of proportion to their numbers, and in these and other ways the Spanish influence still persists throughout the South, and in the Far West.

We have had much, and shall have more, to say of the influence of the frontier on our national life. However, we must not forget that, as has been already pointed out in regard to the form of colonial governments, the influences of institutions and environments are always dependent upon what, for lack of clearer knowledge, we call race. The French voyageurs who paddled their canoes along the streams, or the French farmers who tilled their fields around Detroit and remained almost unchanged Norman peasants generation after generation, did not react to the frontier as did the English. No more did the Spaniards in California, who spent their time hunting on horseback, or with music and games, and, when supply ships came by sea, with balls and gay festivals. The frontier was, perhaps, the most important moulding influence in American life. But that was because the people who came under its influence were for some reason peculiarly receptive to it. Professor Turner performed a great service when he caused the whole of American history to be rewritten in terms of the frontier, but it is well to remember that, just because frontier influence has not been universal, there must also be racial factors in our case to account for our receptivity toward it. That the Americans and, to a lesser extent, the English race everywhere were receptive is all that need concern us now.

The new American frontier that was forming around 1800 was different from preceding ones, and more typically "American," as we have come to consider it. The first frontier of settlement had not really been an "American" frontier at all. All the settlers had England for a background. Poor and well-to-do, learned and unlearned, gentlemen and laborers, were mingled in fairly close contact. As a newer frontier formed at the back of the old settlements, there was, it is true, no European background, but the pioneers were nowhere far from our oldest settled country. To a considerable extent, however, in passing the population through this second sieve, the learned and gentle were left behind, and rawness and lack of culture were increased along the border. The American population has been squeezed through such a sieve over and over again, and, when the first migrations over the mountains occurred, there was another elimination of education and refinement. Moreover, with each successive swarming out from the older settlements the background of culture and beauty became more and more meagre. The first settlers had come from the rich background of old England, its churches and hedgerows and old, old villages, its handicrafts and household arts even in the homes of the small farmers. In the colonies, by the latter third of the eighteenth century, a civilization of no mean order had arisen, as we have seen, but it was different. The good architecture was confined almost wholly to the modest dwellings of the upper class. There were no great buildings of any sort. The churches — with a few exceptions — were everywhere, for the most part barnlike, bare, and ugly. The homes of the poor had begun to take on that unpainted packing-box effect of bare utility with no pretense to beauty that has ever since been one of the depressing aspects of our countryside. In their interiors, all interest in the carving or painting of furniture had disappeared, and a crude utility had obliterated any striving for the æsthetic.

Life had been growing freer and more independent for the poor, but also less cultured in the broadest sense. American advance has always involved a selection. If that selection has meant that the more democratic, the more independent, courageous, and ambitious, — as well, it must not be forgotten, as the more shiftless, — have passed on to the frontiers as pioneers, so has it also meant that those for whom education, the pleasures of social life, æsthetic and intellectual opportunities of one sort and another have counted as more important than a material getting ahead, have for the most part usually stayed behind. They have been deposited in successive "older settlements" like the sediment in a stream in flood.

Although the hunter and Indian trader had always made a blurred fringe ahead of actual settlement in the wilderness, the earlier frontiers had been made up of permanent home builders. Gradually, however, the more characteristic triple advance of civilization began. First went the adventurers, a motley crew of hunters, traders, ne'er-do-weels, restless and discontented spirits, men, also, fired with the spirit of adventure in the untried and unknown. As others of a somewhat more substantial sort followed, the first would feel cramped, sell out their scantily cleared fields, and move on. Behind the second line of advance was a third, whose members came in greater numbers, brought social organization of schools and newspapers and churches, built towns and pushed ahead of them the second line of those who had got used to semi-wilderness conditions, as those, in turn, had pushed ahead of *them* the first liners who felt cramped with neighbors a dozen miles away. But the torch of frontier influence was handed back rapidly from one line of advance to another, and when we speak of the frontier we mean, in general, all three of the lines up to such period as the third began to be "old," "settled," or "conservative."

To a considerable extent, this might happen fairly quickly, and by 1793 there were already three newspapers established to the west of the Alleghanies; but this did not prevent the overpowering influence of frontier life and thought. We have already spoken of the effects of such life on the ideals of democracy, work, and the all-important increase in mere physical comfort. There was another effect as the Americans began to understand better both the hardships and the technique of frontiering. The older and more substantial men became more and more hesitant about venturing, and the frontier rapidly became young. An enthusiastic youthfulness becomes one of its clearest notes. Hope and inexperience combine to emphasize the freedom and democracy of the wilderness and of economic equality. Failures there were in plenty. The whole front of the American advance was strewn with them, men and women who dropped down to the moral, economic, and intellectual level of a hopeless and shiftless poverty. But in the buoyant air of freedom, of youth and of opportunity, it was those who succeeded who gave the tone to the temperament of the frontier everywhere.

Success on the frontier — on the innumerable frontiers that have followed one another across the continent — meant material success, tinged with politics. Almost all those who went to the frontier were poor, and even to buy land at a dollar an acre, work and stock it, meant going into debt. The fundamental problem, which united the whole frontier in a bond of sympathetic understanding, was to make money, or at least to build up the material structure of a home. The mark of that struggle remained on everyone. Material success became a good in itself that could not be questioned. The only other success which the life offered was that of local leadership, becoming a known and followed man in one's community. For that it was essential that one should be able, so to say, to swing an axe, to get one's self on in the rough and hard life, to mix with one's neighbors on a plane of equality, or, if a bit above them, to be that bit only in the abilities they admired, the abilities that enabled one to be a good frontiersman. On the one hand, the man who was merely virile, strong, ambitious in a material sense, was much more apt to make a success in that hard life than the man who by training or environment possessed the manners of good society, who was learned or cultivated and who cared more about such things than about spending his life making a clearing and adding acre to acre. On the other hand, the frontiersmen, possessing none of these things, but others of value, naturally idealized themselves and their qualities, and came to look down upon those different from themselves, as the Puritan had looked down upon those with whom he differed as being morally inferior. Just as American Puritanism had become intolerantly narrow, so was the life of the frontier; and thus two of the strongest influences in our life, religion and the frontier, made in our formative periods for a limited and intolerant spiritual life.

The development of that vast optimism which is one of our characteristics belongs to the next period, but already there was growing up on the frontier that self-confidence which breathes a belief that we know our own business better than anyone else. Life on the frontier was extremely narrow, and success in it called for the combination of a few primal qualities, not of a very high order, save perhaps those of physical courage and dogged perseverance, which, after all, can be found also elsewhere. The fact, however, that a man who was more than this simple type was less likely to be a success in frontier terms tended to make the frontier mistrust his qualities and greatly enhanced its complete trust in its own. Because the frontiersmen had developed the right combination of qualities to conquer the wilderness, they began to believe quite naturally that they knew best, so to say, how to conquer the world, to solve its problems, and that their own qualities were the only ones worth a man's having. Among these came to be aggressiveness, self-assertion, and a certain unteachableness.

Self-confidence was greatly increased by the simplicity of

the frontiersman's problems and of his life. There were none of the complications of an old and settled community. Under the new Land Law of 1800, a settler could buy smaller tracts of land, paying down only fifty cents an acre, the balance of a dollar and a half an acre being nominally spread over four years. Boys usually married at eighteen or twenty, when they had saved a hundred dollars or so, and girls at fourteen to sixteen. The bridegroom might receive as gifts a horse, seed, and a few implements; the bride a bed, perhaps a cow, a few chairs and kitchen utensils. The neighbors joined together to build a rough house in a few days, and the couple were well started. Children, ten to a dozen, and sometimes twenty or more, were welcomed as affording, almost from the time they were able to walk, additional labor for the pair, and almost no expense, though some additional toil. Food came from the farm, clothes were homemade, there were no bills for doctors or schooling, and, when old enough to marry, the children would start out as their parents had. For those settlers who enlarged their economic operations, the problems of money owed to Eastern creditors and of markets for outlet of surplus products might become of bitter importance, but for countless individual settlers life was reduced to its simplest terms.

But, if life was simple, it was almost unbearably narrow. If there was almost no privacy, sometimes a dozen persons living in one room, and every neighbor knowing his neighbor's business, nevertheless there was great loneliness also and little or nothing for minds to feed on. In the life of the colonial Americans, and later of our frontiers in each wave of advance, we can trace the lack of desire for privacy, and the craving for news and gossip of any sort to break the monotony of empty minds, in lives of little variety and in communities where everyone is doing precisely what his neighbor is doing. The simple economic conditions of marriage in America had done away with the European idea of dowries, and American boys and girls "married for love," but the hard, grinding work of daily toil and the incessant childbearing left little time for romance, and both minds and emotions became starved.

Just as William Bradford, in trying to account for the prevalence of unnatural vice at Plymouth, with its religious repression, had suggested that human nature, dammed in one direction, would find outlets in another, so the emptiness of life on the frontier, and to some extent among the poor of the older settlements, led the emotions to find relief in wild orgies. At first the religion of the frontier had been to a great extent the Presbyterian, but about 1800 the less intellectual and more emotional appeal of the Baptist and especially the Methodist faith swept the frontiersmen into those folds. These denominations did not believe in a learned ministry, and their appeals were all to the emotions. The almost incredible camp meetings catered both to the settler's desire for company and to his need for expression in emotional life. The inhibitions of his starved social and emotional life were suddenly removed by the mass psychology of these vast gatherings, at which thousands would exhibit pathological symptoms in unison.

One of the greatest of these, held in Bourbon County, Kentucky, in 1801, was attended by twenty-five to thirty thousand persons, coming from a circuit of a hundred miles. Seventeen preachers, as well as many volunteers, preached continuously from a Friday to the following Thursday, and at one time, it is said, three thousand followers lay unconscious on the ground in religious swoons, while five hundred "jerked" and "barked" in unison. One prayer felled three hundred of them. In the innumerable meetings of the sort during the next half century, in the poorer parts of the East and throughout the South and West, the religious frenzy often passed into a sexual orgy, and as dusk came on, and the preacher played on the emotional natures of his hearers, he would be surrounded by a mass of humanity in which all intellectual control had been released, some falling insensible, some writhing in fits, some crawling and barking like dogs, some having the "jerks," and others throwing themselves in couples on the ground among the trees in frenzies of sensual passion. Although such meetings were greatly objected to by the more substantial men, they were a natural outcome of the abnormal conditions in many sections of American life. Man craves an outlet for his emotions, and these had been completely starved in the monotonous, hard-working, lonely, drab existence of the outer settlements and frontier.

The camp meetings, with all their pathological symptoms, merely throw a lurid light on a more general factor which was beginning to have influence in America. All the way down the stream of European life, from savagery through paganism to the Middle Ages, there had been in most periods various outlets for man's emotional nature. There were the household arts and crafts, in which man's æsthetic emotions, however crude, found some self-expression. There were the religious pageants, services, and festivals, full of color and emotional content, many of them derived unconsciously from those of pagan days. There was much in the communal life of one sort and another that brought people together and gave interest and color to their lives. Almost all of this had disappeared in America. Self-expression in art had, as we have noted, been abandoned under the stress of the struggle for mere material comfort. Owing largely to Puritanism, the religious festivals had been abandoned and all æsthetic emotion had been banished from church services. The early Church in Europe, frowning on many festivals as pagan, had been forced to restore them for the mental health of the people and to bless them in the name of Christianity. There was nothing in the hard-working, drab life of the American poor and pioneers to take the place of all these things. Mind and emotion became ingrowing, and nature took its revenge in the form of occasional outbursts of violent excitement. The camp meeting is a key to much that we shall find even in present-day life, in a nation even yet emotionally starving.

The West was growing rapidly. In 1800 the territory of "Indiana" was set off from the Northwest Territory because of the radicals' objections to the governor, St. Clair. Three years later the State of Ohio was formed and admitted to the Union, with the most democratic constitution of any State yet — judges, for example, being appointed by the legislature, and for periods of seven years instead of for life or good behavior. Population was increasing so fast that there seemed no limit to possible development. There was comparatively little intercourse with the old East, and "the river" gave to the whole of the States now being built up a unity of life and direction of which they were very self-conscious. There was a free West and a slave-owning West, but these sections were bound together by the subtle tie of both being "West" and by the more material one of "Ol' Man River," who brought them all together and promised to be the great common outlet for all their produce.

There was no market in the East, owing to the cost of transporting produce over the mountains. There were only creditors there, for most of the Westerners owed money either to land companies or the government, from whom they had bought their lands on partial payment, or to individuals for the expenses of development. Already the East was beginning to be regarded as grasping, aristocratic, snobbish, dangerous, effete, and undemocratic by those who breathed the free air of mortgage-encumbered acres. Then, suddenly, a rumor came that Spain had ceded the territory of Louisiana, with the port of New Orleans, to France; and that France might bottle up all Western energy and prosperity by closing the mouth of the river!

Back in the East, which was beginning to look small as compared with the boundless stretch from the Appalachians to the Rockies, North and South were developing fast, and, in some respects, far apart from each other and from the West. In the South, the cotton gin had done its work and created a new economic order. Agriculture and slavery had ceased to be unprofitable. In South Carolina, Georgia, and Alabama the cotton kingdom had arisen, with its great estates and its insatiable demands for more land and more slaves. The tobacco planters of Virginia, who a generation before had been willing to talk of emancipation, now found the breeding of slaves for the ever-yawning market more to the south a profitable adjunct to their fields, although prosperity did not return to the great houses. Throughout all the country south of the Potomac, however, the social structure of the ante-bellum period, so well known in song and story, was rapidly crystallizing. Life was utterly different from that in the West, but, because both sections were agricultural and in debt, the political philosophy of each was agrarian. Both feared the growing money power in the North; and the small democratic farmer of the West and the great landed magnate of the South both disliked the Northern merchant and banker socially — one because he had no manners, and the other because he had too much!

Jefferson, as we have seen, trusted the common man, but only — a fact which is now often forgotten — when that man was a farmer, large or small, and had the self-reliant, individualistic, conservative traits that the ownership and working of the soil develop. He had no faith whatever in a city proletarian class. Nor had he faith in a purely moneyed class of the towns. This had been one of his chief reasons for opposing Hamilton's attempt to create such classes, which are always found together. In the South, John Taylor of Caroline gave emphatic voice to the Southern and Western fears. A capitalistic class based on manufacturing, stockjobbing, banking, and speculation was bound, in his opinion, to bring about class hatreds. It would exploit the people at large as ruthlessly as ever royal, noble, or church classes had done, and at the same time be far more difficult to reach or control because it had no distinct legal status or privileges as a class. It would have no legal obligations going with its position and would work subtly underground for its own selfish interest in public opinion or any political party. In the course of time it would ruin the country.

Hamilton, however, had been successful — at least partially so. His policies of refunding, assumption, and of a bank, as well as the tariff to be later adopted, had given an enormous impetus to the building up of a moneyed interest; but that interest, instead of extending throughout the country as he had expected, had become localized in the North, where it was to remain entrenched until the present day.

For the building up of such an interest both labor and capital were necessary. We have already noted the difficulty of getting the former in the North, in the absence of free laborers or slaves. The New Englanders, however, now busy starting their new textile mills, solved the problem for the generation of 1800 onward. For various reasons there was much distress among the small farmers, which accounted for the great emigration to the West. Many, however, could not emigrate, because of abject poverty or other causes. To operate their new machines, the mill owners exploited these conditions by seizing on the wives and children of impoverished farmers. "In collecting our help," wrote one, "we are obliged to employ poor families, and generally those having the greater number of children." Tending machines, wrote another, did not require men, but was better done by girls of from six to twelve years of age. Of these, great numbers were set to work to create the capital required by their employers. In one Rhode Island plant in 1801, Josiah Quincy found one hundred of them at work, for from twelve to twenty-five cents a day, there being a "dull dejection in the countenances of all of them." Possibly three quarters of the operatives were young women, but sometimes an entire family let themselves out. In one case, for example, a man signed a contract for $5.00 a week for himself, $2.00 for his sixteen-year-old son, $1.50 for his thirteen-year-old son, $1.25 for his daughter of twelve, $.83 for his boy of ten, $2.33 for his sister, $1.50 for her son of thirteen, and $.75 for her daughter of eight. With a labor supply thus arranged for, the outlook was bright for the rapid production of capital from manufacturing.

Shipping, however, was producing it more rapidly. It had been discovered that by buying furs for very little on the coast of Alaska and selling them for a great deal to the Chinese, and by repeating the operation with goods bought in China and sold here, large profits could be made. This and other shipping routes began to pile up fortunes for men who came from nothing to affluence in a short time. A mercantile "aristocracy," as its descendants like to call it, was being built up in Salem, Boston, Newport, New York, and other ports. Although we usually hear much more of the Massachusetts ships than others, the greatest fortunes were built by men like Astor of New York and Girard of Philadelphia, who in the first decade of the century became America's first millionaires. Money was coming to count for more in American life and to spell power. Success loomed much larger, and Astor and Girard, whose predatory methods were notorious, became two of the most powerful men in the country, men whose words were respectfully listened to in the Congress now located in the new city of Washington.

Astor was a czar in the Far Northwest fur trade, where his power was greater than that of the Federal government; and a man who, like Girard, could order his London bankers to make a single investment of a half million dollars out of his idle balance was beginning to exert a new sort of influence. The country was getting rich fast, but there were multitudes of men beside John Taylor of Caroline who looked anxiously at the portents in the North. "We have," wrote John Adams in 1808, "one material which actually constitutes an aristocracy that governs the nation. That material is wealth. Talents, birth, virtues, services, sacrifices, are of little consideration with us." He added that the object of both political parties was "chiefly wealth." Connecticut was and always had been, he said, governed by a half-dozen or a dozen families at most.

Looking back later, Emerson wrote, perhaps somewhat too sweepingly, that between 1790 and 1820 there was "not a book, a speech, a conversation, or a thought" produced in the State of Massachusetts. Emerson may have exaggerated, but our intellectual life was at a low ebb. In the North, new men, with no background of culture and no interest in things of the mind, were building up new fortunes to incredible figures for that day, and setting a new pace for all to follow. In the South much more of the Old World lingered, but there also King Cotton was scattering riches so lavishly and in such unexpected and untraditional directions that the pursuit became absorbing. In the West, life was hard and the pioneer qualities had to be exalted lest the weary people faint. The civilization of the eighteenth century had died, and a new America was emerging, whatever it might prove to be. Meanwhile, in spite of the Declaration of Independence, America was not yet free, but was still swirling around in the wake of European States.

In 1797, Washington had been succeeded as President by John Adams, of the Federalist Party, if Adams could be said ever to have belonged to a party. England and France were again at war, and both were preying on our commerce, France being the worst aggressor in this period. In spite of the wise advice in Washington's Farewell Address, the American political parties strongly espoused sides in the European quarrel, the Republicans (then so-called) under Jefferson being insanely pro-French and the Federalists pro-English. John Adams, like Washington, was merely pro-American. The provocations of France, especially in her adding insult to injury in refusing to accept our representatives unless bribed to do so, as was made clear in the X.Y.Z. correspondence, were very great. Pugnacious as Adams could be on occasion, he was as anxious as Washington to keep the country clear of European war, at least for those twenty years which Washington had deemed necessary for us to grow in. Hamilton, however, who considered himself the real head of the Federalist Party, but in reality was beginning to lose his own, had grandiose schemes for declaring war on France and then, in concert with England, for attacking Spain, leading a great army of invasion — with himself in the rôle of conquering hero — into Mexico, seizing the whole Southwest, and allowing England to compensate herself further south out of the spoils of the dismembered Spanish empire.

Adams chafed and fretted, but Hamilton and his Massachusetts followers, the little powerful group of Federalist leaders known as the "Essex Junto," felt that they had the game quite in hand, and were speechifying in the Senate on the armed forces to be raised when, without having taken them into his counsel at all, Adams sent in the appointment of a Minister to France and blew their schemes to atoms. He had learned at last that no trust could be placed in the party leaders; France had given him an opening that might lead to peace; and, though it involved his own political ruin, the President had seized it and saved the country. Hamilton and the Junto were mad with rage, and determined to ruin Adams even though the party should commit suicide. History has upheld both the courage and the wisdom of Adams, whom Hamilton professed to regard as unfit for his office, and Adams himself never wavered in the belief that what he had done was right. Years afterward he wrote that he considered it the most disinterested act of his life, and would have inscribed on his tombstone: "Here lies John Adams, who took upon himself the responsibility of peace with France in the year 1800."

During the excitement, in 1798, Congress had passed the Alien and Sedition Acts, the first authorizing the President to deport without trial any alien whom he should judge dangerous to the peace and safety of the country, and the second providing fine and imprisonment for anyone who should publish false, malicious, or scandalous statements about members of the national government with intent to bring them into disrepute. These Acts brought forth responses in the form of resolutions passed by the Southern State of Virginia and the Western State of Kentucky, claiming that the Acts were in contravention of the Federal Constitution and calling upon other States to consider them void, thus voicing the doctrine of States' rights and nullification.

The Alien and Sedition Acts, together with the Naturalization Act, by which a residence of fourteen instead of five years was made necessary before an alien could become a citizen, all sprang from the Hamiltonian-Federalist distrust of the common man. Even the excesses of the French Revolution had not destroyed Jefferson's implicit faith in him, so long as he remained dependent upon the soil and not upon some capitalist for his living. Whether Jefferson was right or wrong yet remains an open question, for though in political life America's dream and ideal rest on the Jeffersonian faith in the common man, in her economic life she has developed along the lines of Hamiltonian special privilege and moneyed classes. As America grew she tried to serve, so to say, God and Mammon — that is, she insisted upon clinging to the ideal of Jeffersonianism while gathering in the money profits from Hamiltonianism. By building up a great industrial and financial, instead of an agrarian, State, we have cut the major premise from out the logical structure of Jefferson's faith, and applied that faith to conditions under which he distinctly renounced it. On the other hand, we have erected an economic order according to Hamilton, but on a basis of a political philosophy which he did not believe would work. That is the modern American paradox. In 1800, however, America was still at the parting of the ways, and it yet seemed possible that the nation might choose to follow in the pure doctrine of either one or the other leader.

There is no doubt that Jeffersonianism was the American doctrine, stemming straight from the Declaration of Independence, which he had drawn up, and from the whole theory upon which the War of Secession from England had been fought. If the common man were to be submerged beneath a hierarchy of the moneyed class, it was not easy for him to see wherein he had gained by substituting for a political king three thousand miles overseas a creditor king at his cottage door. If America has stood for anything unique in the history of the world, it has been for the American dream, the belief in the common man and the insistence upon his having, as far as possible, equal opportunity in every way with the rich one.

By 1800 the common man was up in arms against the Federalist Party with its openly expressed disbelief in him and its effort to control him. The great debtors of the Southern plantations and small debtors of the Western clearings were equally distrustful of the rising financial powers of the North. They had seen the Northern speculators rake in almost all the profit derived by the Hamiltonian policies of redemption and assumption. Of the national debt, the one State of Massachusetts held more than all the Southern States combined. They had watched the rise under government favoritism of a mercantile-shipping-manufacturing-banking group whose interests they believed, not without reason, to be directly opposed to those of the farmers and planters. From 1796 to 1800 they had seen the expenses of the Federal government mount from $5,800,000 to $10,800,000, while in 1798 the party which had built up the moneyed class by special privilege laid a direct tax on houses, lands, and slaves, the weight of which fell to a far greater extent upon the planter in the South, and the poor everywhere, than upon the new rich of the North. Jefferson had been biding his time, and the general discontent in 1800, combined with the split in the Federalist Party, gave him his opportunity.

The presidential campaign of 1800 was fought with great bitterness, the clergy of Connecticut in particular contributing a most ungodly amount of unchristian lying about Mr. Jefferson. With the almost solid backing of the South and West, and the addition of large numbers from the poor farmer and city laboring class in the North, the Republican (later the Democratic) Party won easily, although, owing to the system then in force, there was a tie vote between Jefferson and Burr for highest place. This was settled in the House of Representatives as provided for by the Constitution, and Jefferson was elected. On the last evening before he retired from office, John Adams appointed a number of Federal judges, as he had shortly before appointed John Marshall as Chief Justice of the Supreme Court, with profound and lasting effect upon the development of both the Constitution and the nation. The judiciary was the only branch of the government from which the Federalists had not been swept clean from office. In the past dozen years they had rendered great services to the country, but their political philosophy of governing by an oligarchy of wealth, talent, and birth was wholly un-American as interpreted by the great mass of the American people. The American philosophy was based on the economics of agrarianism, and agrarianism had won. Farmers, Jefferson had said, "are the true representatives of the great American interest, and are alone to be relied upon for expressing the proper American sentiments." They had responded by expressing those sentiments at the polls with exceptional clarity.

Jefferson's election was a triumph for the American dream. We have seen how, in spite of the vast changes due to following Hamilton in our business life, America even yet clings to the Jeffersonian belief in the common man. This is still an axiom with millions of Americans who have forgotten or never heard of Jefferson's distinction between "common men" of varying industrial pursuits. But subconsciously that distinction seems to have lingered until within a decade or so, for the American farmer has been considered to be the special repository of the American virtues, in spite of the enormous increase in other classes of toilers. Up to the Great War, it was an asset of no small value to a public man to have been raised on a farm, to have been a "barefoot boy, with cheek of tan" — in spite of the fact that nearly half the boys in the nation were by that time being brought up to dodge automobiles in crossing city streets.

The fears of Jefferson's opponents that his entry upon office would usher in a reign of anarchy were wholly without foundation. The disgraceful predictions of the Reverend Timothy Dwight, Congregational "Pope" of Connecticut and President of Yale College, that if Jefferson were elected "we may see our wives and daughters the victims of legal prostitution; soberly dishonored; speciously polluted; the outcasts of delicacy and virtue, the loathing of God and man," simply did not come to pass. As a matter of fact, although he was not a professing Christian, few more genuinely religious men than Jefferson ever entered the White House, although the New England clergy, like all others, subtly influenced by the economic interests of the richer members of their congregations, could not appreciate that fact.

Jefferson insisted upon maintaining the national credit, and upon the payment of all debts, public and private. His first four years were a period of excellent, economical government, illuminated by one of the most brilliant *coups* in international politics that have ever been seen.

By 1800 there were a million Americans settled in the territory which the British government had tried to close to pioneers by the Proclamation of 1763. Every little village and scrub town along the Western rivers — Pittsburgh, Wheeling, Cincinnati, and hosts of others — was dreaming of a future in which it would be a great centre of wealth and population. There is never any past on the frontier, only a future, and one of the most radical changes which frontier mentality undergoes is precisely this complete shift of orientation in time. To dream solely of the future instead of the past is bound to act as a powerful solvent on one's entire stock of ideas and mental processes. The rumor, therefore, that Spain had ceded Louisiana to France and that France was to close "the river" came as a profound shock, not merely to business plans of the moment, but to the whole dream the West had been dreaming.

For two years France repeatedly lied, denying that any transfer had taken place, but at last she was ready to act openly, and in October 1802 the agent at New Orleans closed the river to American commerce. Spain had ceased to be a power in the Mississippi Valley. The future of the West depended again on France, and Napoleon had turned the key on the only door which opened on the world. From flatboat to flatboat, river town to river town, the news leaped frantically up "the river" and along its tributaries. It was carried overland by swift courier from Natchez to Washington, and reached Jefferson in the White House.

The President knew his West. He knew how slight the bond of economic interest was that held it to the East. He knew the dream it dreamed, and that if no help came promptly from the Federal government, the pioneers would take matters into their own hands, rush France out of its slender hold on the Gulf, plunge the nation into war, and perhaps set up for themselves a huge trans-Appalachian State, a United States of the Mississippi. The Federalists hoped a chance had come to break Jefferson's popularity in the West, and howled for war. Jefferson, however, had long foreseen the crisis. Six months before, he had written to the American Minister in Paris that the day France took possession of New Orleans, "we must marry ourselves to the British fleet and nation." First, however, he would try pacific means, and without divulging his purpose he obtained an authorization from Congress of a million dollars for expenses incidental to our intercourse with foreign nations. He then instructed the Minister in Paris to attempt to buy New Orleans and the Floridas, the island of New Orleans alone, or, at worst, the right of navigation.

There were ample reasons, some known and others not (including the imminence of war with England), why at that moment Napoleon was anxious to turn an uncertain liability in the New World into cash in the Old. On April 11, 1803, he defied the British Ambassador and simultaneously offered the American Minister, Robert Livingston, and our special envoy, James Monroe, the *whole* of Louisiana. Terms were quickly arranged, and in less than three weeks the United States had secured the entire continent from the east bank of the Mississippi to the Rocky Mountains, and from northern Texas to the Canadian border, for a total sum of fifteen million dollars. "Ol' Man River" had become American for his whole four thousand miles of imperial extent. A million square miles had doubled the size of the country, three fourths of which was now "the West." By a stroke of the pen, the national centre of gravity had shifted as if by a convulsion of nature.

Meanwhile an event had occurred in Washington which was also to alter materially the development of the nation, although it had none of the spectacular quality of Jefferson's statesmanship. In delivering an opinion in the case of *Marbury* v. *Madison*, Chief Justice Marshall had quietly laid down the principle that "a legislative act contrary to the Constitution is not law . . . that a law repugnant to the Constitution is void." The Supreme Court thus placed the corner stone of its power of legislative review. Congress was not, like Parliament, to express the legislative will of the people. The veto of the elected President could be overridden if desired, but not the judicial veto of a majority of our nine judges appointed for life if their verdict should be, "Unconstitutional."

Jefferson's first term had been amazingly successful. The Federalists were demoralized, and in July 1804, when Aaron Burr killed their leader, Hamilton, in a duel, their power crumbled completely. In the autumn, Jefferson received 162 electoral votes to his opponent's 14.

Whether or not the territory ceded by France included the Floridas and Texas was a moot point. Jefferson wanted Florida, to give us control of the Gulf coast, and the Westerners wanted Texas. In 1806, Burr, now thoroughly discredited, went West and played his hand at some sort of conspiracy which is even yet unexplained. In any case it was a complete fiasco, but other troubles crowded quickly on the President. The war between England and France was bringing in its train the usual insults to ourselves. Among these was the impressment of seamen on our vessels by the British. There was no question but that large numbers of British subjects preferred to serve on American merchant vessels rather than on British ships of war, but the mere claim of a right to stop and search our vessels would have been annoying enough in itself had the British not gone further and frequently taken bona-fide Americans from them. There was much fraud connected with naturalization papers, and the claim to American citizenship did not mean much. The French could have no excuse for a similar procedure, owing to the difference in race and language, so this particular source of irritation was wholly of British origin.

In June 1807, England went even further, and a roar of indignation went up in America when the British frigate *Leopard* overhauled our frigate *Chesapeake* off the Norfolk Capes, fired on her, and took off four men. Had Jefferson chosen to declare war, he would have had a united country behind him, but he preferred to try the coercion of economic measures, and the rest of his term is mainly the story of the failure of his embargo policy, and the rising bitterness of the commercial Northerners against the closing of their ports and the ruin of their shipping by their own government. Meanwhile both England and France were issuing their Orders in Council and decrees, aiming at establishing paper blockades and preventing neutrals from trading with either country. In this respect there was nothing whatever to choose between the two countries in respect to their interference with our rights. Our own country might extend from the Atlantic to the Rockies, but once out on the high seas we were still kicked about by both the European belligerents, and it was not easy to tell which was kicking us harder. Jefferson's policy of standing on the side lines while the Europeans kicked each other, and perhaps forcing their attention to our claims by refusing to trade with them, had been a complete failure, much more likely to disrupt the Union by the Secession of New England than to gain international respect for our rights. There might be little choice between England and France in respect of wrongs done us, but we could hardly enter the fight against both at once when they were fighting each other. We were not at all in the position of the man who can take two squabbling boys and knock their heads together. It might be, as William Pinkney said in 1810, that "war with France is about as practicable as war with the moon," but if we were to choose sides, the side chosen would depend on something more than what they were both doing to us on the seas. As we have said, the centre of gravity of America had shifted, and the real demand for war was to come from the West.

The character of our new acquisition to the west of "the river" was not yet well known, but the exploring expeditions of Lewis and Clark in the Northwest and of Zebulon M. Pike in the Southwest had indicated that the prairies and plains were not of much use to settlers, and thus the western half of the country was to retain its reputation as the great American desert until after the Civil War. Our pioneers were still woodsmen, used to clearing forests, and the treeless wastes beyond puzzled and discouraged them. So the frontier, with its three advances of hunters and traders, of short-stop settlers, and of real settlement, kept on pushing northward into Indiana and the Northwest Territory, shoving the Indians steadily backward. Between 1795 and 1809, by "treaties," the savages had been forced to part with forty-eight million acres of their hunting grounds.

The process was suddenly halted by the emergence of two of the few great leaders who have arisen among the red men, Tecumseh and his brother, the latter called the Prophet, who were sons of a Shawnee. The old trader's method of getting furs cheaply by debauching the Indians with whiskey had been followed on a larger scale, and if possible in a more scandalous way, by the great Astor, and what with this practice, wars, and the change in the habits of their life, the natives had shrunk to perhaps only four thousand in the great rectangle between Pennsylvania, the Mississippi, the Ohio River, and the Canadian border. The two Shawnees determined to save their race without attacking the whites within their own boundaries. They urged that no further cessions of land be made, and preached against the use of strong drink. The land-hungry whites were alarmed. They saw their hopes dashed if the Indians should become moral, law-abiding, and insistent upon remaining upon their lands. William Henry Harrison was governor of the Indiana Territory. He met the situation by making a "treaty" with a few scattered and irresponsible savages who ceded Tecumseh's hunting grounds, and then Harrison, advancing on Tecumseh's camp, provoked a fight, the famous "battle" of Tippecanoe. Tecumseh's "conspiracy" was broken, but the affair was raw enough and had to be glorified. Rumor was spread and gladly believed that the English in Canada had been behind the savage in egging him on to keep the Americans off his lands, and the streams from the vials of moral indignation were diverted from Harrison and the Westerners to the British, who, having been the enemy for forty years, could easily be made the scapegoats for anything. As a matter of fact we know now that they had nothing whatever to do with Tecumseh.

Over the mountains in Washington the new President, James Madison, who was struggling with the international situation and was trying to preserve peace by getting both the belligerents in Europe to rescind their obnoxious Orders and Decrees, seemed to be making some headway. But the new Congress that met in 1811 was destined to be led by the West. Fiery young men came from Kentucky and settlements up to the Canadian border, with Henry Clay at their head, to be joined by John C. Calhoun from the South Carolina frontier. Little by little these "war-hawks," as they were called, fanned the flame of the war spirit in Congress, shouting how Canada could be conquered in six weeks, but mainly giving the war cry of "sailors' rights."

They were strongly opposed by the New England States, which were the only ones that had any sailors, but which much preferred a profitable, if speculative, trade to war, and had no wish to sacrifice that trade for the sake of pulling the Canadian chestnut out of the fire for the benefit of a West which they already dreaded. In fact, they feared the westward shift of power so greatly that Josiah Quincy, of Massachusetts, had solemnly proclaimed in Congress in January 1811, that if Louisiana were admitted as a State — as she was the next year — the bonds of the Union would be dissolved, and that "as it will be the right of all, so it will be the duty of some, to prepare, definitely, for a separation; amicably, if they can; violently, if they must." New England had nullified the Embargo. It now threatened secession. On June 23, 1812, Parliament repealed the Orders in Council. It was too late. There was no cable to bear the news to America, and five days earlier the war-hawks had succeeded. Congress, in compliance with the President's message, had declared war with England on the eighteenth.

The war proved inglorious and indecisive. We were unprepared, and England had her hands so full elsewhere that one more small enemy was not worth bothering about. Land operations against Canada were disastrous for us. On the water we had some good fights and gained some brilliant victories, mostly in duels between single ships on either side, which did much to kindle patriotic enthusiasm here and to breed respect for us in England. Such victories as those of the *Constitution* over the *Guerrière*, of the *Wasp* over the *Frolic*, and of Perry over the English on Lake Erie, were welcome indeed to the young nation. The West threw up a new hero to the surface of American political life in Andrew Jackson, who marched into Florida, and also, after peace was signed but the fact was still unknown to him, inflicted a severe defeat on the British in the battle of New Orleans. Meanwhile the British had captured the city of Washington, and in dastardly fashion and sheer wantonness had burned some of the public buildings and many of our national records.

New England, rapidly being altered by force of circumstances from a maritime to a manufacturing section, was disloyal almost to the point of treason. She discouraged enlistment, refused the services of militia, declined to subscribe to government loans, and threatened secession. So strong, indeed, was the odor of secession and disloyalty around the meeting of Federalist delegates at the so-called Hartford Convention in 1814 that the members never outlived it. At length both nations grew weary of a war which was bringing neither glory nor gain to either of them. Peace was made at Ghent the day before Christmas, 1814, with nothing said about any of the grievances which we had complained of when we began hostilities.

The war, however, was far from having no results, quite aside from our having slipped West Florida into our pocket during the general excitement. We had managed to keep out of European wars for the twenty years that Washington had said were necessary for our growth, thanks to himself, Adams, and Jefferson. At last, pushed into it by the West, we had shown the world that we would go to war if provoked too far. Moreover the English, who appreciate a good fighter, had measured us with themselves at sea, and had infinitely more respect for our abilities than they had had before. Less happily, the war left bitterness on both sides. England, who had felt that she was fighting the battle of freedom against the all-grasping tyrant Napoleon, much as we felt we were making the world safe for democracy by fighting Germany recently, could not forgive us for stabbing her in the back when she was so engaged and throwing our weight on the side of Napoleon, who had injured our commerce quite as much as she had. In America, the belief in England's inveterate enmity, a tradition fostered among us since the Revolution, was given an enormously increased strength by our having chosen her as our enemy a second time in our short national life. It required several generations of research to disprove utterly General Harrison's lies about the English having set Tecumseh on us, and Harrison's later political career as "Tippecanoe" tended to make a legend of British perfidy. Had the Westerners not longed for Canada and Tecumseh's hunting grounds, and had France been a little more accessible as an enemy than "the moon," we might very well have gone to war with Napoleon instead of with England, and the whole sentimental history of our international relations might have been quite different. We are a very sentimental people, but emotions are bad foundations for international relations. Had Napoleon not sold us Louisiana, we should have been dragged into war with him, and "married the British fleet." The War of 1812 began in Napoleon's bathtub, where he was when he made known his inexorable decision to sell Louisiana. It ended on the Atlantic Ocean with America fighting his enemies for him. His legend never came between the American people and that of Lafayette.

One more result of the war was that we had at last gained our independence from Europe. We seceded from it almost completely. Not only were we no longer caught in every eddy of its political contests, but we turned our faces away from it and toward the West. A sense of nationality and destiny, as well as an immense task of material exploitation, began to influence all classes. For the next twenty years we scarcely thought of Europe, except, perhaps, now and then to resent it. Our schoolboys continued to declaim the revolutionary orations against England, because there was as yet not much else in the way of "pieces to speak," and because these orations belonged to our short history as a nation, of which we were becoming very conscious. For the most part, however, we scarcely took our eyes off the colossal task of material development and westward expansion. We decided to our own entire satisfaction that we had just fought a glorious war, and got down to work and making money. During the war, Key had written "The Star Spangled Banner," and it now began to "wave." Emigrants swarmed into the new West, which seemed to be sucking in men from the whole of the old, and now comparatively small, South and North. The new centre of gravity was being ever more heavily weighted. On the other hand, the collapse of the Federalist Party, the disloyalty of New England, the stench — of which the most was made — of the Hartford Convention, all left New England with only a tithe of the national influence it had possessed fifteen years earlier. The South, with its slavery and great estates, many of them wearing out from too incessant cultivation of single crops, was becoming a section apart from the fast-throbbing life of the new nation. Over the mountains the great valley, two thousand miles wide, with its unified river system four thousand miles long, opened an empire such as man had never seen. There was nothing now to stop the American short of the Rockies, except the "Great American desert." The songs of the voyageurs had been hushed. On the slopes of the Pacific the bells tolled on in the sleepy Spanish missions of California, where the dreams were of Heaven or bright black eyes and not of expanding empire. Louder and louder rose the sound of the Saxon. Along the whole front of the moving American "West" a myriad axes swung, *crack-crack-crack*, in ever faster and more dominant staccato, as the trees crashed, and the clearings multiplied with incredible swiftness.

VI

THE SUN RISES IN THE WEST

In 1800 a million Americans were living west of the mountains, and their numbers were increasing so rapidly as to frighten Eastern conservatives out of their wits. Then came the Louisiana Purchase, the war with England, and Indian cessions, throwing open a new empire to settlement. New England had always liked to consider itself the driver of the American coach, and the old die-hard Federalists there fought tooth and nail against the upbuilding of a new section which might threaten its dying influence. Through their mouthpiece in Congress, Josiah Quincy, they had thundered against the addition of French Louisiana and the creation of new States. "You have no authority," Quincy told the members of Congress, "to throw the rights and property of this people into the 'hotch-potch' with the wild men on the Missouri, nor with the mixed, though more respectable race of Anglo-Hispan-Gallo-Americans who bask on the sands in the mouth of the Mississippi. . . . Do you suppose the people of the Northern and Atlantic States will, or ought to, look on with patience and see Representatives and Senators from the Red River and Missouri, pouring themselves upon this and the other floor, managing the concerns of a seaboard fifteen hundred miles, at least, from their residence?" Whether patiently or not, that is precisely what they were going to see.

By 1820 there were two and a half million people instead of one million over the mountains — one quarter of the whole population of the United States, and a million more than there were in New England. By 1830 one third of the American people were "men of the Western Waters," as they liked to call themselves, numbering three and a half million. For still another decade emigration westward was to be wholly of native-born American stock. As we shall note in a later chapter, the vacuum left in the older States by this vast exodus and by the rapidly increasing demand for industrial labor brought about an inflow of foreigners, but these stayed on the seaboard, so that until past the mid-century the Mississippi Valley was racially, as well as in its enforced economic democracy, the real home of Americanism. It was there that the American dream seemed most certain of realization.

Emigration from the seaboard States, mostly Southern, had continued throughout the war, but after peace it became a veritable exodus. From the North, which was also swept by what was called "the Ohio fever," the chief entry to the West was over the mountains and down the Ohio River. The flatboats carrying a nation to empire floated steadily westward. Colonel John May, a rich Boston merchant who was a stockholder in the Ohio Company, watched them pass Pittsburgh, and noted that two had "on board twenty-nine whites, twenty-four negroes, nine dogs, twenty-three horses, cows, hogs, etc. — besides provisions and furniture." Thousands upon thousands floated and poled their way down the Ohio, after having crossed the mountains on foot or in Conestoga wagons. "To-day," wrote Judge Hall, "we passed two large rafts lashed together, by which simple conveyance several families from New England were transporting themselves and their property to the land of promise in the western woods. Each raft was eighty or ninety feet long, with a small house erected on it; and on each was a stack of hay, round which several horses and cows were feeding, while the paraphernalia of a farm yard, the ploughs, wagons, pigs, children and poultry, carelessly distributed, gave to the whole more the appearance of a permanent residence, than a caravan of adventurers seeking a home. A respectable looking old lady, with spectacles on nose, was seated on a chair at the door of one of the cabins, employed in knitting; another female was at the wash-tub; the men were chewing their tobacco, with as much complacency as if they had been in the 'land of steady habits,' and the various family avocations seemed to go like clock-work." So they passed, these men and women of destiny, to the infinite toil of home building in the wilderness. Indian alarms were as frequent as fires in Boston, May wrote in 1805, and he was tortured by myriads of gnats which even got down his throat. On his own land, "a number of poor devils — five in all — took their departure homeward this morning. They came from home moneyless and brainless, and have returned as they came."

Another traveler a decade later noted that after passing the Wabash "there was a complete departure from all mark of civilization." "These lonely settlers are poorly off," he added; "their bread-corn must be ground thirty miles off, requiring three days to carry to the mill, and bring back, the small horse-load of three bushels. Articles of family manufacture are very scanty, and what they purchase is of the meanest quality and excessively dear: yet they are friendly and willing to share their simple fare with you. It is surprising how comfortable they seem, wanting everything. To struggle with privations has now become the habit of their lives, most of them having made several successive plunges into the wilderness: and they begin already to talk of selling their 'improvements,' and getting still farther 'back,' on finding that emigrants of another description are thickening about them."

The haunting problem was that of a market. The settlers could swallow the gnats and drive back the Indians. They could fell trees and build their cabins, but money — where could they get money? And money they had to have. Furniture, tools, books, all the implements of civilization had to come from the outer world into their great valley, over the mountains or up "the river," and had to be paid for in goods or cash, and even "the river" did not yet afford the outlet to a market needed by innumerable small settlers. Money almost every one of them needed, too, to pay for the land itself. Under the Act of 1800, Eastern speculators had taken up vast tracts, twenty thousand to five hundred thousand acres at a time, of some of the best lands, and these they sold to settlers on credit at prices much above that asked by the government.

But even if the settler had bought from the government, there were the unpaid installments. Without markets the best that the farmers could do, as one of them said, was "just not to starve." Default became general. Nearly a third of the land originally contracted for was given up, and, speaking generally, the entire West was in debt to the East, either to individual capitalists or to the government. The government did not evict the settlers, and as the more successful farmers noted this they began to default, for they could not see why they should pay if their neighbor got his land without paying. By 1820 the defaulted payments amounted to over $21,000,000. The whole situation made for demoralization of financial character. Congress tinkered with the law, but so long as the East remained in control, there was little hope of seeing the West's demand for free land accepted as a government theory, the East insisting that the government should derive a profit from the public domain. On the frontier this theory had been discarded by 1820. Free land was demanded as a right for the man who would settle on it and make it worth something. In 1820 an act was passed abolishing the credit system of purchase and reducing the price to $1.25 an acre, and a compromise was reached with defaulters by taking from them the proportion of land unpaid for and giving a clear title to the remainder. The West, however, had been thoroughly and bitterly convinced that it was being exploited for the benefit of the East.

It had also had an experience with banks which it never forgot. The need for cash had been answered by the upspringing of many small banks, managed, even when honestly, all too often by men who knew nothing of the principles of sound banking. Farmers went heavily into debt, believing that land was bound to rise quickly in price. The panic of 1819 found them not only in debt to the East and the government, but to their local banks. The whole community was buried three feet deep in debt it could not pay. If a mortgage was foreclosed, there was no one to buy. Ruin stood sentinel at the door of every farmhouse and at the edge of every clearing. Banks demanded payment, could get none, and merely maddened the people, who stood solidly together in sentiment as they did in debt. The banks then failed like corn popping in the fire, and the West's conception of the money power had taken definite shape. The Eastern land speculator had demanded money; the government had demanded it; the merchants had demanded it; the banks had demanded it; but if the settlers had no market for their surplus products, where were they to get it? The mountain rampart to the eastward made freight rates prohibitive. One could float down "the river," but its strong current made getting back almost impossible by pole or sail. Two questions were becoming clear. Was the Westerner, with his dream of empire, to sink to the level of a serf or a peasant, tilling his land for just enough to sustain life and to be harassed by his creditors? With economic democracy throughout a vast area and manhood suffrage for national affairs, that question had its ominous aspect. Could the Union hold together unless the problem of a market for three million people could be solved? That meant transportation, and the only means of transport ever known to man, horses on roads or sailboats on the water, had both failed.

In spite of a large emigration from the Northern Atlantic States, particularly to Ohio and the Western Reserve, the immigration to the West up to 1820 and even 1830 had been, as we have said, chiefly from Virginia and the States farther south. Most of the families had come from the Piedmont and frontier sections of the Eastern Southern States, small farmers, and this emigration also continued. There was little difference between these settlers and those from the North. Most of them held no slaves and many were extremely poor. We get a glimpse of the latter sort in a note of 1819 which records that there passed through Atlanta, "bound for Chatahouchee, a man and his wife, his son and wife, with a cart but no horse. The man had a belt over his shoulders and he drew in the shafts; the son worked by traces tied to the end of the shafts and assisted his father to draw the cart: the son's wife rode in the cart, and the old woman was walking, carrying a rifle and driving a cow." Not many slaves came in at first, and in any case the question of slavery was not a sectional one in the West for some time. A convention held at Vincennes had petitioned the governor of the territory to suspend the prohibition of slavery in Indiana so as not to divert Southern settlement to Missouri, and as late as 1824 a proposed pro-slavery amendment in Illinois was defeated by only five to four.

After the end of the War of 1812, cotton rose as high as thirty-four cents a pound, and during that decade there was heavy emigration of another sort to the southern part of the West. The larger slave owners bought tracts of several thousand acres each in the belt of rich black soil, and moved out in the fashion of the patriarchs of old, with their families, troops of slaves, and horses and cattle. For the most part they bought land already cleared by the pioneers of the first advance, who were pushed farther ahead. A change was becoming apparent rather than notable by 1815, and increased from then on. In the second advancing battalions of the frontier, population increased in both the north and south of the West, but in the north it was mainly a white population which built up towns where the first pioneers had left hamlets, which founded schools, cultivated farms more carefully, and accumulated property. In the southern part, the white population diminished rapidly in proportion to the total, and slaves replaced the free labor of the first Southern frontiersmen. Instead of towns, plantations sprang up, requiring ever more land and more slaves.

From the beginning the cotton planter had a sure market for his produce, and this was to have an effect we shall note later. But in the third and completely settled stage of the West of that day there was an even more marked difference between the northern and southern sections. The northern towns and farms became more prosperous, and a community life of prosperous people developed. The southern plantations, on the other hand, began to feel the effect of an exhausting single crop. The largest owners, many of whom had become absentees, living in Charleston or Savannah or even in Paris, might buy new land farther west and move their plantation almost bodily forward, leaving an impoverished community behind them; or, more usually, they would stay on in the old place, getting steadily more mired in debt, but keeping up the scale of living to which they had been accustomed.

By 1821 one third of all the cotton raised was on land west of Georgia, but no prosperous and populous communities were being built up. The real Southern frontiersmen had this land-hungry, plantation economy pushing steadily behind them. The "West" in the South was geographically very narrow as compared with the North, and when the Southern pioneer had been pushed across Louisiana he found himself for the first time face to face with the Spaniard. Mexico had revolted in 1821 and declared her independence. In her great province of Texas, land could be bought for twelve and one half cents an acre, or one tenth what the American government charged, and within a decade eighteen or twenty thousand Southern pioneers had pressed over the border and were living under Mexican rule. The waves of the advancing English had finally begun to lap at the doorsills of the Spanish missions. On the open plains of Texas the sound of the American axe was little heard, and the American, now half farmer, half ranchman, listened with Protestant dislike to the sound of the mission bells. Two great racial and religious currents had met at last, and began to swirl in dangerous water.

However different the northern and southern sections of the West might be growing from each other, the West as a whole was a unit as compared with North and South in the East. In twenty years two million people had shared the experience of pioneering. That in itself was a bond as strong as it was subtle. The Connecticut Yankee might talk with a nasal twang and the neighbor who had trekked over the mountains from the upland of Carolina might talk with a drawl, but between them was a common bond of a great experience and of the acceptance of a mode of life. Debt, hardship, independence, a dozen things bound them together and made them brothers when contrasted with the Northern merchant or Southern planter "back East." And the Mississippi, "the river," "Ol' Man River," bound them again. Back East a Yankee farmer never went visiting to a Georgia patch up on the mountain side, but up and down "the river" people traveled and met and mingled. Life was mobile, free, and often lawless. The men of the Western Waters had more than Indians and trees to fell, and debts to worry about. Wreckers and robbers infested the river towns of the Ohio and the Mississippi; the Harpes, Hare, the Masons, "Pluggy" and his lieutenant "Nine-Eyes," among others, were names which brought terror to many a home and town. Picturesque and villainous, living on horseback or on islands in "the river" or in caves in the banks made into fortresses, they brought a new element into the complexity of American life. There had been plenty of lawbreaking back East, but there, for the most part, life had been safe. Life along "the river" was far from safe, and the vast stream which welcomed everything, clutched at everything, received without a sound many a body riddled with holes from ball or knife.

To go back East was to get into another life, a life of crowded population, of drawing-rooms and countingrooms, where the poor were quite safe from the assassin but not from the tax gatherer, and where the cultivated classes were getting very much worried about the threats to their property coming from such outlandish communities as Kentucky and Illinois and Heaven knew what new States which were being "admitted" to outvote them. Besides Kentucky and Tennessee, Ohio had come in in 1803, Louisiana in 1812, Indiana in 1816, Mississippi in 1817, Illinois in 1818, Alabama in 1819; and each of them had as many Senators as Massachusetts or New York or Virginia. What was to be the end of it all? President Timothy Dwight of Yale College gave full vent to his spleen. "The class of pioneers," he wrote, "cannot live in regular society. They are too idle, too talkative, too passionate, too prodigal, and too shiftless to acquire either property or character. They . . . grumble about the taxes by which the Rulers, Ministers and Schoolmasters are supported. . . . After exposing the injustice of the community in neglecting to invest persons of such superior merit in public offices, in many an eloquent harangue uttered by many a kitchen fire, in every blacksmith shop, in every corner of the streets, and finding all their efforts vain, they become at length discouraged, and under pressure of poverty, the fear of the gaol, and consciousness of public contempt, leave their native places and betake themselves to the wilderness."

Poor Dwight! "Regular society" and "the fear of the gaol"! It is time we went back over the mountains to see what all this was about. "Gaol," of course, was the prison for poor debtors who could not pay, which, with its horrors for the poor, was still in vogue in the East; but America was evidently getting to be much more complicated than had been the eighteenth-century seaboard civilization which had so proudly announced to the world that all men were born equal and that all had the right to life, liberty, and the pursuit of happiness. Dwight, being related to the half-dozen or dozen families which ruled Connecticut, naturally saw things in a different light. To him and his like, the American dream was a distressing nightmare.

New England, and, to a slightly lesser extent, the Middle States, were in the grip of a revolution which was completely to alter the life of the sections and set them off in marked contrast to both the South and the West. Manufacturing, as we have seen, had made a start in the earlier period, but until the Embargo and the War of 1812 the economic life had consisted chiefly of small farming and of shipping. Between 1805 and the end of the war, shipping had received a series of blows from which it was long in recovering. On the other hand, conditions fostered the growth of manufacturing at a stupendous rate. By 1810 the total value of all manufactured goods had reached the figure of at least $125,000,000 in the United States, mostly centred in the Northern States. New England textile mills which had been able to use only 500 bales of cotton in 1800 were calling for 90,000 by 1815, and the new industries, like snowballs rolling downhill, kept increasing their size with extraordinary rapidity. Between 1820 and 1831 in Massachusetts alone, the output of the cotton mills rose from $700,000 to $7,700,000, and of her woolens from $300,000 to $7,300,000.

Of less immediate importance than such figures, but of immense significance for the future of America, was the new system introduced by Eli Whitney, who had already profoundly altered American history by his cotton gin. In fact, while history usually deals with political persons, it would be hard to find any statesman or politician of his day who has had a more lasting influence upon our life than this Yankee inventor. Whitney received an order to make muskets for the government during the war. Up to that time a musket, like everything else, had been made by one man, who did it all from start to finish. Whitney, owing to the scarcity of skilled mechanics for sudden large-scale production, conceived the idea of having each man make one part only, — a much simpler matter to learn, — and having all parts interchangeable. It took him two years to perfect his system, but once done, the way was open to mass production at lower cost. The news of the exploit spread over the world, but Europe preferred to continue the old craftsman method, for there was no lack of skilled labor over there. It has been precisely this lack which has determined much in the development of our social and economic life.

For the first two decades or more of the century, it was still an open question whether shipping or manufacturing was the more important New England industry, and as their interests were naturally opposed, there was confusion in political policies. In other respects as well as this, the old solidarity of New England life was breaking down. Population was increasing, the best land had long since been preëmpted, and the small farmer, who had been the backbone of New England, was suffering. He was either moving West to better and cheaper land or becoming a hand in a factory town, although for the most part the hands were still women and children. There was little in common between the man who had owned and worked his own farm and the same man working on low wages for a mill owner in one of the new towns fast springing up. Many of the young women who went into the mills did so for a short time only, to make enough for a small dowry, to help pay a mortgage on their father's farm, or help a brother to go to college or to migrate West. In some mills, notably those at Lowell, the working conditions were considered excellent for that day, though they deteriorated between 1830 and 1840. The working hours were often from five in the morning to seven at night, and a system of corporation paternalism grew up which dictated the time at which the women, who were forced to live in the companies' boarding houses, had to go to bed, enforced their attendance at church, and even prescribed what church they must subscribe to. Liberty and the pursuit of happiness were somehow not progressing under industrialism. In spite of the great number who went into the mills, the problem of securing a labor supply was always acute. "Our greatest difficulty at present," wrote one mill owner in 1832, relating his twenty-five years' experience, "is a want of females — women and children — and from the great number of factories now building, [I] have my fears that we shall not be able to operate all our machinery another year."

If wealth was rapidly accumulating, it was yet more rapidly concentrating. The changing conditions which were fostering the growth of cities in the North were laying the foundations of many of the great fortunes of to-day. The day of the great country magnate even in New York was passing, but that of the city "landlord" had come. The poorer people, who under country conditions had had homes of their own, began to be herded into small quarters in the cities in the hope of finding employment. In 1831, miserly old Stephen Girard died in Philadelphia, leaving $6,000,000, but only three years before, Mathew Carey had written of how thousands of the poor traveled hundreds of miles seeking employment on roads or canals at 62½ to 87½ cents a day; how hundreds died annually from this work under bad conditions, only to have their places taken by others; how the cities had filled with persons who could not make more than 35 to 50 cents a day; and how "there is no employment whatever, how disagreeable or loathsome, or deleterious soever it may be, or however reduced the wages, that does not find persons willing to follow it rather than beg or steal."

Economic democracy was fast breaking down in the North, and the comparative simplicity of an earlier day was passing. There had always been some distinction between town and country, but the two had formerly merged at a dozen points, and in all of the older towns one had had to walk only a few minutes to find one's self in the country. There had been no such difference in the old days as there was now between an Astor and a farmer, even though the farmer, as might easily have been the case, were better educated than the ignorant immigrant who had become the leviathan of American wealth and who defied the United States government from his home on Broadway.

There were, however, more hopeful signs. In New England the hold of the old Congregational Church was being broken. Church and State were at last separated in Connecticut in 1818, and in Massachusetts in 1833. This was the outward and visible sign of a change that had long been taking place. The old Puritan theology and fervor had been dying for many a day. Unfortunately, whereas the former faith had in many cases been an effective builder of genuine strength of character, the sediment that was deposited when it drained off held chiefly the dregs of some of its worst qualities. The two centuries of insistence upon certain rigid forms of conduct, and the equal insistence upon the duty of the community to be the keeper of the conscience of the individual, remained. The Puritan had possessed some sterling traits. His descendant became mainly Puritanical. His belief in himself as the chosen of God lingered long after the relationship had probably become repugnant to the Deity; it certainly had to the New Englander's fellow citizens in other sections.

On the other hand, much that was good remained, and was to serve as a leaven in the educational and community life of many a Western settlement in the wild days ahead. Among the more mediocre minds, the belief that it was incumbent on them to be missionaries, and the welcome given to every crazy doctrine were to strew the country in the next decade with the weeds of thought. Among the better minds, by the change from Congregationalism to Unitarianism, under the lead of Channing, the way was opened to a religion of self-reliance and to a broad humanitarianism. Intellectual preparation was being made in Boston for that burst of optimism, idealism, and a joyous acceptance of life that was to flood the country in the next period. As yet, however, the chief signs of a reviving life for art and letters were to be found in the coterie gathered in New York, with Washington Irving at its head and including Cooper, Bryant, and lesser lights.

While this new life of merchants, manufacturers, bankers, literary men, magnates, and proletarians, increasing urbanization and dwindling agriculture, was rapidly setting the North off against the rest of America, conditions were becoming fixed and idiosyncratic in the South. The old crops of tobacco, rice, and indigo had become completely overshadowed by cotton. Only a small percentage of the Southern whites had owned slaves, but cotton had opened new visions of riches. Since the beginning of the century there had been much to turn our heads from the older and slower ways of building up a property. The breathless speed at which certain manufactures had grown, the easy money to be made in starting banks, the speculation in Western lands, the risks of commerce in the war, the rapid rise in city real estate as population concentrated, and the effect of the cotton gin, had all been breeding a spirit which demanded riches overnight instead of by the efforts of a lifetime of toil.

In the South everyone turned to cotton. "The lawyer, and the doctor, and the school-master, as soon as they earned any money, bought land and negroes, and became planters. The preacher who married an heiress or rich widow, became owner of a plantation. The merchant who wished to retire from the perplexities of business . . . passed his old age in watching the cotton plant spring up from the fresh-plowed ground." But as the slave trade had been prohibited, the price of slaves advanced rapidly. The small man was losing his chance to get even a start in life. It was estimated in 1839 that a planter could get a thousand acres of good cleared cotton land for $10,000, but that it would cost him $50,000 to get the slaves to work it. Had there been a system of free labor, the initial investment would not have been a quarter as much. Once established, the cotton planter was caught in an economic system from which there was no escape. In bad times he could not, like the Northern manufacturer, turn off his hands. They were property, and valuable property, which had to be carried at any cost short of ruin.

Across the sea, England was in full tide of industrial revolution and was becoming the chief manufacturing nation of the world. Between 1820 and 1829, production of cotton in the South rose from 160,000,000 pounds to 365,000,000, a large part of the increase being due to westward extension. Of the total crop, full four fifths was exported to England and France, less than one fifth going to the New England mills. The ships that carried the cotton east to Europe preferred to bring freight back at any low rate rather than come in ballast, and the consequence of this vast and assured foreign market was thus to flood the South with manufactured goods at prices far below those offered by Northern manufacturers. Not only was the South thus building up a culture of its own quite different from that of the North and West, but it was becoming detached from the Northern sections in its whole economic life, Europe being the market in which it both bought and sold to the extent of about 80 per cent.

Slaves had begun to seem as vital to the Southern plantation as machines in a Northern factory, and as the steady press westward of the Southern economic system met the border line of Texas, it was diverted northward much as a glacier meeting an immovable obstacle. Only those who did not mind becoming Mexican expatriates trickled through. The West was still set off against the North and South, but its southern part was becoming slave. The first rumbling of the inevitable conflict was heard with the controversy over admitting Missouri as a slave State in 1819. Slave and free States had been admitted alternately, and there were eleven of each, giving the two economic systems equal power in the Senate. Missouri, however, lay north of the line which had hitherto tacitly been accepted as marking the northern limits of slavery, and the North was thrown into ferment by what seemed a new aggressiveness on the part of the expanding Cotton Kingdom. The matter was finally settled by the "Missouri Compromise," by which Maine and Missouri were both admitted, one as free and one as slave, with the prohibition of any extension of slavery in the Louisiana Purchase north of latitude 36° 30′. John Quincy Adams, with perfect clarity of vision, read in the words of the Compromise the "title-page to a great, tragic volume."

By 1820 there were thus coming into clear alignment three sections, the industrial North, the Cotton Kingdom of the South, and the West, now narrowing somewhat to mean the part north of the new line. Of these, it was in the West alone that the old economic democracy of pre-Revolutionary days still survived and that the Declaration of Independence was still a living gospel for nearly all classes. It was the beating heart of America. Were the functions and interests of each of these sections to prove irreconcilable with those of the others? Was the force of nationalism or of sectionalism to prove the stronger?

We have already spoken of the intense need of the West for markets and transportation, and the apparent absence of any solution to the problem. With the increase in industrialism and the decrease in agriculture, the North needed a market also, and likewise food. One problem could be solved if the two sections could be linked. Invention and daring both came to aid. Since the Roman days of roads made of large blocks of stone, most roads on both sides of the ocean had been mere dirt tracks in which wagons could be mired to the hubs in bad weather. About 1800, the Scotchman McAdam experimented with crushed stone for a surface, and the success of his work made the greatest advance in rural communication until the Ford car. The invention came just in time for the West. The Cumberland Road, following the route of an old Indian trail, was begun before the war and completed from Pennsylvania to Wheeling by 1820, at a cost of a million and a half, provided by Congress. Its solid construction and fine surface at once made it the main entry to the West, but although it served splendidly for communication and as a link, it had not solved the problem of freight.

Another invention, however, came to the assistance of American nationalism. Although John Fitch had built a steamboat as early as 1787, the first successful one was that built by Robert Fulton twenty years later. A new era opened for America, East and West, when the *Clermont* puffed its way laboriously against the current of the Hudson. Within two years Nicholas Roosevelt of New York was in Pittsburgh looking over the problem of Western river navigation. The next year he was back again, and a steamboat a hundred and sixteen feet long, costing $30,000, was launched from a Pittsburgh yard. Having descended the Mississippi, it turned northward again and demonstrated that here at last was something that would go up stream as well as down. The old flatboats and rafts for floating down "the river" continued long in use, one traveler encountering two thousand of them in a twenty-five days' trip in 1816, but this was a one-way traffic.

It was a business, however, on all the Western waters, and one which, like all the many varied occupations of Americans, bred its own characters. The boatman had become a type and had his songs as well as the old French voyageur. The woods along the shores which had echoed back a few generations earlier the

> "Fringue, fringue sur la rivière,"

now resounded to

> "The boatman is a lucky man,
> No one can do as the boatman can,
> The boatmen dance and the boatmen sing,
> The boatman is up to everything.
> Hi-O, away we go,
> Floating down the river on the O-hi-o!"

Much experimenting and many disappointments were still in store before the great period of steamboating on "the river" was to form such a picturesque chapter in American life, but at least the prospect had been opened of an inward as well as an outward movement of freight for the West. Until the Civil War, New Orleans disputed the position of leading port with New York, and would have easily eclipsed it had it not been for the greatest engineering feat Americans had yet undertaken.

It was all very well to have steamboats beginning to pit their strength against that of "Ol' Man River," but that did not avail to link the West any closer to the East, though it did help the unity of the former section. In 1810 it cost $125 to carry a ton of freight by wagon from Philadelphia to Pittsburgh, and $100 to move a ton from Buffalo to New York. Canals had been talked about by many, but Governor De Witt Clinton of New York turned dream into reality against scoffing and skepticism. On the Fourth of July, 1817, he dug a shovelful of earth, and the work on the Erie Canal, from the Hudson to Lake Erie, was begun. In eight years the long trench, three hundred and sixty-three miles, had been dug at the then stupendous cost of over $7,000,000, an amount, however, which was more than repaid by tolls in the first decade of operation.

The effect was amazing. Clinton, like Whitney, had had more influence on the development of the country than 99 per cent of the statesmen in Washington. There had been speeches in Congress nearly as long as the Canal, but the Canal accomplished what they did not. The time of travel from Buffalo to New York was reduced from twenty days to six, and the cost of moving a ton of freight from one hundred dollars to five. In one month of the first year, 837 barges left Albany for Buffalo. Eastern-manufactured goods poured westward; Western farm products poured eastward. Even Western lumber could now be shipped profitably. New England potatoes, at seventy-five cents a bushel, were crowded out by "Chenangoes" at half that price. Flour manufactured on Lake Erie water fronts could be shipped via New York to the Carolinas at less than $1.50 a barrel freight. The West could at last buy and sell to the East. New England farms were abandoned in large numbers, and hustling towns sprang up in western New York, Ohio, and further West. The West was linked to the East not at Charleston, Baltimore, or Philadelphia, but at New York. The Cumberland and other roads could not compete with the all-water route, and in ten years from 1820 the real and personal property of New York City leaped from $70,000,000 to $125,000,000.

Boston, over two hundred miles overland east of Albany, was out of the picture altogether as an *entrepôt* for Western business. Other canals elsewhere were projected and partly built. Philadelphia and Baltimore struggled valiantly to regain their lost position, but there was no other such passage through the mountain barrier as was afforded by the Hudson-Mohawk Valleys. New York was to remain supreme on the Atlantic seaboard. The incomes of its merchants shot up and they themselves could afford to become more exclusive socially. But out on the long waterway the bargemen whom the new business had brought into being were singing, the words coming, as those of folk songs always do, from nowhere:—

> "I 've got a mule, her name is Sal,
> Fifteen miles on the Erie Canal.
> She 's a good old worker and a good old pal,
> Fifteen miles on the Erie Canal.
>
> Low bridge, ev'rybody down!
> Low bridge, for we 're going through a town,

> And you 'll always know your neighbor,
> You 'll always know your pal,
> If you 've ever *navig*ated on the Erie Canal."

It is true that the West was now linked economically with the East. De Witt Clinton had knocked a wide door through the wall which had separated them. The Mississippi Valley was no longer an enclosed empire which could trade with the world only down "the river." Other doors, though not so wide as the Erie Canal, were being opened. But, on the other hand, the interests of the West were not those of the East, and the contending forces of sectionalism and nationalism were far from having reached a point of equilibrium. The Western farmer was not to be a European peasant; this much had been settled; but he was a debtor and a citizen. He was inevitably opposed to his Eastern creditors and might be to his other fellow citizens.

Little by little, the Federal government had been growing more like the vision of Hamilton and less like that of Jefferson. Jefferson himself had, by force of circumstance, given it an impetus in that direction when, wisely allowing the practical needs of statesmanship to overrule the theory of the political thinker, he had forced the western half of the Mississippi Valley down the throat of a Constitution which had never been designed to receive it. Jefferson had a fit of mental indigestion over it, but the Constitution did not. Louisiana slipped down perfectly easily.

In session after session of the Supreme Court in Washington, Chief Justice Marshall was handing down decisions, five hundred and nineteen of which were written by himself, in which he steadily strengthened and extended the powers of the Federal government as against both the people and the States. In phrases which have been quoted innumerable times, Lord Bryce wrote of him that "the Constitution seemed not so much to rise under his hands to its full stature, as to be gradually unveiled by him till it stood revealed in the harmonious perfection of the form which its framers had designed." It would be more accurate, perhaps, to say some of its framers. At any rate, the Constitution owes nearly as much to the interpretation of the great Chief Justice as to its original authors; and it certainly became much less the instrument which, wisely or unwisely, a large proportion, if not a majority, of the people who had originally consented to it would have desired.

The attitude in favor of "loose" or "strict" construction of its clauses — that is, of nationalism versus States' rights — was gradually altering according to sectional economic interest. It is quite unnecessary to go the full length of the economic school of historians, who can see nothing but the economic motive in history, to allow that such a motive is extremely potent. It has always been so in the political history of our own country.

Whitney had given the Southerners the cotton gin. The gin had fastened cotton on them as the chief mode of economic exploitation of the resources of their section. Cotton had fastened slavery on the black, and the black on the back of the white. Slavery was the institution of a section, and that section was in constant and increasing danger of being outvoted in Congress, owing to the disproportionate increase of population in other sections. If additional power were given to the Federal government it would be more and more dangerous to their "peculiar institution" to be a minority. Safety thus lay in limiting the powers of the Federal government over the States. It was clear as a proposition in Euclid. The South in self-defense was bound to stand more and more for strict construction and States' rights, in what was, after all, a matter of opinion and interpretation.

The North was in process of transition. Nullification and talk of secession had been rife in New England for the first decade and a half of the century, but now manufacturing, which was hungry for tariffs and special favors from the government, was competing with shipping, which thrived on free trade. The leader of the section, Daniel Webster, was to register clearly in the shifts of his own opinions the money interests of his constituents.

The West, almost from the start, had been the creature of the national government. Its States had not been independent before the Union, as had those of the East. They had mostly been carved out of the national domain first as territories, then as States. Moreover, the West cared little for finespun theories of government. It had its idealism of individualism and freedom, but was also practical enough in calling for economic help from whatever source could supply it, and the natural source to which it looked was the national government in Washington. The immediate relation of the Westerner to the government was far more direct than that of the citizen of any other section, for in most cases even the title to his home, not always settled, came to him straight from the government of the United States. For the Easterner the government was something aloof from his daily concerns except on election days or when the tax gatherer came around. For the Westerner it was the rock on which his home was built or a landlord whom he was fighting. Roads, canals, internal improvements of all sorts, were essential to the existence and growth of the section. It demanded that the government supply them.

For a while Congress lent willing ear. As we have seen, it had built the Cumberland Road, but it began to have doubts as to whether it could constitutionally appropriate the money to maintain it. In 1816 it chartered the second Bank of the United States, and passed a tariff bill, but President Monroe and the South and North had, severally, constitutional doubts and sectional reasons for calling a halt on Western demands. The South, hoping to build up domestic manufactures, had voted for the tariff; New England, the shipowners still being able to outvote the manufacturers, had voted against it; but a reversal of sectional interests in that respect was to come in another dozen years, and although Northern manufacturers were to welcome tariffs they began to balk at internal improvements for the West.

After a long series of international complications running all the way from England, and the Holy Alliance in Europe, over South America, and up to Russia in Alaska, with all of which the Secretary of State, John Quincy Adams, had been coping with distinguished ability, President Monroe in his annual message in 1823 had announced the doctrine which has ever since borne his name. Briefly stated, this was to the effect that whereas the political systems of Europe and America were different and we would not interfere in the internal affairs of the old continent, neither would we consider the New World hereafter as a sphere for European colonization or permit European powers to extend their system hither. It was a gesture, but a gesture that emphatically meant not only that we had seceded entirely from Europe, but that we had embarked on a policy of the Americas for the Americans. Although the public had been unaware of the dramatic incidents that had led to its enunciation, it was well received by the people and strengthened the feeling of Americanism and nationalism. We intended to keep forever out of Europe and to keep Europe out of the New World. The doctrine became almost as deeply imbedded in our minds as the Declaration of Independence.

It was indicative both of the growth of the West and of its inherent nationalism that the political thinker who at this time brought forward the only plan for overcoming the growing sectionalism was Henry Clay of Kentucky. His plan, which came to be known as "the American System," was simple enough in broad outline, and was based on the old Hamiltonian doctrines. Clay, however, was a popular orator in a day when the American loved oratory and hailed every speaker as a Cicero or a Demosthenes. Clay had a power of cogent presentation that had been denied to the logical but boringly diffuse Hamilton, and protectionists since the day of Clay have merely rung the changes on his speech of March 30, 1824.

Clay's economic policy was distinctly American and national. In the three sections of the country, he saw a North which was becoming predominantly industrial and manufacturing, and a South and West that were overwhelmingly agricultural, but both of which had some nascent manufactures. The panic of 1819 had laid the country, particularly the West, prostrate. Clay saw an increasing agricultural surplus, as the country grew, which would be unsalable in Europe, and he saw the West's need of internal improvements. As a means of making us independent of Europe and of bringing the three sections into economic and political harmony, he proposed a protective tariff that would greatly increase American manufactures, and provide money for roads, canals, and other improvements. He counted on the industrial sections being pleased with the protection afforded, the West with the improvements it demanded, and the agricultural sections to be made generally prosperous by the market for their produce that he believed would come with the increase of the industrial population. The need for a market for the West had become painfully clear. Corn was selling at Cincinnati at eight cents a bushel and wheat at twenty-five. But New England merchants still outvoted the manufacturers, and Webster made a powerful speech against the measure in Congress, while the South condemned it as a "combination of the wealthy against the poor" — that is, of the Northern manufacturer against the Southern planter. Clay carried the bill through by a vote of 107 to 102, but the sectional nature of what he had hoped would be an "American System" was clear. New England cast 15 votes for and 23 against; the Southern West, 13 and 7; while the Northern West was solidly in favor. Four years later, when a new tariff bill came up, the New England manufacturers had won their local struggle, and Daniel Webster thundered as powerfully for the "Tariff of Abominations" as he had against the earlier and less "abominable" one. The measure was carried by all sections except the South, which, under the lead of South Carolina, was so incensed that it threatened nullification, boycott of Northern goods, secession, and even armed resistance.

The West had produced a national leader and a political thinker who had outgrown the frontier, but the West itself had not yet done so. In the election of 1824 there was no party issue. The Federalist Party was completely disrupted and all four candidates for the Presidency were Republicans, the three geographical sections being represented by John Quincy Adams of Massachusetts, William H. Crawford of Georgia, Andrew

Jackson of Tennessee, and Henry Clay of Kentucky. It is notable that the West had two candidates, and that the South produced one from the Cotton Kingdom instead of any successor to the "Virginia Dynasty." Adams, having been Secretary of State, would according to precedent have been the next President, but precedents were failing, and Adams, one of the ablest men the country has ever produced, was austere, wholly independent, and refused a single concession to political chicanery or mob popularity. Crawford had no chance from the start, and the West could have elected Clay had it stood by him. That section, however, preferred action and emotion to thought and logic, and voted overwhelmingly for the dueling, swashbuckling hero, "Old Hickory." Clay did not get a single electoral vote from over the mountains except in Kentucky, Missouri, and Ohio. When the votes were counted, Jackson had 99 and Adams 84, whereas Crawford, who suffered a paralytic stroke, had 41 and Clay only 37. No one having been elected, the choice was thrown into the House of Representatives, Clay having there the power to elect either of his opponents. His choice fell on Adams as the abler man and the one whose policies were nearer to his own. The West had not won the Presidency, but it had made a President.

Adams had been elected by a section, but he tried to carry out his policies without a thought of party or personal political profit. These policies included internal improvements on a considerable scale, and the devotion as well of public funds to educational and scientific purposes, all in advance of his time. The South feared for its slaves in a loose-construction theory of the Constitution; the West haw-hawed at the "intellectual" President; party leaders, looking toward the next election, saw the impossibility of a man who would not cater to hungry claimants for political favors; Adams was aloof, and doomed. In spite of it all, in 1828 he polled 40 per cent of the popular vote, but the South and West beat him heavily. Adams had stood by Jackson when he had raided East Florida, and finally by diplomacy, in 1819, Adams had won that new bit of territory for us from Spain; but Jackson had done the fighting, and anyway he was the sort of man who would be popular with those who liked that sort of man. The West assuredly did; the South was afraid of Adams, the North, and loose construction; and Jackson was easily elected. For the first time a man of the Western Waters journeyed to Washington to take his place in the White House.

The democratic elements of the nation had brought about a mild revolution in 1800 when they elected Jefferson in order to swing the government back to the Americanism of the frontier and the simple citizen, and to stem the tide of Hamiltonianism and Federalism, with their emphasis on privileges and the rich. That movement of revolt, however, was slight as compared with the revolution of 1828. We have merely to contrast the type of Jackson with that of the preceding Presidents — Washington, John Adams, Jefferson, Madison, Monroe, and John Quincy Adams — to realize that new forces would have to be taken into consideration in American life. The scenes at the White House after his inauguration were accepted as a portent, and the crowds who thronged the city to see the man of the people placed in power were likened to the barbarians pouring into Rome. "It was the people's day," wrote an eyewitness, "the people's President, and the people would rule." A disorderly mob crushed their way into the White House, stood on the satin furniture, smashed china and glass in their rush for refreshments. In the press, the President himself was nearly suffocated against a wall and had to be rescued. Tubs and buckets of punch were placed outside on the grounds in the hope of keeping some of the mob out of the house, but they continued to surge at the doors, and those inside could not escape until the windows were opened and the rooms cleared by using them as exits. To dwell on this aspect of what was in reality a great movement would be unfair.

The election had been a victory not merely for a section, but for a class. By 1825 every Northern State had finally provided for manhood suffrage, and Jackson had been the choice of many of the laboring and small-farmer class in the East as well as the overwhelming choice of the West. Ignorant as they were compared with the richer Eastern classes, it was these people who had kept the principles of the Declaration of Independence and the Revolution in their hearts. Americanism in those days had assuredly meant more than mere secession from the British Empire. The common man had believed, and been taught to believe, that it meant a new hope for him, an opening of the door of opportunity for all, a recognition of his rights as a *man* — not simply as an owner of property — to life, liberty, and the pursuit of happiness. He had watched with growing resentment what seemed to him the closing of doors upon him, the rise of privileged classes, and the increasing difficulty or inability for himself to reap profit and benefit from his toil. He feared a leader from a class which he instinctively felt could not or would not sympathize with his own troubles and ideals. He sought a leader of his own sort, and as the West was the heart of this Americanism, it was there that he was found.

But if moving on from frontier line to frontier line had stirred the wits of the settlers in some respects, their experiences had nothing to give them more than the old parochial view of politics which had been held by the men of the towns and parishes of the East. Their contacts with the world at large were so negligible, the problems of their small communities were so standardized and simple, that they could see few difficulties in the way of being provided with what they wished by government. The American doctrine had developed, through the long training of the common man in local politics, that anyone could do anything. Just as he had learned to become a Jack-of-all-trades himself in his daily life, without special training, he could see no reason why public office called for particular qualities or experience. The fact that men had had to turn their hands to everything in communities where life was reduced to its simplest terms, and where there was little division of labor, had tended not only to self-confidence, which was admirable, but to a lowering of the quality of work and thought. Superficiality had inevitably resulted from enforced versatility. Both the demand for a high quality and the need for technical training ceased to be felt. Jackson voiced the almost universal sentiment among his supporters when he declared that "the duties of all public offices are, or at least admit of being, made so plain and simple that men of intelligence may readily qualify themselves for their performance." Mediocrity is one of the prices paid for complete equality, unless the people themselves can rise to higher levels.

The Jacksonian movement of revolt, like most of those which deeply stir humanity, was one of aspiration, not of intellect. The men of the West wanted a leader who would appeal to all of their instincts and traits, not to their minds. The frontier bred equalitarianism, it is true, but at the same time a swaggering individualism. Life had a terrific sameness for all, which made each individual fear to be different, and yet from which he would fain escape by asserting himself. The frontiersman refused to admit that anyone was better than himself, and at the same time, with the ancient instinct of human nature, would stick through thick and thin to a leader. Such a leader, however, must have the frontiersman's own traits glorified, not those of another group. The West agreed with Henry Clay's doctrine of an "American System" as meeting the needs of his section, but the Westerner was not a thinker and could not give his allegiance to one. In Jackson he found the man he needed. At once a born frontiersman, an Indian fighter, duelist, equalitarian, and strong individualist, the conqueror of the British at New Orleans, the man who without a thought of constitutional or international difficulties had marched into Florida and seized it, a man of almost superhuman strength of will, of sterling honesty, uneducated, but with often uncanny good judgment and happy intuition, Jackson provided just the figure the ignorant but hero-loving and idealistic masses could cling to. Tall, lank, raw-boned, picturesque, fearless, honest, stubborn, his legend crossed the mountains as "Old Hickory," and the revolution was accomplished.

There has never been a more devoted patriot than the man he defeated, but the lofty vision of Americanism in the mind of

John Quincy Adams was not the Americanism of the masses. He thought too much in terms of the "superior" man in the best sense of the adjective rather than of the "common" man. Adams did not represent riches, but he did represent intellectual and moral integrity of the highest type. The common man cared nothing for these. Intellectual integrity was an unmeaning phrase to him, and his morality easily included fighting the devil with fire and rewarding one's friends with public office. At the low end of both the economic and the intellectual scale, his material needs bulked large. But he also had his idealism. He did not seek to plunder the rich. What he asked was what he thought America stood for — opportunity, the chance to grow into something bigger and finer, as bigger and finer appeared to him. He did not envisage America as standing for wealth only, and certainly not as standing for culture; still more certainly not as a reproduction of European classes and conditions. Somewhat vaguely he envisaged it as freedom and opportunity for himself and those like him to rise.

Perhaps his Americanism was a dream, but it was a great dream. The common man had dreamed it in 1776 and hoped he had brought it into being. After a quarter of a century of uneasiness over its passing, he had stirred himself and sought to recapture it under Jefferson. Now, more than a quarter of a century later, he had made another effort to realize it. We shall see him do it twice again, before our story ends with its final question. If Americanism in the above sense has been a dream, it has also been one of the great realities in American life. It has been a moving force as truly as wheat or gold. It is all that has distinguished America from a mere quantitative comparison in wealth or art or letters or power with the nations of old Europe. It *is* Americanism, and its shrine has been in the heart of the common man. He may not have done much for American culture in its narrower sense, but in its wider meaning it is he who almost alone has fought to hold fast to the American dream. This is what has made the common man a great figure in the American drama. This is the dominant motif in the American epic.

VII

THE NORTH BEGINS TO HUSTLE

BETWEEN 1830 and 1850 the two great obvious changes in the country were the industrialization of the North and the expansion of the West, the South continuing but little altered. Although manufacturing had got a good start in the North during the Embargo and the War of 1812, it was, as we have seen, not until the Tariff of 1828 that capital in New England had swung over to the factory from the ship to such an extent as to enable the manufacturer to outvote the merchant. From that time on, the character of the North was settled, and we watch the rise of fortunes, of a foreign population, of a permanent wage-earning class.

Until the various financial Acts of Hamilton in connection with the establishment of the national government, "property" in America had, to an overwhelming extent, meant investment in land. This had involved two points: first, the fact that the sort of property owned by nearly all, rich and poor, was of the same sort; and, second, the fact that its ownership entailed a certain sense of responsibility. With the rise of speculation and investment in government and other securities at the end of the eighteenth century, this responsibility tended to evaporate. The owner of a boxful of papers was far less hampered in his relations both to his property and to his community than was the large planter of the South or the small farmer of the North and West. His methods of accumulation and the amount of his wealth were much less open to public knowledge and scrutiny. His occupations and daily life, so different from those of either farmer or planter, bred a different set of qualities. The trader who dealt in securities or who turned over real estate quickly in rapidly growing towns had no need of such qualities as made the New England farmer or such a Southern planter as Washington. His personal interests often became disassociated from those of his fellow citizens, and even inimical to them. Human nature being what it is, he would, consciously or not, tend to view the public interest in the light of his own, just as Daniel Webster, the greatest statesman New England has produced, could turn a somersault on the tariff question when the economic interest of his constituents changed.

Had the growing moneyed class been able to exert their influence only by speech or writing or casting their solitary ballots, they would not have made much difference in the country. Their comparative numbers were very small, and they might have entertained any views they chose as to the American dream. That, however, was not the case. No man can make a fortune by himself. He has to depend in part either on his neighbors making it for him, — as for example in the unearned increment he derives from the increasing value of land, — or he has to employ the labor of others, reserving for himself, in return for his own capital and services, a portion of the return from the labor of each of his serfs, slaves, or workmen. The fact that an individual is shrewd or unscrupulous enough to avail himself largely of these means should not blind us to the fact that he has not made his money solely by himself. He owes the greater part of it to his fellows.

We are here concerned only with the effect of the capitalists' having used the labor of others. There is both an economic and a political question for us in this. The first is, In what proportions should the surplus of labor be distributed between the capitalist and the laborer? The second, What sort of character for citizenship is evolved in the wage earner as contrasted with that of the man who works for himself? So far in our history we have settled the first chiefly by force, and dodged the second.

As we have seen, Jefferson, the apostle of the American dream, did not believe in the possibility of realizing it except in a country in which the vast bulk of citizens were independent farmers, owning their own farms. He believed very firmly that a great self-governing democracy could not survive the rise of a town, wage-earning proletariat. So far as our story has gone, the Jeffersonian democracy was safe. We have seen that its believers had risen twice to repel what they had felt to be attacks on it, and had elected Jefferson himself in 1800 and Jackson in 1828. Because economic and political democracy had advanced together, it was still assumed, putting the cart before the horse, that economic democracy was the result of political, and that life, liberty, and the pursuit of happiness — in a word, "opportunity" in its widest sense — would be assured to the people at large by manhood suffrage. In 1840, out of a total working population of 4,800,000, over 3,700,000 were still engaged in agriculture. The next largest figure, that of nearly 800,000 in manufacturing, was, however, becoming ominous, especially as more than 520,000 of these were concentrated in the Northern States.

It had been becoming increasingly clear that the opportunities for making large individual fortunes in that section centred in the factory. Large-scale agriculture was out of the question; turnpikes, canals, the new railroads, banks, city real estate, might create wealth quickly, but they all depended on increase of goods and population. Manufacturing was the key to both of these. But manufacturing required labor, and the creation of large private fortunes required the profits from a great deal of labor or the unearned increment arising from the efforts of others. Astor, in New York, what with his fur trading, his city real estate, and deals of one sort and another, was setting the pace. As with Ford and Rockefeller to-day, his fortune towered above those of other business men of his time, but when he died in 1848 and left $20,000,000 he showed the business men what "success" might mean. The great fortunes of the early Republic, such as those of Hancock and Washington, had amounted to a few hundred thousand. The pace had been immensely quickened.

The problem was labor. Machinery, markets, transportation, were now ready. But fortunes could not be made without hands who would work for wages. Not only was the supply of native American women and children inadequate, but, as the mill owners became more rapacious and the conditions of work less attractive, the native American was largely driven out of the factories. Although at first girls had come in willingly from the farms to work for a few years, by 1846 we read that "a long, low, black wagon, termed a 'slaver,' makes trips to the north of the state [Massachusetts], cruising around in Vermont and New Hampshire, with a commander who is paid one dollar a head for all [the girls] he brings to market and more in proportion to the distance — if they bring them from a distance they cannot easily get back." Although a few of the mill owners, notably some at Lowell, were high-minded men who did their best to maintain decent conditions for their employees against the pressure of their greedy competitors, the whole situation radically altered in manufacturing between 1830 and 1850.

The pre-Revolutionary immigrants who had come in floods in the middle of the eighteenth century had almost all gone on to the land, and their families had now been in America for nearly a century. They were thorough Americans who insisted on American standards and conditions. Since that great movement had spent its force, there had been comparatively little immigration. From the first census in 1790 to 1825, the inward flow of foreigners averaged only about 8000 a year at all ports, and these were easily absorbed. From

1825, however, the numbers increased annually almost without a break, from 10,000 in that year to nearly 300,000 in 1849, most of them coming into Northern ports. From about 1830 the employer of labor found himself in possession of about 50,000 possible new hands a year. After another decade this had risen to over 100,000, and when the famine in Ireland had done its worst, immigration jumped to between 250,000 and 300,000 annually. Here at last was what the manufacturer had been looking for. At the end of the period, the abortive revolutionary movements on the continent sent a good many educated Germans to us, but for the most part the immigrants who came were extremely poor and ignorant. They had fled from unbearable poverty at home, and had expended everything they had merely to get here. To them America was a land of promise, the one hope left in the world. America was, indeed, a land of promise, but its Eastern section was not so indubitably one for a poor man. Among the economically lower classes many people were fleeing from it as fast as they could. By 1850 over 16 per cent of all persons born in the Eastern and Middle States, and nearly 27 per cent of those born in the Southern States, had gone westward. Again, in the same year, more than 50,000 persons, almost all in the East, were paupers, and 135,000 were supported in whole or in part by the State. More than 66,000 of the latter and about 37,000 of the former were not immigrants, but native-born Americans.

The earlier Irish who came were mostly put to spade work, and to a considerable extent they dug our canals and laid down our railroads. The native American brought up on a farm — Jefferson's good citizen — had an inborn dislike for working for someone else. He had a proper and instinctive dread of losing his independence and the full stature of his manhood. Rather than fall to that, he preferred, if he could, to move West and begin again as his own man. He had not had in the past, however, any feeling that manual work was beneath his dignity as an American. No European race has any such feeling to-day, and, much to their advantage in every way, the

English, French, Germans, Italians, and Spanish perform all the duties in their civilizations from the bottom to the top. The immigrant who came to America was greatly looked down upon, because of his strangeness, frequent uncouthness, and low standard of living. As he took the low-paid manual jobs working for other men, which the American had declined not on the score of their being manual but because of their being for others, the contempt for the foreigner began to be transferred to the work he did, and the American began to establish his tradition that the work, as well as the foreigner doing it, was beneath him. As shoals of Irish women became household servants, the feeling came to include domestic service. In this respect, and most unfortunately, the despised foreigner in the North fed the same superiority-complex tendency in the development of our psychology as did the negro slave in the South.

The negro slave had at least one great advantage over the Northern factory worker. He was property, and had to be taken care of. What the Northern manufacturer considered *his* property was the mill with its machinery, and he came to care no more for the worker than for the bale of cotton. The few mill owners who wished to be fair to their employees had to meet the fierce competition of the unscrupulous. It was characteristic of a good deal to come in our life that the "American System" of Henry Clay was maintained by the manufacturers as a "system," but with no regard for the individuals to whom alone any system could mean anything. Like our modern "efficiency," it forgot the man. The manufacturers did indeed manufacture goods, and so increased population and provided a market for agricultural products. For this they demanded "protection" and other special favors from the national government, but they cared not a rap as to what they were doing to Americans as human beings. Prices to the consumer, on the one hand, were raised as high as the special privileges secured would permit; and, on the other, the native American working class was beaten down in the economic scale as low as possible. The manufacturer was enabled to do this by using the club of cheap immigrant labor.

Recovery from the disastrous panic of 1837 was slow, but in another half-dozen years the mills were making very large profits. By 1845, for example, the Nashua and Jackson mills were paying 24 per cent in dividends, and many were returning heavily on watered stock. Meanwhile, wages had been largely reduced and production speeded up. A girl was expected to handle machinery doing nearly four times as much work in the late 1840's as compared with little more than a decade previously. In the Middle States a ten-hour day had been secured in many lines of work, but New England still clung to twelve or fourteen. It was there contended that "the morals of the operatives will necessarily suffer if longer absent from the wholesome discipline of factory life"! Could Puritan hypocrisy go farther? The legislature was assured that if it lowered the hours of work no limit could be placed to the evils of misspent time by thus leaving the operatives "to their will and liberty." As the mills and factories increased in size, and the mill towns grew in population, both hygienic and social conditions became worse. A petition to the Massachusetts Legislature in 1842 declared that "the population of manufacturing places are now, in great measure, dependent for the means of physical, intellectual and moral culture, upon the will of their employers."

In both Europe and America the period was one of *laissez faire* in economics. The will of the business man, even in the America of to-day, is, by the necessity of the case, a will to make a profit. Only what he may choose to do with his profits beyond a certain point, in the way of business or social service, rests entirely with him, even when the competition of unsocially-minded competitors permits him to exercise that choice. In New England, the will of the employers, with very few notable exceptions, was directed to making every cent of profit possible without the slightest regard for the welfare of their employees or the larger social questions of Americanism in the section. The manager of the largest mill in Fall River announced that, so long as he could find hands to work at the lowest wages, he would get every particle of work possible out of them, and, when worn out, would discard them as he would worn-out machines. The manager of a mill at Holyoke who found his hands "languorous" in the morning conceived the idea of working them on empty stomachs, and succeeded for a while in getting three thousand yards more of cloth a week for the same wages. Had the manufacturers been scraping along on little or no profit, some excuse might have been offered for their cutting costs in order to keep going at all, but dividends were high, and watered stocks were spouting fortunes. The attitude toward labor was thus dictated by pure greed and not by the necessity of the case. By 1850 the good type of native New England men and women who had originally flocked to the mills to work had been driven out.

The highly respected and prosperous merchants and shipowners of Boston and other leading New England ports had proved equally incapable of any vision other than that of lining their own pockets. After the "War for Sailors' Rights" fought against England in 1812, the shipowners reduced wages until in a few decades they had brought them far below those possible for an American workman. The captains and officers were often brutal, and sailors could get no redress when conditions were brought to the attention of owners. Within a comparatively few years the fine Yankee sailor had almost disappeared, and his place had been taken by the lowest and most abandoned of the foreign groups. In 1817 the government had passed a law that at least two thirds of the crews must be Americans, but, as usual when a law conflicted with their supposed interests, the business men completely disregarded this one. On the other hand, after flogging had been made illegal, the Boston Marine Society, composed of the most respected shipping merchants in Boston, at a time when the North was being inflamed over the cruelties to the negro in the South, petitioned the government to restore the right to flog sailors to their work. The great shipowners were making fortunes and laying the foundations for future social snobbery, but in the process they were breaking Federal laws and, by forcing down wages to starvation levels and by wielding the lash, they were driving self-respecting American sailors out of our merchant marine. To a considerable extent the same story could be told of the rest of the industrial North. "The rich, the wise, and the good" of the old Federalist formula had broken down in their leadership, and a class of wage earners new to American society was beginning to look for leadership in its own ranks. Labor began to organize, but for the most part it was merely on the defensive during this period.

Between 1830 and 1850, about two and a half million foreigners had been added to the population, chiefly in the Middle and New England States, giving an entirely different complexion to the problems of self-government and manhood suffrage. Hordes of underpaid ignorant immigrants, with little training in government of any sort, replaced the old American stock with its long experience of town meetings and politics. The new citizens could be led to the polls by "bosses," and the demoralization of the larger municipalities quickly ensued, the rich caring no more for the quality of the electorate than for the welfare of their "hands," provided that the legislatures, like the factories, gave them the desired results. People were no longer thinking in terms of statesmanship and the future, but of private business and the present. Constitutional questions which had perforce been the chief study of the earlier generations for so many decades were considered settled, except perhaps slavery, which everyone thought of as little as possible when allowed to forget it.

The conditions of the period were developing several of those traits which we consider rather distinctively "American," but which really date from this time. The nation was growing at a staggering rate. Whether we pore over the tables showing population growth, manufacturing, commerce, the increase of wealth, or what not, we are struck even to-day by the marvelous changes wrought every year. There seemed no limit whatever to the possibilities. The Federal Census of 1850 estimated that, if the ratio of increase for the preceding decade were maintained, the United States would have a population of 269,000,000 in the year 1930. In a table showing the comparative progress of our population with that of foreign countries it demonstrated that, whereas between 1790 and 1850 the average growth of Prussia, Great Britain, Russia, and France had been only 1.7 per cent annually each, ours had been 8.17 per cent.

We no longer feared any nation on the earth. The West was ours unhampered. The future seemed clear and glorious. A great wave of optimism swept over the country, and reenforced by the material development of the next three quarters of a century, was to become a lasting trait in the American character. America had always been a hopeful country, but, until the middle of the eighteenth century, life had been a fairly serious business. Nothing but parts of the seaboard had been won from the wilderness, and everywhere in the background were French and Indian enemies. The colonies were weak, dependent parts of an empire. By 1750, as we have seen, a very substantial civilization had arisen along the coast, but then came the anxious years of controversy, war, and the weakness of the new independent government for an entire generation. The attitude hitherto had thus been hopeful but serious. From the 1830's on, this changed to a rampant optimism.

If, in view of the somewhat dark picture painted in the beginning of this chapter, it be asked how optimism became so general throughout all classes, the answer is not far to seek. It must be noted, for one thing, that however badly off a large multitude of the new immigrants might be at the lowest rung of the American economic ladder, they were used to a low standard of living, and in almost every respect, not least in the independent political atmosphere, they found themselves far better off than they had been in the countries from which they came. The Germans, of whom we shall speak in the next chapter, mostly went West and prospered. The Irish, poor as they were on first arrival, took to American life like ducks to water and soon rose in the scale of living, becoming foremen, policemen, politicians; and in a few years many of each succeeding crop of immigrants climbed to a level of influence and economic standards undreamed of in the old country. For the native-born who were being worsted in the struggle in the East, there was the West, with its rainbows.

But, most important perhaps of all, there was the complete absence of any legal class distinction. The fact that opportunity appeared at least to be open to everyone kept alive belief in the American dream. After Andrew Jackson every boy was being told he might be President of the United States. In the Old World, luck or genius might raise a man from nothing to eminence, but for the general mass of men there was little hope there of rising above the station in life into which they had been born. In the America of the earlier days, character and hard work might bring a competency, but in an agricultural economy the accumulation of property was for most a slow process, and wealth was attained by very few. On the contrary, in the seething America of the 1830's and 1840's, both immigrant and old American felt that, with just a little luck, fortune might be waiting for him around the corner. Had n't Astor made $20,000,000, Girard left $6,000,000, while men in every community were evidently getting rich on a large if less spectacular scale? Astor had been a foreign immigrant, scarcely able to read and write, yet there he was, rich as Crœsus, and dictating to the government. Native or foreigner, rich or poor, learned or unlearned, the race was free for all, and the prizes were beyond the imaginations of the preceding generation or of European magnates. There was nothing but the mysterious texture of the brain cells that need keep one man below another. But if one were to get ahead of his fellows, if one were to grow rich in a few years, he must hurry. City lots were rising in price with every year of added population, corporations were growing greater all the time, the tap-tap-tap of opportunity at the door seemed to grow louder and more insistent as a man listened, and life was short. For one's self, for one's family, one must hurry.

The older American civilization had been leisurely. Many travelers found Americans rather slow and all too often lazy. Work had been necessary and had been enthroned as a virtue, but when the possibilities of altering one's position were small, and the farmer or storekeeper expected to be farmer or storekeeper all his life, there had been time, and stability. Now there was neither.

Better roads, railways, and steamboats had all speeded up the actual tempo of life a bit, but not sufficiently to account for that nervous haste that from now on was to be another distinctive American trait. New York, wrote one traveler about 1840, "is the busiest community that any man could desire to live in. In the streets all is hurry and bustle; the very carts, instead of being drawn by horses at a walking pace, are often met at a gallop, and always in a brisk trot." "The whole of the population," he adds, "seen in the streets seem to enjoy this bustle, and add to it by their own rapid pace, as if . . . under the apprehension of being too late." Nervousness became a common physical trait. All observers of the period note the new haste with which the Americans gulped down their meals, and hurried from the table. The American jaws began their ceaseless motion, and the chewing of tobacco, precursor of gum, became almost universal. Describing the New Englander, another observer wrote that "when his feet are not in motion, his fingers must be in action, he must be whittling a piece of wood, cutting the back of his chair, or notching the edge of the table, or his jaws must be at work grinding tobacco. . . . He always has something to be done, he is always in a terrible hurry. He is fit for all sorts of work, except that which requires slow and minute processes. The idea of these fills him with horror; it is his hell." "We are born in haste," commented an American of the day; "we finish our education on the run; we marry on the wing; we make a fortune at a stroke, and lose it in the same manner."

The *New York Sun*, in a long article in 1838, noted that the universal mania had spread to the children. "'Try,' is the first word, the meaning of which is thoroughly mastered. Boys are men before they are loosed from their leading strings. They are educated in the belief that every man must be the architect of his own fortune. . . . Dreams of ambition or of wealth, never the arm which drives the hoop — the foot which gives the ball its impetus. Toys are stock in trade. Barter is fallen into by instinct, as a young duck takes to water. There is scarcely a lad of any spirit who does not, from the time that he can connect the most simple ideas, picture to himself some rapid road to wealth — indefinite and obscure, it is true. But he reads the history of Girard, and of others who have amassed wealth. He sees the termini of the race — poverty at one end — affluence at the other, and jumps the intermediate years. He fancies that the course of amassing will be as easy as imagination. He dreams of dashing into a fortune by some lucky speculation. Contentment with competence he learns to regard as a slothful vice. To become rich, and, of course, respected, influential, great, powerful, is his darling object."

It was already noted by foreign travelers that the American did not love money for its own sake or hoard it as did the European, but was careless of it once gained, was lavish in both spending and giving, and seemed to enjoy money-making chiefly as an activity. The American had always been "taking a chance." The most serious of the religious leaders of the Pilgrims and Puritans had taken a great chance when they left comfortable Holland and England for the bleak wilderness. Every trial of new sites for settlement had always been a chance. Every one of the many million immigrants — German, Swiss, Scotch, Irish, English, French, and what not — who had staked their last bit of money in the world to reach the Land of Promise had taken a tremendous chance, for himself and his family. The colonists had taken a chance when they defied the might of the British Empire. Yet, somehow, it seemed that ninety-nine times out of a hundred the dice had fallen right. Taking a chance had got into the blood of the American until by the mid-century we find, as Kipling wrote of him nearly a century later,

> He greets th' embarrassed Gods, nor fears
> To shake the iron hand of Fate
> Or match with Destiny for beers.

The influence of this taking a chance, of matching with Destiny for beers, had been cumulative, generation after generation, but it was the West that had made the winning chances so dazzling even for the Easterner. As we have pointed out, had the continent stopped short at the Appalachian Mountains, the civilization of the seaboard would probably have developed along the lines already so clearly marked out by the middle of the eighteenth century. As it was, that older civilization was almost completely wiped out. American culture and character, moulded by new influences, were to be wholly different. The planter, the statesman, the churchman, the "gentleman" as then understood, the budding poet or artist, were all to be conquered for many generations by the rising man of affairs.

There were two factors which chiefly influenced the new type of civilization. One was the colossal size and richness of the new American empire, which made the prizes to be won so great as to turn the heads of even the most conservative of old Eastern families; and the other was the absence of any impassable social barriers, which made success a free-for-all race, and so intensified the fierceness of competition to the *n*th degree. Man's love of being distinguished among his fellows has been one of the leading factors in raising the level of the whole race. In America, as contrasted with Europe, it was open to every man, theoretically at least, to rise from the very bottom to the top. Wealth in every society has spelled, to a considerable extent, power and opportunity. It was not strange that it should do so in America, after the pioneering stage was over. The difference between Europe and America was that in the latter the prizes of wealth were far larger, they were to be won more quickly and easily, and they were open to all. This naturally meant that the possibility of winning them was in everybody's mind, just as in England to-day, where high and low bet on horses, everyone talks races, or as in a Latin country they talk lotteries. In America, the place of horses and lottery tickets was taken by vast enterprises, the prizes were millions, and the people talked about *them*. Making money became a great and exciting game in which everyone participated. Of course the element of luck was great, but those of skill and ability were also present; and thus, apart from the excitement of the game, and the power and pleasures to be derived from wealth, a fortune, if made by one's self, became also a badge of personal merit in the eyes of the public, our only substitute for a peerage to mark the man of outstanding ability.

If the size of the prizes, and the opening of the race to all, made for much aimless "hustle" and sheer bodily nervousness, they also released an enormous amount of energy in the people at large and directed it into the channels of personal ambition. It was a fact of vast significance that not only, as the *Sun* said, was the word "try" the first of which the child mastered the meaning, but everyone, educated and uneducated, old American or newly landed immigrant, was also expected to "try." For the several million foreigners in particular, to be expected to try, and to have something to try for, was a challenge releasing unsuspected reservoirs of energy and resource.

Some of the effects, however, were not so good. The winning of a fortune in haste required intense concentration. We have already seen how, in spite of the idealism also present, the life of the lower classes in America and particularly on the frontier tended to become absorbed in the pursuit of the material basis of life. In the older sections the pursuit of wealth, although it had its idealistic side, tended likewise toward materialism. In 1834, a by no means unsympathetic traveler noted that scenery meant nothing, that to the American a waterfall "is a motive power for his machinery, *a mill privilege;* an old building is a quarry of bricks and stones, which he works without the least remorse. . . . At the bottom of all that an American does, is money; beneath every word, money." Although he gave much more liberally than the European to useful and public objects, "it is neither enthusiasm nor passion that unties his purse strings, but motives of policy or considerations of propriety, views of utility and regard for the public good, in which he feels his own private interests to be involved."

The American standard of living, except in the notable extravagance in dress, was in some respects as yet below Europe. The cult of plumbing had not come, and an English traveler in 1840 could complain bitterly that even in most first-class hotels, like the Tontine House in New Haven, there was no such thing as a water-closet, guests having to go out of doors to an ill-smelling place at the end of the back yard. With the rapid increase of wealth, however, the standard was rapidly rising, and the American man began to be caught in the endless treadmill of rising family costs. With the great readjustment going on, the limitless possibilities, and the establishing of a new scale of incomes, he must needs indeed have been a brave or quixotic man who deliberately declined to try to make money and who interested himself in other things.

Moreover, there has been one factor in American money-making of deep and lasting importance to American social life and character, present from the start, but becoming more marked in this period. In communities of more or less stable population and resources, a competence is accumulated slowly. The speed with which one could get rich in America was due to the immense increase in population growth, and the exploitation of the continent's unequaled resources. In old countries there would have been a distinct limit to the expansion of a business or the building of cities. In the Land of Promise there seemed to be none. The more men who devoted themselves to the material development of the country, the more quickly it developed, and the greater the chance of everyone to get something out of it for himself. Thus, superimposed on the old Puritan and pioneer raising of work to the rank of a virtue, was the new conception of business as somehow a social and patriotic duty. Accumulated competencies or fortunes were rare. The overwhelming mass of the people, with boundless energies let loose, were anxious to improve their position. The combined mass of their desires, united with the realization that the more rapid the development of the country, the more chance they had individually to realize their hopes, created a public opinion that it was the duty of every man to assist in the development of the nation — that is, to go into business of some sort and to "make business." This, combined with the ordinary temptation to make money and the lack of social pleasures and the resources of cultivated society, made the pressure to think in terms of business almost irresistible.

Even the young heir to a fortune, an observer of the 1830's tells us, "has no conception of living without a profession, even when his family is rich, for he sees nobody about him not engaged in business." The man without a business gradually ceased to have public respect or social standing. One rich young man, "wearied out with his solitary leisure . . . could find no other relief than to open a fancy-goods shop." Even the pulpit, always sensitive to public sentiment, hurled anathemas at the man of leisure, devoting himself to the cultivation of the arts, as a political enemy to his country, and the introducer of aristocracy and of idle and pernicious habits. Here and there the exodus to Europe started, and occasional Americans who could afford to do so, and whose tastes and temperaments could not be satisfied with the new conformity to business, began to appear in Paris, London, or Rome as exiles.

These, however, were rare and unimportant exceptions. For the rest, every possible motive of private desire and public opinion tended to make them swing into line. The fact that the race was free for all, with its resulting fierceness of competition, and the fact that going into business and making money had for the reasons just given been exalted into a sort of religious duty and patriotic virtue, introduced yet another element into the moral condition of the nation. Business ceased to be a mere occupation which must be carried on in accordance with the moral code. It had itself become part of that code. Money-making having become a virtue, it was no longer controlled by the virtues, but ranked *with* them, and could be weighed against them when any conflict occurred. The quick development of an industry or a tract of land, the making of a million dollars to be added to the capital resources of the nation, could be weighed as exhibitions of moral and patriotic virtue against breaches of other exhibitions of virtue, such as justice or honesty. It was the tremendous development of the country, and the opening of the gates of opportunity to all, that had brought this about. Had it not been for this raising of money-making to the moral plane as a virtue in itself, its delinquencies could never have been measured with crimes against other parts of the moral code. As it was, unhappily, they could be, and were.

As we have seen, in the colonial period the American had been tempted into an attitude of lawlessness by the passage of impossible, unwise, or inconvenient laws by the British Parliament three thousand miles away. The colonist had got into the habit of deciding for himself what laws he would or would not obey. As the country had expanded westward, frontier conditions had reënforced this attitude toward law. Of the widespread lawbreaking in the period from 1830 to 1850 we shall speak more at length in the next chapter, but we may here note that another factor, very subtle but very deep-reaching, in the attitude of the American toward law was introduced by the raising of money-making to the rank of a virtue. This, and the fast tempo of the new American life, made it all too easy for the individual to get himself involved in all sorts of moral casuistries. It might, of course, be wrong, so he could argue to himself, to make false statements, even to perjure himself in a report or application to the government, to bribe a legislature, to hoodwink a competitor, to take an unfair advantage; but on the other hand, if by doing so he could put through his deal, if he could make a million in a year instead of in ten, was not that a patriotic service that might well outweigh the personal peccadillo involved in the means of its attainment? Were not the voices of the Church and public praise united in assuring him that by making money fast and "developing" the country he was rendering a patriotic service and performing a moral duty? If the making of a hundred thousand was a moral act, the making of a million must be one of exalted virtue and patriotism. If, in the course of doing so, a policeman or a land-office official in Washington or a few legislators in the State

Capitol seemed to be in the way, it could hardly be immoral to get rid of their obstruction by the simplest and quickest method possible. It might be, as old Ben Franklin had said, that honesty was the best policy, but that meant it was only a policy, and if another policy worked better, why not employ it? If honesty was a virtue, so also was "developing the country." They could be weighed quantitatively against each other, and if the reasoner happened to profit to the tune of a million, that was his luck or God's providence.

As for honest government, municipal or State, "the Fathers" had fortunately set up all the machinery for us. It had, of course, to be kept going just as the machinery in the factories had to, but it was ill-paid work which could be left to a low class of labor just as foreigners were being put to run the machinery in the mills. So long as the government ran fairly well and the cost was not too high, a patriot could be better employed in making a million in his office than in working for $500 a year as a State Senator. If the machinery did not run smoothly, if the cost got too high or the legislative product were not satisfactory, it might be necessary to bother about it; but meanwhile the country had to be "developed," and a practical patriot was busy about more important things than legislating. As to the crime that was becoming rampant throughout the country, there was no use in getting excited about that, and the business man had his affairs to attend to. So ran the ordinary business man's mind.

Indeed, what with the hurry, the illimitable opportunities, and the fierce competition, this new sort of get-rich-quick patriotism was putting a heavy strain on men. Just as in the early colonial days, or out on the advancing frontiers, a good bit of man's culture had to be dropped overboard, so now, in this new sort of struggle in the developed East, it had to be. Each stripped for the race to meet competition. Time was money and could not be wasted on what did not produce money. In the West, culture had come to be looked down upon by the pioneers as effeminate and useless because it did not help to fell trees and make a clearing. So in the East, among a very different class, it began to be disparaged because it lessened the speed in making money. Reading and music began to be left to the women. Men dropped out of society, or if they attended some function would be likely to be found segregated on one side of the room, uninterested in the conversation of the women and in turn incapable of interesting them. Just as money-making had become a manly and patriotic virtue, so an interest in art and letters tended to become a feminine minor vice. It was the frontier over again in fundamental influences, though in a gilded, rococo setting.

As we compare the East of 1850 with that of 1750, I think we find the most essential contrast to be in the field of morals and the scale of values. There is no use in throwing stones at the men of the later period; they were caught in the conditions which surrounded them. We cannot find fault with the pioneer for losing some of the standards of civilized life and developing others under the strain of the type of life he led. In similar fashion these men of the East of 1830 to 1850 were subjected to new and colossal strains. Unfortunately, however, just as the pioneer period on the frontiers left scars on the American mind, along with some excellent legacies, so did the Eastern period. Chief among these was the moral confusion caused by the expansion of the old conception of work as a moral virtue into the further conception of money-making as both a personal virtue and a patriotic duty, with the resultant confusion as to its relation to the rest of the virtues and the whole scale of social and moral values. Emanating directly from the too rapid expansion of the country, I think we must consider it one of the most potent influences for evil in American life. Yet the more one studies it sympathetically with a wish to understand, the less does one see how it could have been avoided. There was assuredly no innate weakness or sinfulness in the American people. We did not love money for its own sake as much as did the Europeans. In accepting the Industrial Revolution, we never brought into being such frightful conditions as ensued in the English manufacturing areas, bad as were our own. Both Jefferson and John Quincy

Adams, foreseeing the evils of too rapid growth, had wished so to conserve the land in the West as to spread the process of development over centuries. Only a despotic government could have forced that policy on a people multiplying with incredible rapidity and bursting with energy. Given the introduction of machinery, the rapid expansion westward, our limitless resources, and our multiplying population, the swift accumulation of wealth was inevitable. In a society without barriers, where there were no established social distinctions, competition would be of unheard-of fierceness, but that was part of the American dream. It was an inevitable corollary of equality of opportunity. That was a legacy of incalculable value, though it has come down to us encumbered by the confusion of moral values which may, happily, not prove permanent. Possibly, neither legacy may prove so.

In stressing the above topic because of its importance, I have thus far given an impression of cultural simplicity to the period in the North which it was far from possessing in reality. The time was one not only of abounding vitality but of vast confusion. In Europe, as well as here, it threw to the surface all sorts of new "movements" and "isms," wise and foolish; but, besides receiving innumerable cranks from the other side of the ocean, we raised a large crop of our own, idiocy, unfortunately, never needing a protective tariff. Mingled, however, with all kinds of absurd experiments to make the world over socially and economically, discussed in books and lectures or put into practice in short-lived "communities," there was much of lasting worth. Imprisonment for debt was abolished, prisons were reformed, the care of the insane was improved, flogging abolished, education provided for the blind, movements started for temperance, world peace, women's rights, abolition of slavery.

One of the most broadly important of the movements was that in education. Even in New England, where opportunities for free education of the very young had been greater than elsewhere, the laws were much better and more liberal than was the actual practice. Chiefly on account of taxation, the rich almost everywhere opposed free education, and the movement developed from the working class. The American system of education is one of the fruits of the practical working of the American dream. In 1830 a workingmen's meeting in Philadelphia unanimously resolved that "there can be no real liberty without a wide diffusion of real intelligence . . . that until means of equal instruction shall be equally secured to all, liberty is but an unmeaning word, and equality an empty shadow." Within the next two decades the present system of free education in the lower grades was established, and colleges likewise multiplied, there having come into being a hundred and fifty small denominational ones alone by the mid-century. Unfortunately, just as our modern system originated among the people and continued to be largely controlled by them, so it bore some of the marks of its sponsors. Not only were instruction and intelligence considered more or less synonymous, as in the above quotation, but the aim and content of education tended to be limited by the cultural standards and outlook of the class which had brought it into being. It was aimed at safeguarding economic and political democracy rather than at the development of the individual, and its content was selected accordingly. To a great extent, largely because our national aims are even yet obscure to ourselves, this original confusion in our educational system has never been resolved.

Innumerable voices seem to come to us from the North in these decades, advancing every sort of business scheme, urging all kinds of social reforms, offering to cure every ill — individualism run mad in an effort to build a society and a nation. They come to us blended in a confused roar like that of a stage mob in the wings of a theatre. In a rapidly running commentary such as this, it would be impossible to distinguish between them by detailed analysis of all the isms and movements, but three voices, all from Massachusetts, sound clearly above the clamor and give expression to three distinct traits of the period — Emerson with his optimism and self-reliance, Garrison declaiming against slavery, Webster pleading for nationalism.

It is useless, with our present small knowledge, to attempt to account elaborately for the appearance of the arts at any given time and place. We have seen that a group of intellectuals, headed by Irving and Cooper, had appeared in New York, and now a much more important one — including Emerson, Hawthorne, Whittier, Longfellow, Thoreau, and others — began to appear in the neighborhood of Boston. This has been called the flowering of the Puritan spirit, and various other things which equally mean nothing. It is easy to bemuse ourselves with words, but the plain fact is that we do not know why, out of the three centuries of Boston history, there should have been a few decades during which an unusual literary group appeared all at once, and never before or after. One or two things may be said. Whatever other by-products it may have had, the Calvinistic theology of Puritanism had trained the New England mind to think — no mean achievement anywhere. Thought as thought, and mind as its instrument, had been held in higher respect in New England than in any other section. The decadence of the old theology had left the people at large indifferent to a great extent, but the release from the conceptions of Hell did not release the old inhibiting influences on thought and instinctive conduct. Among a small group in Boston, however, Unitarianism had served as a rationalizing bridge between the dread Jehovah and a somewhat vague Power for Good at the centre of things. This abstract Power for Good, reënforced by the concrete development of the resources of the West, began to make the world — that is, Boston and its neighborhood — a pleasanter place to live in. If God after all was good, and if the U.S.A. was definitely on the road to becoming the greatest nation on the earth, there was ample material for the highly trained Boston intellect to work on.

All this, and more, does not explain, nevertheless, why there should almost simultaneously have appeared such a group as did appear. Of them all, the most authentically American was Emerson, if we possibly except Thoreau, and there is no comparison between the men in the influence they have exerted. Without any thought-through system, a fact which perhaps has endeared him all the more to Americans, Emerson was imbued completely with the new spirit of American optimism and with the religion of the infinite possibilities in the individual common man. Why all this deference to the great men of the past, he asks, when "as great a stake depends on your private act to-day as followed their public and renowned steps?" "Hitch your wagon to a star," he told his hearers in a thoroughly American metaphor which could thrill them. Probably his most popular essay has always been that on "Self-Reliance," and he has indubitably stirred innumerable youth to high endeavor. In the history of American thought, the further west the Indian was driven, the more remote the Devil became. In Emerson, the Devil, or the problem of Evil, evaporated almost completely. Dr. Channing and the now distant pioneer had done a complete job.

The American dream — the belief in the value of the common man, and the hope of opening every avenue of opportunity to him — was not a logical concept of thought. Like every great thought that has stirred and advanced humanity, it was a religious emotion, a great act of faith, a courageous leap into the dark unknown. As long as that dream persists to strengthen the heart of man, Emerson will remain one of its prophets. On the other hand, noble and simple as his life was, there was much in his doctrine that lent itself all too readily to the emphasizing of American traits already produced on frontier after frontier. Such a quotation as "Do not craze yourself with thinking, but go about your business anywhere. Life is not intellectual or critical, but sturdy," illustrates what I have in mind. His belief in the value of spontaneity, of the intuition rather than the thought-through conclusion, was of the frontier, not of the Puritan. In no other author can we get so close to the whole of the American spirit as in Emerson. In him we sense the abounding vitality and goodness of life, the brushing aside of the possibilities of failure, evil, or sin, the high value placed on the individual, the importance ascribed to the every act of you and me, the aspiration toward the stars and the calm assurance that the solid earth is ours, the worship of culture combined with the comforting assurance that the spontaneous glance may be best, the insistence on a strenuous individuality, the trumpet blasts that call us to high endeavor in the lists of thought and character, combined, for our weaker moments, with the dicta that "we are all wise" and that "culture ends in headache." His volumes are the mirror of the American soul. Every lineament is there reproduced. But American conditions have changed. Steeped as he was in Concord and Boston, Emerson was a product of the development of the West. He belonged to our century of optimism, an appendix to the Tables in the Census of 1850. For him all was good — God, the possibilities of life, the heart of man. To-day we are not so sure, and boys and girls no longer read their Emerson as did those of my generation.

In the vast optimism of the period, men kept their eyes averted as far as possible from the portentous cloud that they saw, and refused to see, slowly rising on the Southern sky — slavery. The South had changed and was buying Northern manufactures heavily now, because the North needed Southern cotton for its mills. Everything had been settled in the Missouri Compromise. The North had talked secession in the War of 1812; the South had talked it later, but we were getting bigger and richer every year. "For Heaven's sake be practical (so ran the popular mind); attend to your business and leave the Southerners alone. They have got to have niggers to raise cotton, and cotton is one of our biggest assets. It is a long time since we had slaves and we don't want them again, but it is the South's affair and not ours; if you make them mad down there, you will ruin business and perhaps smash the Union. Everything in America has worked out for the best in the past, and if only the confounded radicals would learn sense and keep their mouths shut, this slavery problem would work itself out somehow." Thus felt 99 per cent of the Northern business men.

But in Boston in 1831, "in the sight of Bunker Hill and in the birthplace of liberty," as he dated it, William Lloyd

Garrison published the first number of his fanatical weekly paper, the *Liberator*. "I shall strenuously contend for the immediate enfranchisement of our slave population. Urge me not to moderation in a cause like the present. I am in earnest — I will not equivocate — I will not excuse — I will not retreat a single inch — AND I WILL BE HEARD." And he was heard. The Abolitionists, as those of his party and way of thinking came to be called, stirred the country, North as well as South, to a pitch of passion such as has never been witnessed among us before or since. The destruction of printing plants, mobbings, even murders of Abolitionists, marked the next decade and more. Opinion will perhaps always remain divided as to whether in the long run the movement served the genuine good of the negro or not. There can be no doubt, however, that it kept the subject of slavery before the two publics, — Northern and Southern, — which would fain have let it rest undiscussed, and that it sowed the seeds of intense bitterness between the sections.

In our own day we have experienced the strength of feeling aroused among our people by the passage of Prohibition legislation by the fanatical reforming elements. If we can imagine that, instead of having merely deprived a large part of our population — a part that considers itself quite as moral and high-minded as the reformers — of the enjoyment of a social habit, the reformers had threatened in addition on moral grounds to deprive them of so large a part of their property as to ruin them financially, we can get a better idea of the feeling stirred up by the Abolitionists. The general subject of slavery will be discussed later, but we may here note that the two sections were in any case drifting apart more widely and rapidly than was realized. The richer classes in both of them were exploiting labor, as every civilization has always done, as every civilization may, perhaps, have to do. That, in spite of the American dream, is an unsettled question as yet. The Southerner exploited labor in the shape of legal slavery, the Northerner in the shape of wage slavery. Neither was conscious of any moral guilt in adapting himself to the social structure that had been shaped by the economic situation of his own section.

In both sections, the rapid increase of the new wealth had brought new men to the top. The men of the North, who had risen from nothing, without traditions, to wealth and prominence as bankers, merchants, manufacturers, or stockjobbers, could be duplicated in the Cotton Kingdom among owners of great plantations. Planters were far from being invariably of ancient lineage or fine old Southern stock. On the other hand, the social traditions of the South were quite different from those of the North, and the Southern planter, sometimes rightly and sometimes not, looked down on the Northern business man as an uncouth upstart without the manners of a gentleman. There was also at work the dislike of the landed proprietor for the city trader, and of the man of easy-going ways for the business hustler. To have these Yankees, who drove their wage slaves twelve and fourteen hours a day in badly ventilated mills for a few cents' pay, and who never assumed the slightest responsibility for them when sick, old, or out of work, tell the Southerner that *his* form of slavery only was immoral, and thus assume airs of superiority, was galling. The Southerner rightly said that he was not presuming to interfere between the Northern employer and *his* exploited labor, and so what right had the latter to make all these threatening speeches against a perfectly legal economic system which was guaranteed in the Constitution of the nation? To him it was an outcropping again of the inevitable persecuting mania of the Puritan — a sequel to the Salem witches, the banishments and hangings of Massachusetts history.

Every civilization which develops a homogeneous form comes to nourish and depend upon a certain set of cultural values. The South had a distinct type of civilization, and its cultural values were dear to it. Those of a highly competitive, complex industrial civilization are bound to be very different, and as the North became definitely committed to such a civilization, the South began instinctively to feel its own threatened. In the same way, what many of the sanest critics of America to-day object to is not its system of life *per se*, but the distorted and debased cultural values which have resulted.

As the North grew in population and wealth, the South felt that it was trying more and more to exploit the rest of the nation for its own benefit and to extend its system. The tariff, to which the South had become bitterly opposed, was a case in point. When that of 1828 had been passed, South Carolina had threatened secession, asking whether it was worth while to remain in a Union "where the North demands to be our masters, and we are required to be their tributaries." North and South as yet were fairly evenly balanced. Each, to get the better of the other, would have to enlist the West on its side. The balance of power had followed the Cumberland Road over the mountains. Baits were offered. There was much jockeying for position, and the endless speeches in the Senate went on.

Finally the climax came when, on January 26, 1830, Webster made his great reply to Senator Hayne of South Carolina, giving voice to the new nationalism and attempting to sweep away the whole doctrine of the right of a State either to secede or to annul a Federal statute. Denying that the Federal government was a mere compact between sovereign States, he declared, in words which every schoolboy knows, that "it is the people's constitution, the people's Government; made for the people; made by the people; and answerable to the people. The people of the United States have declared that this constitution shall be the supreme law." Defying the right of a Southern State to nullify or secede, the great orator from a State which had itself threatened secession less than two decades before ended with an impassioned plea for unity in the florid oratorical style of the day. "When my eyes shall be turned to behold, for the last time, the sun in heaven, may I not see him shining on the broken and dishonored fragments of a once glorious Union; on States dissevered, discordant, belligerent; on a land rent with civil feuds, or drenched, it may be, in fraternal blood! Let their last feeble and lingering glance rather behold the gorgeous ensign of the republic, now known and honored throughout the earth, still full high advanced, its arms and trophies streaming in their original lustre, not a stripe erased or polluted, nor a single star obscured, bearing for its motto no such miserable interrogatory as 'What is all this worth?' nor those other words of delusion and folly, 'Liberty first and Union afterwards'; but everywhere, spread all over in characters of living light, blazing on all its ample folds, as they float over the sea and over the land, and in every wind under the whole heavens, that other sentiment, dear to every American heart, — Liberty *and* Union, now and for ever, one and inseparable!"

A few weeks later, at the Jefferson birthday dinner, the issue was clearly joined, President Jackson electrifying the Nullificationists by giving the toast of "Our Federal Union — it must be preserved," to which Vice President Calhoun immediately added the challenging one of "The Union — next to our liberty, the most dear." The issue balanced on a knife edge for two years, when the West, having been bought over by favors, gave its support to a new tariff bill, which at once set the State of South Carolina aflame. The Ordinance of Nullification was passed; armed resistance to the Federal government threatened. But the nation was not yet willing to drink the cup of blood. Compromise was effected, and the South was promised a steady diminution of the tariff duties during the next decade. Before that was quite passed, however, the Abolitionists, through the Massachusetts Antislavery Society, had declared that the Constitution, making a slavery compact between North and South, was "a covenant with death and an agreement with hell — involving both parties in atrocious criminality, and should be immediately annulled." A few weeks later, the New England Antislavery Society went on record, passing a resolution by 250 to 24, that it was the duty of every Abolitionist to agitate for the immediate dissolution of the Union.

The South was being more and more goaded. Wild words were spoken there, the mails rifled, lives threatened. It was not merely a question of slavery. It was a question of interpretation of the fundamental compact between the States — a question whether, as in the tariff controversies, one section of the country could be made tributary to another; whether property guaranteed by the Constitution was safe or not if the North objected to an economic system which was different from its own; whether the Southern planter should be forced to take his morality from the Northern business man; whether an agrarian civilization could preserve its character or should be forced to conform to a disliked industrial one; whether a section of the country was to be allowed to maintain its own peculiar set of cultural values or be coerced to conform to those of an alien and disliked section by force of numbers; a question of what would become of liberty if Union were to mean an enforced uniformity. As we look back to-day, — because, from a military necessity in the conflict which we shall have to chronicle in a later chapter, the slave became legally free, — the tendency is to think of the whole conflict of sections in the simple terms of slavery. To do so, however, is to mistake the forces at work. The questions at issue were far more numerous and far less simple. In the life of the nation to-day, overwhelmed by an industrialism and a uniformity that have become subversive of our American dream, those questions have not yet been answered.

Meanwhile, observers refused to look at the black cloud which was coming up in a sky which otherwise seemed to be dazzling blue. If there were anxiety and resentment in the South, the North was humming with industry and its business men were doing their best to hush up the Abolitionists, even by threatening their lives. The West — to which, like the party managers of that day, we must now turn — was exulting in its youth and beginning to glimpse "Manifest Destiny" in the sunset sky over the Western mountains. The plain citizens everywhere felt a thrilling sense of freedom and of power. To a crowd that pressed too closely on a political procession, a gentleman at the head had called out, "Make way for the representatives of the people!" "Make way yourself!" was thundered back. "We are the People *themselves*."

VIII

MANIFEST DESTINY LAYS A GOLDEN EGG

"MAKE way! We are the people!" In Spanish and in English, though not in French, that cry had now resounded on the continent for nearly three centuries. It was only in English, however, that the cry was hurled at any and all that hindered or helped the steady advance of the ordinary man. The fish in the sea, by millions annually, had succumbed to it. The fur-bearing animals in the woods had scurried before it across half a continent. The incredible flocks of wild pigeons in the air had melted before it. The trees of the forest had heard and crashed in helpless obeisance to it. The Indian, native owner of the soil, had heard it, and fought or sickened or fled. The rich had heard it and entrenched themselves more strongly behind political privilege and a Federal Constitution steadily being modified by judicial decisions to bulwark the rights of property against the demands of man.

The English, when America was first settled, had been a seafaring folk. It had been many centuries since the founders of the race had dwelt in the vast forests of Germany and

Britain. When their descendants had crossed the sea, however, they had been confronted by the almost forgotten conditions of the forest. In the two hundred years since the first permanent settlement had succeeded in Virginia, they had learned the technique of forest living and clearing. The American frontiersman was as much at home in the silent forested wilderness as his ancestor had been on the tossing waves. That wilderness had extended from the Atlantic over the mountains, until, in the Mississippi Valley, it gave place to the open prairies and plains. Slowly the American civilization had cut its way through, but when it emerged into daylight again on the Western side, owing to its long forest training it was as uncertain of itself in the face of the great open spaces as a seaman on the land. Moreover, the wide expanse of the plains had been proclaimed by every explorer who had visited it as a waste desert utterly unfit for human habitation. Almost as inevitably as though it had been the sea itself, it seemed to set the bounds to the western advance of the white man.

Throughout the whole history of that advance, the front line had been in constant contact with the retreating rear line of the savage. Occasionally, as in the cases of the Cherokees and the Seminoles in the South, large bodies of the red men had clung to their hunting grounds and been surrounded by the whites and a civilization to which they could not be assimilated. The racial pride of the English had prevented any amalgamation. The impact of one race on the other had not been ameliorated by intimacy and human kindness. The black slave had become a domestic animal, occasionally ill-treated, but more often kindly and sometimes even affectionately used. The red man had remained, in the view of the white, a wild beast of the forest to be exploited or exterminated. In the broad sweep taken through our history by this book, we have been unable to chronicle the incessant local contacts and conflicts, but they had not been without their effect on the psychology of the whites in creating a certain race prejudice and insensibility to the rights of those who were considered inferior, emphasizing that trait of ruthlessness already in the blood. Treaty after treaty had been made with the natives, only to be broken without compunction when the white man wanted more lands for his insatiable demand for expansion. Two centuries of almost yearly conquests over a weak foe had implanted in us a feeling that nothing could stand to block our way. Almost the only "foreigners" we had known had been poverty-stricken Europeans and American savages. Both fed our sense of superiority.

At last the "Great American Desert," as it came to be named, seemed to call on us to halt, and a permanent Indian policy was evolved which contemplated forming the plains into a vast reserve for the red men, who, in spite of war, disease, and stolen hunting grounds, yet numbered between three and four hundred thousand east of the Rockies. The Cherokees and the Seminoles were removed bodily from the South, and with the Plains Indians — the Sioux, Shawnees, Pawnees, Kansas, and others — were forced to sign treaties that they would remain behind the new line of demarcation between the two civilizations. President Jackson in his annual message of 1835 declared that a barrier had at last been raised behind which the Indian would be protected, and that "the pledge of the United States has been given by Congress that the country destined for the residence of this people shall be forever 'secured and guaranteed to them.'" Already, however, the inability to keep the white man from anything he wanted had become evident. The northeastern part of the boundary had been settled by solemn treaty in 1825, but the discovery of lead mines and the pressing in of new immigrants at once made trouble. Without a shadow of right, whites settled on Indian lands and preëmpted their cornfields. A rising under Black Hawk was suppressed by local militia and Federal troops under General Scott, and the Indians were pushed back regardless of treaties. If the great Desert should ever be found to have value, the doom of the natives would be sealed. Meanwhile, westward expansion was diverted from the Desert's inhospitality and the wildness of its savage inhabitants, southward to Texas and northwestward to the Oregon country.

West of the Sabine and south of the Red River lay the great Mexican province of Texas. Mexico had won her independence from Spain in 1821, but neither the vast body of the population, composed of civilized Indians, nor the small Spanish and Creole element at the top, had shown any capacity for self-government. Roads ran from Mexico City to Natchitoches in Louisiana, Santa Fé in New Mexico, and San Francisco in California, but these vast outlying provinces were too huge and distant to be well governed, even had the government been stronger, sounder, and more capable at the heart. Owing partly to national character, whatever that may mean, and partly to the character of the civilization which he had first encountered in the New World, the Spaniard had remained an explorer and exploiter and had never become a genuine pioneer.

Texas was almost uninhabited, and at first the Mexican government welcomed colonization by the Americans. Land grants for that purpose had been made to a Connecticut Yankee, Moses Austin, who died just before independence was won from Spain. His son, Stephen, continued his father's work, and in 1822 planted a colony on the shore of the Gulf. Under the new Mexican colonization laws each married settler could acquire 4428 acres for less than two hundred dollars, and the population rapidly increased, as we have noted previously, the immigration coming mostly from the American South. It was the intention of Mexico that these settlers should become Mexican, and Austin abided loyally by the understanding. In 1831 he wrote confidentially to a friend, saying that he had bid an everlasting farewell to his native country and intended to "fulfill rigidly all the duties and obligations of a Mexican citizen."

Down to about 1834, Austin was able to abide by his pledges, and was the absolute leader of the twenty thousand or so inhabitants of the province, of whom about two thousand were slaves. Mexico had prohibited slavery within her borders, but, as on all frontiers, white labor was almost unobtainable and there were no docile Indians in Texas to be exploited as in Mexico itself. Unless the settlers were to remain peasant farmers, the only recourse was to black slavery, and the Mexican government looked benevolently the other way. The instability of that government, however, the uncertainty as to the status of slave property, the prohibition against further American colonization, and the fact that recently the immigration had embraced a large proportion of reckless and even criminal characters, made no longer tenable the continuance of Mexican loyalty on the part of a State whose population was almost wholly American in origin. Santa Anna exploded the situation when, in 1835, he proclaimed a new constitution for Mexico, abrogating certain States' rights hitherto possessed by the Texans. The settlers in turn proclaimed a provisional government and expelled the Mexican garrison from San Antonio. The military plans were badly bungled, and when Santa Anna appeared in that little town with three thousand troops, the fortified mission house of the Alamo was found defended by less than two hundred Texans, with no rescuers on the way. On March 5, 1836, the building was carried by assault and every defender was massacred, almost every Texan within having been already killed or wounded before the Mexicans reached them. Among the slain were Davy Crockett and the notorious Bowie of hunting-knife fame.

A Declaration of Independence had been drawn up, March 2, by fifty-five Texans, whose average age was under thirty-eight. Sam Houston, who in the autumn was to become President of the new State, defeated the Mexicans in a battle in which the American war cry was, "Remember the Alamo!" A constitution, legalizing slavery, was ratified, and the United States was asked either to acknowledge the independence of the new State or, better, to annex it to the Union. Recognition was granted within a year, but annexation meant war with Mexico and an addition of territory (large enough to carve into five States) to the slave portion of the Union. The revolt had come from natural and almost inevitable circumstances, but voices were at once raised in the North protesting that the whole affair was a plot by the South to extend its power, and in the tension which then existed annexation had to wait.

Meanwhile, the Great American Desert had also been flanked on the north. Fur traders had long been carrying on their trade far up to the Oregon country, and by 1831 the American Fur Company had a steamer which had proceeded up the Missouri River as far as Council Bluffs, and annually the head of navigation was pushed farther. The traders went into the Montana valleys to get the results of the season's hunts, and learned to know the whole terrain of the northern West east of the Rockies, which the first covered wagon had reached by 1830. Trappers, explorers, and missionaries pressed farther northwest to the Snake and Columbia Rivers. Oregon, the title to which was in dispute with England and which had hitherto been reached only by sea around Cape Horn, was now brought into touch with settled America overland.

The "Oregon Trail," across the plains, along the River Platte and through the mountain passes, started from Independence, Missouri, which was the farthest flung *entrepôt* of American business for a while on the Western frontier. From it also the Santa Fé Trail led across the plains southwestward to the settlement of that name in New Mexico. The Spaniards there had money, but the fifteen-hundred-mile haul from Vera Cruz made freight rates practically prohibitive, and the Americans who first drove their wagons over the plains found a market ready to their adventurous hands. The first got through in 1821, and after that the Santa Fé traders started across the plains each spring, traveling in caravans for protection against the Indians until the border of the Santa Fé country was reached, when a mad scramble ensued to see which of the competitors could get there first. At night, the horses would be unharnessed and, with the rest of the live stock, placed in the centre of a corral made by the encircling wagons. The government, however, came to the aid of the traders. In 1827 Fort Leavenworth was established, and in 1829 Major Riley, with a detachment of troops, marched in the spring with the caravan as far as the Mexican border on the Arkansas River, awaiting their return there in the autumn.

In one or two subsequent years there were also armed escorts, but sufficient impression had been made on the Indians to render the route safe when the traders went in bodies.

Measured by the statistics which the American was now coming to adore, all these activities — trapping, emigration to Oregon, trading with the Santa Fé country — were not very important. Their tremendous significance lay in the fact that as the Great American Desert came to be traversed in one direction and another, the myth of its uselessness to the white man was gradually dissipated. Although government surveyors were in future to get a good deal of credit for mapping the region, the fur traders of the northern part came to know the whole territory well, and the trader with Santa Fé soon realized that for at least the first seven hundred miles the land was already susceptible of easy agricultural development. When the honor of the nation had been pledged to the Indian, the frontier had thought that Catlin was right when he said that the whole strip reserved to the savage "is, and ever must be, useless to cultivating man." Unhappily for the red man, the settlers were beginning to find out that Catlin had been wrong. The whole theory of the Desert as a reserve for the natives quietly broke down and disappeared. Had the Far West kept merely to trapping and to passing once a year in a caravan to trade with the distant Spanish, the Indian might not have suffered, but things were happening farther back in the Middle West and the East which were soon to overwhelm the savage, though far beyond his ken or control.

The tremendous growth in population in the United States, the expansion westward, the development of manufacturing and of machinery, had all resulted in wild hopes and created a hectic atmosphere of "prosperity." Although the real railroad age did not begin until about 1848, lines were begun and planned in the early thirties. Everywhere the demand for interchange of goods led to the demand for transportation, and as constitutional scruples had become sufficiently strong to preclude the national government from undertaking to provide transportation facilities, and private corporations were not yet sufficiently developed to do so, an era began in which the individual States, more amenable to the whim of the voter, plunged into the most fantastic extravagances to build roads, canals, and railways. With all this came the demand for currency and credit, and newly chartered banks were scattered over the country like confetti. The more feverish "prosperity" became, the madder the uprush of prices and demand for credit. In 1830 the per capita issues of paper money were only $6.69. By 1837 they had risen to $13.87. The price of land, as well as of other commodities, shot up as a whale spouts. Western lands on which in 1830 a lender might have hesitated to lend a thousand dollars seemed, by their prices, to warrant double that by 1837. But it was not only the West that lost its head. Just as, in 1928, financial advisers were cautioning the gullible public that if it did not buy stocks immediately at any price, it might never have a chance to buy American "equities" again, so all sorts of rumors were put about in 1834 and 1835. It was said, for example, that the timber of Maine was nearing exhaustion, and timber lands jumped in some cases from five dollars up to fifty an acre. Building lots at Bangor soared from three hundred dollars to a thousand. In the South, prices doubled and trebled. Between 1830 and 1835, the assessed value of real estate in New York City jumped from $250,000,000 to $403,000,000. The sales of government land to settlers and speculators rose from less than $5,000,000 in 1834 to over $25,000,000 in 1836, most of the huge sum being borrowed from banks on absurd valuations and hopes.

Quite apart from President Jackson's war on the Bank of the United States and the unfortunate aspects of national finance, the bubble had swollen to such dimensions that the smallest pin could prick it. In May 1837, the banks suspended specie payment by general consent, and the panic was on. All the Western and Southern and some of the Northeastern States had involved themselves in huge bond issues for improvements with no regard to their economic value, and the crash included public as well as private credit. Values melted. In North Carolina, farms could be sold for only 2 per cent of their supposed worth. In Mississippi, slaves who had recently been purchased for twelve to fifteen hundred dollars each were offered for two hundred dollars cash. It was said that in Alabama practically the entire property in the State changed hands, and that 50 per cent of all in the United States did so. Feeling against the banks, which would have been extremely virulent in any case, was rendered more so by a staggering list of defalcations by officers, which grew day by day. New York was like a dead city. Boats lay idle at the docks and all building operations ceased. It took two years for the full effects to be felt in the West, and five before the nation began to recover. The rich saw fortunes swept away and the poor faced absolute destitution. In New York, six thousand men working on buildings were discharged. Within five months from the suspension of payments, nine tenths of all the factories in the Eastern States had closed, and fifty thousand employees in the shoe trade in Massachusetts were idle. From a half to two thirds of the clerks and salesmen in Philadelphia were without work. At New Bedford forty whale ships were laid up. Throughout the entire industrial sections of the country, the suffering of the working class was intense. In the South, plantation owners had to sell slaves for whatever they would bring to buy food to feed the rest. Owners of land, whether speculators or bona-fide farmers, were overwhelmed with debt which it was impossible to pay, and were lucky to keep a roof over them. The debauch was over and the nation lay prone.

Just as earthquakes under the sea cause tidal waves, so the panic of 1837, like that of 1819, caused a great wave of westward migration in the population. It rushed out from the Atlantic seaboard, dropping the uprooted human beings in its course as flowing water lets the heavy particles in it sift downward to rest. For the most part, with each successive hundred miles west, the population became sparser. People would move from one line to the next, which seemed to them to offer more opportunity; settlers on that line, in turn, would move on to the next one.

But far out in the West, on the real frontier line, the wave beat against the already doomed domain of the Indian, and washed up into it settlers and houses and farms, and the Fate that was to overtake the savage. Fort Winnebago, for example, which had been established to protect the Indian in his rights, became the starting point for white invaders to sweep up to the lead district, flood the prairies, or enter the hardwood forests of Wisconsin. No one can even estimate the vast numbers of Americans from the innumerable countrysides, villages, towns, and cities who in these years shifted westward from wherever they started. Michigan, which had a population of 31,000 in 1830, held 212,000 ten years later. Two by two, slave and free, new States came into the Union in a decade or so: Michigan–Arkansas, Iowa–Florida, Texas–Wisconsin. Constitutions of the new members to a great extent showed the hatred of banks, and the steady demand for more democracy.

Towns started before or after the panic were rapidly rising into cities — Keokuk, Burlington, Davenport, Chicago, Milwaukee, Dubuque. The West was in ferment all along the line. Each new community thought it would surely be *the centre* of its territory, but who could say? About 1840 a man who had bought land on the outskirts of Chicago, as then mapped, for a thousand dollars an acre complained that he could not get a hundred dollars for it and perhaps would never be able to get fifty.

America has always been a land of dreams, the "land of promise." The Atlantic has ever been a vast sundering Lethe which has shut out the influence of the past. The only finger which has beckoned has been that of a hope-filled future. Panic after panic — 1791, 1819, 1837, 1857, and so on down — has wrought havoc and destruction, like our Western tornadoes, but the finger has never ceased to beckon with compulsion. For a short space once, in the mid-eighteenth century, we had a summer's day of pause and fulfillment, when we thought our America was bounded by the nearest mountains, and began to take our ease in Zion. But, the mountains overleaped, wider and wider Americas opened before us, and there were never rest and stability and the pause of fulfillment again. We still have fever in our blood.

From the very beginning, the quantitative measure of value assumed a definite place in the American mentality. If one man built a house in the woods, the Indians would probably soon tomahawk him and his family, but if a dozen families settled in a group, there might be comparative safety. In old, long-settled England, if a man prospered he might invest in acres added to his own, or houses to rent, or other opportunities which offered where population was fairly dense and stable. But for the first comers to America there was no chance to get ahead unless others came also, by birth or immigration. Had the earliest settlers at Jamestown or around Massachusetts Bay never increased, the value of their property never would have done so either. They might have made money by trading with the Old World, but there would have been nothing in the New into which to put it. Moreover, newcomers meant new interests and wider social opportunities. All motives — safety, profit, social intercourse, educational opportunities, everything — led the Americans to watch mounting figures of population growth with an eye to all that made life richer and pleasanter.

This was an experience repeated on every successive frontier of the many America has known. Except for the very vanguard itself, — the hunters and trappers and professional frontiersmen, — the American has always wanted to see his community grow. In each beginning such growth has meant safety, social life, better schools, churches, roads, a rising value for his property and scale of living for himself and his family. The man who had bought land in Chicago at what for the moment had proved an extravagant price knew well that the only way for him to recoup was to have Chicago grow. If it grew enough, he might get his money back; if it grew fast, he might be rich; if it grew as it has since grown, his grandchildren would be rich beyond the wildest dreams. In the Old World, landowners had no such chance to multiply their values tenfold in a decade. There the markets for merchants or manufacturers were not multiplying with a population that doubled every twenty years. It was only in America that for the ordinary man the rosiest dreams might turn to truth if his luck were right.

Each of us is likely to be the centre of his own universe. It would be hard for most of us to deny that whatever might bring us wealth, opportunity, consideration, was not somehow in itself beneficent. We are beginning to-day, under wholly altered conditions, to realize that size and quality are not necessarily commensurable, but it is easy to see how the typical American double concept of "bigger and better" came into being. In the last chapter, we noted how the American came to be preoccupied with business to the exclusion of the arts, even that of living, — an exclusion which had begun to develop in the eighteenth century, — and how business had become for him an absorbing game rather than a mere heaping of gold. In much the same way, the desire to make things grow "bigger and better," to make his village into a town and his town into a city, came naturally to be a game. As he lost sight of the real end for which wealth is won, so likewise he tended to lose sight of the real end for which an increase in population may be desired. Like poker chips, his money measured his skill and success in business, and so, again like poker chips, the rising figures of population and Chamber of Commerce statistics measured his success in foresight and struggle in another way. Size, like wealth, came to be a mere symbol of "success," and the sense of qualitative values was lost in the quantitative, the spiritual in the material.

In the frontier stage, size, as also the material development of houses and farms and roads and stores, *did* mean the scaffolding on which a civilized life had to rest; and numerous frontiers burned that thought deep into the developing American soul. Unfortunately the scar which it left has been the transposing of ultimate value to the scaffolding instead of the civilization, and the adoration of business and size for themselves and not as means to lives of cultural value. As a professional athlete loses his sane idea of exercise as the foundation for a sound mind in a sound body, and warps his whole life to developing the physical basis of the union, so the citizenry tended to lose its sense of rational proportion. "Bigger and better" did mean something real at one time, but it was much easier, in a land of unlimited opportunity, to make things bigger than to make them better, and in working for bigness first we came to a great extent to forget the ultimate purpose of humane value.

It was largely in the period from 1830 to 1850, when the nation was growing like a weed, that this conception took its deep root among us, although the germ had always been present. Together with it there grew up naturally another American trait, that of "boosting" and of objecting to criticism as "kicking." This is a perfectly natural, indeed almost an inevitable, double corollary to the need, real or imaginary, of constant and rapid growth. At the positive pole, "boosting" tended to help growth; and, at the negative one, criticism might hinder it. The first, like building up a business, thus became regarded as a patriotic virtue, whereas the second, like leisure, became a sin against the nation.

At one stage of our growth, everything desirable seemed to depend, and to a great extent really did depend, upon steady and rapid increase in size. The man who joined a community and did his utmost to hasten its growth was not simply an additional unit in a population which might have been just as happy and prosperous without his being numbered among it, but he was recognized as adding to the prosperity and furthering the ambitions of every other member who had already cast his lot and invested his work or money in the community. On the other hand, each man who left the community decreased the prospects of success for all the others. Criticism of faults, or even a cold appraisal of facts, might deter others from coming. Especially after the West started on its development, almost every settlement was a wild gamble. A cluster of houses might be a potential Pittsburgh, Cleveland, or Chicago, or after a dozen years of hard work and the sinking of the settlers' capital might relapse into wilderness. Individualists as the settlers were, in many respects, success in State building could come only by coöperation. The man who shouted "bigger and better" coöperated. The man who criticized or went back East was considered not only a "kicker," but a dangerous enemy to growth, who should be overwhelmed with scorn. Such men, as one newspaper said in 1841, were "recreants," "worse than drones, for they impede the labors of the industrious." Men who doubted success in any direction whatever "ought to receive the withering scorn and derision of a nation which claims to have no superiors in knowledge and the arts."

The later odd aversion, in a nation wholly made up of immigrants of one generation or another, toward any of our citizens who expatriate themselves for a while, springs straight from this frontier prejudice. He who went abroad became hated both as a lost unit in a population which must be made ever larger, and also as a critic, albeit even a silent one, who might "give the place a bad name" and hinder others from coming. It was the enormous possibilities of developing the West that enrolled business as one of the virtues. It was the genuine need of our successive frontiers for increased population that, with the materializing of our values, confused for three generations and more the twin concepts of bigger and better, and made the critic a "recreant."

In another respect the frontier did us harm in training us not to see what we do not want to see. The earlier frontiers of the seventeenth century had been made up merely of homes "farther out," homes still intended to be permanent. The Connecticut River Valley, for example, had been first a "frontier" of Massachusetts Bay, but it was not long before it took on an aspect of cultivated permanence, and in a few generations the boast could be made that there was no more smiling landscape in Old England itself. However, as people gradually got the habit more and more of moving on, when more genuine frontiers came to be planted again and again, both the hard work and the sense of impermanence tended to make for a shiftless disregard of surroundings. The first few years of any settlement are years of grinding toil, and while the very foundations are being laid there is no thought or energy to be devoted to such amenities as flower gardens, trees, or even mere neatness and cleanliness out of doors. Such things have to come later; and little by little, as people got used to moving on, to devoting themselves to the quickest exploitation of every settlement and neighborhood, they came to care less and less about general appearances. Like intellectual culture, such things came to be considered foolish ornament for those who were effeminate in taste and not up to a real man's work. How deeply this frontier willingness to overlook one's surroundings entered into the American make-up is evident in all parts of the country to-day. The five hours' railway journey from New York to Washington, from our largest metropolis to the Capital of the nation, is rendered hideous by the survival of this frontier trait, as are our country roads. It is another example of how values tended to become debased on the frontier to the lowest common denominator of utilitarianism.

We cannot understand our traits unless we find their roots, and it was impossible that we should outgrow frontier characteristics so long as the frontier remained a dominant moulding force in our national life. It was the West that had dragged American culture from its eighteenth-century quiet mooring. It was the West that was building up Eastern manufacturing and Eastern fortunes, and it was the West that was dominating the American mind and outlook, in spite of the smug Boston Brahmins and shipowners, New York bankers, or Southern cotton magnates. American life was in full flood, and it was impossible for anyone to keep dry feet. Nevertheless, over all the tumbling waters of materialism, and through the rifts in the clouds of issues that would later have to be faced, shone yet a light of idealism.

The American did not believe he was selling his soul to Mammon, but thought he was merely pledging it for the moment, as he was ready to pledge anything he owned, with the hope of ultimate gain. He could not be quite comfortable about devoting himself solely to business until he had made it a virtue, and he always looked forward to a future which would justify spiritually his intense present preoccupation with the material. Even the transcendental Emerson was swept with the current and wrote that somehow art would come to us in a new form, raising "to a divine use the railroad, the insurance office, the joint-stock company, our law, our primary assemblies, our commerce." We were enjoying the most glorious chance to get rich quick that had ever been vouchsafed to the human race, but we could not eat our meat, as heirs of a civilized scale of values, without its being blessed in the name of mind and spirit. We were boilingly busy. We must make our fortunes while there was still a chance in a new country. Some day you would see. The ways of God were mysterious, and if we only made the insurance office and the joint-stock company profitable enough to ourselves, they would be changed to spiritual values. Just how Astor's twenty millions made him any more of a spiritual asset to the nation than Washington's half million had made him, or his farm and scarce anything else had made John Adams, was not dwelt upon. Nor would it be likely to be, as long as frontier stretched beyond frontier toward the ever-retreating sun. The pot of actual gold was within our grasp. It was the spiritual gold that lay at the end of the rainbow.

Meanwhile, the West was harvesting villages, towns, and cities. "Ol' Man River" swept past populous communities and bound them together in his hundred arms. In the East, short stretches of railways had been built and there were a few in the West, but as yet water and the wagon road held their own. The Fulton–Livingston–Roosevelt combination in New York had tried to monopolize the steamboat building on the Western Waters, but Captain Henry M. Shreve, who built the first "double-decker" on the river, had won his fight against them, and by 1834 so important had the river navigation become that the government employed him to clear the stream of snags with his newly invented "snag boat." In the forties the West had more marine tonnage than the entire Atlantic seaboard, New Orleans alone in 1843 having twice that of New York, our greatest Atlantic port of the time.

By the mid-century there were probably a thousand boats operating regularly on the Mississippi. Even at the beginning of our period, in 1834, the steam tonnage on that river — 39,000 — was nearly half that of the whole British Empire, and it multiplied sixfold in sixteen years. Over the unknown spot where De Soto had been given his watery grave in the midst of a continental wilderness, there now raced against each other great boats, gleaming with lights at night, costing a hundred thousand dollars and more, carrying their picturesque hundred or two of passengers — gamblers, merchants, slaves and immigrants, fur traders, cotton planters, every imaginable type of humanity — and cargoes of every sort of merchandise. Of accidents there were plenty. Even when the fires were not being fed with resin or oil-soaked wood, while safety valves were illegally fastened down, in the races between steamers which were a favorite form of river sport, the snags, sand bars, explosions, and sudden conflagrations of the flimsy superstructures often resulted in heavy loss of life. Boats had to be light, as they were built for speed and shallow water. Indeed, they drew so little that they could almost have floated in the whiskey consumed on them in a single trip. This great period, up to the Civil War, bred a motley and picturesque life. Mark Twain has immortalized the pilots, but, important as they were, they were only part of the varied lot engaged in the river traffic.

As the boat swung out from her landing at New Orleans, the dock would be lined with negroes singing to their comrades, who made up a good part of the crew: —

> "Farewell, brothers, if you 's gwine fo' to go,
> We 'll weep fo' to see you' face once mo'."

The roustabouts, like all who have to do with boats, had their songs for their work, and an Eastern traveler would watch them, amused, as they would take on the wood for fuel with

> "Ducks play cards and chickens drink wine,
> And de monkey grow on de grapevine.
> Corn-starch pudding and tapioca pie,
> Oh, de gray cat pick out de black cat's eye!"

It was not only the ducks who played cards and the chickens who drank wine in those roistering days. Everyone did, almost, and one of the most picturesque features of the river was the professional gamblers who were nearly as much a part of the ship's company as the captain and the crew. They formed here, as throughout the West, a type of their own, easily to be picked out by their faces even when they did not assume the gaudy and flashy raiment of many of the profession. There was little time lost in getting up a game, often at the bar, where the Easterner could be picked out by his whiskey cordial, the Southerner by his julep, and the Westerner by his tumblerful of whiskey straight with no effeminate water after, even if the sectional classification were not made easy by other characteristics.

The gambling gentry frequently abused their privileges, and the term "lynch law" seems to have been coined about 1834 to meet the need of dealing with them, and in particular of hanging one of them at Vicksburg. It may have been difficult to frame a legal case, but at that time we were entering upon the most lawless period we have ever known. We have already noted the various causes which had, for long, bred disrespect for law as law in America. With the period beginning about 1830, however, we enter upon a new phase. Up to that time, almost all our lawbreaking had to do with business transactions. America, as contrasted with Europe, had been singularly free of crimes against the person, and it is not easy to trace the causes of the change. The great distress caused by the panic may have been a small contributing influence, but was assuredly not the cause. The problem was one which concerned the whole country, and, although I treat of it in this chapter, we may also ignore the life of the West as a cause. It is true that the great wave of crimes of personal violence which swept over us in these decades, for the first time, coincided with the very rapid westward advance, just as it did with the great stream of foreign immigration, but I think both these may be dismissed. The frontier always breeds a certain lawlessness in its early stages, but we had been living on successive frontiers for two centuries, and the West of this period was scarcely more lawless than the East or South. Moreover, although there were many mob clashes in the industrial sections between the foreigners and the Americans, in almost every case it was the latter who were the aggressors, and we cannot lay the violence of the period at the immigrants' door. There were scarcely any of them in the South or West, at which sections, on account of their crime, the East liked to point the finger of scorn.

As a matter of fact, there was no section of the country which could play the Pharisee with regard to the others on this score. The *Philadelphia Ledger* had scarcely read Arkansas a moral lecture, because the Speaker of the House of Representatives in that Western State had plunged a bowie knife into a member on the floor, when it had to record a felonious assault of one member of the Pennsylvania legislature on another, also on the floor; and members of Congress went armed in the Capital at Washington. The whole period was punctuated not only by murders, lynchings, and mobs in the South and West, but by similar happenings in the Middle States and New England, directed largely against immigrants, negroes, and Catholics. The burning of the Ursuline Convent near Boston was merely one of the most notorious of these. That at Providence was also attacked, several Catholic churches were burned in New Hampshire, and a priest was tarred and feathered in Maine, while there was serious rioting in New York, Philadelphia, Baltimore, and other Northern cities. In April 1840, a New York journal pointed out that although New York had a population of only 300,000 against 2,000,000 in London, there were seventeen murders in the smaller city to one in the larger. A Philadelphia paper two years before had also noted that there were more murders in the South in one year than in Italy in five.

Even making all allowance for the panic, for the rising passions over the slavery issue and abolition, and other contemporary influences, it is evident something had happened in our country. Lincoln wrote bitterly that "law and order had broken down," that "wild and furious passions" were substituted for "the sober judgments of the courts," and that "outrages committed by mobs form the everyday news of the times," "common to the whole country."

Treading warily in trying to trace the beginning of one of the most sinister forces in our national life, I would hazard three influences as operative — a false ideal of education, the political ideal of citizen as ruler, and the muddling of morals by having given business success the rank of a moral virtue.

In the American colonies the old system of apprenticeship had largely disappeared. As in all new countries, the quality of work counted for less than getting work done, even of makeshift sort. The constant migrating of much of the population had broken down a good deal of the restraint and training of the home, and these had not been supplied by the new educational system. One intelligent foreign observer of this period noted that the children in America were *taught* more and *trained* less than in Europe. The educational system, devised by the people for the people, did not aim at all at training either mind or character, but only at instilling facts useful for making a living.

The American political philosophy, from the discussions of the Revolutionary era onward, has notably dealt with the *rights* of the citizens and not with the *duties* of the subject. The very word "subject" became abhorrent. Yet, even if the people are sovereign, it is evident that the individual is still subject. We may be subject to ourselves in our collective capacity as the "sovereign people," but we are subject. Following the winning of independence, the ordinary American had liked to refer to himself as a "king," but if we are all kings, and no one is subject, the only result is anarchy. There developed, however, especially in these first days of manhood suffrage, an objection to enforcing laws unpleasantly against one's fellow "sovereigns."

An instructive example occurred during a serious riot in Baltimore in this period, when the city was at the mercy of a mob. A body of citizens met in the Exchange and were busy drawing up a set of resolutions in favor of public order while a crowd of drunken men and boys were absurdly threatening the town. An old revolutionary soldier, eighty-four years of age, finally broke in with "Damn your resolutions! Give me a sword and thirty men and I will restore order." "But, General Smith," said the man who was proposing the resolutions, "would you fire on your fellow citizens?" "Those who break the laws, drive their neighbors from their houses, plunder their property, and reduce their wives and children to beggary, are not my fellow citizens!" thundered the old man, who was soon after elected mayor of Baltimore and did restore order. The Americans, as I noted earlier, had during the colonial period got into the habit of obeying only such laws as they chose. It was an easy step for the authorities, when the people became sovereign, to enforce only those laws that would be popular when they were enforced. Even sovereign States, North, South, and West, had constantly threatened nullification of national statutes.

Of the moral muddle into which we got by raising money-making to the rank of a patriotic and moral virtue I have already spoken. This was a cancer that ate deep into the vitals of our life. It meant not merely that profit could be set off against order, — as in one State, which, having calculated the cost of an adequate police force and of a canal, voted for the canal, — but the demoralization of our whole attitude toward law and public life.

The balancing of making money for one's self as a patriotic virtue against obeying law or trying to maintain an incorruptible public service as another patriotic virtue, commensurable in quantitative terms, had completely befuddled our moral conscience. The failure to enforce law, on the part of everyone, from a Western sheriff to the Federal Congress, also confused the issue. We have already seen how the failure of Congress to enforce the law relating to payment for Western lands had brought about such great injustice as to break down to a considerable extent the Westerner's economic integrity. This was repeated in the preëmption laws. Settlement outran the government land agents, and when lands came to be sold at auction the question arose of what to do with the settler who had already squatted on it, preëmpted it. Should he lose all his improvements or pay a high price as against some speculative bidder? To protect him a benevolent but weak government ruled that he should have no competitors at the sale, but be allowed to acquire title at the minimum government price. On the other hand, the bona-fide new settler asked himself, if that were so, why should *he* be forced to pay high against a speculator when he was complying with the law more fully than the squatter? From this situation developed all sorts of illegal methods, often including violence or threats of it, to secure land at minimum prices and prevent any real competition at the auctions. Thus once more the inability of the government to deal wisely and strongly with a far-reaching problem of fundamental importance to vast numbers of our most virile and active citizens had become a force deeply corrupting to public conscience.

Like a disease suffered by a youth of abounding vitality, however, these centres of infection in the body politic were lightly thrown off. With the exception of a few voices of individuals and occasional journals, the general lawlessness and corruption were treated without seriousness and even with levity. It is often only when the youth has reached maturity that the effects of early disease become painfully apparent.

Meanwhile the youth felt the blood coursing in his veins, and he was throwing himself into the work of carving out his future with infinite gusto. The momentary thought of a western boundary marked by a line of forts protecting an Indian preserve had passed almost as quickly as it had arisen. Texas, with a territory as large as France, kept knocking at our doors for admission to the Union of States. The annual caravans which set out from Independence to trade with the New Mexico country carried our minds toward the Southwest and California. The other lines up into the fur country or over the Oregon Trail to the Pacific Coast likewise carried our minds thither. From Oregon, settlers were straggling down the coast into northern California. Like a huge lobster's claws we were beginning to nip the Pacific Coast at north and south, with the Desert and the mountain ranges in between, and as yet but little regarded. In every direction the finger of fate beckoned westward. Someone had coined the phrase "Manifest Destiny" and no one needed to be told that it meant inevitable expansion to the Pacific at any cost. To be sure, we had pledged our national honor to the Indians when we allotted them the Desert, and the Mexicans owned the mountains and the coast, but racial pride classed the Mexican Spanish and half-breeds with the savages, and two centuries of broken treaties with *them* had accustomed us to paying no attention to rights that conflicted with our own expanding energy. The British had tried to confine us within a line along the Appalachian watershed in 1763, and population had poured over the imaginary line like water bursting through a dike. The expansion of population and its westward sweep on the American continent have been one of the greatest movements in the history of the human race — a movement involving tens of millions of individuals, unthinking, collective, unmoral, akin, in all save its incredible swiftness, to the inevitable advance of a glacier.

More and more, American life was taking on the characteristics of a mass phenomenon. Down to 1840, all the men who had been elected President had been outstanding national figures. But the day for these had passed. The system of nomination by Congressional caucus had given way to our present system of national conventions which made it almost impossible for any candidate not a professional politician or in close touch with the party machine to secure a nomination. Moreover, sectional interests and the bulk of the mass began to demand a man on whom all could unite, which meant a man who was sufficiently unknown or sufficiently colorless to have aroused no strong antagonism. In 1840 he was found in the West, and the innocuous old Indian fighter, General Harrison, was swept into the White House in a campaign in which there was no pretense of discussing principles, but which was merely a whirlwind of catchwords. The "hard cider" and coonskin-cap campaign became a landmark in our political history, and the Indians in the Desert, if they knew anything about it, might well have pondered their destiny when they learned that old "Tippecanoe" had been elected as the "Great White Father" largely because of the popularity worked up for his having defeated them in a battle which marked one of the stages of our broken faith.

Although "Tippecanoe and Tyler too" won the election, the old General lived only a month, and four years later a still less known person, Mr. James K. Polk of Tennessee, was nominated by the Democrats. Everyone might ask, bewildered, "Who is Polk?" but he stood for a policy of Western expansion and defeated the brilliant Henry Clay. There was nothing brilliant about Polk. His mind was intensely limited in interests, and there is no evidence that he knew or cared anything for history, literature, or art, or even for many of the amenities of life. Dancing was banished from the White House, where social events became frigid. But although Polk's personality was colorless, it was far from spineless. He could formulate a policy and push it through, and the policy he chose added a half million square miles to the national domain. In his lack of culture and personality, his narrow and undistinguished mind, his unmorality rather than immorality, he typified the movement of expansion itself as a natural force. That movement could override the Indians without government formalities; but, although the settlers might care no more for a Mexican than for a Shawnee, when the Mexican border should be crossed, international complications would ensue. If Manifest Destiny were to reach San Francisco, it would have to do so via Washington. It had been a mass movement, but at last it could act only through an individual. That is the significance of James K. Polk.

Among the demands of the campaign had been the settlement of the Oregon question with England and the annexation of Texas. Polk had nothing to do with the latter, for a week before he entered office Congress passed the necessary Joint Resolution, and the day before he became President his predecessor sent word to the Texan Republic that the way was open for her to become a State of the Union. Polk at once turned, however, to the problem of Oregon. Both England and America had claimed the whole of that country, and there were settlers of both nationalities living there. The campaign cry had been for a boundary along latitude "Fifty-four-forty or fight," and there had previously been several attempts at negotiation. After two years Polk was able to report that a compromise, highly favorable to the American side, had been reached with the British. This gave us practically all of the Columbia River and set the boundary at the 49th parallel, with a clear title out to the Pacific on our northwest. Polk, who had neither love nor fear of England and who was never deterred by scruples of abstract right, might probably have held out for more had he not wished to have his hands free for even larger game — California.

Mexico had protested against our annexation of Texas, whose independence she had never acknowledged, and she had withdrawn her Minister from Washington. That was a natural move and in no way signified war. European nations as well as ourselves had acknowledged Texas as an independent State, and the question whether or not we had any right under our own Constitution to annex another nation, as many denied, was purely a domestic one for ourselves. Mexico had no intention of declaring war. War was necessary, however, for Polk's plans, and would have to be forced. In June 1845, orders were sent to the commander of our naval squadron in the Pacific to be ready to seize San Francisco as soon as he should hear that Mexico had opened hostilities. Our Consul at Monterey was also informed that, whereas we could use no influence to cause California to revolt against Mexico, we would gladly receive her into the United States if she should do so of her own volition. Other mines were also laid.

Polk next turned to claims of somewhat less than five million dollars which American citizens had against Mexico for bonds, concessions, and the usual odds and ends that can be easily accumulated for such a purpose. Polk offered to assume these if Mexico would acknowledge the Rio Grande as the southern boundary of Texas, although for a century that boundary had always been the Nueces River. He offered another five million for New Mexico, and stated, like a corporation lawyer building up a merger of competing plants, that "money would be no object" if Mexico would sell us California. Needless to say, no Mexican government could have accepted such an offer and stood for a moment, the very making of it being an insult to the pride of the Mexicans, a quality which the Expansionists felt the Mexicans had no right to possess. Moreover, in spite of the fact that Mexico had declined to receive a "Minister" although she would a "Commissioner," which was diplomatically correct, Polk had insisted on accrediting his representative as Minister. The latter was refused a reception, and Polk at once ordered General Taylor to advance with troops across the Nueces to the Rio Grande. Mexican territory had now been invaded by our armed forces, but even yet she offered to negotiate our differences. Meanwhile, Taylor had attacked the town of Matamoros, and a small body of Mexicans crossed the Rio Grande and had a skirmish with him. A fortnight later, Polk sent a message to Congress asking for a declaration of war on the ground that our patience was exhausted; that Mexico had invaded our territories; and that she had shed American blood on American soil, although the title to the soil was so uncertain that Polk had just offered to pay Mexico five million for it.

War, of course, was declared, and a month later, on June 14, some American settlers in the Sacramento Valley in California raised the flag of revolt and declared their independence. We need not follow the military events of the conquest. In Mexico, under General Scott, there were brilliant operations, and we could take much pride in the feats of our troops had the cause itself been somewhat clearer on the side of justice. On February 2, 1848, by the Treaty of Guadalupe Hidalgo, we agreed to assume the Mexican claims, later adjudicated at only a little over three million dollars, and to pay Mexico an additional fifteen million in exchange roughly for Texas to the Rio Grande, New Mexico, Nevada, Utah, Arizona, California, and a good part of Colorado. Even the plunder of Cortez paled in comparison, and within a few months California was to yield a store of gold the like of which he had never seen even in Aztec treasuries. With slight rectifications along the border, the continental United States had now assumed its present form. Manifest Destiny had taken nearly a quarter of our continental area at a gulp. A few hundred thousand Indians were merely pepper on the meat.

Even before we acquired title in these two years to nearly a third of our present territory, extending from the Gulf to Puget Sound, and embracing everything from the Plains to the Pacific, a considerable American population had already settled in what has come to be called the "Far West." In 1847 the Mormons, after much persecution in the Middle West of Missouri and Illinois, had trekked into the Mexican wilderness and settled around Great Salt Lake, and within a few months five thousand or more had firmly laid the foundations of a new State under Brigham Young. There were also settlements or stray settlers all up and down the Pacific Coast, and from 1846 to 1849 their numbers were rapidly increasing. With the exception of the Mormons, they were of the usual type of pioneers, but late in 1848 the discovery of gold in the mill race on Sutter's ranch near Sacramento altered not only the history of the State but that of the whole nation. The first discovery was made just a week before we acquired title to the El Dorado from Mexico, and there have been few more striking accidents of coincidence. It soon became evident that the deposits here and there as hurriedly investigated were fabulously rich. At once the greatest gold rush in history began, and the "Forty-Niners," as the first-yearmen at once came to be called, have forever taken their place in our picturesque history with the Pilgrim Fathers, the pioneer, and the cowboy. They came from every part of the country, by overland trail, across the Isthmus of Panama, around the Horn. By 1850, California, which three years before had been a foreign State with its Mexican ranch owners, its Spanish missions, and a few scattered American farmers or ranchers, held nearly a hundred thousand Americans and was in a turmoil.

Thus far every American frontier had been settled by agriculturists after the first advance stage of hunters and trappers and Indian traders. Except for the broad distinction between North and South, slave and free, plantation and farm economies, there had been a marked uniformity of social and intellectual life on all of them. In this respect the settlement of California offered a complete contrast. Every type of citizen of every social grade and profession came, not to hew forests, farms, and make homes, but to get rich as quickly as possible by a happy stroke of luck. Clerks, sailors, lawyers, doctors, farmers, even clergymen, everyone who loved adventure or believed in luck, tramped, rode, or sailed to the newest promise in the Land of Promises. On the coast, the crews of almost every vessel that touched there deserted and scrambled to the "diggings." Back East the exodus became a craze. In a few months San Francisco leaped from a few houses to a city of more than twenty thousand, catering to every sort of vice and extravagance. No town could ever have more belied its patron saint!

For the first few years, the feverish life of gold seeking, the recklessness engendered by sudden gain and as sudden loss, the almost complete absence of decent women, all made for a kind of frontier. In 1850 only 2 per cent of the population of the mining counties were women and it is quite uncertain how many of them would have come under our classification of decent. Most of the men had come with no intention of remaining, but had expected to return home as soon as they had made the fortune which they anticipated would inevitably await them. The first year five million dollars in gold was found, and by 1853, the annual amount had risen to about sixty million dollars, after which it began to decline. There was no machinery for maintaining law and order until the Vigilance Committees undertook the work regularly in 1856, the *Alta California*, a San Francisco journal, noting the next year that between the Americans' taking over of the city and the beginning of the Vigilance Committees there had been twelve hundred murders in the place, with only three hangings.

Everyone had gone armed as a matter of course, and a considerable part of the American people had had another taste of taking the law into their own hands.

The discovery of gold had given our newly won possession on the Pacific a start in population which it would have otherwise taken long to get, but gold was not all. After the first fever wore itself out, many stayed and others came because of the attractions of the climate and the business opportunities. "The coast," however, was always to remain differentiated from all other frontiers. Not only was there a much greater mingling there of all types instead of the uniformity of other frontiers, as we have noted, but also it differed in that its sudden population was made up, not for the most part of people who had come from just a little way back, but of those who had come vast distances, and in large part from the Eastern States. Just as there was less uniformity of origin and occupation, so there was less uniformity of thought, and considerably less equalitarianism socially and politically.

In another point also it differed widely. On all other frontiers, capital accumulated very slowly and had to be borrowed from the older settlements. In California, capital was created in the form of gold dug from the ground almost more rapidly than means to employ it could be found. For this reason a different attitude was noticeable there toward wealth and its possessors from the start. There was none of the psychology which has its root in the problem of the absentee capitalist. The climate, the different form of agriculture, and the hundreds of miles of mountain barrier between them and the rest of the United States, tended likewise to emphasize the sectional characteristics.

By 1850 four sections had thus emerged into clear light — the North, the South, the Middle West, and the Far West. We shall consider in the next chapter more particularly the feelings which had been aroused by the annexation of Texas, the Mexican War, the whole problem of slavery and economics, which were rapidly tending to render the sectional differences more dangerous. Here we need only note that in the Far West a capitalistic system and outlook had sprung up almost overnight as part of the very structure of the new society. In the North, industrialism had completely conquered the old agrarianism. In the South, slavery had built up a type of civilization which was quite different from anything in America in 1776. The old Americanism was to be found in the Middle West, which was yet preponderantly the land of the small town, the small farmer, and the pioneer — "folks." To be sure, the lengthening shadows of eastern North and South had crept over the Valley also, but in its upper portion, what we call the "Middle West" to-day, the old American dream lingered because it still had foundation in the economic and social life of the people.

In spite of the deepening shadow creeping over the whole land, we refused to look up from our preoccupations. We were working more feverishly than ever. California gold had given an impetus to every business and created the basis for another great structure of credit. We were getting richer, more numerous, busier every year. Back in the East, Herman Melville had written an American classic, *Moby Dick*, but no one knew or cared what the "White Whale" signified or whether there was any evil in the universe. We preferred Emerson, who apparently neither knew nor much cared, either, and who asked us to be spiritual and cultured, but hopefully looked, like the rest of us, for spirit to evolve somehow from matter, and blessed our railroads to a divine use. But the dark cloud in the American sky grew blacker and was spreading. It assumed fantastic shapes. Was it smoke from the chimney of a Northern factory, or the gigantic image of a negro slave? In a decade the lightning would leap from it with blinding flashes and the thunders echo on a hundred battlefields. Meanwhile, "Ol' Man River" flowed through the great Valley to its portal on the Gulf. The South stretched its plantations from the Atlantic to the Rio Grande. The North could not live without the West, and the Middle West could not live without its outlet on the Gulf. The dark cloud might be reflected on the broad surface of the Mississippi, but "Ol'

Man River" flowed on; and, whatever might happen to paper constitutions, as long as he flowed there must remain eventual unity on the continent. In his mighty arms he held us all.

> Ol' man river, dat ol' man river,
> He must know sumpin', but don't say nothin',
> He just keeps rollin',
> He keeps on rollin' along.[1]

[1] Copyright 1927 by T. B. Harms Co., N. Y. (Reproduced by special permission of the copyright owners.)

IX

BROTHERS' BLOOD

THERE have always been two opposing forces operating on American life and character. Just as democracy stresses the value of the individual human being yet tends to equalize the economic and social status of all, so we saw in the last chapter that, in spite of the strong individualism generated on the frontier, the State builders found they had to rely upon the coöperation of all to give the individual his largest opportunity of profit and happiness. In order that the individual might prosper, he found it needful to enforce a certain uniformity of effort and outlook on all the other individuals. The same opposition of forces and ideals has always been present in our political philosophy. The Declaration of Independence had announced to the world, not that "these united colonies are, and of right ought to be," a free and independent Nation, but "free and independent *States*." When the old Confederation proved too loose a bond to serve any useful purpose, our Federal Constitution was adopted, tightening up the Union; but, like all compromise documents, it left many points untouched for a more convenient time. Whether a "Sovereign State" was superior or inferior to the Federal government was one of these points, carefully dodged by the Fathers.

The vast westward expansion had operated in the usual double way. It had put an increasing strain on the Constitution and yet was to prove at the most critical point in our history the chief unifying force. The original thirteen States had been sovereign and independent before the United States came into being. There was no doubt about that. Texas had also been so when admitted to the Union. All the rest were clearly the creatures of Congress, although they were admitted with all the rights of the original States. Had we not secured, in all the varied ways we did, the Western domain beyond the Appalachian Mountains, our constitutional and other problems would have been much simpler, and probably our life as a Federal State much briefer. The Sovereign States which had united would have felt comparatively free to withdraw, and although it might have been inconvenient or unwise for a single one to do so alone, yet when so complete a division of interest appeared as between North and South by 1860, a break-up would have been comparatively simple and almost inevitable. The problem, however, was enormously increased by the presence of the West. Practically all the territory across the Appalachian Mountains had been acquired by the *United States*. It was a vast property in common, and if constitutional questions with regard to it were, more than once, nearly to wreck the Union, it was the unifying influence of the Great Valley which was at the last to save it.

The Constitution was silent as to any powers to acquire foreign territory, and, if acquired, as to how to administer it. When Jefferson had been confronted with the need for instant decision as to whether to take the Louisiana Territory when offered or lose it for the nation, he took it, but believing the action to be unconstitutional, and with the expectation that an amendment to the Constitution would be made validating it. None ever was, and John Quincy Adams was equally convinced that we had no constitutional right whatever to incorporate within our government a foreign sovereign State such as Texas. Both statesmen, and those who believed with them, would appear to have been right, unless the wording of the Constitution may be so stretched as to cover anything under Heaven desired by us. Our general theory as to how new and unorganized territory should be developed into States was, as I pointed out earlier, a very wise one, but, as it was wholly extra-constitutional, there were plenty of dangerous *lacunæ* in it.

By the 1840's the question of slavery was arousing more and more bitter feelings between the sections. The agitation by the Abolitionists in the North, the attempt of the Southern members in Congress, by voting against receiving petitions relating to slavery, to abrogate the right of petition guaranteed to citizens in the Constitution, and other factors had roused passion on both sides. By a large party in the North the annexation of Texas and the subsequent war with Mexico had been visualized solely as an attempt on the part of the South to extend slave territory in the Union. Since the Missouri Compromise of 1820, which had prohibited slavery north of 36° 30′, statesmen in all sections had made heroic efforts to keep the question settled, but it was fast getting out of their hands.

The war with Mexico over, and the loot safely lodged in the Union, the usual question of its administration came up. Polk wished wisely that the old line of 36°30′ simply be run westward and no questions raised, but a Pennsylvanian Representative in Congress, David Wilmot, thought otherwise and in time precipitated a crisis. The insatiable Polk was trying to get through Congress a bill to buy a small additional strip from Mexico, and to this Wilmot tried again to insert a provision to the effect that slavery should never exist in territory acquired from Mexico. As the territory was far to the south of the dead line, the Southern members at once, and quite naturally, launched a savage debate. "Wilmot's Proviso," as it was called, was utterly unnecessary and was merely a match tossed into the combustible situation. Never passed, its importance was in reopening the whole question of the powers which Congress possessed over territories, the bitterness of the previous few years now leading the South to make the new claim that there was not only no right to prohibit slavery, but, quite to the contrary, a moral duty to protect it as a property right. The fat was in the fire.

As the months passed, feelings became more embittered. Little by little the cords which had bound North and South together had been breaking under the strain of the Northern attack on slavery and the Southern defense of it. Three of the great church denominations had already split into independent Northern and Southern bodies. The Congress which met in December 1849 was so bitterly factional that sixty-three ballots had to be taken to elect a Speaker in the House. Three of the elder statesmen, worn out by age, were yet present — Webster, Calhoun, and Clay. They came at the end of their years and strength to take their parts in the great debate to save the Union. California had already written freedom into her new constitution, and in any case neither the soil, the climate, nor the occupations of that State or of New Mexico were adapted to any large extension of slavery. But just as the North had been led to believe that in the war the South had planned to extend slavery, so the South had come to feel that the North was trying to extend freedom into slave territory. Secession was being openly talked, as it always had been whenever any section had become disgruntled. The difference was that passions were higher and the threat meant more now. It was clear that secession would mean war. "Peaceable secession!" thundered Webster, old and emaciated as he was. "Sir, your eyes and mine are never destined to see that miracle. The dismemberment of this vast country without convulsion! The breaking up of the fountains of the great deep without ruffling the surface!"

If it was the representative of New England who provided the eloquence, somewhat ponderous as ever, it was the representative of the West who provided the constructive thought. Clay submitted certain measures as a new compromise, the most important being the admission of California as a free State, the organization of New Mexico and Utah as territories without mention of the question, and the passage of a more stringent fugitive-slave law. New England would not have followed the Westerner, but it did follow its own leader, now, however, no longer recognized as such by many in view of his advocacy of the right of the Southerner to pursue his runaway slave into Northern territory. Whittier, an ardent antislavery man, expressed the feeling of a multitude when he wrote: —

> So fallen! so lost! the light withdrawn
> Which once he wore!
> The glory from his gray hairs gone
> Forevermore! . . .
> Of all we loved and honored, naught
> Save power remains, —
> A fallen angel's pride of thought,
> Still strong in chains. . . .
> Then, pay the reverence of old days
> To his dead fame;
> Walk backward, with averted gaze,
> And hide the shame!

Clay, Calhoun, and Webster all died within two years, but, in spite of the Northern inability to swallow the Fugitive-Slave Law, the new compromise of 1850 was to hold the shaking structure of the Union together for another decade, just long enough to ensure that even war could not destroy its permanence. The West had saved us with its new compromise.

Meanwhile the country was extremely prosperous in all sections, and speculation was rife. The injection of the enormous amounts of gold from California would in any case have brought about business activity, but in addition the Crimean War in Europe helped to provide an increased market for our farm products abroad, in which both South and West shared. As usual, also, our population increases, so unlike the slow advances in the Old World, provided rapidly expanding markets for products, and rising prices for real estate. Chicago, for example, jumped from less than 30,000 inhabitants in 1850 to almost 110,000 in 1860. Furiously as the future could be discounted, however, we over-discounted it, according to our sanguine custom, and with the close of the European war came the periodic panic in 1857. The newly invented telegraph assisted the process by instantaneously spreading every piece of bad news everywhere at once. Though not so severe as that of 1837, the crisis was bad, and, as on previous occasions, it started a shift in population toward the West. In a long-settled and fully populated country, there is little for the people to do in a financial or agricultural crisis but remain and suffer where they and their ancestors have lived. In America, on the other hand, such a period has served to set a considerable part of the population on the march to unsettled regions. Such crises have been like pulsations of a vast heart, pumping inhabitants into our unpeopled spaces.

In the course of our narrative, we have now noted many waves of immigration and migration and seen many frontiers, from those of Jamestown and Plymouth to those of Illinois and California. We have seen enough, perhaps, to hazard another generalization. In this matter of migration there were double and opposing forces at work, as in so many other spheres of our national life. We naturally like to stress the courage, hard work, and ability of our empire builders. It is well that we do. But, on the other hand, we cannot fully understand our own national mind and character if we do not ponder the other side of the coin. Almost every man who has migrated from Europe to America, from old settlement to newer, from East to West, has, at the same time that he has shown the qualities noted above, shown also a certain lack of courage when he decided that things had got too much for him "at home" and that he could no longer remain, that he could not fight through to success where he was. The Pilgrim and Puritan leaders who came to America, for example, were but a handful of those in England. Those who migrated preferred the physical discomforts, but political and religious simplifications, of the wilderness to their native land and its insistent problems. We think of them as strong men, but it may be questioned whether those who remained in England, faced the conditions, including possible martyrdom, and fought the Stuart tyranny to a successful finish, were not the stronger. Without indulging in any finespun discussion of that point, I think there can be no doubt that the frontier has always presented a simpler set of social and economic problems for the individual to solve than the more complex ones of the older countries or older American settlements. It was the man who was baffled in the face of such complexities, who could not adjust himself to them, who preferred to substitute for them the simpler conditions of a frontier society even at the expense of physical risk and discomfort, who became more or less the typical American from the days of John Winthrop on. This tendency thus present in millions of individuals and in migration after migration has possibly fostered in us a preference for slipping out from under a situation when it becomes too complex rather than thinking it and fighting it through. It would be a natural result.

Two other psychological traits would naturally flow from such constant emigration away from places where conditions had become too much for the individual to contend with. The fact that the emigrant had been oppressed or made to accept an inferior position in the society from which he removed, whether as a religious protester or merely an economic failure, would tend to make him assert himself all the more when he reached a society in which the weights were taken off his free self-expression. The absurd egotism of the New Englanders, their belief in their own vast superiority, their cruel persecution of those who differed from them, may easily have sprung from such a psychological root, as have also the hoodlumism and utter lack of self-restraint shown by many later comers of another hatching. The Puritan who believed himself the elect of God and lawgiver for mankind, and the Irish policeman who swung his club and puffed out his chest, were both victims of the same psychological reaction on passing from conditions where the ego was squeezed to others in which it could blow up like a balloon. The oppressed or the failures who suddenly rise to power or success are much more apt to feel their own importance and inflict their own views on others than those who have always sat in the seats of the mighty.

Another psychological trait has also resulted from our conditions. The fact that possibly the great majority of Americans have suffered from maladjustment, lack of success, or even actual oppression and tyranny, whether in the lands of the Old World or the older settlements of our own, has caused them to develop a remarkable feeling of sympathy for the "under dog" of any sort, economic, political, social. Lying deep in our subconsciousness, this usually comes to the surface as emotion, and has appeared many times. In international relations it has colored our feelings with regard, among others, to Greeks, Hungarians, Irish, Cubans, and the natives of India, not always intelligently or wisely or with knowledge of the facts. It has colored our attitude toward criminals and politicians. It is a trait which domestic statesmen do, and foreign ones ought to, reckon with. It is an instinctive reaction, not a reasoned position, and derives straight from the life history of millions of individuals. At any moment it may appear against a foreign nation thought guilty of oppression, against politicians who attack a rival too ruthlessly, against the money power or others considered too privileged. On the other hand, because it belongs to our unconscious and is not the product of a trained intelligence or of morality, because it belongs to the realm of emotion and desire, it cannot be counted upon when in conflict with other emotions or desires, as has been exemplified in the case of our treatment of our own Indians. The plight of the red man, for example, left the Abolitionists cold, though they were willing to pull down the whole fabric of America, if need be, to free the black man.

The lack of employment following the panic of 1857 would have loosened a considerable part of the American population from its moorings and blown them westward in any case, but as it happened, with our proverbial luck, the year after the panic wrought its havoc, gold was discovered in Colorado, and a rush started comparable only to that for California. As compared with the diggings of the Pacific Coast, Colorado was easy to reach, and in the spring of 1859 the Missouri River from Independence to Council Bluffs was lined with the camps of the gold seekers. The general cry was "Pike's Peak or Bust," and many attained to both destinations successively or simultaneously. They crossed the plains in covered wagons, carriages, on horseback, and even on foot, pushing their baggage ahead of them in light carts. In two years there were nearly thirty-five thousand persons in Colorado, and Denver was a prosperous city. The West had jumped across seven hundred miles of the American Desert and a new frontier had come into being to impress again on more Americans those characteristics stamped by all the big and little frontiers that had been coming into existence for two and a half centuries.

As one studies our history from the standpoint of influences and not of politicians, one is impressed again and again not only by the double influences always at work, some of which we have spoken of, but by the fact that so often what has promised to be poison has contained its own antidote. The acquisition of the Mexican West was threatening the existence of the Union. But out of that acquisition had come unexpectedly and at once several hundred million dollars in gold. That gold gave a great impetus, among other things, to building railways, and when civil war at last came, and the South counted on the West joining with it on account of their being bound together by the arms of "Ol' Man River" and an outlet on the Gulf, it was the newly completed railways between West and North that enabled those sections to hold together, instead of South and West. The river did indeed make a geographic and national unity of the great Valley. The West could not afford to see the lower half in foreign hands. She would insist on unity at any cost. Had there been no railroads to carry her produce to the East, she might have had to accept unwelcome secession to achieve unity. As it was, they had come just in time, owing to the gold, to enable her to survive, to join the North, and to achieve valley unity through war instead of scission. In 1849, there were no railways of importance in the West. By 1860, the northern West had nearly one third of the 30,000 miles in the whole country, and was not only covered with a network that made marketing of produce easy, but also well connected by trunk lines with the East. Had the West joined the South, the break-up of the nation would have been inevitable. As it was, the railways made it possible for the West to join the North, which it preferred to do in opposition to slavery. Once joined to the North, however, coercion of the South became vital, owing to the essential unity of our great valley. The line of 36° 30′ might divide two civilizations fairly, but "Ol' Man River" held them both and would not let them go.

The theory of that line, however, was fast breaking down. California had been admitted as a free State, and half of it lay to the south of the sacrosanct division between slave and free. New Mexico and Arizona, which would probably both be free, lay almost wholly to the south of the line. By the time of the Clay Compromise of 1850, all of the national domain had been organized into States or Territories except the great Indian preserve which ran from Texas to Canada and from the Missouri border to the Rocky Mountains. Railroad building had been so stimulated by California gold and generous land grants by the Federal government that the question of a transcontinental line was being actively discussed. If it did not cross the Indian preserve, sacredly guaranteed by the government, it would have to pass through Texas and be wholly a Southern line, which the North would by no means agree to. Already the Santa Fé Trail, the Oregon Trail, the settlers of Utah and Colorado, had made havoc of the theory of the sanctity of our treaties with the natives. They were doomed, and we need not enter upon the many details of the final act of the tragedy. From the days when an occasional savage had seen a sail from one point or another on the coast, and fought or welcomed the first settlers, the red men had been steadily pushed back until they were all herded together in the interior of the continent for the last stand. That was marked by broken treaties and open war, but was hopeless from the start.

Caring nothing for the red man, but desirous of permitting a transcontinental railroad to be built from Chicago across the middle of the West, in 1854 Senator Douglas of Illinois tried to push a bill through Congress organizing the central part of the Indian country into a new Federal Territory under the name of Kansas, without excluding slavery from it, just as Congress had not insisted upon Utah or New Mexico being either slave or free. He soon changed his plan so as to provide for two Territories, Kansas and Nebraska, thus making it possible to give one State each to the North and South should their inhabitants decide differently on the slave question. The two were to include the whole of the Indian country except that part which is now Oklahoma. Douglas and the North wanted a Northern transcontinental railway, and he was willing to pay the price to the South — a vast increase in territory in the North open to slavery.

The bill passed on May 25, 1854. The Missouri Compromise had been definitely repealed. Five months later Abraham Lincoln was telling the nation in his speech at Peoria that, although he did not question the constitutional right of the Southerners to hold their slaves in the South, and knew nothing else for them to do under the existing conditions, yet "slavery is founded on the selfishness of man's nature — opposition to it on his love of justice. These principles are in eternal antagonism, and when brought into collision so fiercely as slavery extension brings them, shocks and throes and convulsions must ceaselessly follow." The price we paid for our projected transcontinental railway was broken faith with our savage wards and a nation drenched in blood. Douglas was a mere unconscious link in the endless chain of destiny. The witches' cauldron had long been brewing, and more ingredients than we can analyze had gone into the unholy broth which we were all, North and South, West and Far West, to be forced to drink.

Douglas and his group may have been willing to pay the price to the South, but the North as a whole was not. The debates in Congress had been bitter and had disclosed the depth of feeling on both sides. The North had just been indulging in an orgy of fanaticism against foreigners and Catholics, but the threat to extend slavery threw all minor crusades into the discard. A new political party with an old name, Republican, was formed, and its first platform announced that it was "both the right and duty" of Congress to prohibit slavery and polygamy in the Territories, the latter prohibition, of course, being directed against the Mormons in Utah, who had horrified America and rather bored themselves with a plurality of legal, and legally supported, wives. Frémont, the inadequate candidate of the new party, carried most of the North and West, but Buchanan, Democrat, carried the South and won the election.

Meanwhile, a wholly new sort of frontier was being formed in Kansas. Backed by the Abolitionists and the Emigrant Aid, among other societies, settlers were sent into the new Territory with Bibles and breechloaders, not to make homes, hunt for gold, or raise hogs, but to vote the Territory on the side of freedom and non-slavery. Slave owners did not care to settle without their slaves, and as the blacks were both valuable and volatile property, they did not care to risk them to any extent in the bullet-laden air of the new Territory. They did, however, with their own rifles, ride over from Missouri on election days to stuff the ballot boxes. Frequent clashes occurred with these "border ruffians," as they were called, and more attention was paid to bullets and ballots than to tilling the soil. Nor was all the blood for "bleeding Kansas" shed out there. Senator Sumner of Massachusetts in the Senate at Washington proved himself an ardent partisan, but not a gentleman, in a violent speech on the "Crime against Kansas," and was beaten into insensibility by Preston Brooks of South Carolina, who thus proved the same things of himself. The temperature of the nation had risen to the fever point. A year later, in March 1857, the Supreme Court, in the Dred Scott case, declared that a negro could not be a citizen of the United States and that Congress, without due process of law, could not deprive a citizen of his property — that is, of slaves. Meanwhile the Senate had accepted a constitution for Kansas, rejected by a majority of its citizens, making slavery legal. The South was winning only to lose.

In October 1859, the fanatic John Brown of Kansas, with a following of eighteen men, of whom five were negroes, and in pursuance of an utterly fantastic plan of making war on slavery, seized the Federal arsenal at Harper's Ferry, Virginia, and took some of the townspeople prisoners. The old man's striking physical dignity and impressiveness, as well as his courage when captured and hung, won him admiration among those in the North whose hearts were stronger than their heads. The conflict was coming to the country rapidly enough without such melodrama, and the South could not fail to be yet more embittered by the sight of arms being put into the hands of negroes. The possibility of a slave rising and of a massacre of the whites, such as had occurred in Hayti, was ever in the minds of the slave owners, responsible for the lives of their women and children on widely separated plantations, and Brown's armed advance into the South with blacks in his party was as cruelly insensate as it was childish. Perhaps no man in American history less deserves the pedestal of heroism on which he has been raised, but the North at once enshrined him as a saint, and more than ever convinced the South that there could be no peaceful solution of the conflict between the two civilizations unless it might be found in an unopposed secession.

Meanwhile, in 1858, Lincoln had opposed Douglas in the race for the Senatorship from Illinois. On the night of his nomination, in words now familiar to every American, he had placed the issue squarely before the nation. "A house divided against itself cannot stand," Lincoln paraphrased from Saint Mark, and then continued: "I believe this government cannot endure permanently half slave and half free. I do not expect the Union to be dissolved — I do not expect the house to fall — but I do expect it will cease to be divided. It will become all one thing, or all the other. Either the opponents of slavery will arrest the further spread of it, and place it where the public mind shall rest in the belief that it is in the course of ultimate extinction; or its advocates will push it forward till it shall become alike lawful in all the States, old as well as new, North as well as South." Lincoln, speaking in the name of his party, claimed that slavery was a moral wrong, though he had no intention of interfering with it in the South, trusting to its gradual disappearance there. Douglas claimed that the morality of the question was no one's business, and that each State should determine its status for itself. He won the election.

In fact, there was little likelihood of any further extension of slavery in American territory, owing to soil and climate. Both sides, however, were losing their heads. The North saw the South trying to reintroduce the slave trade and extend conquest to the southward in the West Indies, while insisting on bringing its black property into the North or making the Northerners capture its slaves for it if they escaped thither. The South saw its institution, and more than half of its total property, being threatened. It declared that it would not submit if the Republican Party won the presidential election of 1860, as, in spite of Lincoln's defeat, it had won the Congressional elections of 1858.

The Republicans did win, with Abraham Lincoln as candidate for President. The Democratic Party, which has never been able to carry the country except by combining South and West, had been split into two by the slavery problem, and neither wing had a chance against the new Republicans, who carried every free State, though polling scarcely a vote in the South. The curtain had now been rung up for the central act of the great tragedy. The sharp geographic delimitation of the party votes showed the completeness with which the Northern and Southern sectionalism had finally worked itself out. It was known with practical certainty that the election of Lincoln meant the secession of South Carolina, probably to be followed by at least a number of other Southern States.

What was the real cause, or causes, of the angry, seething emotions which had steadily mounted throughout the nation as the sectionalism became more and more pronounced? The older historians would have replied at once, "Slavery." A wiser and a broader view is now coming to be accepted, although our latest historian, with more of the closet scholar than the statesman on this particular point, goes back to the older view because he finds little but slavery mentioned in the "documents" of the crisis. We surely know, however, that avowed reasons or political battle cries usually simplify, even if they do not conceal, the real complex of influences in a given struggle. There is, of course, no doubt that slavery was in everyone's mind, and that it made the best concentration point for all the vague and emotional substratum of the sectionalism which had now become deadly. The mere abstract morality of slavery, however, would not alone have been adequate to plunge the nation into war.

Perhaps, as we have suggested before, our present situation in regard to the Prohibition Amendment will help our own generation to understand, in much milder form, the complex that lay behind disunion in 1860. We are not split in America to-day solely on the morality of taking a drink which contains alcohol. Mixed with that are questions of social welfare, of economics, of entrenched interests, of class distinction in legislation, of urban against rural communities, of personal liberty, of the real function of a Federal constitution, of the right of one section of the people to coerce another at least almost equally large, of the conflict of different outlooks on life, of different ways of life. To a considerable extent the opposing parties to-day are inextricably mixed throughout the land, drinking as a social custom and a habit not being delimited by soil or climate. If it were, the conflict would be much more sharply defined by having geographic boundaries.

From the beginning of settlement in America, soil and climate *had* fostered a fairly sharp sectionalism of social and economic life.

It was not simply that slavery, which had been universal, had proved economically unprofitable among the Puritans and to a considerable extent in the Middle Colonies, and thus became chiefly confined to the South. It was that, because of differences in soil and climate, a wholly different sort of life developed in the agrarian South of large plantations from that which developed in the industrial North. The South was not all made up of the Southern gentlemen of legend and of fact any more than the North was all made up of Concord sages. There were many sorts of people in both sections, but in the

South they had all pretty much developed a love for a more or less easy-going country life with habits and values of its own, and disliked, even when they did not despise, the hustling, shrewd, business type of men in the North. There, on the other hand, the people looked down on the Southern type, which they could not and did not try to understand.

The slave was the working capital of the Southerner, it is true, just as cash and credit were the working capital of the Northerner, and the attack of the Abolitionists on the morality of holding slaves as property aroused as much anger in the South as a similar widespread propaganda in the South for the confiscation of Northern bank accounts would have raised in the North. But beyond that the Southerner grew increasingly resentful at having his whole way of life attacked by another section, just as many of us to-day are deeply resentful at being coerced in what we shall drink and how we shall entertain, by a portion of the nation which, whether rightfully or not, we consider bigoted and narrow-minded, and in many cases motivated by false ideals and mercenary desires. We object to being told that we cannot judge the morality of our own acts and that we must guide our conduct by the standards of fanatics enacted into Federal laws. The South had always stood for a strict construction of the Constitution, and in its interpretation of that instrument it had quite as good an argument as the North, if not better. To avoid controversy and possible failure to ratify, the Fathers who drafted it had purposely left it ambiguous. According to the Southerners' interpretation of it, not only had their property in slaves been guaranteed, but the Constitution was now being used to threaten their whole way of life, whereas for the most part, for a half century and more, Supreme Court decisions had been modifying it so as steadily to strengthen the Northerners in possession of *their* particular form of property and capitalism.

By 1859, owing to the admission of new States, there had come to be eighteen free against only fifteen slave States, so that the South had become a minority party in both houses of Congress. It was easy for the Abolitionists to shout for immediate emancipation of all slaves, but it was not so easy to say how it could be done, any more than it is easy to-day to clean off the stark and damnable injustices of our present industrial régime. Even Lincoln said that he did not blame the Southerners "for not doing what I should not know how to do myself. If all earthly power were given me, I should not know what to do as to the existing institution." At the Peace Conference of Versailles, America stood firmly for the self-determination of racial and cultural groups, even when it involved absurd national boundaries. The South was a geographic, economic, and social unity. If ever there was a case for self-determination, it might seem as though that section had had a perfect one. After a generation and more of constant attack and of decreasing spiritual unity in the nation, the election of 1860 left the South in the absolute political power of a party which was solely Northern. It is not difficult to see why a large part of the Southern people could see nothing left but peaceable secession.

On the other hand, influences had also been at work in the North. The Abolitionists had long been preaching their moral crusade against slavery with more bitterness than that of the Anti-Saloon League against alcohol in our time. They had denounced the union with the South as a league with Hell, and worked to destroy the Union. Men of another type, like James Russell Lowell, who had believed that the Mexican War was merely a plot of the South to extend slave territory, had increased the feeling against that section by talk and writing. He had ended the first of his enormously popular *Biglow Papers* with

> Ef I 'd *my* way I hed ruther
>   We should go to work an' part,
> They take one way, we take t' other,
>   Guess it would n't break my heart;
> Man hed ough' to put asunder
>   Them thet God has noways jined;
> An' I should n't gretly wonder
>   Ef there 's thousands o' my mind.

At any rate, Massachusetts agitators and men of letters had done their best to see that there should be thousands, and tens of thousands, of their mind. Massachusetts has occupied a singular position in our national history. Settled some years after Virginia had shown that colonizing was practicable, and always the heart of New England, Massachusetts contributed some of the best and some of the worst streams of influence to our national development and character. Unfortunately one of the latter was fanaticism and intolerance, and it was in Massachusetts that Abolitionism had its strongest hold. The Puritan spirit, noble as it was in many aspects, became an uncompromising, fanatical, and dogmatic one. The men of that State have never taken much trouble to understand the point of view of other sections of the country, even when they have known it at all, and have seldom questioned their own. It is significant that Massachusetts has given but two Presidents to the United States, both over a century ago, and that both of them failed of reëlection, despite their sterling character. That this State, and all New England, would take an unyielding attitude on the slavery question, in so far as it appealed to her moral and fanatical inhabitants, was a foregone conclusion, even although they had no solution to offer. Throughout the whole North and West, moreover, the lover of liberty and the underdog complex could be easily played upon, as it was by *Uncle Tom's Cabin.*

But more than these factors were needed also. If the Southerner had not liked the sneers of the Northerner, neither did the small Northern farmer or shopkeeper, clerk or laborer, like the sneers of the Southerner against those who developed the traits of an industrial civilization. The old antagonism of the townsman and the countryman is as old as towns themselves. It runs through all literature and history. It reappears in highly intensified form between industrial and agrarian types of culture, just as it has cropped out again and again between East and West, and is involved to-day between Occident and Orient. Moreover, Republican orators played on the racial and economic fears of the Northern laborers and mechanics, asking how they could expect two dollars a day when Southerners spent but ten cents a day on their slaves. Of course, this was sheer bunkum. One of the chief economic disadvantages of slavery was its costliness and waste. The orators took no account of the fifteen hundred to twenty-five hundred dollars that a slave cost to buy, of the possibility of his death, of the need of keeping him in sickness, off seasons, dull years, of the need of feeding, clothing, physicking him, or of his inefficiency. But the fear served. The Northerner had no love for the negro, who in many ways was treated worse in the North than in the South, even that trouble maker for the South, the free negro, having a better chance to rise above the laborer class in, say, Louisiana than in New York or Connecticut. But the Northern laborer came to fear slave competition.

The fact was that within our political and geographic unity we had been developing two contrasted and antagonistic types of civilization, while at the same time many and powerful factors were dictating that there must be uniformity of conditions and outlook. The railroads, telegraph, increasing mobility of population, easy transportation, interchange of goods and ideas — these and many other factors were binding the lives of individuals closer together. What each section did and thought was of necessity more and more affecting the others. Just as we have seen that even on the individualistic frontier a uniformity of life, desires, and aspirations came to be unconsciously enforced because it spelled greater prosperity for all, so this same more or less unconscious forcing of uniformity came to be felt in national life. In two respects the North was in the line in which the world was moving, away from human "slavery," but toward the exploitation of men and women in highly industrialized communities.

The conflict between North and South, like the American Revolution, had to be rationalized. Just as we can see now that it was not any single item, like taxation without representation, which wrought the Revolution out of a situation that evolved from wholly differing attitudes toward life on the two sides of the water, so it was not simply the moral question of slavery that had been carrying North and South toward the brink of disaster for fifty years. But the whole situation had to be simplified and rationalized, as we have said, and it was characteristic of the North, and especially of New England as the centre of the rationalizing process, that the whole stress should be laid on a single issue which could be moralized. The average Northern workman cared a good deal more about the negro as a competitor than he did about him as a being in God's image who was entitled to life, liberty, and the pursuit of happiness. There was precious little that a negro could do in the way of pursuing happiness in most Northern communities, as Connecticut could bear witness.

The Republican Convention which met at Chicago in May 1860, and nominated Lincoln, had drafted a platform which announced that there should be no extension of slavery allowed into new territory, but neither should there be any interference with it in the slave States. But the Convention was not only being held in the West. It was full of Westerners who had ideas of their own. Illinois and some other Western communities were not so keen on the slavery question as were certain of the Easterners. If a good many people out there did not see why men, even if black, should be made slaves to Southern capitalists, neither did they see why they themselves should be made slaves to Eastern capitalists who made freight and interest rates, and controlled railways and banks. The small West of 1819 had learned hatred of financiers; the larger West of 1837 had had the lesson rubbed in; the West of 1860 had just passed through the panic of 1857. The plain people had risen against the Hamiltonian capitalists when they elected Thomas Jefferson in 1800; they had frightened them out of their lives when they had elected General Jackson in 1828 and destroyed the United States Bank as a result; and they had no intention now, with the panic only three years past and the mortgages still cawing on their roofs, of nominating Governor Seward of New York and the capitalistic East as President. There might be slaves in the South, but were not the capitalists doing their best to make slaves of white men?

Had they not driven good Americans out of our merchant marine? Had they not to a great extent driven them out of our factories? Were they not asking Western farmers to pay high tolls and impossible debts? Were they not beating down Americans with the club of cheap foreign labor and "black lists"? They would take a foreigner without any recommendation, but not an American unless his last employer allowed it. Were they not even going so far, back East, as to give a discharged or voluntarily quitting workman a card, when they saw fit, on which was written that he had "liberty to work elsewhere"? What was America coming to when the "liberty to work" was dependent on the nod of a factory manager? What of the American dream?

Successive migrations, much hard work, no money, and a general social level which raised few men of culture above the mass of plain men and women were not doing the West any good intellectually, to put it mildly. It was not without reason that even the thinking required to be a good Presbyterian had for the most part long been abandoned for the less arduous reactions to emotion of the Baptist and Methodist. But the West feared, and not without cause, the smooth, polished, and mercenary East, as it envisaged it. So the West crashed the gates of the Convention and nominated its own son, Abraham Lincoln, for President, to the bewilderment and horror of Boston, New York, and all points East, which saw in the possible President only a gaunt, coarse, uneducated backwoodsman with no qualifications whatever for high office. The Eastern delegates had gone to Chicago as a matter of form to go through the routine of nominating Seward. They went home with Lincoln. He was as yet a Lincoln comparatively unknown and not yet formed by four years of the heaviest responsibilities and decisions that have ever fallen to the lot of any of our Chief Executives.

Some weeks after the election, the legislature of South Carolina, on December 20, 1860, passed the anticipated formal resolution of secession, unanimously declaring that the union with the United States of America was dissolved. Georgia,

Alabama, Florida, Mississippi, Louisiana, and Texas followed in quick succession, and at Montgomery, Alabama, on February 9, 1861, Jefferson Davis was chosen President of the newly formed Confederate States of America in the convention being held there, scarcely three weeks before Lincoln was inaugurated at Washington. Virginia joined the Confederacy in April, as did Arkansas, Tennessee, and North Carolina in May. The roll of secession was then complete.

Secession, as we have pointed out, had been threatened from one section or another in every decade since the Constitution had been adopted in 1787, just as husband and wife might quarrel and frequently tell one another they cannot stand marriage any longer. Life, however, springs from organic growth and not from documents and contracts. Many a husband and wife, thinking in terms of a legally breakable contractual relation, have awakened to the fact that their union has been made real and unbreakable by a thousand subtle bonds and ties which had been weaving their chain unnoticed. So with secession. As a matter of constitutional interpretation it might or might not be legal, but when it was being faced as an immediate possibility and reality, many awoke to the fact that, whatever quarrels there might be, a thousand subtle ties had made the Sovereign States an indissoluble nation.

There was no longer any question of a written Constitution. We had been quibbling over the interpretation of that for nearly three generations. There was something much more binding — a deep and passionate sentiment of devotion to the Union. Northern Abolitionists might shout until they died that slavery was so foul a stain as to call for the break-up of the nation. Second-rate poets like Lowell might prattle about what God had not joined together. Business men might cast up figures to discover whether a national market was worth a war. But when, on April 12, the South Carolinians fired on Fort Sumter and the following day the Stars and Stripes fluttered down from the masthead in surrender, all such sophistries were swept away in one vast wave of emotion.

Millions of plain men and women, neither poets nor fanatics nor capitalists, men and women of factory and shop and farm, as well as those of birth and breeding and luxurious homes, suddenly realized that deep in their hearts an abstraction and a symbol — Union and the flag — possessed a moving power of which they had not dreamed. The rules of government had been ambiguously laid down in a written document, but a nation had been formed in the silent hearts of its citizens.

Nor was Union sentiment confined to the North and West. The situation was confused on both sides of the old Mason and Dixon's line. There were plenty of hot-heads in the South, as there were in the North, who welcomed secession for its own sake; but many there also felt as did Robert E. Lee when he wrote his son, "I can contemplate no greater calamity for the country than a dissolution of the Union," and yet felt that, the situation having reached the point it had, there was nothing for them to do but sorrowfully to take the side of friends and relatives, of all they had known and all they had held dear. Many did so believing that the only way out was to leave the shelter of that Union from which they were being driven by the blind bigotry of a North which, in its industrial development, had grown away from the old "live and let live" of the Constitution; which now threatened the property of the South, denounced its standards of morality, and was seemingly insanely anxious to create a uniformity of thought and life throughout the whole length and breadth of our great land. The South, too, had loved the Stars and Stripes. It had taken more than its full part in the first founding of the nation. The earliest successful settlement had been on its shores, not on those of New England. The man on whom the success of the Revolution had finally depended had been a Southern slave owner, and had been the first President. In the drafting of the Constitution and the statesmanship of the early Republic, no names had shone brighter than Jefferson, Madison, and Marshall, all Southerners and slave owners. The South felt that *it* had not changed, but that the North had, and that the North was now trying to use its new power of numbers and capital and industrialism to coerce the South into serving as its vassal in modes of thought and life. The parting of the ways had been reached.

There were no large cities in the South, centres of intellectual ferment and influence. In spite of wealth in land and slaves, there had for long been little free capital. There were no colleges to compare in numbers and opportunities with those in the North. Scattered throughout the Southern States were charming homes, where social intercourse was a fine art and where men and women had grace and learning. But little by little the section had been drifting backward in a rapidly moving world. It is too early yet to measure the forces of the nineteenth century in terms of spiritual value, but democracy and the Industrial Revolution were creating a new world, in which we have not even yet found our way, but in which slavery had become an anachronism. No practical way of doing without slaves in the South had been suggested; and confronted with the ruin of its peculiar type of civilization, or with the need for defending it morally and intellectually, the South had for some decades been forced to spend its energies on such defense, and had suffered in consequence. It had got out of touch with the thought of the growing world. It did not realize the strength of the forces dooming slavery everywhere, nor of those building the sense of nationality. It claimed the right not to change, the right to continue to live its own life in its own way. But that was precisely what the magnitude of the blind forces of our modern world do not permit. Like the rest of us, individuals, nations, civilizations, the South was caught in the grip of forces which neither it nor we can understand or control.

Not realizing the force of nationalism, the South hoped for a peaceable secession. Thinking in terms of boats and "Ol' Man River," she thought the West would join her because of the outlet to the Gulf, not understanding the part that the new railways would play. Not realizing, on the one hand, the temporarily overstocked condition of the cotton market in Europe, or, on the other, the strength of the sentiment for democracy and freedom among the cotton-mill operatives of England, she thought that Cotton was King, and that, if it came to war, England and the rest of Europe would have to acknowledge her independence and come to her aid. So, with no industrial organization, with negligible financial resources in cash and credit and banking institutions, her five or six million whites found themselves at last facing in war nearly twenty million in the North and West. The necessity for looking backward and spending their whole energy in defense of the anachronism of slavery had prevented her statesmen from attaining the stature of those of her great period, — who had eagerly looked forward, — and from studying with an open and unbiased mind the forces which were becoming dominant. Yet she felt that she had law and right upon her side. National unity was a sentiment, not a constitutional obligation, and surely, she argued, six million people with a civilization and ideals of their own, inhabiting a clearly delimited territory, should not be coerced and held in permanent subjection by mere weight of numbers among their foes. And so they fired on Fort Sumter, and the Stars and Stripes fluttered down, like a wounded bird.

That was in April 1861. It is not part of the plan of this book to retell in detail the oft-told story of the four years of devastating and bloody war that followed until on another April day, in 1865, General Robert E. Lee, ablest general of the war and noblest of Southern gentlemen, offered the surrender of his sword and the Southern cause to General Ulysses S. Grant, who, when a cheer began from the Union lines, ordered it stopped with the words, "The war is over; the rebels are our countrymen again." That the Southerners' hope of independence and the right to their own way of life had not been fantastic is shown by the fact that, outnumbered more than three to one and incomparably more heavily outweighed in resources, they defended their flag, the Stars and Bars, for four years of intense suffering and heroic effort. Now that the passions of that time have receded into the pages of history from the hot hearts of those who suffered them, we can realize that the courage and endurance of Southern men and women, and the stainless purity and gentleness of the soldier who led their hosts to war, are among the imperishable possessions of our common national past.

It is probable that during the war 620,000 Americans were killed or died from wounds and disease in the military service, 360,000 Northerners and 260,000 Southerners, out of some three million who saw service on both sides. Until the recent World War it was the greatest and most bloody struggle which humanity had known. The first battle, Bull Run, was a disgraceful rout, but before long these men and boys on both sides, who had known nothing of war and never dreamed of going to war, learned to stand fire as well as any veterans of Europe, and perhaps better, for in many of the battles the casualties were higher in proportion to the numbers engaged than in any of the battles of the Napoleonic Wars. It was a civilian's war in a nation which had scarcely known war for nearly a century. The recruiting systems were bad; the use of bounties, the evasion of service by many rich men in the North who paid the poor to take their places, and what came to be known as "bounty jumping," were all scandalous.

But in an age which delights to look at the worst instead of the best in human nature whenever it has the choice, it is all too easy to overstress the sordid side. The fact remains that a great, self-governing democracy maintained the war for over four years by its own decree and fought it to a finish with a dogged courage and a casualty list such as the world had not before seen. We shall discuss the economic aspects of these years better in the next chapter, but may note here that the war vastly increased the prosperity of the North and ruined the South. If the North had lost, nothing would have happened except that it would have failed to keep the Union together by force. The South, on the other hand, was fighting for its very existence, and when it lost, it was prostrate. Both sides gave much, but in the South the highest social class gave *all*, as that in the North did not.

At the start, neither side had any professional army which

amounted to anything. The only training school for officers, West Point, had been in the North, as was also that for naval officers, at Annapolis; but for the most part the graduates followed their States when the war broke out, the South being fortunate in gaining not only the best officer in the army when Lee finally went with Virginia, but such men as Beauregard, Stuart, and the two Johnstons as well. The less fortunate North had to experiment with one general after another until the figure of Grant gradually overshadowed all others.

Even after armed conflict had begun, both sides, as always happens, expected only a short war. Recruits were enlisted in the North for ninety days. However, the disastrous battle of Bull Run, July 21, 1861, completely altered opinion as to the length and magnitude of the struggle. The next lot of volunteers were enlisted for three years. Except for the blockade of Southern ports, nothing further of military importance occurred for nearly eight months, as the armies faced each other and were undergoing organization, until, in the beginning of 1862, Grant secured the unconditional surrender of Fort Donelson on the Cumberland and practically secured possession of Tennessee. In April, Commodore Farragut successfully passed New Orleans and proceeded up the Mississippi, which, however, could not be cleared and held until, a year later, Grant succeeded in capturing Vicksburg.

Unlike Lee, who came of a distinguished Virginia family, Grant came of completely undistinguished small people in a small Middle-Western town. His real name was Hiram Ulysses and not Ulysses Simpson, the change being due to a mistake in his enrollment at West Point. As a young officer in the Mexican War he had served well, but had made an utter failure of everything he had attempted after his resignation from the army in 1853. He was a hard drinker, and when he first volunteered for the Civil War no attention was paid to him. In many ways, as in the entire lack of all interests of a cultural sort and the curious limitations of his mind in other respects, he was a typical product of the small-town life of his day, especially in the West. But he had the particular type of military genius that was called for.

In the East, although McClellan had 100,000 men in the Army of the Potomac, he seemed to be making no progress. Lee had crossed into Maryland and been defeated at Antietam, in September 1862, but the next year had been able to get into Pennsylvania, to be defeated at Gettysburg on the very days that Grant was besieging Vicksburg. Although Lee had been forced back, there was nothing very promising in McClellan's or Meade's merely preventing Southern inroads on Northern territory. In March 1864, Grant was made a Lieutenant General and General in Chief of the Armies of the United States.

In the West, the Confederacy had been cut in half by the clearing of the Mississippi, and "Ol' Man River" was again rolling along for the Union his whole length. Grant came East and took charge of operations against Lee and Richmond. General Sherman undertook the task of cutting the Confederacy in two in another direction, and, starting South from Chattanooga in July, he marched through the South, passing through Atlanta, and, after being lost to the news for a month, at last emerged at Savannah in December 1864. In application of his famous phrase, "War is Hell," he had deliberately caused the widest destruction possible, though the persons of civilian Southerners had been respected.

There is no need to recite the further military manœuvres which led up to the final scene of Southern surrender at Appomattox. Grant, who understood the pride of the Southern officer and the stark need of the private, stated simply that officers should retain their side arms, and that all men who claimed a horse or mule should take it home to work their farms. One's mind reaches forward to a meeting on the Franco-German frontier in 1918, in a freight car filled with distinguished officers with stars and orders on their breasts. . . . The small-town, undistinguished Hiram Grant, uncultured and untraveled, looms above them all as a chivalrous gentleman and a magnanimous conqueror, as in few words in that little farmhouse in 1865, in shabby fatigue uniform, he adds healing to the peace. His enemy, General Lee, recognizes a fellow gentleman in the stocky, stubby-bearded, carelessly dressed man whose terms he has just had to sign. "This will do much to conciliate our people," he says, and it is all over.

As a nation we have been singularly fortunate in many ways and on many occasions. In one respect this luck or fortune, or what you will, has been very good to us in a unique form. The only two great military struggles in which we have been intensively engaged — the War of the Revolution and the Civil War — have left us legacies such as war rarely, if ever, has left to others, legacies of men so surpassingly great in character as to have become, and deservedly so, folk heroes for a people whose history has as yet been so brief. In the Revolution, the South had given us George Washington, and in the Civil War, the West gave us Abraham Lincoln. Usually war gives national history the military hero. Occasionally the great statesman emerges to take a permanent place in the memory of his people. America's fortune has been to receive from our struggles (for the World War for us was a holiday affair compared with the other two) two men whom we think of neither as soldiers nor as statesmen, but as men of such sublime character as to have taken their places among the highest of mankind of all times and races, and to have become enshrined in the hearts and hopes of all humanity.

Lincoln, the man whom Fate had held in store to save the Union, came straight from the common people and the democracy of the West. There is no need to retell the thousand-time-told tale of his ancestry, his hard upbringing in a log cabin in direst poverty, his self-education, his early career as a lawyer and politician, until the year when he entered the White House. Untrained, untried, uncouth, uncultured as the East understood culture, unwanted, the homely "rail-splitter" and backwoodsman undertook in humbleness of mind the task not only of holding the nation together, but of so acting that the bonds of brotherly union should be those of sympathy and understanding and trust, and not of force, even though war might have to intervene for a time.

It had been the plain people who had given him power, and the plain people trusted him. Not so the "rich and wise" of the old Federalist formula. Charles Francis Adams, for example, who rendered inestimable service during the war as Minister to England, and who, in the opinion of his son Henry, had the most perfectly balanced mind of any of that great clan of Adamses, could read the minds of a Lord John Russell or a Palmerston, but failed completely to understand or appreciate Lincoln. Like most of the others of the rich and wise, he trusted Seward instead, because Seward was the type of man and mind they were used to, and they could not suspect that a man who came from backwoods poverty and the rough frontier had more wisdom than them all.

In the weeks before and after inauguration Lincoln displayed that infinite patience of which he was to have such sore need in the years to come. Seward, whom Lincoln had made Secretary of State and who considered that, in spite of a whim of fortune and democracy, he himself could be the actual President, as in his opinion he should have been the titular one, handed the President a memorandum on April 1, 1861, in which he suggested his own method of bringing disunion to an end. One shudders as one reads it to think what the history of our land might have been had the East won in the Chicago Convention and had Seward been elected in Lincoln's place. His idea was that, as the President had not yet evolved a policy for reuniting the nation, that end could be accomplished by forcing an immediate declaration of war against Spain and France, possibly also against England and Russia, and making trouble in Canada, Mexico, and South America! In case the President did not consider himself capable of fulfilling the duties of his office, Seward offered to undertake them himself. Lincoln replied with great kindness that whatever had to be done he must himself do. The measure of the man began to show.

In spite of his belief in its moral iniquity, slavery was protected by the Constitution, was legal in many of the States, and Lincoln considered, always, that he was President of the whole United States in spite of the temporary secession of some of them. Moving slowly, by which caution he saved several of the wavering border States to the Union and prevented further secession, he announced that there should be no aggressive move made by the Federal government, that civil war was in the hands of the South, not his, but that secession was unconstitutional and that the laws of the Union must be enforced by him in all its parts.

When the firing on Fort Sumter brought war on the nation, he kept to the idea that the only object of the war was to save the Union, not to settle the slavery question by force instead of law. "My paramount object in this struggle," he wrote in August 1862, "is to save the Union, and is not either to save or destroy slavery. If I could save the Union without freeing any slave, I would do it; and if I could save it by freeing all the slaves, I would do it; and if I could do it by freeing some and leaving others alone, I would also do that. What I do about slavery and the colored race, I do because I believe it helps to save this Union; and what I forbear, I forbear because I do not believe it would help to save the Union. . . . I have here stated my purpose according to my view of official duty, and I intend no modification of my oft-expressed personal wish that all men, everywhere, could be free." Every act of Lincoln was dictated by his belief in Union, and his hope and duty of restoring not merely a Union of force but a Union of hearts. When he finally came to the conclusion that he must emancipate the slaves, it was because he felt, as he said, that "slavery must die that the Union might live," and when he issued the Proclamation some months later, after the success at Antietam, America realized only slowly that the cause of human freedom was thenceforward bound up by destiny with the cause of the Union.

Above all the din and stench of human misery and blundering and meanness, the profiteering and self-seeking and angry passion and other ills that war ever breeds, two speeches by Lincoln, imperishable possessions for us when we despair of democracy, show the manner of man who could arise from the depth and very heart of democracy when its trial was sorest. In the next chapter we shall have to see democracy at its lowest and vilest, and it is well that we should hearten ourselves with a glimpse of it at its noblest, and listen to how the greatest soul that democracy has yet evolved would have us wage war and make peace.

On November 19, 1863, part of the battlefield of Gettysburg was to be dedicated as a national cemetery. A concourse of people gathered, and for two hours listened to the most polished orator of the time, Edward Everett, who stood for the man of culture as opposed to the man of the people, the ungainly President who was there merely because he was President. No one now ever reads what the polished orator spoke as, without any depth of feeling for the dead or living, but with the thought of himself and the impression he was making, he discoursed on the sin of rebellion. And then Lincoln rose, and quietly spoke, "gracefully for him," as John Hay noted — spoke in words that, now cut in marble in our noblest tomb, may yet outlive the stone on which they are inscribed.

"Four score and seven years ago our fathers brought forth on this continent a new nation, conceived in liberty, and dedicated to the proposition that all men are created equal. Now we are engaged in a great civil war, testing whether that nation, or any nation so conceived and so dedicated, can long endure. We are met on a great battlefield of that war. We have come to dedicate a portion of that field as a final resting place for those who here gave their lives that that nation might live. It is altogether fitting and proper that we should do this. But in a larger sense we cannot dedicate, we cannot consecrate, we cannot hallow this ground. The brave men, living and dead, who struggled here, have consecrated it, far above our poor power to add or detract. The world will little note, nor long remember, what we say here, but it can never forget what they did here. It is for us, the living, rather to be dedicated here to the unfinished work which they who fought here have thus far so nobly advanced. It is rather for us to be here dedicated to the great task remaining before us, that from these honored dead we take increased devotion to that cause for which they gave the last full measure of devotion; that we here highly resolve that these dead shall not have died in vain; that this nation, under God, shall have a new birth of freedom; and that government of the people, by the people, for the people, shall not perish from the earth."

Edward Everett listened condescendingly to the uneducated man who knew only Blackstone, Shakespeare, and the Bible. The trains were waiting. The crowd dispersed. Boston aristocracy and Western democracy had had their say. The aristocrat had taken two hours, the democrat two minutes; and one had become immortal.

A year went by, and for the first time in history a great democracy was called upon to elect a chief magistrate in the midst of a life-and-death struggle. Lincoln was again elected. The following March, when he delivered his second inaugural, the surrender at Appomattox was scarcely a month away, though that could not be certain. In his address, Lincoln held out no false hopes, but always thinking of the nation, and the peace that was to be, he ended his brief address with the words: "With malice toward none, with charity for all, with firmness in the right as God gives us to see the right, let us strive on to finish the work we are in; to bind up the nation's wounds, to care for him who shall have borne the battle, and for his widow and his orphan — to do all which may achieve and cherish a just and lasting peace among ourselves, and with all nations."

Early in April the President went to see Grant, and remained with him until the day before the surrender. To one who urged that Jefferson Davis ought to be hung, he answered, "Judge not, that ye be not judged." Peace was concluded on the ninth, and on the fourteenth the Stars and Stripes were run up the pole at Fort Sumter. In the morning, Lincoln held a cabinet meeting at the White House to consider the reconstruction of the Union. There was, he said, too much talk around of "persecution" and "bloody work." He would hang nobody. As soon as certain simple obligations had been complied with, the seceded States should come into the Union with all their former rights and privileges. "We must extinguish our resentments if we expect harmony and union. There is too much desire on the part of some of our very good friends to be masters, to interfere with and dictate to those States, to treat the people not as fellow-citizens; there is too little respect for their rights. I do not sympathize in those feelings." He was once more in fact, as he had always been in spirit, President of the whole *United* States.

In the evening he and Mrs. Lincoln went to the theatre. He sat in his box, happy and content, the long vigil ended by the side of his broken Union, now reunited, though with wounds which he intended to heal. All eyes were on the stage. Suddenly a shot rang through the auditorium. Lincoln fell forward, unconscious and dying. A half-crazed assassin, waving a knife, leaped from the box to the stage, shouted "Sic semper tyrannis," and fled through the stage door to a waiting horse. The President was carried to a near-by house, laid on a bed, and without regaining consciousness, but with a look of perfect peace and rest on his worn features, passed away in the early morning.

The war was won; the Union was preserved; but peace and love and honesty and brotherly kindness had fled with Lincoln's soul.

X

THE END OF THE FRONTIER

The Civil War was a convulsion so great as inevitably to exert profound effects on the national life. Before considering these, we must turn for a moment to the effects on our international relations.

It was quite obvious that the rise of a great self-governing nation in the New World during the previous three quarters of a century could have been hardly pleasing, to say the least, to the governing classes of aristocratic and monarchial Europe. England was not yet the democracy that she has since become, and Republican France had returned to imperial forms under the third Napoleon. From the day of our national birth, both nations had treated us with scant respect. We had earned some by having at last turned against one of them and fought in 1812, but both continued to accord us as little as possible. Our diplomatic relations with England were frequently strained, particularly when the swaggering Palmerston was in office; and we nearly went to war with France in Jackson's time. In spite of Washington's Farewell Address, however, we continued to be guided by sentiment, and to magnify England's unfriendliness and to minimize or ignore that of France.

The tide of democracy was rising everywhere, and the general revolutionary movements in Europe in 1848 had sent shivers down the spine of the upper and ruling classes. The lower classes looked to America as an example and a refuge, and the upper as a portent and a danger. If the United States should split in two, and the experiment of self-government thus prove to be at least a partial failure, the results would be useful to the European upper classes, and there is no use denying that they were anxious for the success of the South. Unfortunately such liberals among them as might have been on the side of American union were to a great extent alienated by the policy which Lincoln had to pursue with regard to slavery. At first it was thought that our war was one for freedom, but when Lincoln announced that it was solely for union, opinion turned against us. Many foreign Liberals honestly felt that if the war were not to free the slave but merely to coerce a population of five millions to live in a Union which they did not desire, there was no moral issue at stake, and that the North was waging merely the same sort of imperialistic war as had been waged over and over in history. Moreover, it was thought that the North could not win, and that, if she did, she could never hold the population of the South in subjection without making a farce of free government. The Emancipation Proclamation did much to remedy this error, but throughout the war, speaking broadly, English upper-class opinion was strongly against the North, and working-class opinion strongly for it.

On the whole, however, the English government itself steered a neutral and correct course in its official acts, and the letting loose from English shipyards of several successive commerce destroyers bought by the Confederate government was not so much an act of malice as of contradictory and ill-drawn laws, and of official stupidity. When the claims for the damage inflicted by them were at last arbitrated in 1872,

America was awarded $15,500,000. The effect, however, of the depredations of these vessels and of the hostile opinions of English society, which was much more vocal than was the working class, was deeply resented in our North, and did much to strengthen the feeling that England was, always had been, and always would be, our inveterate foe. We had been made irritable for many decades under the gibes of provincial English minds, such as that of Sydney Smith, who in a sneering article had asked in 1820, "Who ever reads an American book?" By the end of the war, we had added a number of classics to English literature, — Emerson's *Essays*, Hawthorne's *Scarlet Letter*, Melville's *Moby Dick*, and Lincoln's *Gettysburg Address*, — but the Englishmen of that day were unable to recognize anything except force as a foundation for respect, and the success of the war opened their eyes for the first time to the fact that a first-class power was arising in America. The world of international relations has always been a world as ruthless and devoid of sentimental attachments as is the competitive world of modern business. We had somehow, in spite of Washington, expected it to be a world of friendliness and sympathy, and always suffered a double resentment when specific instances proved that it was not. We expected more from England than from other nations on account of our origin and the many common ties; but, on the other hand, there was the steady smouldering anger from old days, kept alive by our school oratory, popular histories, politicians who catered to both anti-British Americans and the Irish vote, and by poets like Lowell. The Civil War thus ended with some increase of respect for us in England, and an added bitterness in our feeling against her.

With France the case was different. The French government, unlike the English, was officially hostile toward us, and had it not been for the restraining power of England, Napoleon would have openly backed the South. As it was, he did use the chance of our desperate struggle to invade Mexico and establish an empire there with Maximilian as ruler, a far more overt act of contempt and hostility than any indulged in by England. But the old tradition that France was somehow always our friend led to glossing over such hostile acts and to a quick forgetting of them afterward.

In one respect, some of the English thinkers friendly to us were right. A war to maintain the Union by force of arms only could not fail to have profound effect on our theory of liberty. How were we to reconcile the use of force to bind to us a population of five million whites and over three million blacks with our Declaration in 1776 that governments derive "their just powers from the consent of the governed; that, whenever any form of government becomes destructive of these ends, it is the right of the people to alter or to abolish it"? In the simple agrarian colonies of a century earlier, it had been easy to declare, when we were revolting against imperial power, that it was self-evident that among the "inalienable rights" with which the Creator had endowed all men were those of "life, liberty, and the pursuit of happiness," but what became of this doctrine of "natural rights" when we were coercing with fire, sword, and bullets a full quarter of our white citizens to live under a government which they had decided was destructive of their rights?

There might have been some offset had we entered upon the war to free the three million slaves and bestow the enjoyment of these rights upon them, but that purpose was distinctly disavowed, and forcible union was the only cause officially declared for the war. The doctrine of natural rights had already been breaking down, particularly in the industrial North. It is an extremely inconvenient one for the employer of labor who wants to keep wages low and to control the industrial machine. It was a Jeffersonian and not a Hamiltonian doctrine, and the North, with its banks, tariffs, and manufacturing, had become a Hamiltonian State. The conflict between the old Americanism and modern industrialism had already become apparent in that section. There had always been some confusion of thought in our effort to ride simultaneously the two horses of Jefferson and Hamilton. The increasing industrialization of American society was steadily to increase that confusion in the future. That industrialization was given a tremendous impetus by the war, which at the same time dealt a staggering blow to the old American theory of natural rights and government by consent of the governed. The blow was dealt by the theory of the war, and was succeeded by another series in the decade which followed the peace, as we shall see. They were to leave us with an emotional attachment to the old American doctrine, but, when faced by the complex problems of highly organized industrialism, with no solid intellectual foundation for our theory of government and its functions.

During the war, the prosperity of the North and West greatly increased. At the beginning there was a serious crisis. The South owed the North about $300,000,000, which was, of course, a total loss. Many banks, particularly in the West, were unable to redeem their notes, and in 1861 came the general suspension of specie payments. But once past this period, various causes combined to bring about a great expansion of business. In comparison with the population, a much smaller proportion of Northern and Western men were in active military service than was the case in the South, and immigration went far to make good those losses. Although the number of foreigners arriving dropped somewhat, a total of about 800,000 came in during the five years, about 80,000 of whom went straight through to the West. In the two years 1863 to 1865, nearly 2,500,000 acres of farm land in that section were taken up under the Homestead Act of 1862, which provided that 160 acres could be had free by any intending settler. The war itself called for huge supplies of all sorts, — shoes, clothing, munitions, and so on, — and manufacturing and the invention of new machinery gained a great impetus. Agriculture was also exceedingly prosperous, owing in part to the fact that in 1860, 1861, and 1862 the harvests of England were almost total failures and those of Europe were small generally. Our exports of wheat from the North jumped from 20,000,000 bushels a year to 60,000,000. Two other bits of luck favored the North and West. Oil was struck in Pennsylvania in 1859, and by 1864 fabulous incomes were being made from it. In the same year that oil was found in the East, the famous Comstock Lode was located in Nevada, which was to become one of the richest mines in the world and yielded $52,000,000 while the war was on, to which may be added about $22,000,000 found in Colorado. The great growth in agriculture in the West permitted that section to replace the South as the best customer of the East, and the railroads shared in the general prosperity. Erie stock, for example, rose from 17 to 126½ and paid 8 per cent dividends; Hudson River from 36½ to 164 and paid 9 per cent. Cities grew rapidly. Everywhere there was a "boom," although labor did not fare as well as capitalists and speculators. There was scarcely any fighting on Northern soil, and almost no damage from that source. Unfortunately, on Lee's dash into Pennsylvania, the ironworks of a man whose one idea had been to get rich as quickly as possible were destroyed. They belonged to Thaddeus Stevens, perhaps the most despicable, malevolent, and morally deformed character who has ever risen to high power in America.

When we turn from the North and West, with their prosperity, their fortunes in oil and gold and silver, in manufactures and railroads, their smiling fields and rapidly growing cities, to look at the South during the war, we find a picture so different, so unutterably sad, that an American would gladly turn his eyes away. There had been no immigration, and of the five million whites about one million had served in the army. The war had been fought on Southern soil, and it had been the policy of the Northern generals to cause as widespread destruction as possible. It was boasted that, where Sherman had passed, agriculture could not revive for a generation. Everywhere there were ruined cities and towns. To a great extent, railways had been destroyed or rendered useless. For four years, against overwhelming odds, the Southerners had fought their fight, and yielded only when every resource was gone. A large part of the live stock had disappeared. Georgia and Louisiana, for example, had lost full half of their horses and mules. Everything was lacking with which to begin again. Not until 1880 did the farm acreage of Alabama equal that of 1860. At the end of the war, good land, when it could be sold, brought only a sixth or a fifth of its pre-war price. In seven States, the value of land dropped $1,500,000,000 between 1860 and 1870. With the Confederate debt and currency worthless, every single bank and insurance company was bankrupt. It was estimated that the loss in bank capital was $1,000,000,000. By the emancipation of the slaves, another $2,000,000,000 was completely wiped out. The Southerner was left with his depreciated land, without labor, and without money or credit with which to hire it. At the end of 1865, it is said that in Alabama, Georgia, and Mississippi alone there were a half million whites without means of subsistence.

Planters who had been wealthy before the war began to follow the mule or ox in the furrow and to do their own ploughing of a few acres. The young men — where there were any left — and the boys were so sorely needed for manual work to keep life in bodies that education had to be partly abandoned. The negro, utterly unfit for such a sudden change, did not know how to make his own living. Even had the South been treated, as Lincoln would have had her, with brotherly kindness, or even with mere decency, it would have taken her a generation to recover. As we shall see, she was not so treated, and we have now to enter upon the most shameful decade in our entire national history, and to record a moral collapse without precedent and, let us hope, without successor. It occurred under the presidency of Johnson and the two terms of Grant.

The centre of infection was the North, which had felt the full force of the Industrial Revolution, and in which we have already noted the partial breakdown in the morality of the business man. The evil tendencies inherent in the situation had been markedly reënforced by the slackness of moral fibre which war always breeds. I do not mean that the whole body of the people had become corrupt or even that there were not outstanding examples of probity and sanity among some of the larger business men, but the moral confusion of the preceding decades, which I have previously tried to analyze, had prepared the soil for the rapid growth of the rankest weeds which war could nurture. Such general demoralization as ensued could not have been possible had the heart of public opinion been sound. There has also never been any other period in which sectionalism was so clearly marked as it was in this one, between the industrial North, the agricultural West, and the prostrate South, so we will consider the sections separately, though somewhat at the expense of chronological order.

Although business of every sort was booming after the war, the period was fundamentally that of railway building. To the 35,000 miles in operation in 1865 about 122,000 were added by 1887. These latter included the great transcontinental lines as well as innumerable shorter ones. The first of the former — one of the greatest engineering feats as yet attempted by man at that time — was begun even during the war, in 1864, and one portion, the Union Pacific, was built westward from Omaha while the other section, the Central Pacific, was being built eastward from Sacramento. The labor employed on the eastern one was mostly Irish, and that on the western, Chinese, strikingly typifying the meeting of the two worlds on American soil. On May 10, 1869, the two construction lines met at a point about fifty miles west of Ogden, Utah, and the telegraph clicked the news to the world that the United States was spanned from ocean to ocean, bound together by iron bands of communication and the overhead wires that made the transit of news instantaneous. As other lines followed, the Northern Pacific, Great Northern, and the tens of thousands of miles of short lines in all sections of the country, it was evident that the American people, numbering 38,000,000 in 1870, 50,000,000 in 1880, and 63,000,000 in 1890, had entered upon a new phase. This vast population, occupying an area of over 3,000,000 square miles of contiguous territory, without tariff barriers, all living under one government, easily afforded the greatest opportunities in the world for exploiting a domestic market of unprecedented size and for the growth of vast aggregations of capital in the form of corporate enterprise.

The building of such a colossal network of rail lines stimulated the most varied sorts of business, much as did the rise of the motor industry in the next century, only upon a much larger scale. We hastened, as we always have, to seize as quickly as possible every chance to share in the sudden development. The whole economic structure of the nation was being transformed with amazing rapidity, and the prizes were colossally great. People began to talk casually about millions who before the war had thought only in thousands.

Our progress has never been conservative and orderly. The great periods of rapid advance between our crises of depression have more resembled the rough-and-tumble of gigantic gold rushes. Men, looking only at prizes and results for themselves personally, have not often stopped to consider methods and influences. Four of the great Western railroads were built with government aid, both in cash and in land grants, and in a few years the government gave to these private corporations approximately 130,000,000 acres, or a domain greater than three New Englands. Not content with even this loot, the promoters watered the stock of the roads upon a gigantic scale, and made profits from the construction companies which were organized by the insiders so that their profits might be secure before the risks were passed on to the feverishly speculating and gullible public. The Union Pacific, for example, appears to have been built entirely at the expense of the government and the first-mortgage bondholders, the total cost having been about $50,000,000, whereas the promoters got about $23,000,000 through a subsidiary corporation, the *Crédit Mobilier*. One of the leading figures in the road was Oakes Ames, member of Congress from Massachusetts, who distributed shares in this little gold mine of profit to other members of Congress and public men, "where they will do the most good to us," on the principle, as he wrote, that it would "induce men to look after their own property." When, a few years later, the scandal was aired, the reputation of even such men as James A. Garfield was smirched, and the extraordinary part was that none of them appeared to consider that they had been engaged in any unethical practices. Our Minister to England left a lasting reputation of a sort behind him at the Court of St. James's by using his official position to market the sale of stock in a worthless gold mine to citizens of the nation to which he was accredited.

Everywhere there was close alliance between corrupt financiers and corrupt public officials. The American business man — which meant, speaking broadly, almost the entire electorate of the prosperous classes — had, as we have seen, adopted the plan of allowing his governments, municipal and State, to be run by hired men in the form of politicians so as to leave himself free to pursue more lucrative callings. However, in a world getting rich quickly, the hired men wanted "theirs" also. Bribery and corruption became general. It was the period of the notorious "Tweed Ring" in New York. The Ring, under the lead of Boss Tweed, came into full power in the election of 1868, and by the autumn of 1871 had carried off loot from the city treasury to an amount variously estimated from $45,000,000 to $200,000,000. The scale and openness of the stealing were beyond belief. A courthouse which was planned to cost, complete, $250,000 cost the city over $8,000,000 without being finished. The conditions were generally known, yet such men as John Jacob Astor, Moses Taylor, and Marshall O. Roberts, after a cursory examination of the city's books, lasting six hours, stated that the city administration was in order.

In November 1871 the Guardian Savings Bank, of which William M. Tweed was president, failed in New York City, soon followed by the Bowling Green, National, and Market Savings Banks, all of which were closely affiliated with the local political ring. One of them had been specially designated by the immigration authorities as being desirable for newly arrived immigrants to deposit their money in, and the failures created much scandal. Only $2,000,000 was involved, but as months went by and the scandal grew, the poorer classes more and more lost confidence in all the city's savings institutions, and withdrew an amount estimated by the *Commercial and Financial Chronicle* to have been over $20,000,000.

The story of Jay Gould, Daniel Drew, and Commodore Vanderbilt has become a malodorous classic in American business, and we need not dwell on the details. In the fight between Vanderbilt and the other two for stock-market profits and the control of railroads, Drew, Gould, and Fisk printed $10,000,000 of bogus Erie certificates of stock, broke the price, and fled to New Jersey. The fight was transferred to the legislature at Albany, where Gould bought the members (Senators getting $15,000 each for their votes) and had the issue legalized. One State Senator took $75,000 from Vanderbilt, then $100,000 from Gould, and voted for the latter. In 1868, Gould and Fisk started printing again, and, without consulting the Board of Directors, printed about $20,000,000 in certificates, which they sold for about $10,000,000. They deposited this sum and about $5,000,000 more in banks in New York, and then suddenly called for the entire amount in "greenbacks," or the legal-tender paper money. To save their reserves, the banks had to call loans in a frenzy, and the stock market crashed, while Gould and Fisk bought back the stock they had previously sold. By this time the investors in Erie had nothing but a cast-off snake's skin for their money.

The financial system of the nation had not yet gone back to a gold basis, but gold had to be used in certain financial transactions, especially in international trade. There was thus a market in the metal which commanded a premium above paper money. The year after the last coup, Gould and Fisk determined to bring about a national crisis and reap another fortune by cornering gold. For this, it was necessary to make sure that the Secretary of the Treasury in Washington would not sell government gold and break the corner. Gould thought this had been accomplished. By September 24, 1869, he had forced gold up to 162, and panic reigned throughout the country. On that day, which has ever since been known in our history as "Black Friday," hundreds of innocent commercial firms went bankrupt, and as a later Congressional Committee stated, "the business of the whole country was paralyzed for weeks" and the "foundations of business morality" shaken. The corner was broken by the sale of $4,000,000 gold by the Treasury, but the slimy trail led perilously close to President Grant himself. Gould, who owned certain judges, including the notorious Barnard, saved himself by repudiation of contracts. To put it mildly, Grant was, as has been said, "painfully blunt in his ethical perceptions," and although it is almost certain he did not personally conspire with Gould, his sheltering of malfeasance in office of some of his higher officials on various occasions helped to debauch the public morale. The better sort of business men were caustic in their comments on such doings as we have noted above and all too many others which were rife throughout the nation, but seemed helpless before the pirates and cutthroats of high finance.

The magnitude of our resources on the one hand, and of the market to be exploited on the other, began to usher in our new period of consolidations and the rise of corporations. Railways began to be merged, and dominating figures to appear in certain industries, such as meat packing in the West and oil in the East. To a considerable extent, as in the case of Rockefeller and the Standard Oil, the railways were used, by means of rebates and special favors of one sort and another, to wipe out smaller competitors and to build up the power of the new oil, coal, or meat "barons," and others, of our modern America. In 1879, the Rockefeller group had organized a new form of control to replace the "pools" which had been declared illegal in the courts. Stockholders in corporations were invited to transfer their certificates to "trustees," surrendering their voting power in the individual companies and receiving a participating certificate in the "trust," a majority of the new shares being held, in the case of Standard Oil, by four of the "trustees." Within three years these were in control of between 90 and 95 per cent of the refining capacity of the nation. This was soon followed by the sugar "trust," and others, but it was not until about 1890 that public opposition became strongly aroused. We shall discuss the influences of the trust problem in later chapters.

Amid all this frenzied "prosperity," labor had not fared well. The inflation of prices, due to paper money and the war, had raised wages in terms of money, but although by 1866 wages were about 60 per cent above those of 1860, the workmen were not as well off, the rise in commodity prices having been about 90 per cent, and in rents yet greater. The panic which swept the country in 1873 added to their distress. Eighty-nine railroads went into the hands of receivers and the building of new mileage was largely suspended, throwing a half million laborers out of work. Nearly three hundred of our approximately seven hundred iron and steel plants closed down. Five thousand commercial houses failed in 1873, 5830 in 1874, 7740 in 1875, 9092 in 1876, almost 9000 in 1877, and 10,478 in 1878.

While consolidations and trusts were coming into being, laying the foundations for stupendous fortunes and almost unlimited power over the lives and fortunes of the working people, wages were steadily being forced down, and the industrial communities were "a weary and aching mass of unemployed." In 1877, the first important railway strike in the country occurred on the Baltimore and Ohio at Martinsburgh owing to a 10 per cent reduction in wages, and was suppressed by Federal troops, after the militia had joined the strikers. Shortly after, Federal troops had to be sent to Cumberland, and at Pittsburgh strikers destroyed property of the Pennsylvania Railroad valued at $3,500,000. None of these strikes were called by unions, but this period saw the rise of unions among the working people as it did of trusts among the capitalists. The problems of an industrialized America were obviously arising. The Hamiltonian State was coming of age.

"We must extinguish our resentments if we would expect

harmony and union," Lincoln had said on the last morning of his life. It is probable that he fully realized the strength of the forces of corruption and fanaticism and bitterness in the North which he would somehow have to control if his hope of a nation united in heart and with a minimum of rancor were to find fulfillment. A conspiracy of a handful, led by a half-madman, had destroyed the one man who stood between his country and the powers of evil, and had plunged us all into a sea of infamy and misery. Looking forward to the eventual reëstablishment of the Union with a minimum of friction and ill-feeling, Lincoln had wisely, through many constitutional and international difficulties, held to the theory that the seceded States could not be, and had not been, out of the Union; that secession was a constitutional impossibility; and that they were merely temporarily out of normal relation. As soon as the war was over, he had intended, in the simplest and easiest way possible, to reëstablish the old relations, and allow every State to function normally.

Unfortunately there were forces in the North which would not permit of this, once Lincoln had gone. These forces were of various sorts. There was, for one, the fierce fanaticism that had always been ready to break out in the North from Puritan days, and which had been fanned to fierce flame by the Abolitionists. They had painted the Southern slave owner as a devil incarnate and had created a deep hatred of the South. There were also the stay-at-homes, business men, politicians, and others, who, having taken good care never to risk their precious lives in fighting, made up for their record in the war, or lack of it, by vituperative hatred afterward. This always occurs after every war. No one ever pretends to hate the enemy or covers him with obloquy so deeply as does the man or woman who never met him in fair fight. There was also the Republican party man who realized that as long as the Southern States were kept out of full relation to the Union, and in subjection, the Republican Party would have complete domination of the nation. The Democrats could not win without South and West; and if the South were sterilized politically by being allowed to send no members to Congress, or to send only Republican members by manipulation of the elections, the Republicans had nothing to fear whatever they might do. There were also those who clearly saw that if Congress could dominate the South, instead of reëstablishing her, there would be fat pickings and innumerable political offices for Northerners.

All these and other factors combined to defeat the dead President's hopes of a reunited country. His successor, Andrew Johnson, had originally been a Democrat, but had been the leading loyal Tennesseean when that State seceded, and had been placed on the ticket with Lincoln to win favor in the border States. From the lowliest of beginnings, unable to write until after his marriage, having been left in earliest childhood without a father but with a mother to support, he had risen manfully and had carved out an honorable career for himself. When Lincoln's assassination made him President, Johnson was not a Lincoln, but he was an honest man who, when the first few days had elapsed after the office was so unexpectedly thrust upon him, tried to carry out Lincoln's policy for the South and a reunited nation.

Two men of considerable contemporary importance had already, before Lincoln's death, given the keynote to the policies which the Republicans were to follow — Thaddeus Stevens, the vindictive fanatic born in Vermont whose ironworks in Pennsylvania had been burned by the Confederates, member of the lower House of Congress, and Charles Sumner, Senator from Massachusetts. Sumner had claimed that secession had deprived the South of every right under the Constitution, and that it lay absolutely at the mercy of Congress, which was another way of naming the Republican Party. Stevens had declared that Congress must treat the Southern States as "conquered provinces, and settle them with new men, and drive the present exiles as rebels from this country." Under such leadership, Congress undertook the task of punishing the South, making places and spoils for its henchmen, and ensuring for a generation the national domination of the Republicans. The vindictiveness of Stevens and the fanaticism and egotism of Sumner combined to despoil the nation of that peace which Lincoln would have brought. The electorate gave them all-too-ready backing. For the next decade the South lived under a military despotism from which almost every trace of self-government was obliterated.

In only six of the Northern or Western States did the negroes, whose numbers there were small, possess the franchise, and in 1865 Connecticut, Minnesota, and Wisconsin voted against granting it in their own domains. The next year Congress, as part of its plan to Republicanize the South, drafted the Fourteenth Amendment to the Constitution, heavily reducing the basis of representation in Congress of such States as did not allow the negro to vote. This was adopted two years later. The Fifteenth Amendment, adopted in 1870, forcibly enfranchised, without the slightest preparation, the slaves, who formed about 70 per cent of the Southern population. Just as both political parties in the North had debauched the immigrant voters and led them to the polls in shoals, so the Southern black was now to be debauched.

In 1867, Congress passed the Reconstruction Act, which divided the South into five districts to be administered by Generals of the Federal army. It also provided for the holding of elections, in which the ex-slaves should vote, for delegates to constitutional conventions which should adopt constitutions providing for negro suffrage. These had to be submitted to the blacks as well as the whites for adoption. Until these constitutions had been drafted, approved by Congress, and the Fourteenth Amendment adopted, the Southern States were to continue to be ruled by the army under supervision of Congress. Johnson vetoed the Act, but it was passed over his veto, and when he had proved himself sufficiently a defender of the Federal Constitution and of Lincoln's policy against the radicals in Congress, that body undertook to disgrace the nation and itself by impeaching him on a trumpery charge. The impeachment, under the lead of Stevens, broke down, but Congress continued its mad course.

In the South, conditions developed as might have been expected. A disgraceful horde of office and spoils seekers from the North, known as "carpetbaggers," swarmed over it. Combining with the riffraff of Southern whites, known as "scalawags," and the utterly ignorant negroes, they formed parties, elected the legislatures, and stole with the complete abandon of Boss Tweed and his gang in New York. The taxes rose tenfold and fifteenfold, and debts were created, not for improvements or other legitimate purposes, but to line the pockets of these political shysters. Rhodes, who made as good a case as he could for the North, notes, for example, that in four years of Republican rule in Louisiana the State tax rose 400 per cent and the State debt from $14,000,000 post-war to an indeterminate amount estimated anywhere from $24,000,000 to $50,000,000 post-Republican. Of the $22,000,-000 debt of the city of New Orleans, $17,000,000 had been issued at 35 cents on the dollar. One estate in that city which even after the war, in 1867, was bringing in $70,000 income, could not be rented five years later for enough to pay taxes, insurance, and repairs.

Scenes in the legislative halls of all the States would have been laughable had they not been tragic. Crowds of Northern muckers, and blacks who had been slaves a short time since, swaggered about, smoking and drinking at the States' expense, ruling the South. There is no parallel for the situation in the history of modern civilized nations, and it is almost incredible that it occurred within our own country. No civilized victor was ever more ungenerous. The war had left the South prostrate; Reconstruction left it maddened.

Little by little, however, the South began to pick itself up. The new constitutions and the Fourteenth Amendment were ratified, and one by one, from Tennessee in 1866 to Virginia in 1870, the Southern States again became members of the Union.

The negro was held in check by the Ku-Klux Klan and terroristic methods temporarily. Gradually the labor problem had been adjusted and various ways of employing the former slaves devised and set in motion. The section still remained a single-crop one, but cotton was again, by large yields and good prices, set up as king. The old planter aristocracy was dethroned, but the "poor whites" became more prosperous. In the lower South, the number of farms doubled between 1860 and 1880, showing the extent of the social revolution which had taken place. Within this period there was little of that industrial development which later occurred, but the statistics show steady improvement.

Statistics, however, do not tell much about civilization in many of its aspects. For a generation before the war, as we have noted, the South had come to have less and less intellectual and beneficent influence on our national statesmanship, owing to her having had to devote herself to the task of defending her type of culture, which had become an anachronism. Then came the war, and after that, Reconstruction and its long horror. If, later, the South was to become solidly Democratic in its party allegiance (the black Republican vote ceasing to count), it was as little wonder as that, unfortunately, she could not for a time give to that party the wise leadership that she had given to the country in the early days of our history. It would obviously take a long time, through suffering, poverty, war, social revolution, and the rise of new classes from the bottom, to replace the South in any position of intellectual and cultural leadership. Any group or party conscious of unopposed power is bound to degenerate. The Republican Party, only a decade old, had been put to the test and completely failed. It was essentially the party of tariffs and the industrial interests — that is, of the North. Two parties are essential, and it was a national misfortune that both the South and the West, our agrarian sections, each from its own causes, were unable in the next crisis to produce the statesmanship that was called for. More and more the Republican Party was to become the party of wealth, privilege, education, and power; whereas, lacking these things, the Democrats yet represented genuine grievances and matters of the deepest import to national life and the American dream.

The West had been growing rapidly during the war, the stream of emigration continuing steadily during the struggle. With the return of peace, the sudden mounting again of foreign immigration, the mustering out of the huge Northern army, and the hard times after 1873, population in the Western States and cities multiplied fast. Germans in the Valley and Scandinavians in the Northern States, such as Minnesota, began to alter the hitherto solid Anglo-Saxon character of the people. So quickly did the whole section develop that Nebraska, although one of the least populated Territories, having only about 25,000 at the beginning of the war, could boast not long after of that number in the one city of Omaha alone. By 1870, Missouri had become the fifth State in population of the entire Union, and St. Louis third in size of all our cities. This increase was hastened by the opening of great tracts of land on easy terms. Under the Morrill Act of Congress all the States had received from the public domain grants of land to be sold for the purpose of establishing agricultural and mechanic colleges on the basis of 30,000 acres for each Congressman, New York thus receiving nearly a million acres. There were also the 130,000,000 acres granted to the railroads, which they tried to sell and settle as rapidly as possible, both to get the ready cash and to build up traffic. Lastly, the Homestead Act, granting free farms to settlers, accounted for nearly fifty thousand new farms within a few years.

Until the end of the war, however, there were but few settlers on the great plains, the "American Desert" having baffled the pioneers. In the almost treeless waste, carpeted with bunch grass, swept by hot and parching winds in summer and by blizzards in winter, where long periods of killing drought were punctuated by almost more dreaded torrential rains which flooded dry river beds and lowlands, it seemed as though there could never be anything to allure permanent white settlement. The Indians and herds of bison numbering millions swept over it, and the land-hungry farmer could see no good in it. Some persisted in trying, and by 1867 Abilene, in Kansas, was a far-flung post of those who wanted to establish an agricultural community, but the settlers, discouraged, just managed to hold on without getting ahead. Two railroads, however, had crossed the plains from east to west on their way to the coast, and provided a way to market for anything which could be raised in the Desert. One of these had first been completed as far as Abilene, but there were no crops in Abilene to be shipped, hardly enough to keep the settlement itself alive.

It was a harsh, deteriorating life on the plains in those days, as it had been on frontier after frontier, and there is no use in idealizing it. Everything was restless and uncertain. No one knew whether a town would fail or succeed. There was nothing beautiful in the mud and dust of the Main Street with its unpainted ugly buildings. Women who came from better homes in the East to pioneer with restless husbands found the life so hard that they would perforce grow slack and drab and careless. The hard water made washing almost impossible. In the long dry months of dust and furious winds, the dust was everywhere. It stung the eyes when you walked, seeped through windows and covered furniture an hour after it was dusted, got into hair and stayed there, with only scant water to wash it out. Women who, as Stuart Henry, an early pioneer, tells us, would wash the windows regularly in their old homes got into the way of leaving them for six months at a time.

No one will ever know what the women of all our successive frontiers underwent in hardships and toil of one sort and another, depending in part, like the Western dust and hard water, on local conditions, and in part on the universal conditions of the rough life, incessant childbearing, and physical work. Their courage and loyalty were beyond praise, and their comparative scarcity had two important consequences. One was that their legal status gradually improved with regard to their rights of property, and the other was that they came to possess extraordinary freedom. In the larger frontier towns, particularly such as attracted men with money as miners or cowmen, prostitutes appeared naturally, and there was always a somewhat slack morality among the lower sort of frontier folk. But a woman was always presumed to be virtuous in the sexual sense, and if she cared to remain so, — as, after all, most did, — she was absolutely safe both in fact and in reputation. The conditions of frontier life often compelled a man to be away from home and perhaps take refuge for the night in another house where the man was also absent. For the sake of protection of each man's own wife, a sort of unwritten law came to be universally and absolutely observed. No man would think of approaching an honest woman, and so rigidly was the rule observed that even when men and women, perhaps absolute strangers to one another, thus spent a night under the same roof, no whisper of scandal would be breathed because it was felt there would be no foundation for it. It is possible that in respect to commercialized vice the American has been no more moral than the men of other nations, though that is by no means certain. It is not unlikely that the self-control learned under frontier conditions would exert an influence on his general conduct in this regard. It is certain, however, that until very recent years, notably after the World War, there was a remarkable freedom of social intercourse between the sexes untinged by any thought of immorality, a freedom which had its marked effect on the American girl and woman, who came to feel themselves both free and safe to go anywhere and do as they pleased.

Combined, on the frontier and in small villages everywhere, with the evident need for a strict code mentioned above, there was the incessant tittle-tattle of a small group who had nothing to do when their work was done, and who lived where they could see everyone else. Out in the frontier towns, there was such a dearth of news as to constitute a sort of mental famine condition. Anything would make talk for a week. As Henry notes of Abilene, "a 'bunch' of Indians skirting through, a string of prairie 'schooners' passing, a train an hour late, even a change in the wind, afforded subjects of extended interest. Godsends in the way of news were a dog-fight, a swearing quarrel between two residents, the broken limb of a neighbor tumbling off a new roof." Squalor, lack of beauty in landscape or buildings, hard work punctuated by sheer idleness when work was done, a tendency toward shiftlessness and impermanence, the hope in the incessant flux of towns rising or falling that the farm might in a few years be "city lots" which would make the owner rich whether he farmed well or not, ingrowing minds with nothing worth while to feed on — all these form part of the background of all our frontiers. Had there been only one frontier, which gradually became settled and richly civilized, the effect might have been slight and quickly worn off, but when repeated again and again and yet again for nearly three centuries, the effect went so deep that it will take us long to eradicate it.

Such a frontier town was Abilene in the Civil War, typical of all the other little settlements pushed out on the plains to see what could be made of the fight against the flies, grasshoppers, winds, snows, dust storms, strange soil, uncertain prospects for crops; composed of ne'er-do-weels, hard workers, godly men and women, "bad men," drunks, a Sunday School, saloons, shabby homes; with chances of becoming a city or reverting to prairie grass and silence.

Before the war, Texas had been our great cattle-raising State, but, cut off from the North by secession and from the South by Union armies after the occupation of the Mississippi River, no market remained for the tens of thousands of cattle on its ranges, and the business was ruined. A man in Abilene, Joseph G. McCoy, conceived the idea in 1867 that Texas cattle could be driven up the old Chisholm Trail across the plains, sold at Abilene, and transported over the new railroad to Kansas City. Thus began one of the most picturesque phases of American industrial life.

It was found that cattle could prosper on the plains even if the farmer could not, and vast herds began to be driven northward the whole length of the Desert from Texas to the Canadian border. At first they were merely driven up in the summer to meet the various railways at different points, but as this put the cattlemen at the mercy of the Eastern buyers from the Kansas City, Chicago, and other stockyards, they began to establish ranches where the cattle could be held and sold when the market better warranted. Texas cattle had always had the name of making very tough meat, but fattening on the plains grass and an improvement in the breed obviated that difficulty, and for a couple of decades the profits in the business were enormous. The "cattle kings" began to appear in the "cow towns" where they met their herds driven in by the cowboys, and a new type enlivened the already colorful life of the West, quite different from that of the mining towns. In 1871 more than six hundred thousand cattle, each herd in charge of its cowboys, followed the long trail up from Texas to one point and another in the North. It was hard, dangerous, and difficult work. The Indians occasionally made trouble, and the herd itself was often unruly. Rounded up at night, it might start at the slightest strange noise in a panic of fear and scatter for miles around. The cowboys found that by circling around the cattle while they were asleep, and crooning a song to them, they might be kept from stampeding, and new folk songs came — anonymously, as always — to fill the need of daily work.

> Oh, lay still, dogies, since you have laid down,
> Stretch away out on the big open ground;
> Snore loud, little dogies, and drown the wild sound
> That will all go away when the day rolls round, —
> Hi-oo, hi-oo, oo-oo.

In some of the cowboys' songs, we get marvelously the swing and movement of the horses as they ride, driving the steers along the interminable trail through the clouds of dust flung up by a hundred thousand hoofs.

> It 's whooping and yelling and driving the dogies;
> Oh, how I wish you would go on;
> It 's whooping and punching and go on, little dogies,
> For you know Wyoming will be your new home.

The end of the frontier was in sight, though the cowboy and the cattle king did not know it; and the cowboy was the last, as he was the most brilliant, flash of color in all our varied ways of making a living. He had learned his trade, as he had taken much of his language and dress, from the Spaniards, and the cattle that pounded on the long trails were the descendants in part of those which had come from Spain before there was a white man on our Atlantic Coast.

While McCoy had been making Abilene one of the first of the cow towns, another man there was experimenting with what was to prove a more lasting cause of change in the plains, and to bring on a conflict of ways of life. The cattle business had brought a certain hectic prosperity to Abilene, as it did to other cow towns, but no genuine civilization could rise where a town was full of cowboys, cattle kings, "bad men," prostitutes, gamblers, revolver shots, and whiskey for a few weeks each year, and dead the rest. In mining towns, most of the inhabitants were men, but in these cow towns on the railroads the contrast between the temporary influx of the cattle crowd and the small-town, law-abiding folk who were trying to make a living there twelve months a year was piquant enough.

In another section of the West, stretching up from Illinois to Minnesota, wheat had become the predominant crop, almost as much as cotton in the South. A great wheat kingdom was rising. In 1870, "winter wheat" had brought the highest prices in the markets, and at Abilene, T. C. Henry conceived the idea of trying to raise it in the bottom lands of the plains in the Great American Desert. He sowed it secretly, and to his joy raised his crop. Later, it was to be found that it could be raised on the higher ground also. At last a use was found for the Desert, and the contest was on between the farmer and the cattle king. Overproduction, fierce competition, and other causes were already undermining the prosperity of the cow country, but its lords did not yield without a struggle against farmers, homesteads, and barbed-wire enclosures. They had come to consider the vast public domain as theirs by some sort of divine right to pasture their cattle upon, but the end was in sight. By 1880, the victory was with the farmer and a settled civilization. The Desert could be made to blossom, and the Indian and the cowboy were both doomed.

The West of this period was no longer solely agricultural. In the big cities, St. Louis, Chicago, and lesser ones, great business enterprises and even manufacturing were giving them an industrial aspect, but as a whole the West was a farming community, and the cities were as dependent on agriculture as the farmer himself — the great meat-packing plants, the manufacturers of farm machinery, the great distributing mail-order houses, banks, and others. The city population was only a small part of the total in any case, and the West was democratic, agrarian, old American in ideals. The many foreign strains now becoming numerous only made it more so, from small colonies scattered here and there, such as the Swiss "River Brethren," the "Russian Mennonites," and the Pennsylvania "Dutch," to the great masses of Germans and Swedes and Norwegians. These people had no great wealth. They were for the most part struggling against odds — droughts, plagues of grasshoppers, cinch bugs, debt, and all the ills that can afflict a farmer.

The world was becoming enormously complex. The West had been built up largely by transportation — rivers, pack trails, roads, canals, and now railways. America as a nation was in the full swing of industrialism and capitalism. The farmer was no radical as to property as he saw it, no communist or anarchist, but he wanted a square deal and a chance to get ahead. There were bound to be genuine conflicts of interest between industrialism and agrarianism. The Republican Party was dominant and was that of the industrial East, the East of banks and railway ownership, of absentee capital in all its forms. It would be difficult perhaps, in any case, for the opposition party, that representing the exploited — the farmers and laboring class — instead of the exploiters, to command the brains that the party of wealth could command. Such a party would have to find its main strength in the laboring class in the East and in the agricultural South and West, chiefly the latter two. The problems to be solved and the conflicts to be resolved were genuine, and were due to the impact of the new

Industrial Revolution on a world which had never before known industrialism on a large scale. They were emphasized with us by the intensity of exploitation of our resources and the immensity of the prizes to be won by those who could exploit them on a large scale. No hope could be expected from the party of tariffs and banks and manufacturing and special privilege. Even with absolute purity of intention, which we need not say we do not expect to find in any political party, it would of necessity be biased by the standpoint of its members. It would be more inclined, as it did, to "wave the bloody shirt" by proclaiming itself the savior of the Union in the war and denouncing the rebel South than to understand or remedy the abuses under which whole sections of the people outside its fold were suffering. Unfortunately, as we have seen, one section which would make up a large part of the strength of an opposition, the South, had been set far back on the intellectual road by circumstances. The other, the West, had not yet advanced very far on the same road.

Life in the West for all newcomers had been hard, terribly hard. To stake out a claim and bring it under cultivation had meant physical toil of such a sort as to leave little energy for thought and education. Although there had been innumerable exceptions, the great majority of pioneers and settlers had been men and women of comparatively little background, education, or experience of the complications of modern industrial problems. In the hard toil of community building, not a little sentiment had sprung up against education in the frontier settlements. As one of the first settlers of Abilene tells us, it was felt that too much book learning somehow might interfere with success under the conditions of the life that must be led, and that it removed one from his fellows. The frontiersmen felt that the mere fact of being Americans gave them superiority, and that knowledge of how to meet "well enough" the problems of their daily round made education superfluous if not harmful. Unfortunately, the problems of the daily round were being complicated by modern business in a way that the farmers began to see, but could not fathom.

I do not mean that there was no desire for education in the West. There was, and schools and State "Universities" were springing up. By the end of the war, the University of Wisconsin, now one of the best institutions in the country, was already in existence, but it was housed in a couple of dilapidated buildings, with a tiny library, and was declared to be not much more than an academy for the village of Madison. In 1873, in fact, there were only 23,000 college students in the entire United States, and the bulk of these were naturally in the East. When we speak of the "West," we understand, of course, that there were innumerable "Wests," all the way from the snug, comfortable towns of Indiana or Illinois, some of which could not have been distinguished from identical ones in New England or New York, out to the roughest group of new shanties along a "Main Street" that was alternately mud ruts or blinding dust, lined with a few saloons and unpainted, unbeautiful boxes for human habitation. Life might be virile, but it was narrow, and for the great mass of the people there was little contact with the world back East over the mountains. Even to-day, when one gets into the great Valley, one feels that one is in an empire so vast as to make a world of its own, and the other worlds we have left, Europe and the American East, seem to diminish in importance and interest as they disappear into more and more thousands of miles of distance. Crossing the mountains to the westward of this empire, again, and reaching the Pacific Coast, we come to our fourth distinct section, but in this period it was not of primary influence on the nation.

That the West would of necessity be behind the East in intellectual attainments and opportunities was inevitable from its being a new country as contrasted with an old and now wealthy one. If we allow that premise, we can judge of the barrenness of the West better by observing that even in the East, until after 1870, not only were there no postgraduate schools or courses, but in leading universities there was no political science or sociology taught, as at Yale, nor practically any history, as at Columbia. At the latter institution, one unfortunate professor had to teach moral and mental philosophy, English literature, such history as was called for, political economy, and logic. If this was the best that some of the oldest institutions of the East could offer, it is not hard to imagine what would be found in the newly established struggling State Universities of the raw West. In the main it was to the South and the West that one had to look for an opposition party which would speak for the rights of the plain man rather than of capital. We should expect to find a good many errors in the consideration of complex social and economic questions, mixed with a good deal of plain common sense.

Every class in power, whether an aristocracy, a plutocracy, or the lower economic strata in a democracy, naturally sees things much from the angle of its particular desires and prosperity, and finds it difficult if not impossible to transcend them. During and after the war, the capitalists — the old ones and the swarms of new — were rapidly entrenching themselves by means of the tariff, the forming of corporations, and the control of courts and legislatures. There was plenty of corruption in Western legislatures as well, but for the most part the really great corporations, such as the railroads and the new "trusts," were owned and operated from the East, where a new type of corporation lawyer emerged to assist the process. The general issue, not yet settled, was beginning to be clear.

In 1873, the Chief Justice of Wisconsin, Edward G. Ryan, one of the abler leaders of the West in that period, posed the problem clearly in his address to the graduating class at the University in his State. "There is looming up," he said, "a new and dark power. I cannot dwell upon the signs and shocking omens of its advent. The accumulation of individual wealth seems to be greater than it ever has been since the downfall of the Roman Empire. The enterprises of the country are aggregating vast corporate combinations of unexampled capital, boldly marching, not for economic conquests only, but for political power. For the first time really in our politics, money is taking the field as an organized power. . . . The question will arise, and arise in your day, though perhaps not fully in mine, 'Which shall rule — wealth or man; which shall lead —

money or intellect; who shall fill public stations — educated and patriotic free men, or the feudal serfs of corporate capital?'" This was the authentic voice of the West, and wholly justified in its prophecy. Diffused power, as we have learned over and over again in our politics and legislation, counts for little. It is concentrated pressure that counts, whether exerted by a railroad lobby, a trust, or an Anti-Saloon League, and the concentration of certain capitalistic interests in vast corporate form undeniably brought new problems into our national life.

Two things were of supreme importance to the West. One was transportation and the other payment of debts. The day of driving a wagon from the farm to the market town over a road free for all had gone forever. The horse was now a locomotive; the wagon was a long line of freight cars; the market town was the world at large. One might as well burn the farmer's crops as deny him fair play in transportation costs. Every new country which needs development faster than capital can be accumulated locally must go heavily into debt. This has been true of every one of our frontiers except California. If, during the existence of the debt, a fluctuation in the purchasing power of the currency in which payment is demanded *increases* the purchasing power of money, it is equivalent in the eyes of the debtor to an increase in his *debt*, an increase made by him involuntarily. If it takes two dollars to buy a bushel of wheat, a farmer can pay a one-thousand-dollar debt by selling five hundred bushels, but if the value of the currency rises so that one dollar will buy a bushel, then the farmer will have to sell twice as much to pay the debt. No Western university may have boasted a chair of economics, but every farmer had firmly grasped this simple proposition. If the "money power" did not play fair in selling transportation or if it seemed to do anything to make money less "cheap," it would certainly hear from the farmers.

In the matter of the railways, it did not play fair. In the early years of our railway age, the abuses were flagrant and both the small business man and the farmer suffered. Although the roads could invoke the right to run their lines across a farmer's fields, although the government had granted them 130,000,000 acres of the people's land and tens of millions of dollars of the people's money, they were regarded by their owners as mere private investments untinged by public use. They had in many cases been dishonestly built, and, when built, their stocks had been outrageously watered. In less than two years after 1867, one group alone increased its share capital from $287,000,000 to over $400,000,000, on which it claimed the right to earn dividends. The rates charged were both exorbitant and discriminatory. In 1869, with wheat selling at 76 cents in the East, it cost the Western farmer over 52 cents for transportation, leaving him only about 24 cents for his risk and labor. The railways could also make or break sections and businesses. The early rise of the Rockefeller fortune, for example, was notorious in this respect. Not only did the railroads carry his oil for less than they charged his competitors, but in one case, where they charged him 10 cents and his competitors 35, they even went further and paid to him the 25 cents extra they charged his competitors!

At first the West tried to remedy the situation not by founding a political party but through a voluntary organization called the Patrons of Husbandry, commonly known as "the Grange," which by 1873 had a membership of 1,600,000. Through the influence of the "Grangers," laws were passed in some of the Western States establishing railway rates and in other ways attempting to curb the abuses. The capitalists claimed that the foundations of property were being undermined and did their best to make the Grangers out as enemies of law, order, and society, dangerous cranks. When Minnesota passed its law regulating rates, the president of the Chicago, Milwaukee and St. Paul had the effrontery to write to the Governor that the company would disregard the laws until the courts had passed upon them. The courts did pass on them, all the way up to the Supreme Court of the United States, and upheld them. It was admitted that private property was not supreme, that the people had their rights as well as capital, and in 1887 Congress passed the Interstate Commerce Act. The Western movement was a turning point in governmental policy. Less spectacularly than the political uprisings under Jefferson and Jackson, the people had scored. The doctrine was Western, and sound as wheat.

The West had other grievances, such as the misuse of grain elevators, and high interest rates, — running up to 15 and 20 per cent, — but the chief of these was the alteration of the money in which the farmer was expected to repay his debts. During the war, specie payments had been suspended and the government had issued paper money. The West had borrowed its money payable in "dollars," and when in 1866, in the laudable desire of returning to a sound currency basis, Congress authorized the cancellation of $4,000,000 in "greenbacks," or paper money, a month, and the currency began to appreciate, the West felt it was being used unjustly in being called upon to pay its debts in dollars of increasing value. It was on this point that the West went wrong, tragically wrong, as it was later to prove, for it ruined the party of protest that the nation has bitterly needed.

It was necessary for the government to return to a gold basis, which it did in 1879, but it was also true that the steady advance of the dollar to par in gold wrought great hardship to all such classes everywhere, notably in the West, as had incurred debt during the period of depreciation. On the other hand, the depreciation had also wrought great damage among the creditors, small as well as big, while it was progressing. It was part of the cost of the war, of every war, just as much as taxation; but, unlike equitable taxation, its incidence was not spread evenly over the population, and its injustice seemed obvious to whichever class successively suffered from it. In 1868, both the Democratic and Republican parties split along more or less sectional lines between sound money and the "cheap money" heresy. In 1874, a convention was held from which later emerged the National Greenback Party of the Presidential campaign of 1876. However, this party accomplished nothing, and with the gradual return of prosperity the issue temporarily lapsed.

The year 1876 was notable in many respects. In celebration of the centenary of the Declaration of Independence, a World's Fair was held in Philadelphia, which gave both foreign nations and our own citizens an opportunity to take stock of our achievements in many lines. If in some respects the exhibits of our machinery and inventive skill were the most notable, our advance in other directions was also worthy of note. It was still the Victorian–Civil War period of execrable taste in architecture and interior decorating, but in painting we already had works to show by such men as La Farge, Winslow Homer, Alden Weir, Thomas Moran, and other contemporaries, as well as our earlier Peales, Copleys, Stuarts, and other eighteenth-century men. Over three million visitors, scarcely any of whom had ever been in Europe, had the chance to see something of the products of other countries. Being held, as it was, on so important a centenary in our history and within a few months of the complete reëstablishment of the Union by the reinstatement of the last seceded State, it greatly helped to deepen the sentiments both of Union and of nationality, and although it was but one factor, we may date a very genuine advance in our cultural life from the early part of this decade. Under such men as Charles W. Eliot of Harvard, James McCosh of Princeton, Daniel Coit Gilman of Johns Hopkins (which was opened for instruction in 1876), our university life emerged from the high-school stage, and the new colleges for women were beginning a revolution in feminine outlook.

It was also in this year that democracy, just a century old, was put to a severe test from which it issued triumphant. The scandals of the Grant régime in national politics, and the general stench which arose from most of our municipalities, had at last begun to arouse the nation to a sense of shame, and the Democratic Party had an exceptional chance to return to power. The alarmed Republicans nominated an honest but rather colorless candidate in Rutherford B. Hayes of Ohio, and the Democrats put forward Samuel J. Tilden, a statesman with an admirable record for reform. The contest was close, and with some frauds on both sides. It was at first accepted as certain that Tilden was elected, and the announcement was so made in all the papers next morning. Two sets of returns, however, came from Oregon, and a slight change in Florida, Louisiana, and South Carolina would swing the election to Hayes. In that immediate post-war period there were few, if any, reputable Southerners who would vote the Republican ticket, for obvious reasons, but there were the disreputable ones and the negroes to count on. Tilden's popular majority over his opponent had been a quarter of a million, and when the people awoke to the fact that the Republicans intended to claim the victory popular indignation rose to a high pitch. An Electoral Commission was appointed by Congress to pass on the returns from the four disputed States, and after many weeks, during which the country was held in suspense, it made its report, the decision having been taken on strict party lines, giving all four States to the Republicans. The careful studies which have been made of the episode long after the heat of the battle had passed indicate that Tilden was deprived of his rightful election as President.

With magnanimity and a high sense of patriotism, however, Tilden acquiesced, and requested his followers to do so, in the announcement of Hayes's election made on March 2, 1877, only two days before one or the other would have to be inaugurated. Considering the magnitude of the fraud, and the depth of passion aroused, this peaceful acquiescence of a majority of the nation in the forms of law and their refusal to precipitate any further strife constituted a landmark not only in our own history but in that of self-governing democracies. The Civil War had proved that the great democracy could preserve its Union against disintegration; the Hayes-Tilden election proved that it could maintain self-control under enormous provocation. The following year the New York Civil Service Reform Association was formed, and slowly a higher ideal of public service began again to be developed.

The issue of slavery and the Union, which had brought about the birth of the Republican Party, was now dead, and new issues had not crystallized. As has been well said, the struggle between the parties now degenerated for a while into nothing more stimulating than the contest of rival railroads for traffic. The election of 1880, in which the Republicans were again successful, raised no issues and decided none. In 1884, the Democrats under Grover Cleveland came into power for the first time since the war, but the new President, with absolute honesty and a bulldog courage, managed to antagonize many interests. His desire to reduce the tariff made enemies of the protected manufacturers and others; his nullification of illegal leases of Western lands, by which he restored fifty million acres to the people, irritated strong cattle interests; his vetoing of pensions bills, which had become a national scandal, antagonized all those who had hoped to feed at the public trough; his unsuccessful effort to stop the free coinage of silver made enemies of the silver kings; his yielding to the irresistible pressure of Democratic politicians for the spoils of office after twenty-eight years in the wilderness alienated the reformers. In 1889 the Republicans returned to the White House with Benjamin Harrison.

By 1890, a profound change had occurred in our conditions which was to usher in for the next few generations problems of a wholly different sort, though not immediately noticeable. The Census Report of that year pointed to the fact that the frontier had by then disappeared. "The unsettled area," it stated, "has been so broken into by isolated bodies of settlement that there can hardly be said to be a frontier line." Unless we have been in error throughout this book in ascribing potent influence to the factor of the frontier in our development of national life, thought, and character, this disappearance of our frontier line would obviously close one era and open another for the nation.

Now and then a new and dynamic idea has been introduced into our conceptions of the historic process, such, for example, as that of the influence of climate and general geographic environment or of the economic interpretation. The tendency at first is to make such ideas explain too much. Such was the idea of the frontier as first given to us by Professor Frederick

J. Turner, which, with the possible exception of the economic interpretation of all history, has caused more reconsideration of American development than any other single suggestion.

It is quite obvious that no single factor, neither climate, terrain, economics, religion, the frontier, nor any other, is all-important in influence; and I have in the course of this volume ventured to suggest that, because the frontier does not bring about the same reactions with other races and in all other places as it brought about in the United States, we must therefore allow for other factors as well. The frontier is no complete explanation, but it has assuredly been a most important element. We have had not merely one frontier to be settled before an older civilization became established, but such a succession of them as might almost be numbered by hundreds. We can check the factors involved in one and the influences radiating from it by comparing them with those in a continuous succession of others. It seems to be incontrovertible that the frontier has exerted much the influence on our life which has been noted thus far in this volume.

Recently a distinguished historian has minimized the importance of the end of the frontier by stating that he does not find that it made any difference in the "fundamental rhythm of American life," a somewhat vague phrase. He adds that in fact the frontier did not come to an end, as the government stated, claiming that the number of acres taken out under the Homestead Act since 1890 greatly exceed the number patented before. He admits that his figures are misleading, as they take no account of the railroad or State grants. How misleading they are is indicated by the fact that the railroad grants were 130,000,000 acres and the State grants probably several tens of millions more. This goes far toward invalidating his argument, but what he apparently fails to see, when he speaks of the large amount of land taken up after 1890 and even of the "cheap abandoned farm lands in the East and the South that go begging for buyers," is that such lands do not constitute a "frontier." The genuine frontier was not merely a staked claim to a farm; it was a state of mind and a golden opportunity. The men and women who trekked westward, advancing the edge of civilization from over the Alleghanies across the three thousand miles of continent — empty, except for Indians — to the Pacific, came under influences entirely different from those of a man of to-day who, tired of being a laborer or clerk, tries the experiment of buying an abandoned farm on some New England hillside within easy reach of the village and the whole of modern American civilized life. The latter has none of that feeling of vast open space, of pushing ahead of the van of older civilizations, of empire building, of a freer and better chance, of a more democratic ordering of his society, of the possibility of rapidly rising in a new community, or of the opportunities which come with the development of a wholly new country where cities may spring up almost overnight and make him rich and a leading citizen in wealth or political power. To take up a bit of land to-day, East, South, or West, is for the most part simply to change one's residence or perhaps one's occupation. It is to become an ordinary farmer, not to share in a great adventure of State building and to have golden dreams of a possible future if one has the luck to strike it right. The psychological conditions are wholly different.

If the influence of the frontier has been what most historians now consider it to have been, then, from the time of its passing, we can look for a slow but gradual change in American life. When "going West" ceased to be a great adventure shared by thousands all the time, a sort of mass movement led by dreams, and became a mere solitary venturing for a better job or a better piece of land somewhere else, evidently a great incentive would be removed. For a century and more, our successive "Wests" had dominated the thoughts of the poor, the restless, the discontented, the ambitious, as they had those of business expansionists and statesmen. With the establishment of full State government everywhere, with — speaking broadly — a more or less uniform life throughout the country, with increasing centralization of population and industrialization of our people, the character of our problems and thought would naturally come in time to be different. The influences of the frontier would steadily decrease in power and we should come under those of altered conditions of living and outlook.

For a century and a half we had been occupied in conquering and exploiting a continent, and by 1890 the task was complete. It had been an adventure of youth. Now it was over. There were plenty of empty spaces left to be filled, chinks in the structure, but the country was ours, peopled, bound together, politically organized from coast to coast. Henceforth the work would be one of consolidation rather than expansion. The problems would be those of ruling a vast population with divergent interests, not of organizing new States; the economic and social problems of the new world era of machinery and the conflicts between capital and labor; the problems of world markets and world contacts; the supreme problem of whether a Jeffersonian democracy could survive in a Hamiltonian economy.

The day was passing when the people could simplify their problems and escape from an environment too perplexing or too inimical by the simple process of going West. The day was coming when, East or West, they would have to stand and face the issues with no escape by a mere shift of ground. Perhaps that was one of the most far-reaching results of the passing of the frontier. Our intensified problems would henceforth permit of no escape. America began to near the day when she could no longer be vaguely optimistic and youthfully buoyant. She would have in time to become maturely self-critical and thoughtful. She would have to face all the issues courageously and with no easy avenue of escape to the "great empty spaces." Those might take care of a little surplus population or become playgrounds when we came to enjoy Nature instead of exploiting her. But they were no longer a solution of our problems, no longer dreams to relieve the sick bed of injustice or discontent. The colt had been roped and thrown. Thereafter he would have to get used to the harness of a complex civilization. It would take a long time, but a generation in the lifetime of a nation is short, and the most important change in direction in our history had occurred, almost unnoticed at the moment.

XI

THE FLAG OUTRUNS THE CONSTITUTION

In the continuous process which we call history, it is all too easy to point to specific dates and to speak of "turning points" when in fact all that happens flows from what has been into what is to be, with a lack of sharp divisions which is annoying to the chronicler but true to all living processes. When in 1890 the Census Bureau announced the fact that the frontier was ended as a dynamic factor in our life under the conditions with which we had been familiar for two and a half centuries, it merely called attention to a particular stage reached in what had been a long evolution. Successive frontiers had been established and ended, more territory acquired and more frontiers begun and ended, for many generations. We had stretched the process from the Atlantic to the Pacific in a broad band which was now bounded on the North by the dominions of a powerful European Empire and on the South by a settled nation which held no offer of a frontier condition.

Just as we had been a long time reaching this stage in our development, so would the effects of our altered condition be a long time working themselves out completely. It would be absurd to expect that, because the Census Bureau made its announcement in 1890, we must expect great changes by 1891. The end had not suddenly come overnight, nor would all its effects be apparent next morning. Moreover, we must be careful not to make the mistake of thinking that world tendencies localized in one country require too localized explanations. Other nations felt the impact of the Industrial Revolution, the problems of the machine age, the trend toward urbanization, the vast increases in population due to the industrialization of society, and the resultant urge toward overseas possessions and imperialism in politics and trade.

Nevertheless, I think it reasonably clear that all these and other factors were modified in our country, both in character and in the matter of time, first by the existence and then by the ending of the frontier. The point is so important that I may be forgiven for emphasizing it. Although, for a couple of centuries and more, pioneering had inculcated upon us an unusual versatility and inventiveness, and although Americans lead all nations in their fondness for, one might almost say worship of, machinery of all sorts, it is well accepted that we did not feel the full effects of the Industrial Revolution until considerably later than Europe did. This was owing in large part to our free land, to our agrarian economy, and to the much greater opportunity here as contrasted with England for the laboring man to lead a free life on a farm instead of being forced into wage earning in factories. The full effect was thus delayed here until our population and domestic market had become so vast as to offer exceptionally tempting chances for consolidation, power, and wealth on a vast scale. Moreover, the first great impact of an industrial era on our life came at a time when the old Americanism of the democratic ideal, the American dream that life should be made richer and fuller for everyone and opportunity remain open to all, had been kept alive by constant waves of thought and emotion flooding back from our successive frontiers. Industrialism was to encounter the mentality not of a people emerging from feudalism, but of one emerging from the exceptionally free and optimistic life of the frontier.

If we wished to be doctrinaire, we might try to estimate what effects would flow from the ending of the frontier experience and from the closing of that avenue for the outpouring of the surplus energies of our restless and energetic population. There was yet, of course, free land to be had, but there were no more great empty States where settlers as they looked over the uninhabited wastes could picture in their imaginations a magic change into flourishing farms, villages, populous cities, arising within a few years by the efforts of the pioneers. There were no longer in imagination empires holding riches and opportunities for us and our children where only the Indian or the bison and the coyote roamed. The *élan* of the great westward trek was gone, gone like the Indian and the bison. We might expect, then, talking as doctrinaires and playing with our interpretation of conditions, that, irrespective of conditions in Europe, we should see a change in the type of our immigrants, that we should get fewer in proportion of the Germans, English, and Scandinavians who had come by the millions to build up the Western empire, and more of the types who would become wage earners in the seats of industrialism, men still motivated by the hope of bettering their position but without the dreams of the now-vanished "West." We might also say that, with the passing of the frontier, the influence of the democracy of that section, or that state of mind, would come to have less political effect on the nation as a whole. Again we might suggest that without the safety valve of Western empire building, and with increasing density of population, the conflict between capital and labor would probably become intensified as the evils of an industrial age were felt by a population singularly unprepared to lie down under them. Once more, we might say, somewhat cynically, that having lost our hunting ground for adventure, and having now seized and peopled all the continental land we could get, we should probably, like other nations, find some excuse for an imperialistic adventure overseas.

In point of fact, all these things came to pass within the decade we have to discuss in this chapter. Immigration did alter within the ten years for which the Census announcing the end of the frontier was prepared. The "West" which had won in each generation, under Jefferson, Jackson, and Lincoln, went down to defeat under Bryan; the struggle between capital and labor became more bloody and fierce than it had been before or has been since; and we went to war with a European nation, took her colonies, and became an imperial power stretching far into the Orient.

I do not wish to be guilty of the fallacy of *post hoc, ergo propter hoc.* On the one hand, these are the things that we might reasonably have predicted from the gradual ending of the frontier influence. On the other hand, if we assume that the frontier had not ended, but that there had stretched on beyond to the westward another valley like the Mississippi to offer scope for a new agrarian empire, to consume our energies, to offer freedom and democracy, to open new frontiers, to afford space and adventure to untold millions more, I do not think that the things noted above *would* have happened. It would seem, therefore, as though we might take the ending of the frontier as one of the really great turning points in our history. Hereafter our problems would take different form and become much intensified as economic and social ones. If there were no diminution in our energies, we should, in time, be forced into the international life and complications of the world on a scale hitherto unknown. With huge cities springing from Hamiltonianism and with no longer a steadily expanding agrarian section to offset them, we should have to face the problem of how to reconcile our Jeffersonian philosophy of democracy with conditions steadily swinging further and further from Jefferson's postulates, and with no hope of return.

Like "Ol' Man River," the stream of our history flows ceaselessly on. He had seen it all; he had known the day of the savages for untold ages before the white man came and "Ol' Man River" took De Soto to his bosom in the dark of night; he had seen the Spanish explorer and the French priest and voyageur; he had seen the English hunter and trapper, the trader, and the farmer; he had borne their children's ships and commerce; he had held the North and South together when they were locked in deadly hate and when the new railroads threatened to be more powerful than he; he had flowed through forest and prairie, past log houses and Southern plantations; and now our people had built great cities on his banks and a new time had come. He had heard the voices of all of us, his children, — missionaries, drunkards, trappers, miners, farmers, planters, savages, slaves, gamblers, roustabouts, millionaires, prostitutes, lovers, Presidents; English, Swedes, Germans, French, Irish, Hungarians, Czechs, Italians, Poles; Methodists, Catholics, Mennonites, Quakers, — all the infinite variety of our America, and in the Great Valley held in his arms they had hoped the hopes and dreamed the dreams of the old America of Jefferson who had given "Ol' Man River" to the nation. What would he see in the new America, the America of the city, the machine, the trust, the incalculable fortunes, that was now forming?

> He must know sumpin', but don't say nothin',
> He just keeps rollin',
> He keeps on rollin' along.[1]

The great middle section of the Valley had been settled to a great extent by Germans. Such cities as Cincinnati and Milwaukee were strongly German and the national flavor of the old French St. Louis had changed from one side of the Rhine to the other. For the most part, however, these newcomers had gone on the land and become substantial farmers, as had almost wholly the great swarms of Scandinavians who had swept over the Northwest and made a Scandinavian empire of Minnesota, the Dakotas, and parts of other States, an empire which survives to-day and is slowly absorbing, instead of being absorbed by, the older Southern and Northern American stocks, while developing as sound an Americanism

[1] Copyright 1927 by T. B. Harms Co., N. Y. (Reproduced by special permission of the copyright owners.)

as exists anywhere on the continent. The end of the frontier, noted by the government in the decennial Census of 1890, had occurred between 1880 and that date. If we look at the two decades prior to that one, and at the two following it, we find that in the former the immigration from all parts of Europe other than the Northern and Western made up less than 5 per cent of the total. In the two decades following 1890, Eastern and Southern Europe provided over 60 per cent of the total. Between 1860 and 1880 less than 250,000 Eastern and Southern Europeans came to us; between 1890 and 1910 they numbered over 8,000,000.

These Slavs, Poles, Hungarians, Greeks, Italians, Russians, Lithuanians, Jews, and others, representing many races and their blends, were of a very different type from the Irish, British, Germans, and Scandinavians. It was not merely that about 35 per cent of them were illiterate as compared with only 3 per cent of the earlier immigration. With our American worship of "book education," we can easily lay too great stress on mere literacy. But these people were much more "foreign" in their background and outlook than those who had come previously, and less easily assimilable to our social life and institutions. The earlier European immigration continued after 1890, though in decreasing numbers, and took up unoccupied lands in the West, but with each decade this addition to our population formed numerically a smaller proportion of the whole. On the other hand, the more "alien" immigration of the new races rose rapidly to 6,225,000 in the decade 1900–1910, and the influence on our national life was keenly felt. Although to a considerable extent these newcomers were peasants who had lived on the soil in their native countries, when they arrived here they did not seek to become farmers and to establish homes in the country, but congregated in huge racial groups in the larger cities, or became operatives in factories and mines outside of the great centres.

There were various reasons for this phenomenon, which seems to have puzzled some writers. We may suggest for one that these people at home had to a great extent been more dependent upon the simpler social groups of family, church, and village than had the British, Germans, and Scandinavians. They were more dependent upon close group solidarity than were the former, in a land where they felt, and were made to feel, more alien than the earlier races. Again, although various factors combined in Europe to foster the emigration thence, perhaps the chief one in starting this different migration to the New World was the demand by the new great industrial corporations here for cheap and ignorant labor which might prove more docile than the restive American laboring man, and more helpless. Importation of foreign labor was the answer of the industrial capitalists to the demands of native labor, just as had been the use of the Irish a half century and more earlier on a smaller scale. At first, large numbers of these new immigrants were brought in under contract and taken straight from the steamer to work in some industry. In 1892 occurred the great Homestead strike of the men in the Carnegie Steel plants. Within fifteen years, by 1907, 75 per cent of the workmen in this great American industry were foreign born. By about the same year the coal mines of Pennsylvania were being operated by a similar percentage of Southern and Eastern European immigrants. Apart from labor contracts, other newcomers of the same races would tend to concentrate where there were already colonies of their nationals who spoke the same language and formed one of those social groups upon which these aliens were dependent.

There was also another important factor in the situation that made these European peasants turn operatives or city dwellers in America. Unlike the earlier immigrants, they did not come with the intention of remaining permanently. Large numbers of them expected to stay a few years, accumulate a little money, and then return to their own lands with more capital and a better position than when they had left. All those who came with this intention would naturally not wish to assume the responsibility of getting and working a farm, but preferred to accept day wages, maintain their old low standard of living, and even go below that, to save as much money as possible in a short time and to keep themselves free from entanglements so that they might return as soon as the happy day dawned when the size of their savings bank account permitted. The earlier immigrants had come to make homes, raise their standard of living, and become citizens; these new ones came as birds of passage, quite willing to lower their standard temporarily in order to raise it when they got home again in Poland or Hungary or Italy.

This also kept them from the desire to assimilate themselves to American social life, to learn English, and to adapt themselves to American ways. As a matter of fact, although great numbers did return home after a few years, they often found themselves out of adjustment there also, owing to their American experiences. After New York, Pittsburgh, or Chicago, even in their worst phases, as these people experienced them, it was too much of a wrench to settle down again in their native villages as peasants. Many did not try the experiment, and, of those who did, many returned here. The whole emigrant movement became more and more mobile. But those who returned here, and those who came for the first time, sought out their own social groups, which had become rather definitely established as workmen in mines and cities rather than as members of agricultural communities. The problems of great slums and of unassimilable racial groups often numbering several hundred thousand in a single place had come upon us, thanks, to a great extent, to the shortsighted selfishness of the great industrial employers who cared only for cheap and "manageable" labor. It is needless to say that this vast floating mass made the maintenance of a fair wage much more difficult for the native workman, who had already inaugurated the period of the greater strikes in an effort to get his reasonable share of the profits of industry, even before this stream of immigration rose to its highest flood. In time these new laborers, who had neither gone home nor become assimilated to America, would come to demand their share, and the difficulty would thus be increased again. The earlier demand for slave labor had left us with the free-negro problem. This later demand for cheap white labor left us with another racial problem, although one somewhat less serious, since, after a generation or two, these people can be absorbed, whereas the negro cannot.

When the first Astor died in 1848, the $20,000,000 fortune left by him was a milestone in American financial and social history. When "Commodore" Vanderbilt died in 1877, he left $105,000,000, and when his son died eight years later his inheritance had grown to $200,000,000, and he had boasted that he was the richest man in the world. We do not have to think of Vanderbilt's most quoted remark, "The public be damned," to realize that none of these men, nor most of those who at that time were laying the foundations of the great inherited American fortunes, ever for a moment thought in terms of social or national welfare. Occasionally a multimillionaire would compound with his conscience or attempt to placate public sentiment by leaving some of his money after his death, when he could no longer enjoy it, to a charitable purpose. Even the rascally Daniel Drew founded a theological seminary in his will. But for the most part these early financial *conquistadores* were as ruthlessly unsocial in their activities as any pirate who ever trod a bloody quarter-deck.

The rapidly rising figures for fortunes which could be and were being accumulated, however, marked the faster tempo of life and acquisition. Not seldom their owners, at death, were perniciously held up by newspapers and clergymen as models for ambitious American youth. They did indeed have to have daring and courage, as does a pirate or a bootleg king, as well as ruthlessness. What gave them the chance to operate upon their new scale was the increasing size of the nation itself — the railroad system, the domestic market, the natural resources, and the vast population of ordinary citizens with their necessities and desires. The tools with which they worked were corporations, the tariff, the stock market, special privileges in railway rates, corrupted legislatures, controlled banks, and the rest of the machinery of the new economic age. Money was power, and control over all these tools grew rapidly with the increasing wealth and power of individuals, groups, or industries. One does not have to be either a communist or a socialist to recognize the enormous possibilities for evil inherent in our system, and the need for control if we are to stave off the different evils of socialism and communism.

In 1888, for the first time a national campaign for President was fought mainly on the tariff as an issue, and two years later, under the successful candidate, Harrison, the McKinley Bill was passed by Congress, raising the average duties to about 50 per cent. Of course, it was said to be necessary, to maintain the high standard of living of the American workman; but as the employers were fighting tooth and nail against the trade-unions, and were willing to import the new immigrant labor to reduce wages, this could not be taken quite seriously. There were in that year about 4,250,000 wage earners in America, and the multitude of farmers in the South and West, who were not sharing in the prosperity of the manufacturers. There was a very deep feeling of unrest throughout the country and a growing opposition to trusts, for fear lest they should monopolize business and the sale of the necessities of life into their own hands, and control the lives of ordinary small citizens. In the same year that Congress served up the McKinley Bill for the protected manufacturers, it threw a sop to the discontented in the form of the celebrated Sherman Anti-Trust Act, which was supposed to make illegal the evils complained of by the people, but which was so drawn as to mean very little until interpreted by the courts.

The ordinary American unfortunately had never been very much offended by corruption. As we have seen, in a land that was, emotionally at any rate, believed to be overflowing with opportunity, and in which the under dog of one day might become top dog the next, in which the scale of values had to a considerable extent become materialized, and ethical concepts of business blurred, no one cared much whether or not someone else "got away" with something shady, provided that the field of opportunity were still left open. For a long time the West had seemed to keep it open, no matter what was being done.

But things were changing. The wave of prosperity which had begun in 1879, and which had shut off Western discontent for a while, had spent itself by 1884, when a panic occurred and carried down the house of Grant and Ward, in which the ex-President was a partner. Things picked up a bit afterward for a few years, but by 1890 the farmer was in serious trouble again from prices. Roughly, from 1873 to 1893 we were in a period of deflation and of falling production of gold, with a more or less steady fall in prices and rising value of gold currency, which had brought about the discontent noted in the last chapter. But there was more to it than that, though the fact of the usual approximate twenty-year cycle in business should be kept in mind.

By 1890, opportunity no longer seemed to be limitless. In this respect the psychological effect of the end of the frontier was probably important. If one wanted to plod as a farmer, one could yet go West and take up a quarter section, but the old freedom was gone, and the mirage of a city arising at any crossroad. Small farming in itself was merely the making of a hard living; it was not boundless opportunity.

Moreover, the farmers had begun to see that they were not getting a square deal. The fact was that the change in the life of the nation, and the weight of numbers and influence, were beginning to tell against them. In 1790, nine tenths of the population had been farmers, and the farmer was listened to. In 1890, only three tenths were farmers, and it was the other seven tenths who were being listened to. In 1850, farm wealth was over half the nation's total; in 1890, it was but a quarter. Around 1890, everything appeared to be conspiring against the farmer — nature, in a series of droughts and other disasters; sound economic theory, which had caused the burden of debt to become unbearably heavy by the appreciation of sound money; the great corporations, by their discriminations and high charges; the declining gold production, which, with world over-production, was lowering the prices for farm produce to levels which would soon spell disaster. The droughts continued in parts of the West for nearly ten years, and the annual production of corn in Kansas and Nebraska alone declined from over 287,000,000 bushels in 1885 to 110,500,000 in 1889. By 1890, farm mortgages had increased to the astounding figure of $1,086,000,000, and there were whole Western counties in which 90 per cent of all farm lands were under heavy mortgage. Owing to falling prices, the cost of raising wheat and corn became actually greater than the amounts received for it. In Kansas over 11,000 mortgages were foreclosed in four years, and by 1895 between 75 per cent and 90 per cent of the land in fifteen counties of that State taken for examination had passed from the owners into the possession of loan companies.

The passage of the McKinley tariff in 1890 had seemed the last straw to the suffering agricultural part of the nation, and in 1892 the Democrats won, reëlecting Cleveland as President for four stormy years. In the same year that the Republicans had passed the tariff and the Anti-Trust Act, they had also passed an act providing for the purchase by the government of 4,500,000 ounces of silver bullion each month, issuing for it legal-tender Treasury notes payable in either silver or gold. McKinley himself was a free-silver man, but the Party must assume responsibility for this measure. The business cycle had just about come to its full round, and the over-speculation in part of the country's business and the bad basic conditions in others would have precipitated a crisis in any case; but the Republican Silver Act brought it about almost as soon as Cleveland was installed. Between 1890 and 1893, the silver dollar had dropped in comparison with gold from eighty to sixty cents. By means of the Treasury notes which the Republicans had created, business men could take silver certificates to the Treasury, exchange them for Treasury notes, and then demand gold in exchange for them, putting in approximately sixty cents and drawing out a dollar. As Cleveland said, "an endless chain" had been set in motion to drain all the gold out of the United States Treasury.

The chain operated. The $100,000,000 gold reserve began to dwindle, and panic seized the entire country as repudiation faced the government. The Free-Silverites in Congress tried to prevent any remedial legislation, although they were forced to consent to the repeal of the silver purchasing clause of the Sherman Act in 1893. Cleveland assumed the responsibility of acting under an almost forgotten statute, sold bonds on four occasions, and staved off a breakdown of government credit. By doing so, and especially by the terms of one of the sales which was made through J. P. Morgan and Company, he aroused intense opposition among the Free Silver wing of his party, which was mostly in the West. By securing the passage of an income-tax measure he alienated the capitalists, and by his handling of the Pullman strike he likewise lost support among labor.

The hard times had brought much suffering to the wage earners, and in 1892, under Cleveland's predecessor, Harrison, there had been a great strike at the Carnegie Steel Works at Homestead, Pennsylvania, the men demanding a revision of the wage scale and recognition of their union. Steel was heavily protected in the tariff on the plea of protection of the American workingman, but the steel plants have been consistent opponents of the unions, and the demands were rejected. Three hundred Pinkerton detectives were engaged to guard the works, and a clash occurred with the men in which ten were killed and sixty wounded. With the aid of eight thousand State troops the strike was won for the company. At the same time, President Harrison was ordering Federal troops to suppress a strike of miners in the Cœur d'Alêne district in Idaho.

There were numerous strikes in 1894 after the panic, involving about three quarters of a million workmen, the most serious being at the Pullman plant in Chicago after Cleveland became President. Pullman had built a so-called "model village" in which he housed his workmen, and then cut wages so low as to leave them nothing above the rents which he demanded. The American Railway Union supported the striking Pullman men by refusing to haul trains with Pullman cars attached. The railway magnates refused to consider arbitration. For the first time in our history in a labor dispute, the government secured a blanket injunction against interfering with the movement of the trains. Governor Altgeld of Illinois had ample State troops ready for emergency, but he himself was greatly disliked by capital because of legislation which he had secured and because he had pardoned certain men involved in the Haymarket bomb affair in 1886, though it is now known they were innocent. As the Governor refused to comply with the Federal government's wish to maintain rail service by use of Federal troops, Cleveland, under cover of protecting the mails, sent two thousand troops to Chicago, the Governor claiming that, if the President could order troops into a State to obey his orders against those of the State authorities, constitutional government had broken down. The men lost the strike. Cleveland's wish had been to preserve law and order as he saw it, but he had played into the hands of the railway managers, and by the use of the injunction had involved the courts in labor disputes. As we shall presently note, they had also become involved in another way.

Although we can see now that by the end of Cleveland's administration the trade cycle would have run its course, and, aided by an unpredictable increase in the world's output of gold, prosperity would have returned with a rush, the misery into which the panic of 1893 had plunged the country, and the new contest between organized capital and labor, brought about the last political conflict between the West and the East, between agrarianism and industrialism.

Neither the American farmer nor the American workman has been a radical as that term is understood in Europe. Indeed, as we look back at the issues for which they fought at various times in the second half of the nineteenth century, we see that for the most part they were essentially conservative. The terror aroused among the larger capitalists and by them transmitted to the smaller business men seems difficult to understand if it was genuine. What the larger capitalist feared, in fact, was the loss of one iota of his steadily increasing control over government and the means of piling up colossal wealth. The contest was not at all one between capitalists and socialists or communists, but between classes both of whom were firmly committed to a belief in capitalism. It was between the big men and the little men, the grasper after excessive wealth and power and the man who demanded merely opportunity to make his living and live his life.

It was a conflict as old as the American Constitution — indeed, as the American Revolution. In the propaganda of the Revolution and the Declaration of Independence, the common man had been cajoled to fight by being told that he was very much more important and capable than the leaders really believed him to be. The Constitution, which had been a compromise in so much else, had also been a compromise in this. It had, for example, never been intended that the people at large should choose a President, a choice so unnatural to the conservatives of that day that, as Colonel Mason of Virginia said in the Convention, they considered "it would be to refer a trial of colors to a blind man." "Mankind when they are left to themselves," Washington had commented, "are unfit for their own government."

Little by little the common man successfully claimed for himself the position designated to him in the Declaration. There is nothing harder to maintain for long in human affairs than a nicely adjusted balance. Speaking of government, Hamilton had said, "Give all the power to the many and they will oppress the few. Give all the power to the few and they will oppress the many. Both ought, therefore, to have the power, that each may defend itself against the other." From the beginning there had never been such a perfect balance, but gradually the many had been gaining, especially in the three epochs following Western invasion under Jefferson, Jackson, and Lincoln. On each occasion the conservatives had feared for their control, and with that for their opportunities to do as they liked and were accustomed to doing. It had seemed to take about a generation each time for the pent-up forces of democracy to seek an outlet in political action, and the time had now again arrived. The movement seemed to be as periodic as the business cycle. So far as the democratic movement was linked with economic ills and sufferings, this is easily understood, but it was always much more than that. A steady working out of the doctrines of the Declaration of Independence to their conclusions had always gone hand in hand with the problems of prices and the mortgage on the farm. Economic ills were also suffered by the growing class of wage earners, but the larger significance of each revolt lay in what was in the minds of the farmers, the defenders of the beliefs of their cultural ancestors.

The West and South had been growing more and more restive. Over and above the economic grievances which threatened their existence were larger issues of Americanism. It began to seem as though Hamilton's second supposition were coming true: "Give all the power to the few and they will oppress the many." The farmer and workman had had their several experiences with banks, money lenders, political parties, corporations. The general life of the nation seemed, in spite of elections, to be rapidly passing into the control of a mysterious few operating behind the scenes. Wisconsin was described at this time as being "ruled by a handful of men who had destroyed every vestige of democracy in the community. They settled in private conference practically all the nominations for important offices, controlled conventions, dictated legislation, and had even sought to lay corrupt hands on the courts of justice."

Apart from corruption, the courts, which were the last resort of the people, seemed to be wholly on the side of the capitalistic few. In case after case they had been building up a mass of decisions which had no regard to any interest of the nation except the strictest construction of the rights of property. In New York they had prevented any effort to reform the sweating of labor in homes, and held up tenement-house improvement for twenty years. They had in various States prevented enactments dealing with hours of labor. In the case of Debs and the Chicago strike the Supreme Court had stretched the Constitution beyond the dreams of Hamilton in order to keep Debs in jail; although in 1880 it had upheld an income tax, in 1895, when Joseph Choate was calling such a tax "anarchy," it had reversed itself and declared it unconstitutional; it had made the Sherman Anti-Trust Act almost void by its ruling in the Whiskey case and by denying in the notorious Sugar Trust case that control of 98 per cent of an industry constituted restraint of trade, because "manufacturing" was not "commerce."

In 1890 the Farmers' Alliance in the West had elected three United States Senators and fifty members of the House, and in 1892 the "People's Party" was formed to unite the wage earners of the East with the Western and Southern farming elements. In the convention at Omaha, the "Populists," as they were called, adopted a platform assailing the old parties and demanding free coinage of silver, a graduated income tax, government ownership of railways and telegraphs, shorter working hours for city laborers, the initiative and referendum, direct election of United States Senators, postal savings banks, restricted immigration, and the Australian ballot. The Farmers' Alliance was trying to save the American dream, but a howl of rage and fear went up from the Eastern capitalists and all dependent on them. It is difficult to understand why, with the exception of the free-silver plank, the platform should have been construed as so subversive of civilization and property rights. There is nothing any more radical about government ownership of railways and telegraphs than there is about such ownership of canals and roads, and some conservative countries do own them. It is solely a question of efficiency and of number of officeholders. As for all the other planks named, every one of them has been subsequently enacted into our laws either by State or Federal statutes or by amendments to the Federal Constitution, and most of them under the benediction of the Republican Party, which assuredly cannot be called "radical."

This final revolt of the West must be considered in its entirety, and precisely as were the preceding and successful ones, as a genuine push along the line of democracy. It was not an attack on property, but a demand that the rights of man should go hand in hand with the rights of property, lest property should cease to be a benefit and become a menace to the generality of men. It was all precisely in line with the specific contributions which every frontier, ever since there had been one, had been making to Americanism. Every such push had seemed dangerous and radical to those who had at each stage managed to get themselves a little more firmly entrenched in property rights than had their neighbors. As for the silver heresy, such financial heresies are the natural products of the debtor-frontier condition. It had been one of the grievances of the American colonies that England had prohibited them from printing as much paper money as they wanted when all the colonies were a frontier of empire. As the forms of "cheap money" alter, — paper money, bank notes, silver, — a debtor class can always be counted on to demand the cheapest. As the problem becomes more complex, its solution becomes more uncertain.

For many years the silver-mine owners, whose particular form of capital on a large scale seemed to demand free silver, had been flooding the West with literature educating it to the silver form of the heresy. The West was not alone, however. Such Eastern minds as those of Henry Adams and the President of Brown University shared the heresy, as did William McKinley, who was soon to appear as the standard bearer of the Republican Party in its assault on the dangerous radicalism of the West. In fact, it is by no means certain that the stage to-day may not be set for such a heresy to arise again. The average man in all our modern democracies is no more of a trained economist than our Westerners were in 1896. With the immense fall in the price of silver and the declining production of gold, which the League of Nations states will reach a crisis in 1940, with the world loaded with debts payable in the currency values of 1918 or so, with declining prices and trade, it may well be that we shall hear before 1940, or that we are already beginning to hear, of the demand for a new and more "scientific" basis for currency — that is, a cheaper money to cause inflation for trade and make the payment of debts easier for the debtor. In a sense, Europe is to-day the new economic frontier of America.

Before continuing the story of the final reflux of the frontier on American civilization, we must turn to glance at another aspect of our life in that period. Man is no more solely a creature of economics than he is of politics. Religion and art have always been two of the mainsprings of his being, strange or crude as they sometimes have been. As we have seen, the budding colonial arts of the mid-eighteenth century had been blighted by the Revolution and the decades of preoccupation with material expansion over the West. In the 1830's and 1840's there had been a sudden blooming in Massachusetts of the most distinguished local group we have had in American letters. None of these men, however, with the exception of Emerson, had glimpsed the real essence of Americanism and its dream of democracy. Hawthorne had harked back to the problems of the early Puritan conscience and was a *revenant* from two centuries earlier, though he left us a classic of the Puritan heart. Longfellow was merely a graceful professor-littérateur; Thoreau was less of a democrat than an impossibly extreme individualist; Lowell, in spite of his chatter about democracy, never really understood the ordinary American's love of it and remained essentially the snob at bottom; Whittier, though he gave us a classic of an American province in "Snow-Bound," was too concerned with the problem of the slave, and like Lowell, who would have sacrificed the Union because of his dislike of the South, saw America too much in terms of a sectional evil.

A little later, Whitman, as no one else before or after, caught a vision, so vast he could not master it, of the whole of America and of its tumultuous democratic dreams. Great poetry, he claimed, was always the "result of a national spirit, and not the privilege of a polish'd and select few," and he determined that "without yielding an inch the workingman and the working woman were to be in my pages from first to last." The Greeks had sung of their gods and the mediæval poets of their lords and ladies, but as he saw it "the justification and main purpose of these United States" were "plowing up in earnest the interminable average fallows of humanity." Here at last was a clear attempt to put into winged and singing words the authentic American dream. America was not to be merely an old Europe in a cruder and less finished setting. Something new had come into being, the belief that something fine and noble, something higher than the world had ever seen, would be harvested from "plowing up in earnest the interminable average fallows of humanity." If America were to make any peculiar contribution to the history of the race and not be merely another nation in the endless rise and fall, it would be in forging out something new and uncommon from the common man. The selfish leader of industry, using the masses to accumulate his private millions, could not see it. The "statesman," grown cynical in deals and committees and caucuses, could not see it. The comfortable scholar of European tradition could not see it. It had come into being from the wedlock of the common man and the frontier, a marriage consummated over and over again in our history. The brood born from those who dreamed the dream grew and increased. But there would be nothing in the dream unless the new life for the common man could be made uncommon, unless out of the womb of democracy could come forth beauty of art and living that should fill the spirit with gladness and make the daily round of living something more than a perpetual subduing of the soul's wilderness for material purposes as we had subdued the wilderness of the continent.

Little by little, it seemed to be nearing us. In spite of all the shoddiness and bad taste of the eighties and nineties, the latter decade marked the highest point we have touched in the illustration of magazines for popular circulation. Abbey, Pennell, Crane, Frost, and others were illustrators who would have been notable in any country. Novelists and story-tellers no longer went abroad for their subjects, but a whole multiple group — Joaquin Miller, Bret Harte, James Lane Allen, Joel Chandler Harris, Mary Wilkins Freeman, Sarah Orne Jewett,

George W. Cable, Lafcadio Hearn, Mary N. Murfree, and others — formed the "local color school" in our literary history and painted the local scenes of New England, Virginia, Louisiana, Kentucky, the Far West, until the American reader came to realize the infinite variety in our national unity. Perhaps the most lasting of those named, from a literary standpoint, was the New Englander, Miss Jewett, and it is notable that she painted for that section a society that was essentially static and calm, one that suffered no more from the tumult of American life and uneasy dreaming. On the other hand, the greatest of all came from the West, a young pilot on a Mississippi River steamboat who assumed for his pseudonym the pilot's call in taking his soundings, "Mark Twain." *Tom Sawyer*, *Huckleberry Finn*, and *Innocents Abroad* were redolent of the American life and outlook of the ordinary man. Something new had come from the waters of "Ol' Man River."

And in the Great Valley something new was suddenly to arise, to dazzle us all for a few months and then to disappear, like a magic city from Aladdin's lamp. It had been four hundred years since the island savage in the West Indies had watched with mingled fear and curiosity the landing of the white stranger and the unfurling of the ensign of Spain. Four short centuries, and now the continent from shore to shore was occupied by nearly 65,000,000 people of all races. Times were hard and getting worse, but we decided to invite the nations to join with us in celebrating that momentous landing of Columbus on the beach of that little island in the Bahamas. We planned the World's Fair at Chicago. Our sculptors, architects, landscape gardeners, painters, and others united, and when in 1893 the world came, it was to hold its breath for a moment in amazement at a vision of beauty which has rarely been equaled. Compared with it the Paris Exposition of 1900 was an inchoate jumble of incongruous monstrosities. It was even more a revelation, possibly, to ourselves than to others. We had been busy apparently with exploiting our riches, with our contests between capital and labor, with our dirty politics, and with all the welter of a too fast growing material development, and yet men among ourselves had produced this city of dreams, shimmering beside the lake where only a few generations earlier there had been nothing but the savages and a few traders in furs. It had risen like a dream and was as transient. In a few months the buildings were torn down and the "White City" evaporated as magically as it had grown.

It is true that the architecture and composition were classical and not distinctively American, but the great point was that a democracy apparently wholly immersed in making livings or fortunes could suddenly fling up this thing of beauty for the world; and the millions who went to see it from little New England farms, from small homes in great ugly industrial cities, from shabby towns in the South and raw ones in the West, caught for the first time a vision of what might be such as they had never conceived. In the city which had hitherto been noted chiefly for the stockyard brutality of its business, this thing of form and loveliness had come and gone, a flashing glimpse of what might lie hidden in the inchoate vastness of our common-man democracy, as one might glimpse a diamond through the heavy enclosing matrix of rough and common stone. As it vanishes, we turn again to the daily round.

In some ways it was a new West and a new South which drew up in the battle for democracy against the East in 1896. It was a West which needed far more capital than the earlier ones, for farm machinery cost money and the modern farmer had to be something of a capitalist himself, and at every turn he found himself fighting a corporation — railroad, bank, farm-machine manufacturer, or what not — which was without human form and which seemed to be almost beyond human reach. The cinch bug, the grasshopper, the refractory soil, the Indian, and most of the other enemies of earlier days had been reachable, but who could reach these corporations which were everywhere and yet nowhere, which covered their tracks in bought legislatures, courts, charters, and interpretations of the Constitution protecting property?

The South also was facing new conditions. At the Cotton Exposition at Atlanta in 1881, a few of the weavers had come down from the Appalachian Mountains and showed their hand looms by which a weaver working ten hours a day could weave eight yards of cloth. The machinery of the modern mills, which was also exhibited, could produce eight hundred yards per human tender in the same time, or a hundredfold. And the mills had been producing too fast. There was world over-production, and the planters found that cotton was no longer king. For a decade they were in sore straits to pay the annual loans made to raise their crops. Neither West nor South was any longer wholly agrarian. There were great commercial and industrial cities in the West, and the smoking chimneys of the ironworks at Birmingham and other signs showed the beginning industrialization of the South.

The East also had changed. The steady industrialization of that section had gone on and vast accumulations of wealth were now dependent on government favors and special privileges. The Supreme Court had been deciding questions wholly in favor of the great corporations, and in the Debs case had even asserted that in the absence of statutes it had the power to prevent interference with interstate commerce, an unexpected stretching of the Constitution which brought profound satisfaction to entrenched wealth. The tariff, which had not only protected "infant industries" but made possible the earning of colossal returns upon real and watered capital, had been extended to heights undreamed of by Clay in his "American System." The East, in a word, had come to lay tremendous stress not simply upon the protection of property rights under law, as contrasted with the rights of man, but upon what it had gradually come to consider its vested rights in governmental favoritism. At every turn, in one way and another, its wealth was more and more coming to depend on legislation and governmental action of various sorts. The McKinley tariff of 1890 had resulted in the return of the Democrats in 1892, and the following year the Democratic tariff bill had both lowered duties somewhat and included the nightmare of the income tax. The moneyed interests of the East were determined that their hold should not be relaxed again if they could help it.

In each rising in the past, there had been some impossible notions mixed in with the sound democratic doctrines and strivings. Economic life had become far more complex, however, and the issue of free silver, following so soon on the experience under Cleveland of the "endless chain" drain on gold bequeathed to him by the Republicans, frightened the entire creditor class, and properly. As a result both of that and of manipulation, free silver soon loomed up as the major issue of the campaign in 1896. The boss of the Republican Party, Marcus A. Hanna, a wealthy capitalist from Ohio, dictated the nomination of his protégé McKinley (who was under heavy financial obligations to him of an honest sort) for President on the Republican ticket. His election would ensure, as far as might be, a tariff satisfactory to the East, but unfortunately he was a free-silver man. However, he had good precedent for changing a religion to gain a crown, and when nominated he accepted the plank in the platform which demanded the preservation of the gold standard. The Populists merged with the Democrats, and with Bryan as leader came out for the free coinage of silver at the fixed ratio of sixteen to one. The silver question, which had cut sharply across party lines, as in the case of McKinley himself, caused a split in both major parties, the pro-silver Republicans passing to the Democrats, and the gold Democrats nominating a separate ticket. Even the Prohibitionists split and put gold and silver candidates in the field. The Populists had merged with the Democrats only with the greatest reluctance, feeling that the real questions in the campaign other than that of silver were being completely overshadowed.

McKinley had stated a few days after his nomination that the tariff was the issue, that the money question was becoming unduly prominent, and that in thirty days no one would hear of it. In fact, however, in less than that time one heard nothing else. The East and the moneyed interests everywhere were whipped to frenzy by terror. I well recall the members of the Stock Exchange marching in a body up Broadway, and the general sense of untold horrors overhanging the whole country if Bryan were elected. I have never known another such wave of emotion catching up whole communities, not even our entry into the Great War or Armistice Day. Bryan, in his famous but not extempore Cross of Gold speech, had not only stampeded the Democratic Convention, but made the gold issue the only one in the campaign that was heard of at all.

An honest man of extremely limited mind, Bryan cannot for an instant be considered in the same category as the three men — Jefferson, Jackson, and Lincoln — who had led the common people in the earlier revolts, but he made a colossal impression. The Republican moneybags were bulging, the great corporations pouring out contributions at the nod of Hanna, whereas the Democrats had nothing. According to Mrs. Henry Cabot Lodge, writing at the time, the McKinley forces had $7,000,000 against Bryan's $300,000. "The great fight is won," she wrote to Cecil Spring-Rice after the election. It was a fight, she added, "conducted by trained and experienced and organized forces, with both hands full of money, with the full power of the press — and of prestige — on one side; on the other, a disorganized mob at first, out of which burst into sight, hearing, and force — one man, but such a man! Alone, penniless, without backing, without money, with scarce a paper, without speakers, that man fought such a fight that even those in the East can call him a Crusader, an inspired fanatic — a prophet! It has been marvelous. Hampered by such a following, such a platform, — and even the men whose names were our greatest weapon against him deserted him and left him to fight alone, — he almost won. . . . We had during the last week of the campaign 18,000 speakers on the stump. He alone spoke for his party, but speeches which spoke to the intelligence and hearts of the people, and with a capital P. It is over now, but the vote is seven millions to six millions and a half." "When a man polls as many votes as he has received for the Presidency, I suppose there must be something in him," remarked Whitelaw Reid less lyrically. Or in the cause for which he stood, we may add. If the man could elicit such comments on the day of victory from such hide-bound Republicans as Mrs. Lodge and Mr. Reid, there must have been, we might say, a good deal all around in spite of the limited mentality of Bryan himself.

The campaign issue was simplified for the average Republican voter, who cared little about the great network of vested interests working behind the scenes for purposes of their own, but everything for the safety of his own property and job or business, which was in jeopardy from free silver. No one who recalls the campaign in the East can forget the grisly fear that peeped from every ballot box that November day in 1896. For the Democratic voter the issue was only in part that of silver. It is true that he considered it a panacea for many of his ills and that Bryan unduly stressed it, but the wave of frantic emotion which swept over the West and South was of the same sort which had swept them in earlier uprisings. Gold was only the symbol of a power which the common man felt to be strangling both him and his Americanism, his dream of democracy and of the rights of man against the claims of privilege. To consider that the Southern and Western farmers who had their all invested in that most inconvertible of all forms of property, farm lands and implements, wished to attack the rights of property is absurd. What they were demanding was the right to enjoy and employ *their* property as independent citizens, getting only a square deal from those who had *other* forms of property. Their monetary theory was wrong, but so was that of Henry Adams, President Andrews of Brown University, and of a good many conservative Easterners, as well as of the Republican candidate himself, McKinley. That was neither here nor there. What did matter for those in revolt, and matter to the bottom of their hearts, was that the money power and corporations — "the interests," as they were beginning to be called — should not conquer and ruin America for the ordinary everyday common man. The demand was valid and just, and if the intelligence of the nation could spare only a Bryan to lead them, the reflection was rather on the nation's intelligence than on them. Mrs. Lodge, womanlike, could see only the individual and not the issue. Reid, like a certain type of capitalist, could see only the politician and not the people. What none heard was the voice of the American, of the American farmer who had stood behind the stone walls as the redcoats retreated from Lexington and who took pot shots at them, of the farmer who had gone to the Connecticut River, and then to western New York, and then to Ohio, and then to Illinois, and then to Kansas, or followed the same western trek in the South; the voice of the early Americans who had been promised "life, liberty, and the pursuit of happiness" by Thomas Jefferson while the conservatives of his day raised their eyebrows and smiled questioningly.

It had been the frontier of each succeeding epoch from which that voice had always risen most clearly and emphatically. When the forces of each generation had accumulated to the bursting point, it had been heard and listened to. But in 1890 the government had noted briefly that the frontier was ended. In 1896, for the first time, a revolt of the frontier failed. Something had gone out of American life. Something new had entrenched itself against attack. In the East, when the news was known the morning after election, there was wild jubilation.

In the West, "Ol' Man River" rolled sombrely to the Gulf. Yes, the East was right on gold and sound currency, as it had always been except in the earliest days when it itself was England's "West," and it had been heretical, but there was so much more than that. This dream that "Ol' Man River" had heard his children dreaming for so long, this dream that at last man was to be worth more than gold, what was to become of that? What of that boy "Mark Twain," who had known and understood him so well and done so much, and then had gone East, bitten, to make a fortune like others, and who was now struggling with bankruptcy and Shylock creditors? What of it all? Across the Gulf in Mexico, Spaniards had come long ago for gold, and more gold. But "Ol' Man River's" children had dreamed of better things as well. Was it only a dream after all? Could they not be satisfied with the gold of mines and forests and fields and honest commerce without digging it from the souls of men? And "Ol' Man River" rolled on to the Gulf.

In spite of the fact that the Republicans had been elected by the terror of a repudiation of the gold standard, they waited three years and a half before passing any legislation on the subject, — in the Currency Act of 1900, — but immediately on election McKinley announced that he would call Congress in special session to raise the tariff. The bill presented by Congressman Dingley, in accordance with the mandates of the manufacturers, passed the House after a purely perfunctory debate of a fortnight in spite of the protests of such men as Worthington C. Ford, chief of the Bureau of Statistics, as to its economic unsoundness. The people, having been panicked by the bogie of the currency, were rewarded for their votes with an increase in the cost of living. As Mr. Ford said, many of the new rates were not merely protective but prohibitive, and the new tariff had emphasized a change in policy from revenue with incidental protection to protection with incidental revenue.

At the entrance to the Gulf of Mexico, only a hundred miles due south from the tip of Florida, lay the large and rich island of Cuba, still in the possession of Spain after four centuries. Its population was chiefly made up of Scotch, English, and American planters of sugar and coffee, of some pure-blood Spaniards, and of a great mass of mixed bloods compounded of Spanish, negro, and Indian. On the one hand, there had been bad misrule by the Spaniards for many years. On the other, many of the Cuban revolutionists — who warred, from time to time, in the worst South American fashion against the ruling power — were as corrupt as the Spaniards themselves. In 1895, one of the interminable revolutions was started again, and Spain named as Governor a "hard-boiled" army general, Weyler, who adopted an unstatesmanlike policy of repression. The sympathy of the American public — always sensitive, as we have noted, to the "under-dog complex" — was deeply aroused by the newspaper accounts of Weyler's atrocities. We have always felt, quite irrespective of local conditions and characteristics, that any and every people is not only entitled to self-government, but capable of it — an altruistic and idealistic but extremely dangerous belief. As I watched the income account of a large sugar estate, in which I happened to have personal interest, being bled by bribes to the Spanish authorities on the one hand, and by yet heavier blackmail by the Cuban "patriots" on the other, to keep them from burning the sugar cane, — sometimes ten thousand dollars at a time being paid to their representatives in the third-story back room of a building in Front Street, New York, — the scales of injustice seemed to me somewhat more evenly weighted than they did to those who thought of the Cuban "patriots" in terms of our 1776.

Affairs drifted on, and, partly in view of the strong American feeling toward the end of 1897, Spain promised home rule to Cuba and reform. Unfortunately we had sent a battleship, the *Maine*, to Havana harbor, and while at anchor there, on February 15, 1898, she was blown up by an explosion, the real cause of which has never yet been ascertained by the public. Spain immediately urged investigation by an impartial tribunal, and arbitration. We declined both, though we had always stood for arbitration of international disputes. An American investigating board announced on March 28 that the ship had been blown up from the outside; a Spanish board, which was not permitted to visit the ship and which had to judge from the outside, announced that she had been blown up by an internal explosion. Subsequently the United States Government had her towed out to sea and sunk so deep that no commission will ever be able to investigate her again.

Inflamed by the yellow newspaper press led by Hearst, the public meanwhile had gone mad. Roosevelt, always bellicose, and then Assistant Secretary of the Navy, demanded that the Spaniards be driven from the New World. McKinley was for peace, but was weak and feared that he would disrupt the Republican Party and interfere with the smooth-running machinery of tariff making and other interesting functions of government if he tried to lead the country and stem the tide of insane jingoism. He noted a year later that if he had been left alone he could have secured the withdrawal of Spain from Cuba without a war. Presidents of the United States can hardly expect to "be left alone," but some of them have had the courage to stand alone and to lead, as did John Adams when he saved us from war with France. What McKinley said, however, was true enough. When he sent an ultimatum to Spain the day after the American commission reported that the *Maine* had been blown up from the outside (which, even if true, did not necessarily determine that it had been by the orders or connivance of the Spanish government), General Woodford, whom I happened to know and who was an honest man, cabled to McKinley within forty-eight hours that Spain knew Cuba was lost, that she was willing to let her go and do everything possible to placate the United States as rapidly as might be consistent with avoiding revolution in Spain itself. Shortly after that he cabled again that he could secure, before August 1, the acquiescence of Spain in either the independence of Cuba or even the annexation of the island to the United States, and that Spain was loyally ready to make any concession. The next day after receiving this cable, McKinley sent a message to Congress asking for a declaration of war. Perhaps he had been too deeply stung by Roosevelt's remark that he "had no more backbone than a chocolate éclair," and so proved the positive in trying to prove the negative.

Senator Lodge wrote to Roosevelt, who had contemplated the capture of the Philippines six months earlier, that we intended to have Porto Rico and he thought that the administration was "now fully committed to the large policy which we both desire." The frontier was closed, but Porto Rico and the Philippines, with a population of over ten millions and enormously rich natural resources, were good pickings. Congress, not mentioning these matters, promptly passed a self-denying ordinance announcing to the world that we had no intention "to exercise sovereignty, jurisdiction, or control" over Cuba, and that after it had been pacified we would "leave the government and control of the island to its people," a statement nullified by the insistence later on Cuba's accepting the Platt Amendment which gave us coaling stations in the island for our navy, the right to intervene in her affairs for the preservation of order, and a veto over both the diplomatic and the fiscal relations of the Cuban government with any foreign power. Recently, in our dispute with the Cunard Line about running ships between New York and Havana, we took the ground that such business was our own "coastwise commerce." Yet, when it comes to the tariff on sugar, Cuba is an independent foreign State. It would appear to have been given its independence by us on rather anomalous terms, and would probably have been far more independent had General Woodford secured that independence by negotiation, as he could have done, instead of McKinley's securing it by war. But in that case we should not have got Porto Rico and the Philippines, Roosevelt would not have had the chance to take his "Rough Riders" for the "charge" on "San Juan Hill" and would likely not have been President, and many things would have been different for us as well as the Cubans.

Of the war itself, not much needs to be said. The Spanish navy was old and in bad shape. Dewey became a national hero for a few months by defeating the part of the Spanish fleet in Manila Bay, and Admiral Cervera was defeated when he tried to make a dash out of the harbor of Santiago in Cuba. The land forces were easily overcome, and the whole affair was a picnic. Without counting the real odds, every victory was received with wild enthusiasm, tempered by the scandals of gross mismanagement in the army and the heavy toll of deaths by preventable diseases.

By the first of October, the peace commissioners were meeting in Paris to make the treaty which would end the affair. Cuba received her independence, the wings of which were to be clipped by our Congress two years later, and we took Porto Rico and the Philippines, paying Spain $20,000,000 for the latter, or about two dollars apiece for each Filipino. When the Peace Treaty was presented to the Senate for ratification, much opposition had developed in the country to the annexation of foreign territory inhabited by peoples who did not speak our language and who could not be assimilated to our institutions. The treaty was ratified only after Senator Lodge had pointed out to his fellow Senators that it would be disgraceful not to ratify what the President had negotiated at Paris, an opinion which he was conveniently to forget on another occasion twenty years later when another President, Mr. Wilson, had also been negotiating at Paris.

Most Americans had enjoyed the war immensely. There was no draft, there were only 223,000 volunteers in service out of a population of 76,000,000, and the casualties were slight. We overlooked the gross incompetence of the army chiefs and such trifles as that, owing to inferior rifles, it took 6500 Americans three hours to subdue 600 Spaniards at El Caney. Victories seemed to come as easily as picking ripe strawberries, and we were amused at making Germany angry and pleased to have England, for the first time in our history, voluntarily come and stand by our side, as at Manila Bay when Admiral Chichester of the British fleet intimated to the German Admiral Diederich that he had best not interfere with Dewey.

The spoils of the war, however, left us with new problems. In some respects, such as the efforts of Major Walter Reed and later of Major W. C. Gorgas, which completely exterminated the dreaded scourge of yellow fever, we accomplished a notable amount of good for all the new islands in our possession; and our administration, though far from flawless, has on the whole been excellent and attended with good results. The Filipinos, however, seemed no more anxious to be governed by us than the Cubans had been to be governed by Spain, and an insurrection cost us more lives than the war itself. For the first time we glimpsed the fact that, even when people want to govern themselves, they may not be capable of it — when *we* want to govern *them*.

Before these new acquisitions, we had seized only empty land, — for Indians never counted, — and the land when filled with our own settlers could be carved up into Territories to become States. Possibly that could eventually be done with Porto Rico, but the Philippines were different. Did the Constitution apply to these ten millions or so of "little brown brothers," as Mr. Taft called them? Were the new possessions part of the United States or not, and if not, what in the world were they?

As might have been surmised, the question assumed an immediate practical aspect through the tariff. The American sugar producers demanded a tariff on imported sugars from the islands, but how could this be placed on them if they were part of ourselves? I understand that at present the independence of the Filipinos is being advocated so that this question can be settled satisfactorily to American producers and prohibitively for the Filipinos. It emerged at once in 1899. If we had had an unwritten and elastic constitution like the British, all might have been easy sailing; but we had a written document which had always to be interpreted with some dynamite to allow us to annex new territory, and which assuredly gave us no light at all on how it would allow us to govern ten million people who did not want us to govern them, whom we did not intend to make citizens, and whom we did so much want to tax.

In 1901 the problem was passed on to the Supreme Court, and it was found, as Mr. Dooley said, that "no matter whether the Constitution follows the flag or not, th' Supreme Court follows the illiction returns." By a decision of five to four, even the five disagreeing among themselves as to the reasoning by which they had arrived at their partial unanimity, it was decided for us that "Porto Rico is a territory appurtenant — but not a part — of the United States." So that was that, and the rest followed. What we had we meant to keep, and we meant to do as we liked. Our new population was judicially declared to be neither American nor foreign, because, as Mr. Dooley also said, "the flag was so lively no constitution could follow it and survive."

What interests us particularly here is that for a generation and more our political philosophy had been showing a marked divergence from that of the days of the Declaration of Independence and the drafting of the Constitution. The first major breakdown had come with the Civil War. It had always been an anomaly that, with our political philosophy asserting that government derives its just powers only from the consent of the governed, we had held three million slaves in subjection. It was still more of an anomaly that when five million or more white citizens no longer consented and withdrew we forcibly obliged them to return. And now we had taken on over a million in Porto Rico and about ten million in the Far East, and the latter, who had been bought for cash, so far from consenting, had staged an insurrection which had had to be put down with a very bloody hand.

McKinley had been overwhelmingly reëlected in 1900 with the Cuban War hero, Roosevelt, as Vice President, and the country had endorsed the war and the annexations, and the Supreme Court had had to rationalize a *fait accompli*. How difficult was the feat was shown by the fact that, as Mr. Justice Brown was parodied as saying, the decision was handed down by the nine justices, "dissenting fr'm me an' each other." They could do nought else; but deep gashes in a national political philosophy or a constitution do not heal without leaving marked scars any more than they do in a man's body. The old Americanism of the frontier had grown from belief that in the early days we had meant what we said when we announced that just government could only be by consent of the governed, and that all citizens were entitled to certain rights. We had always had to shut one eye when we looked at the negro, and after 1865 we had had to shut it also when we looked at the South and those in it who objected to being "reconstructed." We had had slaves, and we had had "rebels," and now over 10 per cent of our population were "subjects." It was getting a bit hard to maintain the fiction of the free man giving his free consent to a free government; and if that were no longer to be held by us as the one infallible political philosophy for freedom, might not the inroads on the old conception extend yet further? If the slaves were to do as the masters told them because *they* had the power, and the South were to do as the North said because *it* had the power, and our islanders were to do as we said because *we* had the power, why should not the little citizen do as the big citizens and the corporations said because *they* had the power? Mr. Alexander Hamilton had evidently led us a long way off from Mr. Thomas Jefferson on his hilltop at Monticello.

On March 2, 1901, Messrs. J. P. Morgan and Company announced the formation of the United States Steel Corporation, and four weeks later stated that its amended capital would be $1,100,000,000. The "billion-dollar trust" had come. On September 6, President McKinley was shot by a mentally unsound anarchist, and on his death, eight days later, Roosevelt became President of the United States and its "Insular Possessions."

XII

THE AGE OF THE DINOSAURS

In what is known as the Jurassic period in the geological history of the earth, there suddenly developed in the course of animal evolution a vast number of huge reptiles which numbered among their species the largest animals ever known, some of them fifty feet long or more. A fortuitous combination of evolutionary factors produced these new rulers of the sea, land, and air which by sheer bulk, physical strength, and weapons of offense seemed destined, once they had appeared, to dominate the world. They roamed the continent æons before our story begins, and even now their fossilized skeletons in our museums, of terrifying size and with jaws filled with two hundred or more teeth, appall us. But nature proved that mere size was not a final factor in development, and somehow these colossal creatures failed in efficiency and adjustment, and passed from the scene.

In the same way, in our own age, a combination of elements suddenly brought into existence in our social and economic world huge business combinations in the form of corporations of a hitherto undreamed-of size, which seemed destined, like the dinosaurs of old, to rule the land. In bulk, strength, and weapons of offense it appeared that nothing could oppose them. Whether they also will develop weaknesses in efficiency and adjustment for which their mere bulk is no compensation, and disappear in their turn, is as yet an open question. It is probable that the dinosaurs passed because of lack of brain power. The difficulty of supplying our modern economic monsters with sufficient power of intellectual direction at the top has already become evident. Whatever the eventual outcome may be, it became clear to the smaller but intelligent and life-loving individuals when these new colossi suddenly rose among them that there was a fight to be waged for all that they had felt made life worth living.

The United States Steel Corporation was merely the greatest among the new economic monsters. A conservative estimate in 1904 showed that 5300 formerly distinct plants had been combined into 318 trusts with a capital of $7,246,000,000, whereas another estimate placed the capital of a larger number of combinations at over $20,000,000,000. While these combinations were being effected in the industrial world, similar ones, eliminating competition, were going forward in railroads. Yet more menacing was the concentration of power proceeding in the banking world, which even the conservative, capitalistic *Wall Street Journal* described in 1903 as "not merely a normal growth, but concentration that comes from combination, consolidation, and other methods employed to secure monopolistic power. Not only this, but this concentration has not been along the lines of commercial banking. The great banks of concentration are in close alliance with financial interests intimately connected with promotion of immense enterprises, many of them being largely speculative." It added that the banking power was passing to the control of men who were less interested in legitimate banking than in stock promotion, watering, and manipulation.

All of these new mammoths were controlled in the last analysis by an extremely small group of men, mostly in

New York City. The members of the Morgan and Rockefeller groups together held 341 directorships in 112 banks, railroads, insurance and other corporations, having aggregate resources under their control of $22,245,000,000. In an after-dinner speech one of the group made the tactical mistake of declaring that it had been said that the business of the United States was then controlled by twelve men, of whom he was one, and that the statement was true. This remark, made among friends, was deleted from the printed report of the speech when given to the public, but the public was well enough aware of the general situation without such admission. Never before had such colossal power concentrated so rapidly into the hands of a few, whether we consider the resources and income at their command, the population affected by their orders and acts, or the millions of persons in their direct employ.

Frequently uninteresting individually, collectively the study of the mentality of the new business leaders is extraordinarily interesting from a social point of view. Charles Francis Adams, who as president of the Union Pacific Railroad had known many of them well, wrote of them that he never cared to meet one again in this world or the next, "nor is one of them associated in my mind with the idea of humor, thought, or refinement. A set of mere money-getters and traders, they were essentially unattractive and uninteresting. The fact is that money-getting, like everything else, calls for a special aptitude and great concentration."

These men were far less crude than those of the William H. Vanderbilt, Jay Gould type of the preceding generation. For one thing, manners had improved in the nation at large, and for another, a type of corporation lawyer had developed which would have scorned to have clients resort to such spectacular rawness as Jay Gould's printing press for "illegal" stock certificates, flight to New Jersey with his money, and the rest of the melodramatic incidents of the post-Civil War period. Whenever possible, the new hands were gloved. Moreover, that odd dichotomy of the mind of great American business men had begun to show itself on the grand scale. What they might do as men and what they might do as "business men" bore little moral relation to one another. A man might be a pirate in business and a beneficent god in bestowing gifts on his native village or on some pet charitable or educational institution.

For example, one well-known Wall Street man who bore the nickname of "Hell Hound" in the financial world was worshiped by his native villagers and a few other beneficiaries of his golden drippings. Andrew Carnegie, who had fought his workmen's reasonable demands for better living conditions and had replaced native American labor by foreign immigrants for the sake of more complete control over their destinies, had begun to distribute millions for his libraries, buying a cheap notoriety on terms so onerous that more than one town or city, including the one in which I happened to live, declined to accept the money in accordance with them. Even before he had sold his works to the United States Steel Corporation, his personal share of the profits had begun to amount to more than $25,000,000 annually. Rockefeller's income was apparently much greater than that, and he who had been ruthless in business also began to scatter largess among the people in his non-business hours.

Perhaps the broadest and most constructive mind of the whole crowd was that of the elder Morgan. One would venture to interfere with him only at the peril of one's financial life, yet he could be singularly generous on occasion, as I have good reason to know. One day there was a money panic in Wall Street, and after rising to an interest rate of 1 per cent a day, or 365 per cent annually, money disappeared. There was none to be had on any terms even for the borrower with the most gilt-edged security. My father had to have $50,000 before three o'clock, or his firm would fail. He could not get a dollar from any bank, though his collateral security was of the soundest. As a last resort he went with an introduction to Mr. Morgan, who was a total stranger, but who at once lent him the money. When on leaving, after an interview which had lasted scarcely two minutes, my father asked him what the rate of interest would be, Morgan, without looking up from the papers to which he had already turned, replied gruffly, "Six per cent — Morgan and Company never charge more than that." Morgan had not the slightest interest in my father, the failure of whose house would not have left a ripple on the stormy waters of Wall Street that day. The gesture was that of a monarch who reprieves an innocent man from death, and passes to other things. Morgan alone in that day made such gestures. As contrasted with him, many of the other "great" bankers, with whom I was occasionally mixed up in episodes as intimately personal as the above, had the souls of pushcart peddlers.

Then there were the so-called "Empire Builders," men of the type of Harriman and Hill, the railway magnates. Different in many respects as all these men were, they had certain traits in common. For one thing, there was the American idea already noted that there was somehow virtue in making money and "developing" the country as fast as possible, which had as its corollary the belief that the main point was to get a thing done regardless of how it was done or its larger social implications. This had become a marked American characteristic, inherited from the frontier "get rich quick and develop fast" state of mind. It was as marked in Roosevelt, who fought the big business leaders, as it was in those leaders themselves. We shall note later his grab of the Panama Canal Zone, but may quote here his alleged remark, when circumventing an Act of Congress in regard to the building of the canal, "Damn the law. I want the canal built." That was precisely the spirit of the men who were ruling the world of business in America at the same period.

With this spirit went an autocratic belief in their own right to rule the people, to develop the country when and where it suited their own convenience, by methods of their own choosing, and to prevent any interference of any sort with their own plans — in a word, to become benevolent despots, if we grant them the courtesy use of the adjective. When, in the great coal strike of 1902, the men were striking against gross abuses of power on the part of the owners, the spokesman of the latter, George F. Baer, declared, "The rights and interests of the laboring man will be protected and cared for, not by the labor agitators, but by the Christian men to whom God in His infinite wisdom has given the control of the property interests of this country, and upon the successful management of which so much depends." Hamiltonianism had gone full circle to divine right; and the rights of man in the Declaration of Independence had collided with the new doctrine of the divinity that doth hedge a capitalist if he is big enough. To such men, the American dream was drivel.

The Hamiltonian system had run completely amuck, having lost its balance wheel. But could the Jeffersonian one function any better? What was left of that base of free farmers owning their own homes and lands on which Jefferson had rested it? In 1900, our population was about 76,000,000. Of this number, somewhat less than 5,000,000 were classed as farmers and planters; 2,550,000 as wage-earning farm hands; another 2,550,000 as wage earners in domestic and personal service; over 3,000,000 in trade and transportation; and nearly 19,000,000 in manufacturing and mechanical pursuits. Over 6,000,000 persons over ten years of age were wholly illiterate, and more than half of these were not immigrants but native-born Americans. The comparatively simple social and governmental problems of 1787 had become so overwhelmingly complex that it is a question to-day whether we or any other nation are going to be able to solve them by intelligence or whether we shall become the victims of uncontrolled forces. In the early days men received a political education in town meetings, and most of their problems were close to their homes. By 1900, the organization of the political system had become such that it seemed to run with as little chance for the individual to influence it as the dynamo in a central power plant.

The fact was, though we did not recognize it then and do not want to to-day, that the forces let loose by the Industrial Revolution and the age of applied science were causing new patterns to be made in the nations, patterns in which coöperation and socialization on a hitherto undreamed-of scale would have to replace to a great extent the old individualism of the eighteenth century and of that American frontier which had continued that century for us long after the calendar had proclaimed it ended. The American workman, the factory wage earner, the horde of salaried men in corporation employ, the farmer raising wheat in Kansas and selling it in London or Bombay in competition with Russia or the Argentine, the capitalist controlling billions of resources in enterprises that affected vitally the lives and happiness of millions of men, women, and children — all still dreamed of living the individualistic lives of the colonial American farmer of New England or Virginia. Each group felt itself hampered by the others. When an Oregonian who wanted to develop the interior of his State found that a Harriman would allow no one to build a railroad into it until he got ready to do so himself, there was heated resentment against the power of the magnates. When the government stepped in, as in the dissolution of the Northern Securities railway merger, the magnates would complain bitterly, as did Hill against Roosevelt, saying it was outrageous that the big business men should have to "fight for our lives against the political adventurers who have never done anything but pose and draw a salary."

Our training and education had not fitted us to solve the new problems. The folkways and life about us, which properly constitute a large part of training, had all been on the side of individualism, ruthless competition, money made quickly by any method, disregard of law and of the social results of individual acts. We learned "patriotism," but not good citizenship. As for our "book education," Woodrow Wilson came close to the mark when he said, in 1907, "You know that with all our teaching we train nobody; you know that with all our instructing we educate nobody." Hamiltonianism was breaking down because the powerful were trying to grasp all power. Jeffersonianism was breaking down because the nation was no longer composed of freemen and freeholders, competent to grapple with the problems of their social environment and forces. Education, by which we had thought to keep the electorate competent for self-government, was breaking down because we had no scale of values and no real objective in our educational system. For the masses, at its best, it had become a confused jumble of "book learning" that gave them neither values to strive for nor that knowledge and intellectual training which might have been of help in understanding the complexity of the forces with which they had to deal intelligently. Yet the American dream was still cherished in millions of our hearts, not least among the common people of farm and factory and shop; and rightly so. What we needed was a leader with sympathies and understanding as broad as his vision might be keen. How deeply the people felt that need had been shown in their whole-hearted devotion to Bryan for his democracy and his belief in the American dream, in spite of his errors — intellectual, social, economic.

The nation was still sectional in that the North, South, West, and Pacific Coast had each its own demands and types of life; but the frontier had gone, and the country was fast being integrated. Of the railway kings, for example, Harriman ruled his Western system from New York, Hill his from Minnesota, and Huntington his from California. The problems had become national as well as sectional. The most pressing of these was the conflict not so much between capital and labor as between the ordinary small American — whether laborer, farmer, or small shopkeeper — and the new class of great magnates who had come to look upon the country as their personal property to be run according to their own ideas. Beyond the first ten or twenty millions which they accumulated for themselves, they were not so much lustful for money as for power and resources with which to "play the game." It was much the same feeling that makes a boy's heart throb as he races his car with another, at highly illegal speed and risk, and wins. Incidentally, as in the case of Harriman and his rehabilitation of the Union Pacific, they might perform services by which the whole community benefited. On the other hand, they might wreck properties, or, in their struggles occasionally against each other, destroy any number of smaller men. Meanwhile, through control of the great corporations, they controlled the destinies of millions of us. Many who had never heard the darkies singing in the South would have at once felt the sting in the words

> The old bee makes de honey-comb,
> The young bee makes de honey;
> Colored folks plant de cotton an' corn,
> And de white folks gits de money.

On every hand the ordinary American citizen was uneasy and looking about for leadership in the fight against "the trusts" — which meant the apparently unreachable controls over his daily life and business.

Suddenly the shot was fired in Buffalo which killed McKinley and made Roosevelt President. Reform was already in the air, but there was no national leader. La Follette had for years been doing fine work, but he was distrusted in the East as a demagogue and his strength was chiefly confined to the Northwest. Roosevelt was as yet something of an unknown quantity in spite of his career as Governor of New York, Assistant Secretary of the Navy, and in minor offices. He had been a reformer and had acquired popularity in the Spanish War. Born a New Yorker of moderate wealth and good social position, he had spent much time on his ranch in Montana and had won his literary laurels by his *Winning of the West*.

It soon became evident that, although a party man, the new President intended to pursue his own policies and not to be ruled by the National Committee and its chairman. His first great opportunity came as a result of the Northwestern railway situation. The Harriman group, in control of the Union-Southern Pacific lines, angry because they had not been allowed a half interest in the Burlington system by the Morgan-Hill group, made a gigantic play to capture the Northern Pacific (carrying a half interest in the Burlington) from their rivals by open purchase in the stock market. The dramatic story, culminating for the public in the Northern Pacific corner and panic of May 9, 1901, when for a couple of hours half the firms in Wall Street were insolvent, is well known. The rivals decided to compromise, and from the negotiations the Northern Securities Company was born.

Under the Anti-Trust Act, the lawyers considered it would be dangerously illegal to merge the competing Great Northern and Northern Pacific into one property, but evolved the idea that one owner could not be considered to be conspiring with himself. A holding company was formed in New Jersey with a capital of $400,000,000 which bought by exchange of its stock the controlling interests of both lines, Harriman having a large interest in the new company as well as control of the two Southern transcontinental roads. If this legal trick should prove successful, there was evidently nothing left to the Anti-Trust Act.

The Northwest, which saw its two competing roads thus merged into one by a subterfuge, legal or not, was up in arms at once, and the excitement became intense by the end of 1901. The following March, Roosevelt having gone over the case with Attorney-General Knox, the government brought action for the dissolution of the merger, eventually winning its suit. Within a short time the President also succeeded in having an act passed by Congress which gave priority in the courts to such cases against the trusts, and another forbidding unfair and discriminatory rebates by railroads to favored shippers. In February 1903, the Department of Commerce and Labor was organized, its head having a seat in the Cabinet with the duty of watching over the economic interests of the people at large. The ordinary small American citizen, East and West, felt that he had at last found a defender in the President, whose popularity became unbounded and who was overwhelmingly reëlected in 1904.

It was not only the Western farmer who was grateful for a new leader, but the laboring class in the East as well. In the same year in which the Northern Securities Company was sued, there occurred the great coal strike in the anthracite fields, under the able leadership of John Mitchell, which continued for months without violence. By his fine character and great ability, Mitchell had won the devotion of the men, mostly foreigners, in the mines. It was in the course of this strike, bitterly fought by the owners, that Baer made the remark already quoted as to the rights of the workingman being cared for by the Christian men to whom God in His wisdom had given the property of the United States. In a ballad sung by the men we get the point of view of another sort of American.

> Now you know Mike Sokolosky —
> Dat man my brudder. . . .
> Now me belong t' union, me good citizen.
> For seven year, me livin' here
> In dis beeg America.
> Me workin' in de Prospect,
> Workin' Dorrance shaft, Conyngham, Nottingham [1] —
> Every place like dat.
> Workin' in de gangway, workin' in de breast,
> Labor every day, me never get a rest.
> Me got plenty money, nine hundred, maybe ten,
> So shtrike kin come, like son of a gun —
> Me Johnny Mitchell man!

The owners, considering that God had given them their property, which they held in the form of great corporations, absolutely declined to employ men who dared to form themselves into a union, to combine their own resources of labor, which perhaps more rightly God might have been considered to have given *them*, into an organization for greater effectiveness to meet the corporations on more even terms. As the summer passed and autumn came, the deadlock continued. Public anxiety, with the winter coming on, was acute, and sympathy was largely with the miners, who were behaving well. Roosevelt had determined to send the army into the fields and mine coal for the public, appointing a commission to consider the case if the owners continued obdurate. At last they yielded so far as to meet Mitchell with the President in the White

[1] Names of collieries.

House. There the owners and the President became so angry at each other that nothing was accomplished, Mitchell, as the President afterwards admitted, being "the only one who kept his temper and his head," but a fortnight later the owners yielded to public opinion and submitted the dispute to a commission, resuming work at the mines.

In one way and another for the next four or five years public attention was continually occupied with the problem of "big business" in relation to the ordinary citizen. In 1904 Miss Tarbell published her *History of the Standard Oil Company*, which gave the people a sound, documented account of how that trust had acquired its power. Revelations of corporate misdoing came out from time to time in official inquiries and court proceedings. Disgusting scandals were laid bare in the investigation of the great insurance companies; it was found that the Standard Oil Company of Indiana was receiving rebates in spite of the new law; that the Sugar Trust, not content with its practical monopoly and high tariff, was deliberately swindling the government by paying duties on underweighing at its docks. Novelists, journalists, and the new and cheaper magazines, all contributed their share to what came to be called "muckraking." Although this tended to degenerate into mere scandalmongering, the revelations which were authentic served to arouse the public conscience and resentment. America for the first time was beginning to take stock of the morality of its everyday business life. Roosevelt, in speech and writing, hammered away at such simple but much needed topics as the "square deal" and business ethics. Slowly the people were getting genuine education, and reaching an adult point of view. It was as though our youth had gone with the frontier and we were growing up, taking a man's serious view of his world, in which reality is no longer seen in the golden haze of inexperience.

All this led us to understand our situation and condition better, but did not point the way to remedy. We began, however, to see somewhat more clearly that we should have to reckon with new forces. Mere "trust busting" was no solution. It was as sensible as it would have been æons before to apply a tape measure to the dinosaurs after a decree that none should exceed five feet in length. A world in which a Kansas farmer shipped his wheat fifteen hundred miles by railroad and then three thousand by steamer, in accordance with prices quoted by cable, could not be run with the same instruments, political or economic, that had been adequate a couple of generations earlier when he drove his produce into town over five miles of dirt road that he and his neighbors kept in order. It would accomplish nothing simply to break up great corporations. A distinction began to be observed between "good" and "bad" trusts. On the other hand, the individual citizen was too powerless when faced by the new corporations with their millions or billions of resources and their power. Evidently it was to be either socialism, which has never made any wide appeal to us and at best is a most unpromising remedy, or use of our government to stand between us and the corporations in order to see that they helped and did not crush us.

We began to follow this new path with such laws as the Pure Food Act and the Hepburn Act, both passed in 1906. In the days when the housewife bought and prepared all the food used in a household, she could assume responsibility herself for its quality, but when our meat came from great slaughterhouses, and much else came in bottles and cans, she lost control of quality and purity. The government had to step in to secure both. In the same way, it had to step in, as it did in the Hepburn Act, to assure the shipper fair rates, the bill placing the power to make rates in the hands of the Interstate Commerce Commission. The first of these new acts made every household, in the simplest way possible, feel itself under the protection of the Federal government; the second made the magnates feel its power. The days of unrestricted individualism were fast passing. Even "Ol' Man River" felt the new curb, and when the great dam at Keokuk was built he no longer flowed unchecked to the Gulf.

With the closing of the frontier had come something of a

realization of the fact that our resources were not illimitable, and within a year after the announcement was made in 1890, Congress had authorized the Executive to withdraw forest lands from homestead entry. Up to the death of McKinley, nearly 47,000,000 acres had been withdrawn, but during Roosevelt's terms that was increased to over 172,000,000, and a few weeks before leaving the Presidency he appointed a National Conservation Commission against the opposition of Congress. Minerals and water power were considered as well as forests, and the discussion of the questions involved brought forcibly before us the change that was coming from the old frontier ideals of quick exploitation and unregulated grabbing of every natural resource for personal gain. We did not want socialism, as popularly conceived with a big S, but we were learning that in the new world we should have to submit to social control of a more drastic sort than any to which the frontier would ever have yielded. It might involve some adjustment of our old American ideals of personal freedom to do what we liked, but it was still government of the people, by the people, for the people, and preferable to government by the few "Christian men" who considered that God had given them the country for a private club, and so we began to think in new terms and to get used to new ways. Efforts were made to frighten the nation with talk of anarchy, Socialism (big S), and communism, but it declined to be panicked.

When in 1907, as a result of bad financing and worse banking, a glut of undigested securities brought on a real panic in Wall Street, the older type of capitalists, who had not seen the light, tried to make Roosevelt responsible in the eyes of the public. The President hurled back at them the epithet of "malefactors of great wealth" and stood his ground. Big business called on him to "let us alone," but it could not be let alone because it could not let *us* alone, but entered into our homes at every chink and cranny. The old pioneer who kept moving on into the wilderness so as never to have a neighbor nearer than ten miles away could cry, "Let me alone," but the day of the frontier was past. Big business could not play the frontiersman any longer in a forest where the trees were men.

While this new orientation of our domestic problems had been proceeding, we had also begun to play a different part in the international world. Little as we were inclined to recognize the fact, our expanding commerce and the possessions we had gained in the Spanish War had made us a world power. The year following the Peace of Paris, we had been drawn into the Chinese situation of that period, and while John Hay was Secretary of State we had joined with the British to force on the not very willing Continental European powers concerned the doctrine of "the open door" in China instead of a practical partition of that country. The next year our troops had joined those of other nations in putting down the Boxer Rebellion, but after receiving our share of the mercilessly large indemnity demanded of China, we returned $11,000,000 of it to the government of that country, which applied it to the sending of Chinese students to America for education. Whether, with our idealism, we thus contributed to the too rapid Westernization of that country and its subsequent troubles, still in being, may be a question as open as John Hay's "door."

In 1899 we had taken an active part in the formation of the Hague Tribunal for International Disputes, and in 1902, when England, Italy, and Germany had declared a blockade of Venezuela in an effort to collect certain claims, we suggested that the question be referred to the Tribunal for settlement. Germany refused until Roosevelt sent our entire American fleet under Dewey to "manœuvre" in the Caribbean, when Germany accepted arbitration. Unfortunately, whatever prestige and friendliness might have accrued to us among our South American neighbors by our defense of Venezuela were quickly lost by Roosevelt's treatment of Colombia. He was very keen to signalize his Presidency by the building of a canal across the Central American isthmus, and in 1902 Congress authorized $40,000,000 for the purchase of the old French De Lesseps syndicate's rights in the canal which it had started to build, unsuccessfully, across the Colombian province of

Panama. Congress stipulated, however, that Colombia would have to cede jurisdiction to the United States of the strip on which the canal was to be built. Through Hay, Roosevelt offered Colombia $10,000,000 cash and $100,000 a year for a hundred years' lease of the strip, which Colombia was slow in accepting. Whatever the ins and outs of Colombian politics may have been, the nation had, of course, a perfect right to delay as long as it wished in making a treaty with us, though as a matter of fact it apparently intended to make it on our own terms. It intended also, however, to collect $10,000,000 from the French syndicate, which could not sell its rights without Colombian consent, and that amount would be added to our bill.

To make a long story short, with the connivance of Roosevelt a revolution was staged in Panama; the province seceded; American war vessels prevented Colombian troops from landing to quell it. We recognized the new nation of Panama almost overnight, and made a treaty with her by which we leased the "Canal Zone" in perpetuity. The rawness of such imperialistic methods beat almost anything that Europe had been guilty of or anything which the worst of our "Christian men" might have attempted in the business world. It hurt our reputation seriously throughout South America, and eighteen years later we made partial amends to the pride of Colombia by granting her $25,000,000, or two and a half times the extra sum which we might have had to pay for the Canal Zone in Roosevelt's time with honor. It is only fair to add that within ten years after we began the work of digging we were able to open the Canal to traffic, and, owing to the extraordinary ability and skill of Colonel Goethals, we made what had been a pesthole, morally and physically, into one of the healthiest and most decent spots on earth. The pity of it was that Roosevelt could not be patient enough to do it honestly.

In 1905, however, he accomplished a genuinely great feat of diplomacy in bringing the belligerents in the Russo-Japanese War together at Portsmouth, New Hampshire, and causing the meeting to eventuate in peace largely through his own diplomacy and tact. Two years later an American naval fleet, including sixteen new battleships, left Hampton Roads for a cruise around the world, returning fourteen months later, in February 1909, without a single mishap, and after causing a distinct impression of our growing power and position in the navy bureaus throughout the world.

Within nineteen years after the official notice of the close of the frontier we had thus witnessed our greatest conflicts between capital and labor; had launched on a policy of conservation instead of limitless exploitation; had begun to be self-critical of our business morality and methods; had fought a European nation and acquired island possessions, extending to the Far East, with 11,000,000 inhabitants; had gone afield to build the Panama Canal; had interfered beneficently in world politics in China and elsewhere; had helped notably to establish the Hague Tribunal; and our battle fleet had been seen around the globe. In applied science we had been making great advances, especially in the technology of mass production, which was just getting into its stride. In our willingness to scrap old methods of manufacture and to experiment in every field we were to provide the world with a striking exhibition of economic courage; but it has been an odd trait in us that, whereas we are among the most courageous of economic innovators, we have been as great fundamentalists in many other respects as Bryan himself was as a Bible student. While we were willing to stretch economic change to the breaking point, we were unwilling — or those at the head of our great economic enterprises were unwilling — to alter in the slightest our social and political arrangements to correspond with the new economic ones. Partly as a consequence of this, — or perhaps as a cause, — the old conditions adapted for a more or less equalitarian society, combined with the new technology, began to create an unprecedented gulf between the wage earner and the incipient billionaire. It is true that, as we have seen, the size of individual fortunes had been growing with each generation, but our new methods both of manufacture and of distribution were to emphasize this tendency in an alarming degree. Even yet we have found no method of control, partly because of our inherent fear of social change, a fear which the fortunate beneficiaries of the system exploit and inculcate to the utmost. Taft — weak, amiable, and with a legal mind — had been subject to it. Not so, however, was the new President, though by no means a radical by any standard other than that of our economic fundamentalists.

Roosevelt had served as President for seven years, and he considered that the wise tradition which limits the holding of the office to two terms applied in his case. In character he cannot be compared with either Lincoln or Washington, but the mere necessary statement of that negative proves his stature. In dealing with the greatest problem of his time, which was that of how to reconcile economic and political democracy with the inevitable appearance of the dinosaurs in a nation as huge as the United States, it cannot be said that he offered any very deep or coherent solution.

He did, however, perform a service of the first magnitude, which no one else at that time was competent to perform. Just when we were feeling the full impact of the forces growing to explosive tension, owing in part to the end of the frontier, he provided a sane leadership to which the most oppressed and discontented could rally. Regarded by the leaders of big business as a pestiferous radical, he was in fact a godsend to them. He was the lightning rod to carry off harmlessly the pent-up fury of the storm which might otherwise have caused vast havoc. More than that, in spite of his own shortcomings, he was a vital force in helping toward a higher ethics of business life and in keeping alive the American dream for the ordinary citizen during perhaps the most critical period in the history of our democracy. If he cannot be ranked with Lincoln, he was undeniably the greatest Republican President since Lincoln, though cursed by the leaders of his own party.

Declining to run for a third term, he dictated the nomination of his successor, Taft. For the next four years the new President, although he was merely weak and not a reactionary himself, allowed the reactionary forces to regain headway. In some ways the nation was undergoing profound changes. Many of them were felt rather than perceived by the ordinary man. For one thing his ballot, cast into the box on election day, was decreasing steadily in value and influence. Public opinion was beginning to be more and more manipulated by means of subtle and high-cost propaganda, until it has been said, not without show of reason, by those familiar with the most recent advertising methods, that only cost limits the delivery of public opinion in any direction desired on any topic. The more money available, the larger the slice of opinion that can be duly delivered. Moreover, organizations, groups, and powerful minorities of all sorts, well backed financially, were beginning to exert more control over legislators than the wishes of the unorganized voters. Over five hundred such organizations have been listed recently as having offices in Washington for the purpose of bringing direct pressure to bear upon legislation. The Anti-Saloon League is merely the most notorious and one of the most successful. The influence of such groups, and of the lobbies of the great economic ones, — railroads, electric and water power companies, manufacturers of all sorts with tariff axes to grind, and so on, — was beginning its undermining of the mere vote of the ordinary citizen. Much of this sort of invisible governing was beginning to be notable in Taft's day, and he proved incapable of dealing with forces which in many cases, perhaps, he scarcely recognized. One of the most powerful bodies in the country to-day, the United States Chamber of Commerce, was, indeed, formed at his suggestion.

Various matters had conspired to weaken the friendship between Taft and Roosevelt, who had returned to America from his African and European trip some time before the campaign of 1912. Unfortunately for his reputation, Roosevelt allowed himself to believe that he should contest the renomination which Taft desired, and when defeated in the convention, where the rulings and proceedings were discreditable alike to him and to Taft, he organized a separate party, the "Bull Moose," and broke with his own. With the Republican vote split between Taft and Roosevelt, the way was cleared with ease for the election of the Democratic candidate, Woodrow Wilson, former President of Princeton University and Governor of New Jersey, an able man and distinctly a Progressive.

In one respect the election marked the end of an era in our country. For the first time every citizen in every section of the continental United States save the District of Columbia was able to vote as a citizen of an established State. There were no longer any territorial governments left, the last two Territories, Arizona and New Mexico, having been admitted as States in the closing months of Taft's administration. Alaska, acquired from Russia in 1867, and Hawaii, annexed in 1898, were the only Territories remaining, and they, like the islands acquired from Spain, were outside the limits of the old continental United States. If 1890 marked the end of the frontier, 1912 marked the end of that long process of expansion and State making for which the foundation had been laid by the Northwest Ordinance of 1787. None could have been so farsighted as to see then, when our population of about 3,750,000 was confined within national limits which extended only to the Mississippi and did not even include Florida and the Gulf coast, that in exactly a century and a quarter a population of over 95,000,000 would have extended over the entire area to the Pacific, every portion populated densely enough to warrant a State government, and that the original thirteen States would have grown to a sisterhood of forty-eight with the centre of population in the Mississippi Valley instead of on the Atlantic Coast.

These facts, however, were merely the physical and statistical symbols of the completion of a great process and of a change in direction. A population multiplied nearly thirtyfold, a frontier ended, a nation completed of forty-eight States with no more territorial status, pointed to a fundamental and colossal alteration.

In his brief inaugural address, after speaking of the reasons for the overturn in the national administration, Wilson clearly recalled the people to consider again the vision of what America might and should be. "We have," he said, "been refreshed by a new insight into our own life. We see that in many things that life is very great. It is incomparably great in its material aspects. . . . It is great, also, very great, in its moral force. We have built up, moreover, a great system of government. . . . But the evil has come with the good, and much fine gold has been corroded. We have squandered a great part of what we might have used. . . . We have been proud of our industrial achievements, but we have not hitherto stopped thoughtfully enough to count the human cost, the cost of lives snuffed out, of energies overtaxed and broken, the fearful physical and spiritual cost to the men and women and children upon whom the dead weight and burden of it all has fallen pitilessly the years through. The groans and agony of it all had not yet reached our ears, the solemn, moving undertone of our life, coming up out of the mines and factories and out of every home where the struggle had its intimate and familiar seat. With the great Government went many things which we too long delayed to look into and scrutinize with candid, fearless eyes. The great Government we loved has too often been made use of for private and selfish purposes, and those who used it had forgotten the people. At last a vision has been vouchsafed to us of our life as a whole. We see the bad with the good, the debased and decadent with the sound and vital. . . . There has been something crude and heartless and unfeeling in our haste to succeed and be great. Our thought has been, 'Let every man look out for himself, let every generation look out for itself,' while we reared giant machinery which made it impossible that any but those who stood at the levers of control should have a chance to look out for themselves. . . . We have come now to the sober second thought. . . . We have made up our minds to square every process of our national life again with the standard we so proudly set up at the beginning and have always carried in our hearts. . . . We shall restore, not destroy. We shall deal with our economic system as it is and as it may be modified, not as it might be if we had a clean sheet of paper to write upon. . . . And yet it will be no cool process of mere science. The Nation has been deeply stirred, stirred by a solemn passion, stirred by the knowledge of wrong, of ideals lost, of government too often debauched and made an instrument of evil. . . . This is not a day of triumph; it is a day of dedication."

Here once more was the authentic voice of the great American democracy; here once more was the prophet speaking of the American dream, of that hope of a better and richer life for all the masses of humble and ordinary folk who made the American nation. It was the voice once more of the democratic frontier, of Jefferson, of Jackson, of Lincoln. But there was a difference. There were still the "plain people" to appeal to. There was still the American dream in their hearts. But the frontier was gone. Had the old frontier been there, with its illimitable opportunity, the President's words would have fallen strangely upon it when he declaimed against squandering our natural resources, against our haste to be rich and great, against the doctrine of every man for himself. These had been of the essence of the frontier, and that a denunciation of them could find answering welcome meant that the frontier was coming to an end in our thought as it had done two decades earlier in physical fact.

The failure of Wilson's efforts at the end of his second term should not blind us to the accomplishments of the first. The hearts of the ordinary citizens had been strengthened by Roosevelt's fight on their behalf and by his preaching of the simpler virtues which had come to be lost sight of in our feverish industrial life. Whatever may have been Roosevelt's faults, and they were many and open to all men's view, I think it cannot be denied that he left the heart of the nation sounder and more wholesome than he had found it; and that is something of which few statesmen can boast. Taft, in spite of his virtues, and they were many, was unable to inspire the nation, but after the slack water of his four years Wilson for a time gave once more to the people — in a measure greater than Roosevelt's — a vision of nobility and importance in their life and destiny that none save Washington and Jefferson and Lincoln had yet been able to kindle for them.

Nor was it the mere idealism of the impractical dreamer. In his first term he could point to a notable number of things accomplished. The Underwood Tariff was the lowest since the Civil War, and to it was appended our first graduated income tax. The Federal Reserve Act, under which our banking system now operates, was passed a few months later, and marked the greatest advance toward sound banking that had been made in our history. The Federal Trade Commission was created and given wide powers with respect to corporations and interstate commerce, though its functions were chiefly those of investigation and advice. The Clayton Act, with a full set of teeth, greatly strengthened the government's hands in dealing with corporations and unlawful monopolies. In addition it strengthened the position of labor by declaring that injunctions could not be issued in labor disputes except to prevent irreparable injury to property, and by making trade-unions, boycotts, strikes, and picketing legal.

The President also succeeded in having Congress repair a breach of national good faith with England. Under the Hay-Pauncefote Treaty of 1901 we had agreed that there should never be any discrimination against the ships of foreign nations if we built the Canal and fortified it ourselves. Subsequently Congress had passed an act exempting American shipping from the tolls which we charged foreign vessels, and although efforts had been made to secure the repeal of this obvious act of bad faith, Congress had been stubborn. Owing to the revolutions in Mexico, Wilson was having a difficult time in maintaining his policy with regard to that neighbor. Great pressure was brought to bear upon him by the oil and other business interests of this country and by the oil interests in England. As the price of a free hand granted him by that country he agreed to secure the repeal of the unjust tolls law, and did so by appealing to Congress not only on the score of national self-respect, but on the ground that there were matters in the foreign policy of the country with which he would be unable to deal unless Congress granted the request.

Wilson's Mexican policy was probably a mistaken one, and of course his administration could claim no credit for the announcement in 1913 of the passage of the Constitutional Amendments providing for the income tax and for the direct election of Senators, both of which had been started on their process of ratification during the previous administration. But it could justly claim to have accomplished more constructive work in a couple of years toward the readjustment of American ideals and life to the new conditions imposed upon them than any previous administration since we had started in our new orbit in 1890. Not only that, but the President had also shown unexpected ability in handling the political problems of his office and had become the undisputed head of his party as well as of the nation. We had set ourselves earnestly to the work of correcting abuses and of reconstructing the possibilities of the American dream in the new world of economic dinosaurs, of billions of capital and millions of employees, of the radio, the telephone, the motor car, the aeroplane, the whole infinite complexity in which there seemed room for everything except the heart of man and the old independence of the individual to work out his own life and scale of values. But we had made great progress. We had, as Wilson said, been refreshed with a new insight into ourselves. We wished to be fair to capital, but we wished to set man himself in the higher seat. How far we might have gone toward reëstablishing the dream in the new setting had we been given not only the leadership but the time needed, we shall never know. As we swung our axe above our head to bring it down on the roots of our evils, a grisly hand from behind seized our wrist and held it firm. Then there was darkness.

In April 1912, the world's greatest ship, the *Titanic*, sailed from England in all the pride of her maiden voyage. With every device of modern engineering, she seemed impregnable to the perils of the sea. Halfway across, the submerged portion of an iceberg tore her from bow to stern, and in a few moments she sank below the waves with the loss of fifteen hundred lives. The next year, with money contributed by Carnegie, a palace was built at The Hague to house the peace of the world. Then, in the summer of 1914, a pistol shot rang out at Sarajevo and an Austrian Archduke was murdered. Austria declared war on Serbia. Mobilizations followed swiftly on European frontiers. The nations quickly followed one another into the bottomless gulf — Germany, Russia, France, Belgium, Great Britain. Like the sinking of the *Titanic*, it all seemed to come without an instant's warning. The earth, which we had thought safe and solid to work and play and dream our dream on, suddenly sank beneath our feet. The waves closed over all that had been known and familiar and loved. The lights of the world went out.

XIII

AMERICA REVISITS THE OLD WORLD

In those days of August 1914 the first reaction of America was one of stunned amazement. Except for the half-holiday episode of the war with Spain, we had almost all of us forgotten that such a horror could raise its head in our modern world. Only the oldest generation among us, men past sixty, had even the faintest childhood recollections of our Civil War or the War in Europe of 1870. War seemed an incredible anachronism. For the past decade we had had our minds intently focused on moral problems and the effort to work out ways and means of making our own land a better and cleaner one in all its aspects. The muckraking in business, the efforts to improve the slums led by such men as Riis, the progress that was at last being made in Congress in controlling instead of destroying big business, all seemed to promise the nearer fulfillment of the American dream. Suddenly the whole of Western European civilization appeared to have burst into flames.

Nor was our bewilderment rendered any the less by our having clear notions of what it was all about. Why should all Europe be so instantaneously at each other's throats because an Austrian Archduke had been murdered in Serbia? Why should Austria refuse any possible solution but war? Why the Russian mobilization? Why should Germany instantly invade Belgium to attack France, all on account of a mysterious murder of one individual? Although heretofore we had scarcely regarded England as the defender of small peoples, we could understand her entry into the conflict in order to comply with her guarantee of Belgian neutrality, but the rest of the whole business was beyond us.

In fact, there is not the slightest reason why we should have understood. The ordinary man in the street in Europe or on the farms of Europe was almost as bewildered as we ourselves, nor have the scholars as yet, fifteen years later, with all the documents before them, been able to agree as to the "causes" of the war. Of the stresses and strains of the European system we knew little and cared less; nor did we bother ourselves about European quarrels centuries old. The problems involved in developing in a little more than one century from a small people of about 6,000,000 to a world power of 110,000,000, the epic sweep of carrying a civilization across three thousand miles of empty continent from the Atlantic to the Pacific, the building up of our government, the absorption of alien races, had all been enough to consume the energies of our own or any people.

Europe was infinitely far away. On the Atlantic seaboard, and to a less extent elsewhere, there were many individuals who frequently went abroad and who had European contacts and interests, but they belonged to a relatively small class. Most of our people, even in the East, scarce gave Europe a thought in their daily lives. Across the mountains, in the great Valley of the Mississippi, Europe disappeared almost entirely, except as the thoughts of immigrants or the children of immigrants went out sentimentally to their homelands of Germany or Norway or Sweden or Russia, or whatever they might be. There was no more reason why the farmers and shopkeepers and professional men of this empire-in-itself of

"Ol' Man River" should have accurate knowledge of European politics and business than why they should have busied themselves with China. Across the next mountains again, and on the Pacific slope, indeed, China became far more important than Europe, and our minds, like our ships and trade, went out to the Orient with never a thought of the European world. Perhaps, at that, we knew more of Europe than Europe did of us. If we were provincial, so had Europe been, wrapped up in a sense of its own superior importance. With a few notable exceptions, such as Bryce or Jusserand, even educated and presumably cultured Europeans had paid as little attention to us as we had to the New Zealanders. The ignorance was not all "made in America."

If there was not much knowledge of Europe among us, however, that did not mean that there was not plenty of emotion and prejudice concerning particular countries there. First, there were those prejudices of fairly broad American spread, dating back to the Revolution of 1776. Perhaps the most widely held was the purely sentimental affection for France due to the legend of the sister Republic in Europe, the State that had helped us gain our independence, that country of Lafayette who had become a sort of folk hero among us. So strong had these emotional appeals been that no action of France subsequently, however hostile, had succeeded in changing them. The attitude toward England was more mixed. There was a small Anglo-maniac group, mostly in the East, and a larger and rabidly anti-English group, with a large percentage of the whole people hesitating between moderate dislike and the feeling that after all we were of English descent as a nation and had more in common with her than with other peoples. Until the Spanish War, however, we could not deceive ourselves into believing that the England of the ruling classes had thought in friendly terms of us. The Revolution, the War of 1812, Palmerston's bullying threat of war in 1841, the attitude of upper-class opinion and of the press in the Civil War, all had left a very bad impression on top of the natural effects of our schoolbook history and oratory.

In addition, we had the feelings of smaller groups. The Irish, always influential politically, hated England and had long been accustomed to use feeling against her in political fights and campaigns. We had also nearly 9,000,000 inhabitants who were either German-born or had one parent at least who was a native German. They had made excellent citizens, and there was much friendly sentiment in the country both for them and for their nation. There were other racial groups of large size and importance. New York alone, for example, contained more Italians than any city in Italy. The great numbers of Scandinavians in the Northwest were naturally more allied in sympathy to Germany than to England.

As the war got under way we were deluged with propaganda, much of which was designed to appeal to the base emotions rather than the intellect, and much of which has subsequently turned out to have been deliberately false. All the warring powers tried thus to influence us, though the Germans proved particularly clumsy in their efforts. On the other hand, it is now admitted that such an item as that sent out by the British showing photographs of the Germans hauling the bodies of soldiers to the soap factory was an absolute falsification intended to influence the Chinese. The stories of cutting off the hands of the Belgian children were fabrications. Our own Admiral Sims has declared that on investigation the stories of atrocious cruelty of submarine commanders, with one exception, were falsehoods. The French executed two war nurses under almost the identical circumstances of the German execution of Nurse Cavell, but we were not told. Naturally the emotional Allied or German propaganda was accepted respectively by those who believed in the Allies or in the Germans, but was infuriating to those whose opinions were the reverse. On the whole, perhaps, it all tended to confuse rather than to clarify our honest sentiments and thought.

Little by little, however, certain broad facts began to emerge in our consciousness, although not in that of all the racial groups. What the reasons were we did not know, but apparently the Central Powers had made the first move toward war and had refused to delay for any possible mediation. The invasion of Belgium was distinctly a crime against international law, and the famous "scrap of paper" phrase made a great impression on us. However, there was no reason for us to involve ourselves in one of the interminable wars of Europe. If the Germans under the Kaiser were trying to upset the balance of power in Europe, it was just what the French had done under Napoleon. If the Kaiser had tried to give us digs at times, Germany had never been so overtly unfriendly as had Louis Napoleon during our Civil War, when he wanted to acknowledge the South and had seized Mexico for Maximilian. There had obviously never been anything in England's attitude toward us for a century and a half that would call for us to fly to her assistance when she declared war on powers with which we were at peace. Belgium was unquestionably suffering from a crime against law, but we had not been signatories of the treaty guaranteeing her neutrality, and there was no reason why we should be expected to act as policeman for the globe. Had we, with Chile, Brazil, and the Argentine, guaranteed the neutrality of Uruguay and then had we suddenly violated her territory, certainly neither England nor France would have felt bound to go to war with us to right a moral wrong on the other side of the world among a set of nations of an entirely different political system.

Moreover, and this was important, for more than a century it had been the corner stone of our international policy that we should keep hands off Europe absolutely and that Europe in turn should keep hands off the New World. Unless we were ourselves directly attacked, for us to intervene in a European quarrel would have been to stultify our whole national policy and invite European intervention in the Americas. Except by a few hotheads of high station or low, the neutrality proclamation of the President was universally welcomed in America as the only proper course to take. Incidentally, we were doing our best — almost quixotically, as many thought — to keep the peace with Mexico under much provocation, and a good part of our small standing army was then stationed on our Southern border.

Even if we remained neutral, however, it was at once obvious that we were to be profoundly influenced. The New York Stock Exchange was forced to close on August 1, and to remain closed for ten months. The Federal Reserve Board, under our new banking system, had hurriedly to be created, and the President announced that $500,000,000 in emergency currency would be available. Practically all the ships which had connected us with Europe as by a frequent ferry were foreign-owned, and commerce and passenger service almost ceased for a while. Imported goods quickly soared in price. Naturally, however, as production declined in Europe, owing to the vast numbers of men called to the colors in every belligerent country, the demand for American goods of all sorts — foodstuffs, ammunition, manufactures of every description — rose by leaps. Two things became clear. One was that the war was likely to act as a forced draft under our whole system of production; and the other was that, as the most important neutral in a time of very complex commerce, we were likely also to have to face and deal with all the problems of neutral trade that we had had to deal with in the Napoleonic Wars and since. The doctrine of the freedom of the seas for which we had always stood was going to be put to severe test.

Throughout our whole history we had been facing westward. Until very recent years, when emigration had tended to flow back and forth somewhat, practically every emigrant to America had come because of oppression or suppression in his European homeland. He had come for greater freedom of religious and political thought or of social and economic opportunity. As we had plunged into the forests, and then farther and farther westward across prairies and plains and mountains to the Pacific, our eyes had ever been turned to the sunset and the future. The dreams and efforts of the great Western railway builders, the Harrimans and Hills, had crossed the Pacific to where the rainbow rested on the shores of Asia. Our tourists came from Europe in European ships, but we launched our own to carry our commerce to China and Japan and the Philippines. With the coming of the war, it was as though someone had roughly seized us by the shoulder and dizzily spun us round. The daily headlines in the papers concerning the most catastrophic drama in history held our attention. Our desire to learn sent us to books of European history and politics. The stream of propaganda was bewildering and unwelcome in a way and to an extent that a European can scarcely be expected to understand. Vaguely we felt that we had left Europe — years or centuries ago — because we or our ancestors were through with it. We had asked to be let alone and we had not been. We had fought for our independence and won it. We had had to fight again. In the Monroe Doctrine we had told Europe we would let her alone over there if she would let us alone in our New World. Europe had scarcely ever expressed the slightest interest in us or friendly sympathy for us. When we had been young, weak, raw, and struggling, European critics had sneered. We had gone our own way and asked no favors. We had built up not only a great nation, but on the whole a happy and contented one. And suddenly, on account of obscure influences and events in which we had had neither part nor lot, Europe seemed to be pursuing us overseas. We had been wholly intent on ourselves.

We were unfair in some ways. We saw that on our own continent forty-eight sovereign States could live in peace; that, as fellow citizens in them, French and Germans and Russians and Austrians and English and scores of other races could live and work in friendly fashion. As we looked oversea into the torrid crater of European hatreds, it seemed as though the world had gone back centuries, whereas we, in frontier fashion, had been thinking in terms of the future and of a happier fate for humanity. The shock of the shift in view was no less profound because it was largely subconscious.

In fact, in its broad aspects, Europe's case, dissimilar to our own as it was in outward circumstance, appears to have been fundamentally much like it. Whatever the immediate causes of the war, the basic one would seem to have been the impact of the Industrial Revolution upon a closed frontier. Our own expansion had taken place up to 1890 with a minimum of explosive violence. To the world at large the pushing back of the Indian had meant little more than the extermination of the bison or the prairie dog. Several huge additions to the national domain had been secured by purchase as easily as if we had bought some new cottages. The wars to secure the rest had not been of world importance. In much the same way, for a couple of centuries or more, certain great European powers such as England and France had secured vast colonial empires in Africa and Asia. Germany, with her rapidly increasing population due to industrialism, had come too late on the scene to get her share. As H. J. Mackinder had pointed out in the *Geographical Review* in 1904, Europe, after having been hemmed in by strong barbarian powers in the Middle Ages, had subsequently been able to expand around the world until it had again come to be faced by completely preëmpted territories and a "closed political system."

We have already noted the profound effects on our own life of the close of our frontier. We have seen how we began to expand forcibly beyond the old limits, even though our land were as yet not densely populated. The tension of the repressed forces in Europe was far greater than with us, and the explosion came in 1914. This does not relieve the Kaiser or other actors on the scene of their immediate responsibility; but just as in our own daily lives there are the immediate motives for what we do and the whole background of our life and character which also determine our conduct, so there were both the immediate and the underlying causes for the debacle of civilization in Europe. In much the same fashion as the American capitalists did not have the mentality requisite for adjusting economic conditions to the legitimate demands of the smaller but ambitious men, so the imperialistic nations who had all the power of overseas possessions they wanted had failed to realize that the responsibility was in part theirs to devise some adjustment of the world situation that would satisfy the legitimate desires of the new and young nations that in turn demanded *their* opportunity. The old always think the young too aggressive. The rich think the rising poor too excessive in their demands. Those who hold power yield only reluctantly a share of it to others. The situations are as old as human nature. The solution of the problem was difficult, — perhaps impossible, — but the crux of the problem was fairly simple in its stark outlines.

The European international situation repeated almost feature for feature our own domestic situation on the ending of the frontier. This we began to sense after a while also. In spite of what may seem a paradox in view of our own military adventures, we were at heart a peaceful, almost a pacifist, people. We did not condone the war, but on the other hand we were also a youthful nation which had had to fight for its place in the sun against the established empires of the Old World. Our sympathy had always gone out to those who had likewise fought them, as in the case of the South American Republics and Spain. In Africa and Asia we had seen England and France build up imperial possessions founded upon force against natives. There did not seem anything very sacred as to rights of property or government in such European empires, especially with the atrocities in the Belgian Congo in our minds. If Germany in turn chose to challenge the rights of the others by force — well, that had been the way of the whole European world, and of our own. We had no conception of the magnitude of the struggle that had been initiated; nor, for that matter, had Europe itself. Everybody everywhere thought it would be over in a few months. Some colonial possessions might change owners, some boundary lines might be redrawn, some indemnities might be paid, and then the world would go on again much as before.

Meanwhile the orders for goods came from overseas like tidal waves. From 1914 to 1916, our exports of explosives rose from $6,000,000 to $467,000,000. The exports of steel and iron doubled. Wheat at high prices flowed from the West in an endless stream. By July 1916, we had bought back, chiefly from England, about $1,300,000,000 of securities sold to her when we needed capital for development. Farms and factories were busy as never before, and prices were going steadily up and up. For a decade we had been concentrating for the first time on how to bring our business life into better harmony with the American dream. With the feverish activity and colossal profits suddenly thrust upon us, there was no longer time, opportunity, or mood for that. The most hectic gold rush of frontier days had been nothing to this rush from Europe to give us dollars. The new and sober vision of ourselves which Wilson had said had been vouchsafed to us drifted away like a puff of smoke before the frenzied demand of Europe for everything we had at any price we placed on it. It was not our fault. It was Fate. The same evil which was ruining Europe, sowing death and hate among the nations, turned away our hand just at the moment when it had been deliberately set to the task of harmonizing our American dream with the changed realities of our new age. For Europe the war was an economic debacle; for us it was a moral calamity.

The difficulties which we anticipated as neutrals soon multiplied thickly around us. Not only did most of the old problems arise again in aggravated form, but science, by completely changing the nature of war, had provided innumerable new complications without providing any solution for them. The Napoleonic Wars had been fought by professional armies, leaving the civilian populations, outside the immediate theatre of operations, largely untouched. The war of 1914 was a war in which the civilian behind the lines was almost as much of a combatant as the soldier at the front. The old and simple list of what constituted contraband articles of war could no longer in honesty suffice, but there was no new international law defining the new contraband. If, as was true, the civilian workman was as much a factor in the war as was the soldier, almost everything needed in our new complex industrial life became closely related to winning or losing.

Moreover, there was the complication that an immense proportion of the goods we claimed the right to ship to neutral countries obviously was going to belligerents. For example, our exports to Denmark rose from $558,000, in November 1913, to $7,100,000 in the following November; to Sweden, from $377,000 to $2,550,000; to Norway, from $477,000 to $2,300,000; to Italy, from $2,300,000 to $4,800,000. If we consider that these figures are for thirty days only, the magnitude of this dubious "neutral trade" is clear. In the same way the problem of mails arose. By parcel post large amounts of contraband were being sent to Germany, a few mails examined yielding, for example, over three thousand packets of raw rubber alone, and in two months the British censorship seized letters containing about $10,000,000 worth of securities and nearly $25,000,000 in drafts and money orders for the Central Powers.

Science had made a new world, but the laws of war had been made for the old one. That England, as the chief naval belligerent, infringed those laws over and over there is no question, just as there is no question that the whole code of law needed remodeling to meet the new age of applied science. On the other hand, we were placed in an extremely difficult position. When citizens complained to our government that their legal rights were being interfered with by belligerents, it was the duty of the government to make the proper representations. As the most powerful neutral in the world, and as one which had always maintained the rights of neutrals in war, a heavy responsibility rested upon us. The Allies complained that we often took a narrowly legalistic view of their illegal but, it must be confessed, necessary acts. It may well be asked, however, now that the passions of the time have partially cooled, What else could we do? Even if the sympathies of our citizens had all been on one side, which they were not, we could not alter the laws of war in the middle of a war in favor of one side without ceasing to be a neutral. If we winked at some laws for the benefit of the Allies, it would be only fair to wink at others for Germany, and our policy, instead of being based on the fairly well-defined law of neutrality, would have become an incoherent succession of decisions dictated by our emotional sympathies.

Busy as we had been with the development of our continent, and materialistic as Europe had chosen to think us, we had long been contending for a more reasonable law of nations. From the middle of the preceding century, American citizens had presented plans at various European Congresses, — Brussels, Paris, Frankfort, and London, — and if no progress had been made for a Court of International Arbitration and for a recodifying of international law, it had not been our fault. If Europe had declined to assist us in such undertakings, it could hardly accuse us of lack of sympathy because we could not alter the laws to suit its purposes in the midst of a war in which we were neutral. At the same time, there was no doubt that the old laws did not fit the new situation, and the complications were almost inextricable. Nations fighting for their lives could hardly be expected to keep to the old laws in strict letter any more than they could be expected to use only sabres and breechloaders. On the other hand, we should have to stand by the old laws or cease to be neutral. If we ceased to be neutral, we should have to enter the war on one side or the other.

Owing to circumstances, the stopping of our cargoes and the opening of our mails fell mostly to the lot of the English. On the other hand, the breaches of neutrality by the Central Powers became even more glaring in the shape of plots in our own country and in the use of the submarine. The sinking of the *Lusitania*, with the loss of about 1200 persons of whom 114 were Americans, was merely the most dramatic episode in the new policy of submarine warfare developed by the Germans. It is as impossible as it is unnecessary to tell in detail the whole story of our gradual reaching to the point at which neutrality no longer became possible for us.

In January 1916, Wilson made a tour of the Middle West, which was largely German in sympathy, to impress upon the people the dangers of the situation. "I know that you are depending upon me," he told one audience in the German city of Milwaukee, "to keep this nation out of war. So far I have done so, and I pledge you my word that, God helping me, I will — if it be possible. You have laid another duty upon me. You have bidden me see that nothing stains or impairs the honor of the United States. And that is a matter not within my control. . . . There may be at any moment a time when I cannot both preserve the honor and the peace of the United States. Do not exact of me an impossible and contradictory thing, but stand ready, and insist that everybody who represents you should stand ready, to provide the means for maintaining the honor of the United States." In Des Moines, he told the crowd, "There is danger to our national life from what other nations may do." Urging preparation for war, he added, "Do you want the situation to be such that all the President can do is to write messages, to utter words of protest? If these breaches of international law which are in daily danger of occurring should touch the very vital interests and honor of the United States, do you wish to do nothing about it? Do you wish to have all the world say that the flag of the United States, which we all love, can be stained with impunity?"

Wilson had been negotiating with Germany for amends for the damages already inflicted on us and for a renunciation of that nation's submarine policy. At one stage Germany agreed to our terms, and there is little doubt that our country was in favor of peace if it could be maintained and if, at the same time, the belligerents could be forced to respect neutral rights. Thus far the Allies had restricted themselves to interfering with our property, whereas the Germans had attacked our lives. Except for certain racial groups, who were powerful but in a minority, the public generally had steadily been coming to recognize the moral justice of the cause of the Allies even apart from Belgium, and when we should enter the war it had become clear on which side it would be. However, the 8,000,000 or more Germans were naturally on the side of Germany as yet, as were the Irish and their sympathizers. The Socialists, who had polled well on to a million votes in 1912 and were supposed to be stronger in 1916, were strongly opposed to war, as was a very strong pacifist element throughout the nation generally. As we have seen in other connections, — for example, the frequently contrasted attitudes of the American as a "man" and as a "business man," — the American mind bears within itself at the same time a strong idealism and a strong realism. In the opposition to our entering the war, both strains operated often in the same individual at the same time. Idealistically these people believed in peace to the very last ditch at which it might become impossible; and realistically they believed it criminally unpractical to plunge a nation of 120,000,000 people into the fires of the European holocaust because 120 had already been killed, if there were any possible other way of making the belligerents consent to respect our rights and the law. Until it had been proved beyond doubt that no such way could be found, they would not enter wholeheartedly into the war. Whether or not Wilson provided us with the wisest possible leadership under the circumstances, these were some of the conditions which confronted him, and which men like Roosevelt, with no official responsibility, did not sufficiently weigh.

At last, however, it was proved beyond question that there was no other way. In the election of 1916, Wilson had been reëlected, although at first it was thought that his opponent Hughes had won. On January 31, 1917, a month before the President's second inauguration, the German Ambassador announced that Germany was to resume unrestricted submarine warfare. Three days later Wilson announced to Congress that diplomatic relations with Germany had been severed. At the same moment the Ambassador was being given his passports. Germany, which in May 1916 had solemnly agreed to accept our conditions as to submarines, had now repudiated the agreement, and the President requested other neutrals to follow our example. Germany again tried to negotiate at the very moment when she was absurdly plotting to embroil Mexico in war with us, but on April 2, 1917, before the Congress which he had called in special session for the purpose, the President asked for a declaration of war.

After reciting the acts which Germany had committed against

the rights of mankind, he continued, "We have no quarrel with the German people. We have no feeling toward them but one of sympathy and friendship. It was not upon their impulse that their Government acted in entering this war. . . . It was a war determined upon as wars used to be determined upon in the old, unhappy days when peoples were nowhere consulted by their rulers and wars were provoked and waged in the interest of dynasties or little groups of ambitious men who were accustomed to use their fellow men as pawns and tools. . . . We have no selfish ends to serve. We desire no conquest, no dominion. We seek no indemnities for ourselves, no material compensation for the sacrifices we shall freely make. We are but one of the champions of the rights of mankind. . . . It is a fearful thing to lead this great, peaceful people into war — into the most terrible and disastrous of all wars, civilization itself seeming to be in the balance. But the right is more precious than peace, and we shall fight for the things we have always carried nearest our hearts — for democracy, for the right of those who submit to authority to have a voice in their own government, for the rights and liberties of small nations, for a universal dominion of right by such a concert of free peoples as shall bring peace and safety to all nations and make the world itself at last free. To such a task we dedicate our lives and fortunes, everything that we are and everything that we have, with the pride of those who know that the day has come when America is privileged to spend her blood and her might for the principles that gave her birth and happiness and the peace which she has treasured. God helping her, she can do no other."

Perhaps no other great nation had so struggled, against every provocation, to remain at peace, until every possible means of moral suasion had been utterly exhausted. Certainly none other had ever before denied to itself any possible spoil of war before entering the arena. It was with no illusion as to the shortness of the contest or the glory of it that we threw down our glove. The stark, grim, miserable Horror of it had been before the eyes of humanity for nearly three years, and there was no prospect of its ending for another three. When the news of our decision reached England, a day of solemn thanksgiving was proclaimed, and the King and Queen took part in a service at St. Paul's Cathedral to give thanks "to Almighty God on the occasion of the entry of the United States of America into the great war of freedom." The Stars and Stripes were flown from the Victoria Tower of the Houses of Parliament, the first time that any foreign flag had there been displayed. In the House of Commons, Asquith, in concluding a speech on our entry into the struggle, said, "I doubt whether even now the world realizes the full significance of the step America has taken. I do not use language of flattery or exaggeration when I say it is one of the most disinterested acts in history."

The Allies were jubilant, but it was a grim America which now bent its energies to carrying out the necessary job on which it had started. The floodgates of propaganda addressed to emotion and sentimentalism were opened wide. Every string was played upon — Lafayette and the France of '76; hatred of the "Hun"; the union once more of the "English-speaking peoples"; all that those who lived in those days recall so well. But we were uneasy. The nation whose flag flew from Parliament Buildings was not an independent English colony grown up. We had not been the world's "melting pot" for naught, nor lived for three centuries on the frontier of a "New World." Once the die was cast, the foreign-race groups sank their personal feeling for their native country in an honest patriotism toward their new land, but much of the slushy propaganda addressed to some could only make others question or be sad. Not to mention those of foreign parentage, over 13,000,000 of our people were foreign-born themselves — 1,500,000 from Southern Europe, 1,800,000 from Eastern, 4,250,000 from Northwestern, including the Germany-sympathizing Scandinavians, and 4,200,000 from Central Europe. Of our male citizens over twenty-one years of age, over 1,250,000 had been born in Germany and the Austro-Hungarian Empires, and they now saw the day when they would have to fight against their own kin.

Even to many not thus influenced by birth or descent, the war came as a great calamity — not because it was war, but because it entangled us once more with Europe. Just a century earlier, at the end of the War of 1812, we had turned our faces resolutely westward. We had tried to build a civilization from which the inherited hatreds and quarrels of Europe should be banished. And now not only had these crossed the sea to disturb the harmony of our household, but also we were to turn back on the policy which had become engrained in us and involve ourselves in the Old World system which was none of ours. It was not that we were unsympathetic toward Europe. Our more cultivated citizens enjoyed her life and appreciated her art and letters. We had shown our humanitarian wish to be helpful by organizing the Belgian Relief and contributing $35,000,000 toward it. Before the war, gifts from our immigrant citizens had flowed in a steady stream of hundreds of millions annually to help their relatives in the homelands. But for a century every American child had been brought up with the belief, buttressed by Washington's "Farewell Address," that we belonged to a different world and that we must keep ourselves clear as a nation of the whole European political system of feuds and alliances; and now we were in it to the hilt. The Spanish War had brought no such questionings. It had had nothing to do with Europe, and everything with the New World or the westward expansion, which had become our natural direction. The fact that the suzerain of Cuba had been a European State had been mere accident, which scarcely was noticed by us. But to make the greatest effort in our history, and to direct it not constructively westward but punitively toward the Old World, was so unnatural as to leave a feeling of unreality about it throughout the struggle, and a desire to be through with it and back into our normal way of looking at the world. The feeling found expression in our never calling ourself an "Ally," but merely an "Associated Power."

Once in, however, we devoted ourselves to helping to win the war with whole-hearted thoroughness. It is impossible to detail all the economic and military measures taken. Our War and Navy expenditure, which had normally been about $300,000,000 a year, rose to over $7,000,000,000 in 1918 and $11,000,000,000 in 1919. Between the Declaration of War and the Armistice, about nineteen months, we raised $11,280,000,000 by taxation, spent $26,000,000,000, and lent the Allies nearly $9,500,000,000. By the five campaigns for the sale of "Liberty Bonds" we added nearly $21,500,000,000 to our national debt. The figures for man power were nearly as staggering. For the first time in our history no reliance was placed upon volunteering, the numbers needed being colossal, and a universal draft act was passed, which finally included all men fit for military service between the ages of eighteen and forty-five, the total number of men registering being over 24,234,000. The whole industrial structure of the nation was coördinated to serve the same purpose. In December 1917, the government took over the administration of the entire railroad system of the country, nearly 400,000 miles of track being turned over by private owners to the single management of the "United States Railroad Administration." Various other boards, notably that of "War Industries," undertook and performed the difficult tasks of directing the economic life of the nation in every aspect into a single machine for war purposes. In May 1918, Congress gave the President practically the powers of a dictator with regard to expenditures within the limits of the total appropriations.

In view of the submarine menace, one of the crying needs at our entry into the war was for ships. The very yards themselves had to be built, but within a few months ships had begun to slip from the ways, and by July 4, 1918, we were able to launch one hundred on that single day. The submarines could not sink them as fast as that. The number of men mobilized in the army, 4,355,000, also required accommodations for what was the equivalent of a population almost double that of the city of Chicago. With our small permanent standing army, the problem of officering and training these sudden millions drawn from civil life was also a serious one. Of the 200,000 commissioned officers we had in the war, only 5791 had received training at West Point. By July 1918, over 1,000,000 soldiers had reached the shores of France, and troops began to pass to the Old World at the rate of a half million a month. By November we had 2,000,000 in France, of whom over 1,100,000 had been transported by the British Navy, which only four generations before had been transporting troops westward to crush the rebellious colonies. The eighteenth-century debt to France was paid. The whole American population which she had helped to free in 1778 was less than the number of Americans now in the army to defend her borders.

Suddenly the end came. The German morale crumbled; the German army sued for peace. The adventure was over, and the Central Empires had lost. The situation behind the German lines had long been growing desperate, more than flesh and blood could stand. Owing to the time necessarily required for the raising, equipping, training, and transporting of an army of millions over the longest lines of communication ever attempted on a great scale in the history of war, our troops had taken part in actual fighting on the front to only a modest extent before the guns stopped on that memorable eleventh of November. Where they did have their chance, however, — at Château-Thierry, in the Argonne, at the Saint-Mihiel salient, and elsewhere, — they gave excellent account of themselves. We had made a tremendous effort, and coming into the war with fresh and enormous resources at a time when it had become a stalemate between the evenly balanced contestants, we were able to bring victory to the side to which we threw our added weight.

On the other hand, it is well to bear in mind that our losses were comparatively trifling, whether we contrast them with those of the European nations or even with our own in our Civil War. Economically, in the latter, half of our country had been left ruined and prostrate, as was a large part of Europe in the Great War, whereas the years 1914–1918 brought us temporarily great profits. In the Civil War, when our total population was about 35,000,000, we lost by death in both our armies nearly 600,000, whereas in the World War, when our population had risen to over 100,000,000, we lost only about 126,000 men. We may contrast this figure with the following: Turkey, 325,000; Rumania, 335,000; Italy, 650,000; British Empire, 908,000; Austro-Hungary, 1,200,000; France, 1,363,000; Germany, 1,773,000; Russia, 1,700,000. Our total casualties, including wounded who recovered, were about 350,000 out of our 4,355,000 men under arms, while, without counting the "missing," Europe had over 8,500,000 dead and over 21,000,000 wounded, out of the grand total of over 60,000,000 men who had been mobilized over there.

The war had thus brought about a vast alteration in the centre of gravity of the political and economic world. Through neither fault nor prevision of our own, we had emerged on the far side of Armageddon with our man power scarcely touched, while Death had harvested the flower of almost an entire generation in Europe. Taken as a whole, our national wealth had increased, whereas nation after nation abroad suffered economic collapse, even France never yet having been able to pass beyond the repudiation of four fifths of her currency value. From the position of a debtor nation to the extent of several billions, we had become the greatest creditor the world had ever seen, having bought back almost our entire indebtedness to Europe and come to hold her obligations in turn for over $10,000,000,000. There were other sides to the picture which we shall note presently, but the waves of Fate had borne us to this position. Unhappily they had not been the waves of general plenty and honest industry throughout the world, but waves of blood and hate and misery, and the air of the world, our own included, was tainted with strange new unhappinesses, mistrusts, dislikes, and fears.

When the Peace Conference assembled in Paris, America was at the pinnacle, apparently, of her power and influence. Wilson, who had perhaps unwisely determined to head the American delegation in person, was received with a delirious acclaim from the ordinary people of the Allied nations such as had never been accorded a leader before. The American dream, however much European statesmen or the "rich and wise" of our old Federalist phrase at home might scoff at it, had been not only a dream for a large part of the European masses, but one realized by sons and brothers who had emigrated to the New World. The lofty idealism of Wilson's various statements as to war aims and the nature of a peace which should usher in a happier era, and if possible banish war, had seemed to make the dream hover over Europe as well as America. The psychological atmosphere was abnormal everywhere. Nerves had been strung to the breaking point by four years of the intensest strain that civilized mankind had ever been called upon to bear. With the sudden release of the Armistice, almost anything seemed possible, even to the opening of the heavens and the vision of the new Jerusalem.

Unhappily there was much more in the psychological situation than that. Wilson had gone to Paris with the same hopes in his breast that had stirred Lincoln as he had pondered how to reunite the Union with healing and permanence. Wilson, with too little appreciation of the age-long complexity of the European political patterns, had hoped for a just and a fair peace which should remedy old abuses and, by the establishment of the League of Nations as an integral part of it, should provide a new organization of humanity which might usher in a long reign of peace and coöperation among all the nations of the world. We had solemnly notified the world beforehand, a pledge that we kept to the letter, that we would ask nothing for ourselves, either lands or indemnities, and with the aid of this disinterestedness Wilson hoped to plead for the new world order. It was a noble dream and it *was* disinterested, for, the enemy crushed, we might have made our separate peace while the Allies made theirs and have gone our way. Wilson elected instead to try to use his immense prestige for the purpose of securing fair play for all nations, enemy and friend alike, and to use the desire of the common men in all of them for a better order to establish in Europe and the world at large the beginning of some such organization as might permit of the nations living together with the same harmony as did the American States.

We have seen what had happened to Lincoln's dreams for our own war-torn land in 1865. Possibly even had he lived, the politicians of his party, bent on hates and spoils, might have been too much for his loftier vision. Less happy than Lincoln, Wilson had to meet the avengers face to face. The very place chosen for the Conference, Paris, was the centre of the most virulent hatred then in Europe, and the choosing of it was in itself a gesture of the pride of triumph and revenge rather than of genuine effort toward lasting peace. The story of the Conference has often been told and is steadily being pieced together more and more coherently by the publication of the memoirs of those who shared in it. America had looked into the crater of Europe at war; now, as never before, she looked into the European system of diplomacy. She discovered the secret treaties, dividing spoils of war to the victors, entered into the midst of the struggle which she had been told was solely for self-defense and the freedom of free peoples. Wilson himself had done untold harm in fanning the flames of racialism and nationalism by his doctrine of "self-determination." In the atmosphere of *Realpolitik* at the Conference, the race became more and more one for spoils, revenge, security. Some wrongs were righted and many more were created. The League of Nations, however, was saved.

But there was also the psychology of America to be reckoned with. While Wilson was negotiating with the foreign statesmen in Paris, a steady stream of American soldiers was passing westward back to America. These boys and men from the mountains of Tennessee, the farms of Iowa or Dakota, the orange groves of Florida or California, the villages and cities from the Atlantic to the Pacific, who had been swept into the great war machine and carried overseas against an enemy anywhere from three to six thousand miles from their homes, in a quarrel which many of them could hardly sense as being in any way their own, had done their job. But they had been homesick, more or less vague as to what it was all about, — except that the "world was to be made safe for democracy," — and to a considerable extent had gained an unpleasant opinion of their allies instead of a better understanding and sympathy regarding them. They had seen France at her worst, and it may as well be frankly confessed that great numbers of them discovered that, in spite of Lafayette, they did not like the French when they met them. It was by no means all the fault of the French. Many unavoidable circumstances made the conditions the worst possible under which the two nations should be made to appreciate each other, and a good many of our men who left France in 1919, vowing that they would never set foot in her land again, a decade later began to think they would rather like to see her once more.

During the six months that the negotiations at Paris dragged along, America was fast turning away from Europe. The war has been called the "Great Adventure." It never was that. For most of our millions it was merely a piece of work entirely out of our line which seemed to bear no relation to the normal course of our national life. We had no particular love for our allies and no hatred of the German people. In fact, of our soldiers who were quartered in Germany after the Armistice, many much preferred the Germans to the French. As far as we could see, a group of men in the Central Empires, the Kaiser and a few others, had brought this horror to pass, had attacked our ships and killed our citizens until we had had to go overseas and help destroy the gang. That had been done, and the whole affair had been more or less unreal from the start. Forced against our will to break our national policy and way of thinking for a century, and to meddle in Europe, the feeling grew that we wanted to forget the whole affair. It was notable that the men who had been "across" would not talk about it when they came back. They wanted to forget, and the easiest way to forget was not to talk even about Europe. Our curious attitude toward the war and our quick revulsion from it were exemplified in the fact that no military leader became a political possibility for any office of the slightest importance. The Revolution had given us Washington for President; the War of 1812, Jackson; the Mexican War, Taylor; the Civil War, Grant; and the Spanish War, Roosevelt. After the

World War, there was hardly even a janitor's job for an ex-General. We wanted, almost in a panic, to get back to our problems, our familiar ways of life and familiar way of looking at America as having her own future in the New World and to the West, as independent of Europe altogether.

Moreover, statistics when used nationally can be very misleading, and although it was true that the national wealth had been enormously increased and that the country was "prosperous," the new wealth was very unevenly distributed. Many of the great corporations, which we had been trying to curb when the war interrupted us, seemed fairly bursting with assets piled up by war business, and luxury was rampant, as always in such a period. On the other hand, high prices had played havoc with people dependent on investments of the sort that before the war had been considered most conservative, and with those living on salaries. Even the wage earners felt they had not been getting their share. During 1919, over 4,000,000 men were on strike at one time and another, and in view of the colossal earnings of the United States Steel Corporation another effort was made, unsuccessfully, by the men to get recognition of their Union. While the owners had been making huge profits, the men had genuine grievances. In some cases they would have to work twenty-four hours at a time, and the methods used by the managers to crush the strike were unjust and un-American, including instructions to agents to provoke all the racial hatred possible between different groups of workmen.

Unfortunately this strike, like many others of that disturbed period, was marred by somewhat revolutionary action, and the collapse of Russia, the fear of Bolshevism, and the growing violence of strikers led to a veritable panic in the country with regard to "Reds." During the war, the government propaganda service had fed the people with stories of enemy plots among ourselves, some of which were true and many of which were not. The Espionage Act of 1917 had been used to jail many persons unjustly, and feeling ran high between their defenders and the panic-stricken supporters of the government.

In 1919, several Socialists legally elected to the New York State Legislature were refused their seats. The whole state of mind of the nation, including many elements in it which should have kept their heads, was disgraceful, but tended strongly to alienate us from Europe, with its Bolshevism and what was considered, somewhat vaguely, its sources of infection for Socialism and Communism.

The sudden end of the war had left us, so to say, emotionally unsatisfied, whereas it had found Europe emotionally exhausted. For two years we had been devoting ourselves with the energy of fever to building up a great fighting machine; the propaganda services had skillfully played on every nerve to concentrate emotion on fighting; and then, just as we were ready to leap in earnest at the enemies' throats, a hand had suddenly pulled us back. Abnormality was bound to ensue from this extraordinary situation in mass psychology. The mob demanded sacrificial victims and found them in all who differed in any way from the conservative and the stereotyped. As news came of more and more revolutions in different European countries, fear of European entanglement grew.

Aside from this psychology of the mass, there was the psychology of politics to be reckoned with. The Constitution had provided, somewhat ambiguously, that the President "shall have power, by and with the advice and consent of the Senate, to make treaties, provided two thirds of the Senators present concur." No one knows just what is intended by "advice," but "consent" is obvious, and every treaty made by a President has had to run the gauntlet of the exceedingly jealous Senators. It had been made clear to Wilson before he went to France that a powerful group in the Senate would oppose any effort to incorporate a League of Nations in the treaty. Roosevelt, who had more and more been losing his political balance since the "Bull Moose" campaign, had come to hate Wilson with a bitterness that blinded him to any good whatever from that Democratic source. The President quite properly, on the advice of his military advisers, had declined to allow Roosevelt to raise and command troops in France as a separate unit, whereupon Roosevelt had sneered that "it was a very exclusive war," failing to see that the desire for "exclusiveness" was on his own part. Joining with Senator Lodge, as the two had joined before the Spanish War to secure Porto Rico and the Philippines, he worked to defeat any treaty which Wilson might make. Other Senators, including Borah and Harding, formed a group of "irreconcilables."

On October 25, Roosevelt had telegraphed to Lodge and a number of other Senators that the "Fourteen Points" which Wilson had announced in August as essential to a lasting peace were "thoroughly mischievous," and Wilson had unwisely countered with the request for the election of a Democratic Congress. The elections took place the following week and the Senate became Republican by a very narrow majority, including Senator Newberry, whose election was vitiated by such gross fraud as to cause him to be unseated after his immediate usefulness to his party was over. Lodge became Chairman of the Committee on Foreign Relations. Wilson's handling of the tactical political situation was bad. He appointed no Republican of importance on the Peace Commission, Henry White not being in that category from a party standpoint. Above all, the President ignored the Senate by not taking a member of that body to Paris with him to share the negotiations. He believed that when the time came he could exert enough pressure either on the Senate directly or through the force of aroused public opinion to carry his treaty through.

It was signed in Paris on June 28, 1919, and on July 10 Wilson, who had sailed immediately for America, presented it to the Senate for ratification. Month after month the treaty was discussed in Committee and in the Senate. The reservations proposed were unacceptable to Wilson, though they would probably have been accepted by the other powers in Europe. In early September the President started on his trip through the West to arouse the country. Making little impression at first, he was gaining ground when he suffered a stroke, and for months was incapacitated for public business. The country was left without a head, and the Senate, sixteen months after the Armistice, finally rejected the treaty. In July 1921 a simple resolution was passed to the effect that "the state of war declared to exist between the Imperial German Government and the United States of America by the joint resolution of Congress approved April 6, 1917, is hereby declared at an end." The previous November the Republicans, with Harding for President, had come into power with the astounding plurality of 7,000,000 votes, and this resolution was their method of ending the greatest war in history. It was like hearing the squeak of a timid field mouse after the thunder of battle had rolled away. Faced by the responsibilities of a moral leadership in the world such as had never before come to any nation, America backed out of the room frightened and stammering.

The story of our present decade must be but briefly sketched. It might be described succinctly by saying that Harding had to liquidate the war; Coolidge had quietly to liquidate the scandals of the Harding régime; and Hoover is now watching the liquidation of the "Coolidge prosperity."

The official end of the war was hardly noticed. For many months we had been in the midst of the inevitable post-war deflation. The sudden ending of actual hostilities had left us with huge inventories of goods, and after a year or so the crash had occurred. This was quite in accord with the precedents of economic history, as would also be a renewed prosperity with a genuine panic of unusual proportions due about 1927 or 1928.

For a while, during the war, American idealism had been raised high under forced draft, and the Prohibition and Woman's Suffrage Amendments, after they had been ratified by the necessary number of State legislatures, were declared parts of the Constitution in 1919 and 1920 respectively. Both had long been before the public as issues, but their incorporation in the Constitution was due to the general psychology of the time, although the second of the Amendments would probably have not been long in coming. With regard to the moral, legal, and other difficulties into which Prohibition has plunged us, it may be noted that it is symptomatic of the breakdown of genuine party government not only with us but everywhere that neither party has yet dared to take a strong stand on what is unquestionably the most discussed issue of the time. Largely owing to the change in our conception of government, according to which a representative has ceased to be expected to use his own mind and has become a mere mouthpiece to express the surmised opinions of a majority of his constituents, the parties have come to dodge the real issues which may be counted on to divide public opinion, instead of seeking for them.

Senator Harding was a colorless candidate for the Presidency when put forward in 1920, with Calvin Coolidge as his running mate for Vice President. Although put into the race by Lodge and the Old Guard, he tried to straddle on the questions of the treaty, the League of Nations, and others having to do with our participation in world affairs. Avoiding every positive stand, he urged a return to what he termed "normalcy." Bewildered by her new position in the world, panicky over the "Reds," caught in the midst of the deflation crash, about the only decision that could be traced in America's voting was that she wanted to play safe and sit tight. Soon prosperity, which is considered "normal" with us, did return, as might have been expected.

The America of the beginning of the last decade was a very different one from that which entered the war. The idealism that had been rapidly making progress in accomplishment under Roosevelt and under Wilson in his first term had largely disappeared. A certain recklessness had taken its place. Although lynching tended happily to decrease, in other respects crimes of violence became more and more common. Speculation became rampant, as always in war and post-war periods. The campaigns to sell government bonds during the war had resulted in 65,000,000 persons having become the owners of securities. Multitudes of these became familiar with the machinery of stock markets and quotations for the first time, and it is not unlikely that this fact accounted in part for the subsequent widespread participations in the excited stock markets of 1922 to 1929. The size of personal fortunes had taken another stride forward, and the country could name billionaires instead of mere multimillionaires. Before the decade was over, Henry Ford was to have the opportunity of declining to accept a check for $1,000,000,000 for his interest in his motor-car company.

Meanwhile he, more than any other man, had introduced the theory and practice of mass production and the high wage scale to increase the consuming power of the masses and thus the market for mass-produced goods. To be profitable, such a system called for standardized products and ever-enlarging demand. Various forced drafts — higher wage scales, advertising of hitherto undreamed-of proportions, "high-powered salesmanship," and the partial-payment plan — were all applied to the public in the effort to get them to buy more and more of the mass-produced goods of factories that had been geared to war production. Both the war, and mass production after it, had dislocated the old economic relations of classes. Prices had risen rapidly, upsetting the family budgets of all of us. Partly to protect the high wage scale of labor, partly because of our new distrust of alien races, partly because of the millions who wished to emigrate from a war-desolated Europe to America, we had heavily restricted immigration. The task was beyond us to remain the asylum for all mankind. The rise in wages and the disinclination to enter domestic service made a revolution in the homes of the ordinary people — professional and other — of moderate means. To a considerable extent the home ceased to function in the old way. Many women found the combined tasks of wife, mother, cook, and housemaid too many for them, and the drift into small, labor-saving apartments became general, when possible.

The demand for more money to meet the increasing cost and advancing scale of living became incessant. Hard work and thrift did not seem to solve the problem as well as lucky speculation. The old desire to control the great corporations in the interests of the American dream became changed into a desire to see their stocks go up so that we could make market profits and pay our bills.

Perhaps the most striking change was in the position of the Indians, which we mention rather for its own intrinsic interest than for its national importance. Ten thousand of them had served in the war. Over a third of the total 244,000 were American citizens, and, owing to the discovery of gas and oil on the lands assigned to them and now held for them, the value of their property in land alone was estimated in 1923 to be over $1,000,000,000. Thirty-seven thousand of them farm one million acres of land, and another 47,000 raise live stock worth $38,000,000. Perhaps no other change in our amazing country has been greater than that in the situation of its original owners. In the years immediately preceding 1921, they were spending about $2,500,000 annually for homes, barns, and modern farm implements, even after they had been defrauded of tens of millions.

The general restlessness of the age was best expressed in the universal desire for a motor car, and in California, at least, the aim of one to a family on the average had been achieved. America was on the move. Out on the old Santa Fé Trail, Vachel Lindsay saw it all pass by.

> Cars in a plain realistic row.
> And fair dreams fade
> When the raw horns blow.
>
> On each snapping pennant
> A big black name: —
> The careering city
> Whence each car came.
> They tour from Memphis, Atlanta, Savannah,
> Tallahassee and Texarkana.
> They tour from St. Louis, Columbus, Manistee,
> They tour from Peoria, Davenport, Kankakee.
> Cars from Concord, Niagara, Boston,
> Cars from Topeka, Emporia, and Austin.
> Cars from Chicago, Hannibal, Cairo.
> Cars from Alton, Oswego, Toledo.
> Cars from Buffalo, Kokomo, Delphi,
> Cars from Lodi, Carmi, Loami.

Ho for Kansas, land that restores us
When houses choke us, and great books bore us!
While I watch the highroad
And look at the sky,
While I watch the clouds in amazing grandeur
Roll their legions without rain
Over the blistering Kansas plain —
While I sit by the milestone
And watch the sky,
The United States
Goes by.[1]

In the government of Harding, likable but weak, scandals piled up for which one member of his Cabinet, in which two future Presidents were also sitting, would later be condemned to State's prison and a fine of $100,000. But no one cared. We wanted "normalcy" and money. When Harding died in office, Coolidge succeeded to the Presidency, and the steady work of paying off the national debt and of manufacturing prosperity continued. We asked for nothing better than higher and higher prices in the stock market. We initiated conferences for reducing armaments, the last two of which accomplished little or nothing. Some of the Great Powers adhered to our so-called Kellogg Pact to "outlaw war," though it is somewhat difficult to discern just what may have been gained by that idealistic gesture. In international affairs our participation remained much that of the "darling daughter" who was allowed to go swimming providing she "hung her clothes on a hickory limb and did not go near the water." No influential statesman dared urge our joining the League with which we had saddled Europe, and suggestions that we should adhere to the World Court for the settlement of international disputes, though we had formerly been forward in such movements, fell on deaf ears. Public opinion, at the first real touch of international responsibility, appeared to have shut up like a "sensitive plant," the leaves of which close together tightly at the touch of the human hand.

We had accepted the great corporations, partly because we

[1] From Vachel Lindsay's "The Santa Fé Trail," by permission of The Macmillan Company, Publishers.

were making money in the rise in their stocks and partly because we realized that the needs of modern business on a world scale somehow called for their existence. Our mass production was insisting on world markets, and our greatest industries, such as motor-car manufacture and moving pictures, rested in part on certain essentials which could only be procured in foreign countries. We were trying to force our goods on every nation. Our great business enterprises, such as the International Harvester, Standard Oil, Ford Motor, and others, were building plants and investing tens of millions of dollars in France and England and Germany and other countries. Our banks were opening branches in London, Paris, Buenos Aires, everywhere. But we still were trying to live in the frontier stage of thought and believed we could live to ourselves by saying we would. To a great extent, we had given up counting on our State Commissions of many sorts, and had come to realize that under modern conditions only Federal regulation would serve. We still insisted, however, upon dividing the world into water-tight compartments in spite of every evidence that it had become a unified organism in which each part depended upon free circulation with all other parts. Under President Hoover, who had been considered to be the great engineering mind applied to the problems of modern business and government, we enacted a tariff that almost staggered ourselves with the prohibitive height to which duties were raised, in spite of the fact that we insisted upon collection from other nations of over $11,000,000,000 in loans even the interest on which could only be paid by selling goods to us.

The battle cries of Roosevelt and Wilson in the struggle to realize the American dream had been changed into the small-town Chamber of Commerce shouts for "Coolidge prosperity." We were told by our leaders that a new era had dawned in which we were forever to lift ourselves by our own bootstraps and everyone could buy whatever he chose as long as his credit held out with bank or salesman. The wild speculation in the stock market, which sucked in not only the old semi-gambling elements but stenographers, elevator boys, barbers, every type of individual, — even hitherto cautious men and women who were beginning to be unable to make both ends meet under the insistent demands of our "high standard of living," — rose to more and more fantastic heights. When sane voices were raised in protest, the President or his Secretary of the Treasury would make a statement assuring the public that all was well. The latter, Mellon, with his wealth that was popularly estimated at several hundred millions, carried great weight, owing to his public position and presumed private shrewdness. When Coolidge, at the end of his second term, declined to run again, Hoover was elected on his promises of a still greater "prosperity" which was to be put on a scientific basis and to last forever. Poverty was to be abolished, and we were to live in an economic paradise. In spite of religious and other issues injected into the "whispering" campaign against his opponent "Al" Smith, — an able executive but son of an immigrant, a "Wet," and a Roman Catholic, — the real issue was the continuance of the wild speculation and of that business "prosperity" which in fact had begun to crack before Hoover was elected, in spite of the denials of the highest officials in the government.

At length, after a few months more, the inevitable crash which had long been foreseen by sane business men came. Hoover struggled against both adversity and truth, and Mellon soon wrapped himself in silence and his millions. The people paid, and the wake of ruin was as broad as the land. The situation was not merely American. It was world-wide. We had hung our clothes on the hickory limb, but it had done us no good. We had tried not to go near the water, and the water had rushed over us. It was the surge of that world panic and depression which was as inevitable after the great destruction of capital in the World War as severe weakness would be in a man after amputation of both his legs. This had been predicted for months in print by the ablest bankers in Europe and America while the American government had encouraged the college professors and stenographers and bootblacks to pay their way by carrying stocks on margin.

It is as incredible that the two Presidents and the Secretary of the Treasury did not know the situation as it is that they should have deliberately deceived the people. Both horns of the dilemma are equally serious for them as leaders of a great nation. In no case could the nation, or whatever party might have been in power, have avoided the inevitable, but the country need not have been advised to crowd on every rag of extra sail as it headed into the hurricane. We had got tired of idealism and had been urged to place our destinies in the hands of the safe realists, hard-headed business men who would stand no nonsense about "moral issues," of which we were told we had had enough, and who would be practical. Our most conspicuously successful manufacturer, Mr. Ford, announced in his new book in 1930 that "we now know that anything which is economically right is also morally right. There can be no conflict between good economics and good morals." As the successful business man would consider himself the best interpreter of good economics, he thus set himself up as the best judge of national morals. Long ago we noted the beginning of the confusion in the American mind between business and virtue. That confusion by 1930 had gone full circle. By then it had become complete. If what was economically right was also morally right, we could surrender our souls to professors of economics and captains of industry.

But, having surrendered idealism for the sake of prosperity, the "practical men" bankrupted us on both of them. We had forgotten, though no post-war leader dared to remind us of the fact, that it is impractical to be only "practical." Without a vision the people perish. The waste of war is always spiritual as well as material, and post-war decades are ever periods in which the fires of noble aims flicker but feebly. By 1930 our post-war decade and our post-war prosperity were over. Let us hope that our post-war materialism may also pass. We have yet to see what shall come, but the task clearly lies before us to

> Rebuild in beauty on the burnt-out coals,
> Not to the heart's desire, but the soul's.

EPILOGUE

We have now traced, in very meagre outline but let us hope with a reasonable emphasis on essentials for our purpose, the course of our story from that dateless period when savages roamed over our continent, coming from we know not where. We reached time and dates with the records of the rich but cruel civilization of Mexico and Central America. We have seen the surprise with which the first white men were greeted when they landed on our islands and coasts, coming thereafter with increasing frequency and in larger numbers. We have seen the strivings and conflicts of French and English and Spanish. We have seen the rise of our own nation from a handful of starving Englishmen in Virginia to a people of 120,000,000 made up of all the races of the world. Beginning with a guard scarce sufficient to defend the stockade at Jamestown against a few naked Indians, we grew until we were able to select from nearly 25,000,000 men of military age such millions as we would to hurl back at our enemies across the sea, only nine generations later. A continent which scarce sufficed to maintain a half million savages now supports nearly two hundred and fifty times that number of as active and industrious people as there are in the world. The huge and empty land has been filled with homes, roads, railways, schools, colleges, hospitals, and all the comforts of the most advanced material civilization. The mere physical tasks have been stupendous and unparalleled. Supplied at each important stage of advance with new implements of science which hastened our pace; lured by such rewards for haste and industry as were never offered to man before; keyed to activity by a climate that makes expenditure of nervous energy almost a bodily necessity, we threw ourselves into the task of physical domination of our environment with an abandonment that perforce led us to discard much that we had started to build up in our earliest days.

Even so, the frontier was always retreating before us, and sending its influence back among us in refluent waves until almost yesterday. In the eighteenth century we had an established civilization, with stability of material and spiritual values. Then we began our scramble for the untold wealth which lay at the foot of the rainbow. As we have gone ever westward, stability gave place to the constant flux in which we have lived since. Recently a distinguished English man of letters complained to me at dinner that we made too much of the frontier as an excuse for everything. It is not an excuse, but it is assuredly an explanation. We let ourselves be too much deflected by it from the building of the civilization of which our forefathers laid the foundations, and the frontier has stretched from our doors until almost yesterday. When my great-grandmother, an old lady with whom I frequently talked as a young man, was born, the United States extended only to the Mississippi, without including even Florida and the Gulf Coast. Both my grandfathers were children when Thomas Jefferson, who carried our bounds out to the Rockies, died. When my father was a baby, the entire country south of Oklahoma and from the Rockies westward was still Spanish territory. When I was born, the Sioux and the Nez Percés were still on the warpath. I was five when the Southwest was first spanned by the Southern Pacific, and twelve when the frontier was officially declared closed.

While thus occupied with material conquest and upbuilding, we did not wholly lose the vision of something nobler. If we hastened after the pot of gold, we also saw the rainbow itself, and felt that it promised, as of old, a hope for mankind. In the realm of thought we have been practical and adaptive rather than original and theoretical, although it may be noted that to-day we stand preëminent in astronomy. In medicine we have conferred discoveries of inestimable value on the world, which we have also led along the road of many humanitarian reforms, such as the treatment of debtors and the insane. Until the reaction after the World War, we had struggled for a juster law of nations and for the extension of arbitration as a substitute for war in international disputes. If in arts and letters we have produced no men who may be claimed to rank with the masters of all time, we have produced a body of work without which the world would be poorer and which ranks high by contemporary world standards. In literature and the drama, to-day, there is no work being done better anywhere than in the United States. In the intangible realm of character, there is no other country that can show in the past century or more two men of greater nobility than Washington and Lincoln.

But, after all, many of these things are not new, and if they were all the contribution which America had had to make, she would have meant only a place for more people, a spawning ground for more millions of the human species. In many respects, as I have not hesitated to say elsewhere, there are other lands in which life is easier, more stimulating, more charming than in raw America, for America *is* still raw, and unnecessarily so. The barbarian carelessness of the motoring millions, the littered roadsides, the use of our most beautiful scenery for the advertising of products which should be boycotted for that very reason, are but symptoms of our slipping down from civilized standards of life, as are also our lawlessness and corruption, with the cynical disregard of them by the public. Many of these matters I have discussed elsewhere, and may again. Some are also European problems as well as American. Some are urban, without regard to international boundaries. The mob mentality of the city crowd everywhere is coming to be one of the menaces to modern civilization. The ideal of democracy and the reality of the crowd are the two sides of the shield of modern government. "I think our governments will remain virtuous . . . as long as they are chiefly agricultural; and this will be as long as there shall be vacant lands in any part of America. When they get piled upon one another in large cities, as in Europe, they will become corrupt as in Europe," wrote Jefferson in the days of the Bourbons.

If, as I have said, the things already listed were all we had had to contribute, America would have made no distinctive and unique gift to mankind. But there has been also the *American dream*, that dream of a land in which life should be better and richer and fuller for every man, with opportunity for each according to his ability or achievement. It is a difficult dream for the European upper classes to interpret adequately, and too many of us ourselves have grown weary and mistrustful of it. It is not a dream of motor cars and high wages merely, but a dream of a social order in which each man and each woman shall be able to attain to the fullest stature of which they are innately capable, and be recognized by others for what they are, regardless of the fortuitous circumstances of birth or position. I once had an intelligent young Frenchman as guest in New York, and after a few days I asked him what struck him most among his new impressions. Without hesitation he replied, "The way that everyone of every sort looks you right in the eye, without a thought of inequality." Some time ago a foreigner who used to do some work for me, and who had picked up a very fair education, used occasionally to sit and chat with me in my study after he had finished his work. One day he said that such a relationship was the great difference between America and his homeland. There, he said, "I would do my work and might get a pleasant word, but I could never sit and talk like this. There is a difference there between social grades which cannot be got over. I would not talk to you there as man to man, but as my employer."

No, the American dream that has lured tens of millions of all nations to our shores in the past century has not been a dream of merely material plenty, though that has doubtless counted heavily. It has been much more than that. It has been a dream of being able to grow to fullest development as man and woman, unhampered by the barriers which had slowly been erected in older civilizations, unrepressed by social orders which had developed for the benefit of classes rather than for the simple human being of any and every class. And that dream has been realized more fully in actual life here than anywhere else, though very imperfectly even among ourselves.

It has been a great epic and a great dream. What, now, of the future?

From the material standpoint, it is probable that the extreme depression will pass in a year or two, barring social and political overturn in some countries, which might delay recovery. I am not here concerned with the longer economic problems raised by the relations of world distribution and consumption under mass production. The problems, fundamental and of extreme seriousness, have been amply discussed elsewhere and by those more competent. But whether, in the next decade, we shall have again to face a furious economic pace or whether we shall be confronted by a marked slowing down of our economic machine, the chief factor in how we shall meet either situation is that of the American mind. One of the interesting questions with regard to that is whether our long subjection to the frontier and other American influences has produced a new type or merely a transient change. Can we hold to the good and escape from the bad? Are the dream and the idealism of the frontier and the New Land inextricably involved with the ugly scars which have also been left on us by our three centuries of exploitation and conquest of the continent?

We have already tried to show how some of the scars were obtained; how it was that we came to insist upon business and money-making and material improvement as good in themselves; how they took on the aspects of moral virtues; how we came to consider an unthinking optimism essential; how we refused to look on the seamy and sordid realities of any situation in which we found ourselves; how we regarded criticism as obstructive and dangerous for our new communities; how we came to think manners undemocratic, and a cultivated mind a hindrance to success, a sign of inefficient effeminacy; how size and statistics of material development came to be more important in our eyes than quality and spiritual values; how in the ever-shifting advance of the frontier we came to lose sight of the past in hopes for the future; how we forgot to *live*, in the struggle to "make a living"; how our education tended to become utilitarian or aimless; and how other unfortunate traits only too notable to-day were developed.

While we have been absorbed in our tasks, the world has also been changing. We Americans are not alone in having to search for a new scale and basis for values, but for several reasons the task is more essential for us. On the one hand, our transplantation to the New World and our constant advance over its empty expanse unsettled the old values for us to a far greater extent than in Europe; and, on the other, the mere fact that there were no old things to be swept away here made us feel the full impact of the Industrial Revolution and the effect of machinery, when we turned to industrial life, to a far greater extent than in Europe, where the revolution originated.

It would seem as though the time had come when this question of values was of prime and pressing importance for us. For long we have been tempted and able to ignore it. Engaged in the work of building cities and developing the continent, values for many tended to be materialized and simplified. When a man staked out a clearing, and saw his wife and children without shelter, there was no need to discuss what were the real values in a humane and satisfying life. The trees had to be chopped, the log hut built, the stumps burned, and the corn planted. Simplification became a habit of mind and was carried into our lives long after the clearing had become a prosperous city. But such a habit of mind does not ignore values. It merely accepts certain ones implicitly, as does our most characteristic philosophy, the Pragmatism of William James. It will not do to say that we shall have no *a priori* standards and that the proof of the value of a thing or idea shall be whether it will "work." What do we mean by its "working"? Must we not mean that it will produce or conduce to some result that strikes us as desirable — that is, something that we have already set up in our minds as something worth while? In other words, a standard or value?

We no longer have the frontier to divert us or to absorb our energies. We shall steadily become a more densely populated country in which our social ideals will have to be such as to give us civilized contentment. To clear the muddle in which our education is at present, we shall obviously have to define our values. Unless we can agree on what the values in life are, we clearly can have no goal in education, and if we have no goal, the discussion of methods is merely futile. Once the frontier stage is passed, — the acquisition of a bare living, and the setting up of a fair economic base, — the American dream itself opens all sorts of questions as to values. It is easy to say a better and richer life for all men, but what *is* better and what *is* richer?

In this respect, as in many others, the great business leaders are likely to lead us astray rather than to guide us. For example, as promulgated by them, there is danger in the present popular theory of the high-wage scale. The danger lies in the fact that the theory is advanced not for the purpose of creating a better type of man by increasing his leisure and the opportunity for making a wise use of it, but for the sole and avowed purpose of increasing his powers as a "consumer." He is, therefore, goaded by every possible method of pressure or cajolery to spend his wages in consuming goods. He is warned that if he does not consume to the limit, instead of indulging in pleasures which do not cost money, he may be deprived not only of his high wages but of any at all. He, like the rest of us, thus appears to be getting into a treadmill in which he earns, not that he may enjoy, but that he may spend, in order that the owners of the factories may grow richer.

For example, Ford's fortune is often referred to as one of the "honestly" obtained ones. He pretends to despise money, and boasts of the high wages he pays and the cheapness of his cars, yet, either because his wages are still too low or the cars too high, he has accumulated $1,000,000,000 for himself from his plant. This would seem to be a high price for society to pay even him for his services to it, while the economic lives of some hundreds of thousands of men and women are made dependent on his whim and word.

Just as in education we have got to have some aims based on values before we can reform our system intelligently or learn in what direction to go, so with business and the American dream. Our democracy cannot attempt to curb, guide, or control the great business interests and powers unless we have clear notions as to the purpose in mind when we try to do so. If we are to regard man merely as a producer and consumer, then the more ruthlessly efficient big business is, the better. Many of the goods consumed doubtless make man healthier, happier, and better even on the basis of a high scale of human values. But if we think of him as a human being primarily, and only incidentally as a consumer, then we have to consider what values are best or most satisfying for him as a human being. We can attempt to regulate business for him not as a consumer but as a man, with many needs and desires with which he has nothing to do as a consumer. Our point of view will shift from efficiency and statistics to human nature. We shall not create a high-wage scale in order that the receiver will consume more, but that he may, in one way or another, live more abundantly, whether by enjoying those things which are factory-produced or those which are not. The points of view are entirely different, socially and economically.

In one important respect America has changed fundamentally from the time of the frontier. The old life was lonely and hard, but it bred a strong individualism. The farmer of Jefferson's day was independent and could hold opinions equally so. Steadily we are tending toward becoming a nation of employees — whether a man gets five dollars a day or a hundred thousand a year. The "yes-men" are as new to our national life as to our vocabulary, but they are real. It is no longer merely the laborer or factory hand who is dependent on the whim of his employer, but men all the way up the economic and social scales. In the ante-bellum South the black slave knew better than to express his views as to the rights of man. To-day the appalling growth of uniformity and timorousness of views as to the perfection of the present economic system held by most men "comfortably off" as corporation clerks or officials is not unrelated to the possible loss of a job.

Another problem is acute for us in the present extreme maladjustment of the intellectual worker to the present economic order. Just as the wage earner is told he must adjust his leisure pursuits to the advantage of business in his rôle of consumer, so there is almost irresistible economic pressure brought to bear on the intellectual worker to adjust his work to the needs of business or mass consumption. If wages are to go indefinitely higher, owing to mass-production possibilities for raising them, then the intellectual worker or artist will have to pay the price in the higher wages he himself pays for all services and in all the items of his expenses, such as rent, in which wages form a substantial element. His own costs thus rising, owing to the rising wage scale, he finds that a limited market for his intellectual wares no longer allows him to exist in a world otherwise founded on mass-production profits. He cannot forever pay rising mass-production costs without deriving for himself some form of mass-production profit. This would not be so bad if mass consumption did not mean for the most part a distinct lowering in the quality of his thought and expression. If the artist or intellectual worker could count on a wide audience instead of a class or group, the effect on his own work would be vastly stimulating, but for that the wide audience must be capable of appreciating work at its highest. The theory of mass production breaks down as yet when applied to the things of the spirit. Merging of companies in huge corporations, and the production of low-priced products for markets of tens of millions of consumers for one standard brand of beans or cars, may be possible in the sphere of our material needs. It cannot be possible, however, in the realm of the mind, yet the whole tendency at present is in that direction. Newspapers are merging as if they were factories, and daily, weekly, and monthly journals are all becoming as dependent on mass sales as a toothpaste.

The result is to lower the quality of thought as represented in them to that of the least common denominator of the minds of the millions of consumers.

If the American dream is to come true and to abide with us, it will, at bottom, depend on the people themselves. If we are to achieve a richer and fuller life for all, they have got to know what such an achievement implies. In a modern industrial State, an economic base is essential for all. We point with pride to our "national income," but the nation is only an aggregate of individual men and women, and when we turn from the single figure of total income to the incomes of individuals, we find a very marked injustice in its distribution. There is no reason why wealth, which is a social product, should not be more equitably controlled and distributed in the interests of society. But, unless we settle on the values of life, we are likely to attack in a wrong direction and burn the barn to find our penny in the hay.

Above and beyond the mere economic base, the need for a scale of values becomes yet greater. If we are entering on a period in which, not only in industry but in other departments of life, the mass is going to count for more and the individual less, and if each and all are to enjoy a richer and fuller life, the level of the mass has got to rise appreciably above what it is at present. It must either rise to a higher level of communal life or drag that life down to its own, in political leadership, and in the arts and letters. There is no use in accusing America of being a "Babbitt Warren." The top and bottom are spiritually and intellectually nearer together in America than in most countries, but there are plenty of Babbitts everywhere. "Main Street" is the longest in the world, for it encircles the globe. It is an American name, but not an American thoroughfare. One can suffocate in an English cathedral town or a French provincial city as well as in Zenith. That is not the point.

The point is that if we are to have a rich and full life in which all are to share and play their parts, if the American dream is to be a reality, our communal spiritual and intellectual life must be distinctly higher than elsewhere, where classes and groups have their separate interests, habits, markets, arts, and lives. If the dream is not to prove possible of fulfillment, we might as well become stark realists, become once more class-conscious, and struggle as individuals or classes against one another. If it is to come true, those on top, financially, intellectually, or otherwise, have got to devote themselves to the "Great Society," and those who are below in the scale have got to strive to rise, not merely economically, but culturally. We cannot become a great democracy by giving ourselves up as individuals to selfishness, physical comfort, and cheap amusements. The very foundation of the American dream of a better and richer life for all is that all, in varying degrees, shall be capable of wanting to share in it. It can never be wrought into a reality by cheap people or by "keeping up with the Joneses." There is nothing whatever in a fortune merely in itself or in a man merely in himself. It all depends on what is made of each. Lincoln was not great because he was born in a log cabin, but because he got out of it — that is, because he rose above the poverty, ignorance, lack of ambition, shiftlessness of character, contentment with mean things and low aims which kept so many thousands in the huts where they were born.

If we are to make the dream come true we must all work together, no longer to build bigger, but to build better. There is a time for quantity and a time for quality. There is a time when quantity may become a menace and the law of diminishing returns begins to operate, but not so with quality. By working together I do not mean another organization, of which the land is as full as was Kansas of grasshoppers. I mean a genuine individual search and striving for the abiding values of life. In a country as big as America it is as impossible to prophesy as it is to generalize, without being tripped up, but it seems to me that there is room for hope as well as mistrust. The epic loses all its glory without the dream. The statistics of size, population, and wealth would mean nothing to me unless I could still believe in the dream.

America is yet "The Land of Contrasts," as it was called in one of the best books written about us, years ago. One day a man from Oklahoma depresses us by yawping about it in such a way as to give the impression that there is nothing in that young State but oil wells and millionaires, and the next day one gets from the University there its excellent quarterly critical list of all the most recent books published in France, Spain, Germany, and Italy, with every indication of the beginning of an active intellectual life and an intelligent play of thought over the ideas of the other side of the world.

There is no better omen of hope than the sane and sober criticism of those tendencies in our civilization which call for rigorous examination. In that respect we are distinctly passing out of the frontier phase. Our life calls for such examination, as does that of every nation to-day, but because we are concerned with the evil symptoms it would be absurd to forget the good. It would be as uncritical to write the history of our past in terms of Morton of Merrymount, Benedict Arnold, "Billy the Kid," Thaddeus Stevens, Jay Gould, P. T. Barnum, Brigham Young, Tom Lawson, and others who could be gathered together to make an extraordinary jumble of an incomprehensible national story, as it would be to write the past wholly in terms of John Winthrop, Washington, John Quincy Adams, Jefferson, Lincoln, Emerson, Edison, General Gorgas, and others to afford an equally untrue picture.

The nation to-day is no more all made up of Babbitts (though there are enough of them) than it is of young poets. There is a healthy stirring of the deeps, particularly among the younger men and women, who are growing determined that they are not to function solely as consumers for the benefit of business, but intend to lead sane and civilized lives. When one thinks of the prostitution of the moving-picture industry, which might have developed a great art, one can turn from that to the movements everywhere through the country for the small theatre and the creation of folk drama, the collecting of our folk poetry, which was almost unknown to exist a generation ago, and other hopeful signs of an awakening culture deriving straight and naturally from our own soil and past. How far the conflicting good can win against the evil is our problem. It is not a cheering thought to figure the number of people who are thrilled nightly by a close-up kiss on ten thousand screens compared with the number who see a play of O'Neill's. But, on the other hand, we need not forget that a country that produced last year 1,500,000 Fords, which after their short day will in considerable numbers add to the litter along our country lanes as abandoned chassis, could also produce perhaps the finest example of sculpture in the last half century. We can contrast the spirit manifested in the accumulation of the Rockefeller fortune with the spirit now displayed in its distribution.

Like the country roads, our whole national life is yet cluttered up with the disorderly remnants of our frontier experience, and all help should be given to those who are honestly trying to clean up either the one or the other. But the frontier also left us our American dream, which is being wrought out in many hearts and many institutions.

Among the latter I often think that the one which best exemplifies the dream is the greatest library in this land of libraries, the Library of Congress. I take, for the most part, but little interest in the great gifts and Foundations of men who have incomes they cannot possibly spend, and investments that roll like avalanches. They merely return, not seldom unwisely, a part of their wealth to that society without which they could not have made it, and which too often they have plundered in the making. That is chiefly evidence of maladjustment in our economic system. A system that steadily increases the gulf between the ordinary man and the super-rich, that permits the resources of society to be gathered into personal fortunes that afford their owners millions of income a year, with only the chance that here and there a few may be moved to confer some of their surplus upon the public in ways chosen wholly by themselves, is assuredly a wasteful and unjust system. It is, perhaps, as inimical as anything could be to the American dream. I do not belittle the generosity or public spirit of certain men. It is the system that as yet is at fault. Nor is it likely to be voluntarily altered by those who benefit most by it. No ruling class has ever willingly abdicated. Democracy can never be saved, and would not be worth saving, unless it can save itself.

The Library of Congress, however, has come straight from the heart of democracy, as it has been taken to it, and I here use it as a symbol of what democracy can accomplish on its own behalf. Many have made gifts to it, but it was created by ourselves through Congress, which has steadily and increasingly shown itself generous and understanding toward it. Founded and built by the people, it is for the people. Anyone who has used the great collections of Europe, with their restrictions and red tape and difficulty of access, praises God for American democracy when he enters the stacks of the Library of Congress.

But there is more to the Library of Congress for the American dream than merely the wise appropriation of public money. There is the public itself, in two of its aspects. The Library of Congress could not have become what it is to-day, with all the generous aid of Congress, without such a citizen as Dr. Herbert Putnam at the directing head of it. He and his staff have devoted their lives to making the four million and more of books and pamphlets serve the public to a degree that cannot be approached by any similar great institution in the

Old World. Then there is the public that uses these facilities. As one looks down on the general reading room, which alone contains ten thousand volumes which may be read without even the asking, one sees the seats filled with silent readers, old and young, rich and poor, black and white, the executive and the laborer, the general and the private, the noted scholar and the schoolboy, all reading at their own library provided by their own democracy. It has always seemed to me to be a perfect working out in a concrete example of the American dream — the means provided by the accumulated resources of the people themselves, a public intelligent enough to use them, and men of high distinction, themselves a part of the great democracy, devoting themselves to the good of the whole, uncloistered.

It seems to me that it can be only in some such way, carried out in all departments of our national life, that the American dream can be wrought into an abiding reality. I have little trust in the wise paternalism of politicians or the infinite wisdom of business leaders. We can look neither to the government nor to the heads of the great corporations to guide us into the paths of a satisfying and humane existence as a great nation unless we, as multitudinous individuals, develop some greatness in our own individual souls. Until countless men and women have decided in their own hearts, through experience and perhaps disillusion, what is a genuinely satisfying life, a "good life" in the old Greek sense, we need look to neither political nor business leaders. Under our political system it is useless, save by the rarest of happy accidents, to expect a politician to rise higher than the source of his power. So long also as we are ourselves content with a mere extension of the material basis of existence, with the multiplying of our material possessions, it is absurd to think that the men who can utilize that public attitude for the gaining of infinite wealth and power for themselves will abandon both to become spiritual leaders of a democracy that despises spiritual things. Just so long as wealth and power are our sole badges of success, so long will ambitious men strive to attain them.

The prospect is discouraging to-day, but not hopeless. As we compare America in 1931 with the America of 1912 it seems as though we had slipped a long way backwards. But that period is short, after all, and the whole world has been going through the fires of Hell. There are not a few signs of promise now in the sky, signs that the peoples themselves are beginning once again to crave something more than is vouchsafed to them in the toils and toys of the mass-production age. They are beginning to realize that, because a man is born with a particular knack for gathering in vast aggregates of money and power for himself, he may not on that account be the wisest leader to follow nor the best fitted to propound a sane philosophy of life. We have a long and arduous road to travel if we are to realize our American dream in the life of our nation, but if we fail, there is nothing left but the old eternal round. The alternative is the failure of self-government, the failure of the common man to rise to full stature, the failure of all that the American dream has held of hope and promise for mankind.

That dream was not the product of a solitary thinker. It evolved from the hearts and burdened souls of many millions, who have come to us from all nations. If some of them appear to us to have too great faith, we know not yet to what faith may attain, and may hearken to the words of one of them, Mary Antin, a young immigrant girl who came to us from Russia, a child out of "the Middle Ages," as she says, into our twentieth century. Sitting on the steps of the Boston Public Library, where the treasures of the whole of human thought had been opened to her, she wrote, "This is my latest home, and it invites me to a glad new life. The endless ages have indeed throbbed through my blood, but a new rhythm dances in my veins. My spirit is not tied to the monumental past, any more than my feet were bound to my grandfather's house below the hill. The past was only my cradle, and now it cannot hold me, because I am grown too big; just as the little house in Polotzk, once my home, has now become a toy of memory, as I move about at will in the wide spaces of this splendid palace, whose shadow covers acres. No! It is not I that belong to the past, but the past that belongs to me. America is the youngest of the nations, and inherits all that went before in history. And I am the youngest of America's children, and into my hands is given all her priceless heritage, to the last white star espied through the telescope, to the last great thought of the philosopher. Mine is the whole majestic past, and mine is the shining future."

INDEX

Printed in the United Kingdom
by Lightning Source UK Ltd.
126692UK00001B/39/A